Women in Coloni
America, 1526 t

Texts and Contexts

For Ann

Women in Colonial Latin America, 1526 to 1806

Texts and Contexts

Edited, with an Introduction, by

Nora E. Jaffary and Jane E. Mangan

Hackett Publishing Company, Inc.
Indianapolis/Cambridge

21 20 19 18   1 2 3 4 5 6 7

For further information, please address
    Hackett Publishing Company, Inc.
    P.O. Box 44937
    Indianapolis, Indiana 46244-0937

    www.hackettpublishing.com

Cover design by Rick Todhunter
Interior design by Elizabeth L. Wilson
Composition by Aptara, Inc.

Library of Congress Cataloging-in-Publication Data

Names: Jaffary, Nora E., 1968- editor. | Mangan, Jane E., 1969- editor.
Title: Women in Colonial Latin America, 1526 to 1806 : texts and contexts /
    edited, with an introduction, by Nora E. Jaffary and Jane E. Mangan.
Description: Indianapolis, Indiana : Hackett Publishing Company, Inc., [2018] |
    Includes bibliographical references and index.
Identifiers: LCCN 2018009234| ISBN 9781624667503 (pbk.) |
    ISBN 9781624667510 (cloth)
Subjects: LCSH: Women—Latin America—History. | Women—Latin
    America—History—Sources. | Latin America—History—To 1830. | Latin
    America—History—To 1830—Sources.
Classification: LCC HQ1460.5 .W627 2018 | DDC 305.4098—dc23
LC record available at https://lccn.loc.gov/2018009234

∞

Contents

Contents

List of Maps

Acknowledgments

Preparing this book was at once easy and difficult. First came the material. (Easy!) Twenty years of archival research has allowed for the accumulation of a cache of intriguing case studies, a few of which I am happy to have had the chance to reproduce here; and twenty years of teaching has shaped my thinking about how to help students approach such stories. Next came the collaboration. The expertise and the companionship that my co-editor, Jane Mangan, brought to this project also made it easy. Previously, I had only admired Jane's research and pedagogical accomplishments from afar so it was a privilege and a pleasure to learn from her up close as we worked together on this book. The efficient staff at Hackett, particularly our editor, Rick Todhunter, and copy editor Simone Payment also eased the process, as did the scholars who either contributed several of the following chapters (Mariana Dantas, Caroline Garriott, Jane Landers, Sarah E. Owens, and Nancy E. van Deusen) or who generously shared their source materials (Bianca Premo) with us when we came asking. Jane and I are grateful to Hackett's anonymous readers who helped us improve our document choices and our framing of these texts, and to several historians who also shaped both choices (Allyson Poska, Lupe García, Zeb Tortorici, and Tamar Herzog). Research assistants Ana Fasold-Berges and Frida Osorio facilitated some of our translations and, many years ago, José Manuel Vázquez Ruiz assisted with a paleographic transcription. I thank the support of Concordia University and my departmental colleagues. As always, I also thank my family, especially my partner, Ed Osowski, whose steady material, emotional, and intellectual support makes my work on such projects possible.

The difficult part of this book, for me, was its timing. My mother, Ann Jaffary, became critically ill and then died unexpectedly while Jane and I were in the midst of preparing our penultimate manuscript for submission. Reading women's wills and considering how women in the past had used such documents to shape their legacies, care for their offspring, and attend to their own spiritual well-being became poignant for me in this period in a way it never had before. Although my mother was, in totality, like none of the women whose lives are recorded in this collection, shades of her show up in many of them. Like her, these women showed themselves at various times to be vulnerable, dutiful, protective, forthright, intrepid, self-interested, and outrageous. So, to the memory of Ann Jaffary, a great teacher, mother, and friend, I dedicate this volume.

NEJ

In addition to our editor and fellow historians whom Nora thanks above, I am grateful to Davidson College for institutional support as well as student input. Thanks to the Boswell Faculty Fellowship, I was able to travel to Montreal to work face-to-face with Nora on translations and editing. Closer to home, I am deeply indebted to my fall 2017 Race, Sex, and Power in Latin America class—Lalyz Anchondo, Ruben Barajas Ruíz, Max Bazin, Emma Blake, María Bravo, Alexa Cole, Cassandra Harding, Daniel Hierro, Alisha Kendrick, Gina Martinez, Aukse Praniviciute, Natalie Skowlund, and Saadia Timpton. These Davidson College students commented on numerous chapters. Their insightful questions and good humor helped shape several chapter introductions from the perspective of the audience Nora and I most hope to reach with this book. Finally, I am grateful to Nora for inviting me to collaborate with her. Nora's leadership, organization, and encouragement made the work of this book mostly easy and definitely fun. The challenges of the past year could easily have thrown us off course, but Nora's fortitude and commitment kept the project on track and made a lasting impression on me of how to embrace life's tough moments with integrity.

JEM

Map I: Locations Featured in Documents

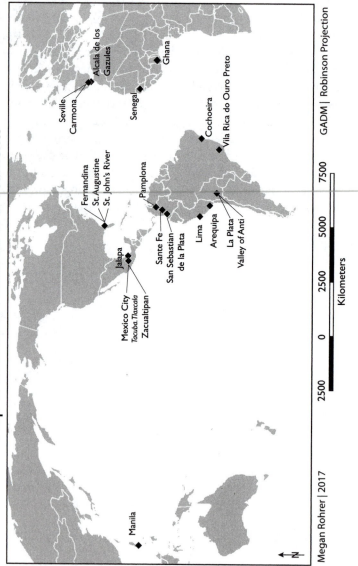

Seville
Carmona
Alcala de los
Gazules

Ghana

Senegal

Cochoeira
Vila Rica do Ouro Preto

Fernandina
St. Augustine
St. John's River

Pamplona

Sante Fe
San Sebastian
de la Plata

Lima

Arequipa
La Plata
Valley of Anti

Mexico City
Tacuba, Tlaxcala
Zacualtipan

Jalapa

Manila

Megan Rohrer | 2017

2500   0   2500   5000   7500
Kilometers

GADM | Robinson Projection

N

Introduction

Women in Colonial Latin America, 1526 to 1806: Texts and Contexts presents scholars and students with a much-needed collection of primary sources in translation. With a view to depicting the diversity of women's experiences, we have selected twenty-one episodes about individual women's lives that span the colonial period. These texts, most of which have never been translated or published before, document the lives of women of European, indigenous, African, and mixed-race descent from Spain, Mexico, the Andes, Spanish Florida, Colombia, and Brazil. The texts reveal the experiences of elite and plebeian women in both urban and rural settings. Every case study will enliven readers' encounters with colonial Latin American women's history through the inherent interest each tale holds. The selected episodes range from the details of the last will and testament of a mid-sixteenth-century indigenous market woman to the criminal trial of a prostitute of Spanish descent in early nineteenth-century Mexico exonerated for the crime of infanticide in 1806. The documents depict the internal contradictions and complexities of women's lives that will challenge students and scholars to move beyond superficial glosses of women's past experiences.

The materials in this collection are ordered chronologically but also conceived of thematically in terms of their framing devices. Each documentary chapter is preceded by an introduction that situates the source temporally and geographically and that highlights interpretive or linguistic challenges the texts present. In our translations, we have modernized punctuation and sentence breaks because the original sentences were often so long that they were difficult to easily comprehend. For clarity, we have also normally modernized capitalization, spelling, and prose. In the many judicial cases included here, we have maintained contemporary scribes' common practice of rendering witness testimony in the third person.

Chapter introductions also invite students, scholars, and instructors to consider possible interpretive questions applicable to each reading. Along with suggestions for further reading, each chapter is also followed by a list of central themes treated in the source, facilitating cross-comparative discussions. The identified themes treated in these texts, central to both the historical record and to current scholarship treating the history of colonial Latin American women are: the family, labor, law, migration and mobility, property, race and ethnicity, religion, sexuality and gender, and slavery.

Historiographic Overview

The nine themes we focus on have evolved over time in the historiography on Latin American women and now overlap; each theme informs the others in recent scholarship. While select works appeared earlier, scholars continue to view two volumes edited by Asunción Lavrin as the seminal works on women in colonial Latin America: *Latin American Women: Historical Perspectives* (1978) and *Sexuality and Marriage in Colonial Latin America* (1989).[1] The former, the first volume of its kind, included several chapters on women in the colonial era and treated such topics as ethnicity, economy, class, religion, the press, and women's participation in the independence movements. *Sexuality and Marriage* asked how institutions such as the church, the crown, and the courts affected norms for women's behavior as well as how women and men resisted those norms. Since its publication, multiple scholars have studied the themes of marriage and sexuality with increasing attention to behaviors outside the norms articulated by colonial institutions.

A recent collection on sexuality edited by Zeb Tortorici invited Asunción Lavrin to comment on the shift in the field between then and now.[2] Lavrin celebrated recent work in which historians "open up to topics that appeared threatening decades ago," including analysis of same-sex relations, bestiality, and masturbation.[3] Two essays in Tortorici's volume, by Chad Black and Tortorici and by Ronaldo Vainfas, use Inquisition cases against women for same-sex relations in order to explore institutional and cultural attitudes around lesbian sexuality. The work of Pete Sigal on sexuality in colonial Yucatán has established an important subfield on male homosexuality.[4] The case of Gregoria La Macho, featured in Chapter 18 of this volume, offers students a primary source through which to engage in these newer trends in historiography.

In addition to the "deviant" topics that seemed out of bounds for Lavrin and her generation, scholars have enriched our understanding of heterosexuality, marriage, and family in the colonial era. Family patterns and practices

---

1. Asunción Lavrin, ed., *Latin American Women: Historical Perspectives* (Westport, CT: Greenwood Press, 1978); and *Sexuality and Marriage in Colonial Latin America* (Lincoln: University of Nebraska Press, 1989).
2. Zeb Tortorici, ed., *Sexuality and the Unnatural in Colonial Latin America* (Oakland: University of California Press, 2016).
3. Tortorici, xii.
4. See Pete Sigal, *From Moon Goddesses to Virgins: The Colonization of Yucatecan Maya Sexual Desire* (Austin: University of Texas Press, 2000); *The Flower and the Scorpion: Sexuality and Ritual in Early Nahua Culture* (Durham, NC: Duke University Press, 2011); and Pete Sigal, ed., *Infamous Desire, Male Homosexuality in Colonial Latin America* (Chicago: Chicago University Press, 2003).

influenced choices about work and housing; they shaped realities with regard to economic status and experiences of material culture. As relationships changed, through birth and death or through new marriages and extramarital relationships, women and men redistributed their resources. Attachments and emotions accompanied the interactions between women and their children, their siblings, their parents, and their spouses or partners. Thus, while legal documents represent a majority of the documents in this collection, we frequently see that issues of family are woven into legal documents in terms of both their original causes and the relations between the actors of a given legal drama. Indeed, one could argue that family serves as a foundational theme in a majority of studies on women in the colonial era.

The subject of families in colonial Mexico enjoyed popularity in the 1990s and early 2000s.[5] Historians of colonial Brazil offer detailed analysis of family structure and kin networks especially among women of Portuguese descent, which the will of Thereza de Jesús Maria Jozé in Chapter 16 allows students to analyze.[6] The experience of children within families and society moved to the foreground of social history, too.[7] Alongside these studies of normative family, work on bigamy and illegitimacy emerged to reveal the many historical actors who made choices outside of institutional norms.[8] For example, such woman as *doña* Francisca de Marquina (Chapter 12) might elect to alter her domestic circumstances by seeking an ecclesiastical divorce. Moreover, although legal and community norms discouraged violence, it, too, was part of the fabric of couples' and families' relationships as the spousal abuse case in Chapter 8 illustrates.[9]

---

5. The work of Pilar Gonzalbo is especially important in this regard. See Gonzalbo, *Familias iberoamericanos historia, identidad, y conflictos* (Mexico, DF: El Colegio de México, Centro de Estudios Históricos, 2001).

6. Alida C. Metcalf, *Family and Frontier in Colonial Brazil, Santana de Parnaíba, 1580–1822* (Stanford, CA: Stanford University Press, 2005). Muriel Nazzari, *Disappearance of the Dowry: Women, Families and Social Change in São Paulo, Brazil, 1600–1900* (Stanford, CA: Stanford University Press, 1991).

7. In particular see the work by Bianca Premo, *Children of the Father King: Youth, Authority and Legal Minority in Colonial Peru* (Chapel Hill: University of North Carolina Press, 2005).

8. Other examples include Richard Boyer, *Lives of the Bigamists: Marriage, Family, and Community in Colonial Mexico* (Albuquerque: University of New Mexico Press, 1995); María Emma Mannarelli, *Private Passions and Public Sins: Men and Women in Seventeenth-Century Lima*, trans. Sidney Evans and Meredith D. Dodge (Albuquerque: University of New Mexico Press, 2007); and Ann Twinam, *Public Lives, Private Secrets: Gender, Honor, Sexuality and Illegitimacy in Colonial Spanish America* (Stanford, CA: Stanford University Press, 1999).

9. See Nicole von Germeten, *Violent Delights, Violent Ends: Sex, Race and Honor in Colonial Cartagena de Indias* (Albuquerque: University of New Mexico, Press, 2013) as well as Steve J. Stern, *The Secret History of Gender: Women, Men, and Power in Late Colonial Mexico* (Chapel Hill: University of North Carolina Press, 1995).

Scholarship on colonial women has also revealed the significant changes in indigenous families and households due to the transition between the pre-Columbian and colonial eras. For example, practices of polygamy and trial marriage came under attack by the church in ways that upended traditions that marked women's lives.[10] If family structures and households shifted, so too did women's networks for childbirth and childrearing, for marital support, and for domestic economies of sustenance.[11] These works collectively suggest that although the informal practices around family often went unrecorded in legal sources, the institution of the family powerfully shaped women's lives and society at large.

If families have emerged as an important topic in the field of colonial Latin American women's history, religious institutions stand out as an equally important place to study women in colonial society. Histories of conventual life illuminate cloistered existence as well as the politics of convents in society.[12] The founding of a convent for indigenous women, documented in Chapter 13, highlights these politics. Yet these works also reveal that nuns did not always behave predictably. Nuns were busy workers as Kathryn Burns has shown, even running banks out of their convents.[13] Further, women's religious practice could present in ways that threatened colonial norms.[14] The writing of female religious, exemplified by *Sor* (Sister) Ana in Chapter 9 of this volume, was a significant literary force in the early modern Iberian world and one that often addressed the issue of empire.[15] As Chapter 10 in

---

10. For these topics generally, see the discussion in Susan Kellogg, *Weaving the Past: A History of Latin America's Indigenous Women from the Prehispanic Period to the Present* (New York: Oxford University Press, 2005), 71–81. On trial marriage in the Andes, see Ward Stavig, *The World of Túpac Amaru: Conflict, Community, and Identity in Colonial Peru* (Lincoln: University of Nebraska Press, 1999), 24–27 and for Mexico, see Deborah Kanter, *Hijos del Pueblo: Gender, Family and Community in Rural Mexico, 1730–1850* (Austin: University of Texas Press, 2008), 83–84.

11. On networks, see Kanter, *Hijos del Pueblo*, Chapters 3 and 4 as well as Jane E. Mangan, *Transatlantic Obligation: Creating the Bonds of Family in Colonial Era Peru and Spain* (New York: Oxford University Press, 2016), especially Chapter 5.

12. Asunción Lavrín, *Brides of Christ: Conventual Life in Colonial Mexico* (Stanford, CA: Stanford University Press, 2008).

13. Kathryn Burns, *Colonial Habits: Convents and the Spiritual Economy of Cuzco, Peru* (Durham, NC: Duke University Press, 1999).

14. Nora E. Jaffary, *False Mystics: Deviant Orthodoxy in Colonial Mexico* (Lincoln: University of Nebraska Press, 2004); Margaret Chowning, *Rebellious Nuns: The Troubled History of a Mexican Convent 1752–1863* (New York: Oxford University Press, 2005).

15. Electa Arenal and Stacey Schlau, *Untold Sisters: Hispanic Nuns in Their Own Works* (Albuquerque: University of New Mexico Press, 1989; rev. 2010); Kathryn Joy McKnight, *The Mystic of Tunja: The Writings of Madre Castillo, 1671–1742* (Amherst: University of Massachusetts Press, 1997); María de San José, Kathleen Ann Myers, and Amanda Powell, *A Wild Country Out in the Garden: The Spiritual Journals of a Colonial Mexican Nun* (Bloomington: Indiana University Press, 1999).

this volume illustrates, spiritual biography could also serve as an important vehicle of expression for oppressed women of color like Úrsula de Jesús.[16] These mystic writings alternately reinforced and contested women's role within religious patriarchy. Historians of women have made excellent use of the copious records of religious institutions to reframe this subfield over the past twenty years.

Both religion and family are topics that readers might associate with fixed locations, such as the church or the home. Yet, in the context of the European expansion, the fall of indigenous empires, and the slave trade, migration and mobility prove to be significant themes for understanding how women experienced colonial life. Such was the case for a number of women whose lives are treated in the present volume (see Map 2). Ida Altman's pioneering research examined the centrality of women and families to Iberian expansion.[17] Karen Powers delved into the subject of mobility within the Andes for indigenous families adapting to, and resisting, colonial rule.[18] A sizeable literature exists with regard to the capture and forced migration of enslaved Africans in the Atlantic slave trade, with works on the circum-Caribbean especially illuminating for the case of Spanish empire.[19] Primary sources of the era reflect the pervasive nature of mobility and migration as students will note in several chapters that follow, including Chapter 5, which features letters sent between spouses and lovers in Spain and Mexico, as well as Chapter 19, which focuses on the financial and social status of the former slave Ana Gallum.

Turning an eye to colonial legal records has been equally fruitful for unearthing women's experience in the colonial world. As the many legal sources in this book reveal, women initiated cases, served as witnesses, appeared as victims, and sought redress.[20] They also sought to obtain or

---

16. Nancy van Deusen, *The Souls of Purgatory: The Spiritual Diary of an Afro-Peruvian Mystic, Ursula de Jesús* (Albuquerque: University of New Mexico, 2004) and Mónica Díaz, *Indigenous Writings from the Convent: Negotiating Ethnic Autonomy in Colonial Mexico* (Tucson: University of Arizona Press, 2010).

17. See both Ida Altman, *Emigrants and Society: Extremadura and America in the Sixteenth Century* (Berkeley: University of California Press, 1989), and Altman, *Transatlantic Ties in the Spanish Empire: Brihuega, Spain and Puebla, Mexico, 1560–1620* (Stanford, CA: Stanford University Press, 2000).

18. Karen Powers, *Andean Journeys: Migration, Ethnogenesis, and the State in Colonial Quito* (Albuquerque: University of New Mexico Press, 1995).

19. See, for example, Daniel L. Schafer, *Anna Madgigine, Jai Kingsley: African Princess, Florida Slave, Plantation Slaveowner* (Gainesville: University Press of Florida, 2003).

20. For a primary source collection devoted exclusively to women and the law in New Mexico, see Linda Tigges, ed., and J. Richard Salazar, trans., *Spanish Colonial Women and the Law: Complaints, Lawsuits, and Criminal Behavior; Documents from the Spanish Colonial Archives of New Mexico, 1697–1749* (Santa Fe, NM: Sunstone Press, 2016). On women and the law in the

Map 2: Transatlantic & Transpacific Journeys

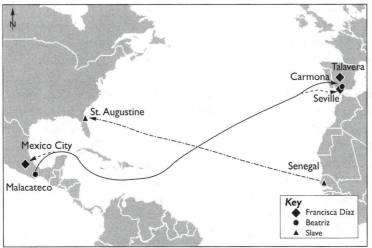

Note: Francisca Díaz travels from Talavera to Mexico City; Mexico City to Seville; and then Seville to Mexico City.

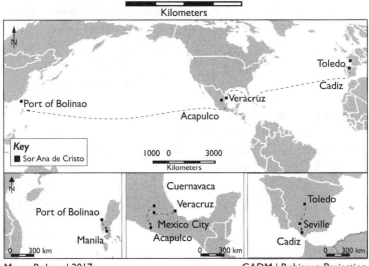

Megan Rohrer | 2017

GADM | Robinson Projection

protect real estate and other valuables in their wills and in other notarial and judicial texts. Students can compare four such wills in Chapter 3 of this volume. Some studies have focused on particular demographics within the

northern Spanish borderlands, see Susan M. Deeds, "Double Jeopardy: Indian Women in Jesuit Missions of Nueva Vizcaya," in *Indian Women of Early Mexico*, ed. Susan Schroeder, Stephanie Wood, and Robert Haskett (Norman: University of Oklahoma Press, 1997), 255–72.

colonial population or particular legal trends based on legal innovation or cultural shifts. For example, when the New Laws of 1542 outlawed enslavement of indigenous peoples, this legal change led to a groundswell of cases by enslaved indigenous men and women, such as occurred in the lawsuit initiated by Beatríz, *india* (indigenous woman), presented in Chapter 2.[21] The varied and persistent legal strategies of enslaved Afro–Latin American women seeking freedom or protecting family and property have been studied across the colonial era; Chapters 15 and 17 contain detailed examples of two such women, one in Colombia and one in Peru, both from the late colonial era, a period in which recent scholarship has particularly focused.[22]

Within the field of women's history, the issues of race and ethnicity have served as significant areas of historical investigation. Early publications in colonial women's history tended to focus exclusively either on pre-Columbian indigenous women or women of European descent.[23] Thus, scholars examined indigenous women as a group to analyze how their lives changed with the arrival of the Spanish. Some works were influenced by feminist anthropology of the 1970s insofar as they followed a model of declension relative to women's status in society before and after European conquest in the Americas.[24] More recent scholarship has instead approached this history by examining women's experiences across ethnic divisions and by re-envisioning, as Camila Townsend does in her historical biography of the indigenous interpreter Malintzin, the complexity of Mesoamerican indigenous women's experience of conquest.[25] In this volume, Chapter 1 offers a primary source insight to the experience of an indigenous woman who was a contemporary of Malintzin. Other works on Mexico have helped to paint a full picture of indigenous women's legal status, marriage choices, and crime.[26] Latin American women's

---

21. Nancy E. van Deusen, *Global Indios: The Indigenous Struggle for Justice in Sixteenth-Century Spain* (Durham, NC: Duke University Press, 2015).

22. Michelle A. McKinley, *Fractional Freedoms: Slavery, Intimacy, and Legal Mobilization in Colonial Lima, 1600–1700* (New York: Cambridge University Press, 2016). Bianca Premo, *The Enlightenment on Trial: Ordinary Litigants and Colonialism in the Spanish Empire* (New York: Oxford University Press, 2017).

23. See, for instance, María Rostworowski, *La Mujer en la época prehispánica* (Lima: Instituto de Estudios Peruanos, 1988).

24. Irene Marsha Silverblatt, *Moon, Sun, and Witches: Gender Ideologies and Class in Inca and Colonial Peru* (Princeton, NJ: Princeton University Press, 1987).

25. Camilla Townsend, *Maltinzin's Choices: An Indian Woman in the Conquest of Mexico* (Albuquerque: University of New Mexico Press, 2006).

26. Susan Schroeder, Stephanie Wood, and Robert Haskett, eds., *Indian Women of Early Mexico* (Norman: University of Oklahoma Press, 1997); Kellogg, *Weaving the Past*; Lisa Sousa, *The Woman Who Turned Into a Jaguar, and Other Narratives of Native Women in Archives of Colonial Mexico* (Stanford, CA: Stanford University Press, 2017); and Kanter, *Hijos del Pueblo*.

history could not be fully addressed without critical attention to ethnic identity.[27]

Indigenous women's history of labor also developed into a significant topic. It will come as little surprise that the majority of women in colonial Latin America worked, whether for their own subsistence or for other masters. More recently, historians have delved into this subject in ways that revolutionized what we know about how women worked in colonial society. Through this work we see how women shaped society, as Karen Graubart argued with regard to indigenous women's labor patterns under colonization in Peru.[28] Studies from the late 1970s on market women's labor in cities spawned in-depth analyses that highlighted the varied types of work women did in urban versus rural areas.[29] Some women's work, especially as healers, positioned them for social control within their communities.[30] Several chapters in this volume, including Chapters 4 and 11, which treat midwifery, and Chapter 6, which addresses domestic labor, highlight examples of women's colonial-era paid labor.

Women's history, while long addressing the history of women's labor, was somewhat slower to engage with the experiences of Afro–Latin American women, both free and enslaved. Initial publications studied marriage (and its absence) to examine the idea of community formation.[31] Among enslaved men and women, for whom marriage was often an impossibility, the formation of community and kin networks outside of marriage has proven to be a fruitful area of study.[32] A rich primary source that explores this issue by examining the experiences of the Afro–Brazilian woman Rita de Souza

27. One of the most influential works on the subject of how race and gender inform each other is María Elena Martínez, *Geneological Fictions: Limpieza de Sangre, Religion, and Gender in Colonial Mexico* (Stanford, CA: Stanford University Press, 2008).

28. Karen B. Graubart, *With Our Labor and Sweat, Indigenous Women and the Formation of Colonial Society in Peru, 1550–1700* (Stanford, CA: Stanford University Press, 2007).

29. Elinor Burkett, "Indian Women and White Society: The Case of Sixteenth-Century Peru," in *Latin American Women: Historical Perspectives,* ed. Asunción Lavrin (Westport, CT: Greenwood Press, 1978), 101–28; Kimberly Gauderman, *Women's Lives in Colonial Quito: Gender, Law and Economy in Colonial Spanish America* (Austin, TX: University of Texas Press, 2003); Jane E. Mangan, *Trading Roles: Gender, Ethnicity, and the Urban Economy in Colonial Potosí* (Durham, NC: Duke University Press, 2005).

30. See Martha Few, *Women Who Live Evil Lives: Gender, Religion and the Politics of Power in Colonial Guatemala* (Austin, TX: University of Texas Press, 2002), as well as Joan Cameron Bristol, *Christians, Blasphemers, and Witches: Afro-Mexican Ritual Practice in the Seventeenth Century* (Albuquerque: University of New Mexico Press, 2007).

31. Herman L. Bennett, *Africans in Colonial Mexico: Absolutism, Christianity and Afro-Creole Consciousness, 1570–1640* (Bloomington: Indiana University Press, 2003).

32. The work of Rachel O'Toole offers in-depth analysis of enslaved women and men's networks in Trujillo, Peru. See O'Toole, *Bound Lives: Africans, Indians, and the Making of Race in Colonial Peru* (Pittsburgh, PA: University of Pittsburgh Press, 2012).

Lobo is presented in Chapter 14. The legal strategies that enslaved women employed, especially when they attempted to seek manumission, is a critical topic within the field of Afro–Latin American women's history.[33] Often these works highlighted the violent discrimination Afro-descended women faced in such contexts, as exemplified in Chapters 17 and 20. Simultaneously, the field expanded our historical understanding of enslaved women's resistance, such as strategies for manumission or purchasing freedom, that existed alongside oppression.

The rich and varied history of colonial women in Latin America is united by a set of key issues that can be traced in part back to the questions posed by Asunción Lavrin's first edited volume. How did women experience Latin American institutions (government and church) relative to men? The implicit power structure therein is colonial patriarchy. Historians writing in the decades since Lavrin have offered myriad answers to the question of how patriarchy affected women's lives and, in particular, have complicated the narrative by increasing attention to class, race, and sexuality. The collective body of work reveals inherent tension in the absolute power of institutions and the negotiations by women in their day-to-day lives. The documents in this reader offer students a first-hand account of the ongoing actions by women to claim degrees of autonomy for themselves throughout the colonial world.

Apprehending Women's History through Legal Sources

The majority of the texts included here are drawn from legal settings. Legal records constitute the most comprehensive sources by which women's experiences in colonial Latin America (the period between 1492 and the completion of the revolutions of independence in 1825) can be reconstructed. While such sources are central to the reconstruction of women's history across the West in the Early Modern period, using such material is particularly appropriate in the Latin American context because of the extent to which the law constituted Iberia's overseas empires in the colonial period.[34] By "the law" we refer, first, to the many layers of legislation issued at all levels of government in Spain and Spanish America, all the way from the lofty proclamations Spanish

---

33. McKinley, *Fractional Freedoms*; María Eugenia Chaves, "Slave Women's Strategies for Freedom and the Late Spanish Colonial State," in *Hidden Histories of Gender and the State in Latin America,* ed. Elizabeth Dore and Maxine Molyneux (Durham, NC: Duke University Press, 2000), 108–26.

34. Both Kathryn Burns, *Into the Archive: Writing and Power in Colonial Peru* (Durham: Duke University Press, 2010) and Angel Rama, *The Lettered City* (Durham, NC: Duke University Press, 1996), make this argument.

monarchs issued in their *reales cédulas* (royal decrees) down to the minute administrative matters treated by the resolutions of *cabildos* (city councils). Second, we refer to the application of law in judicial contexts—ecclesiastical, civil, and criminal courts—and third to the enormous body of extra-judicial legal transactions by which elites and commoners, through the intercessions of notaries, organized and officiated their public and private lives.

In the Latin American context, the law, as opposed to other entities (the military, the church, the entrepreneurial population, or peninsular elites) orchestrated Iberia's claims to its overseas empire to an exceptional degree. As several researchers in the past fifteen years have also demonstrated, Spanish America is also unique in terms of the dramatic extent to which the non-European populations as well as women enthusiastically and effectively embraced the rights and privileges the law afforded them. Within ten years of the conquest, indigenous communities began using legal channels to petition the crown, and eventually the Real Audiencias (the central district courts in Spanish American viceroyalties) as well as to local magistrates for redress of fiscal, political, and personal grievances.[35] Enslaved Africans, both male and female, used the protection of the law to secure their rights to personal property, to limit corporal punishment, and to regulate their rights to self-purchase. Women in Latin America used the law to address domestic violence, to secure legal separation from husbands who were not fulfilling their financial or physical obligations, and to arrange for the distribution of their possessions to their heirs. Indeed, Bianca Premo has recently argued that it was through the venue of tribunals that marginalized Latin Americans—women, those enslaved, and indigenous people—constructed the Enlightenment by using courts as a means to redress social and legal injustice.[36]

The law was central to the lives of colonial Latin Americans, but legal sources present various kinds of interpretive challenges to those of us trying to apprehend the past through such materials. What kinds of experiences of the law can historians access? What kinds of materials are contained in the texts themselves and what problems do these texts present? Judicial cases often document the experiences of women who came to the attention of judicial authorities because they were exceptional in some way, or because they took exception to colonial institutions and conventions. The very contrariness of such women lends itself to the suggestion that colonial-era women were, as a

---

35. See, for example, Steve J. Stern, *Peru's Indian Peoples and the Challenge of Spanish Conquest: Huamanga to 1640* (Madison: University of Wisconsin Press, 1993); Brian P. Owensby, *Empire of Law and Indian Justice in Colonial Mexico* (Stanford, CA: Stanford University Press, 2008); Graubart, *With Our Labor and Sweat*; María Elena Díaz, *The Virgin, the King, and the Royal Slaves of El Cobre: Negotiating Freedom in Colonial Cuba, 1670–1780* (Stanford, CA: Stanford University Press, 2002).
36. Premo, *The Enlightenment on Trial*.

rule, fearless troublemakers or unrepentant deviants. Students encountering only these kinds of sources might be forgiven for formulating the impression that the women of colonial Latin America should best be understood as a collection of defiant rabble rousers.

Contributing to this impression, historians of women have uncovered substantial evidence in the past two decades of the ways that the law and legal processes empowered Spanish American women, particularly when their positions were compared with women from other European countries. For one thing, *patria potestad* (the legal right of the fathers to determine the fiscal and legal contours of those under their protection) notwithstanding, in Iberian law, women had the independent right to inherit, own, and bequeath property. Second, regulations governing inheritance did not discriminate between men and women as was the case for other European powers. Legitimacy and the degree of blood relationship to the deceased, rather than sex, determined inheritance rights. Finally, within marriage, at least theoretically, women retained independent financial control of their own assets, consisting of the dowry and the arras. Dowries were financial gifts their families presented to their daughters at marriage, which husbands were permitted to manage. The arras was a lump sum gift representing a maximum of 10 percent of his personal wealth that a groom often presented to his bride at marriage as a symbol of estimation in which he held the union. The value of both items along with accumulated interest was returned to women, at the time of death or legal separation from their husbands. They bequeathed such wealth independently to their heirs. In recognition of these practices, Spanish and Spanish American women did not always relinquish their own surnames at marriage.[37]

Furthermore, widows and single women over the age of twenty-five enjoyed legal rights identical to those of men to make contracts, litigate, and administer their own property.[38] But even married women may have exercised such rights more often than the law would suggest at first reading. Both Kathryn Burns and Karen Gauderman have also observed that although the law may have declared that married women could not act independently of their husbands in legal or fiscal matters, women frequently circumvented such restrictions. Burns suggests that women may have acted autonomously despite the law's official restrictions. While she describes frequently located

---

37. For more on women and the law in colonial Latin America, see Silvia Marina Arrom, *The Women of Mexico City, 1790–1857* (Stanford, CA: Stanford University Press, 1985), Chapter 2; Matthew C. Mirow, *Latin American Law: A History of Private Law and Institutions in Spanish America* (Austin: University of Texas Press, 2004), Chapter 5.

38. Susan Migden Socolow, *The Women of Colonial Latin America* (Cambridge: Cambridge University Press, 2000), 9–10; Gauderman, *Women's Lives*, 27, 30.

cases in which women represented themselves in legal transactions, she has never found emancipatory documents suggesting they had obtained permission from their husbands or fathers to do so.[39] Further, Gauderman found that women who had not obtained licenses from their husbands to engage in independent commercial transactions occasionally legitimated their actions through retroactive licenses obtained from their husbands. If a husband refused to grant such a license, Gauderman reports, "the courts could compel them him through fines and imprisonment, and if this were not sufficient, the judge alone could grant the woman a license."[40] Judicial documents also document the extent to which both Habsburg and Bourbon legal practices offered sometimes surprising protections, or occasionally, useful indifference, to the legal plights of colonial women.

The impression that the law empowered colonial Latin American women who effectively defied their subordination to men usefully counters an opposite portrait of women's status that emphasizes the lawful victimization of women in colonial contexts.[41] Women's legally subordinate status is suggested by some elements of Spanish law: married women and female minors could not by law initiate legal or contractual proceedings without the permission of their husbands or fathers. Women, like children, were also limited in their personal and fiscal decisions by the legal and social concept of *patria potestad*, literally, the power of the father to govern the minors of his household. This power, according to the *Siete Partidas,* the thirteenth-century code that remained the most important foundational legal philosophy governing the law in the colonial era, defined *patria potestad* as "the power fathers had over their children," and withheld such power from mothers, and women, like servants and slaves, ideally remained under the authority of male heads of household.[42] Further, the legal privileges that men held over their wives is apparent in Spanish and Spanish American regulations concerning adultery. Although the law theoretically supported women's suits for legal separation from husbands who engaged in wanton adultery, men who caught their wives in flagrante delicto, were lawfully empowered, depending on the code

---

39. Kathryn Burns, "Forms of Authority: Women's Legal Representations in Mid-Colonial Quito," in *Women, Texts, and Authority in the Early Modern Spanish World*, eds. Marta V. Vicente and Luis R. Corteguera (Aldershot, UK: Ashgate, 2003), 149.

40. Gauderman, *Women's Lives*, 41.

41. This is the thesis Karen Vieira Powers advances in *Women in the Crucible of Conquest: The Gendered Genesis of Spanish American Society, 1500–1600* (Albuquerque: University of New Mexico Press, 2005).

42. See Premo, *Children of the Father King*, 25–27.

consulted, to either murder both parties, or to murder the man alone, while turning the wife over to judicial authorities for punishment.[43]

The document choices in this collection reveal that Spanish American law, like the social context in which it developed, served at once to empower women and to inhibit them. A binary model that casts women alternatively as victims or rebels does not accurately convey their experiences or social realities as they operated to achieve their goals amongst networks of allies (and opponents) of both sexes. We attempt to offer a more nuanced portrait of women's experiences within the colonial legal system with our documentary selections in two ways. We hope to provide an indication of the range of women's colonial experiences—from the extraordinary to the representative—through our selections of notarial in addition to judicial records because the former type of documentation helps create a more representative model of experiences common to many women's lives. Such sources contain such social historical matters as details of family relations, property holdings, and governance, but can also be used to understand more esoteric issues, including for instance the assessment of individuals' articulations of their connections to both European and indigenous cultural, material, and spiritual realms.[44] Second, we hope students and scholars will be able to use these materials to better understand both the specific mechanisms by which women used the law to their own advantage, and those circumstances in which the law disadvantaged women, or was powerless to assist them.

Reading Strategies and Interpretive Questions

We close with a discussion of four interpretive strategies and five broad interpretive questions through which the following source selections may be apprehended. First, tracking texts for various kinds of omissions—temporal delays, unexplained gaps of information, or matters left unsaid—is a useful strategy for the interpretation of any kind of historical documentation. Readers, for instance, might consider the meaning of significant lapses in time occurring between different stages of a judicial case. What might account

---

43. Some sources of Castilian law, including the *Fuero de Cuenca* and the *Fuero de Sepúlveda*, empowered men to kill both parties. The *Siete Partidas*, however, limited the husband to the right only to kill the man who had challenged his honor. Albrecht Classen and Connie Scarborough, eds., *Crime and Punishment in the Middle Ages and Early Modern Age: Mental-Historical Investigations of Basic Human Problems and Social Responses* (Göttingen, Germany: Hubert & Co., 2012), 231.

44. Karen B. Graubart, "Catalina de Agüero: A Mediating Life," in *Native Wills from the Colonial Americas: Dead Giveaways in a New World*, ed. Jonathan Truitt and Mark Christensen (Salt Lake City: University of Utah Press, 2015), 21.

for such lapses? Do they reveal something about the behavior or motivations of the historical subjects under study, or might they be indicative of bureaucratic or institutional practices? Documentary omissions can also assume other guises, including issues that appear important in one portion of a case or to one party, that are subsequently neglected by others. If various witnesses concentrate in their testimony on one issue, what might it mean if this matter did not feature in a judge's assessment of a case? Another revealing type of omission involves those matters that historical subjects, whether state officials, or humble commoners, considered so commonplace that they did not merit comment in the text. What do the texts collected here reveal about the kinds of practical, spiritual, cultural, or legal knowledge were of such an uncontested nature that they required no explanation in the documentary record? What sorts of attitudes, beliefs, laws, or behaviors were so accepted that they literally went "without saying"?

A second interpretive strategy involves tracing aberrations and deviations from documentary templates. Legal sources, whether notarial or judicial, share the attribute of adhering to formulaic patterns of procedure and language. In various passages within individual types of documents, lengthy sections of text follow a standardized "boilerplate" template. These include such legal formulas as the text of the oaths to which witnesses before the Inquisition must adhere, the standardized questions to which witnesses testifying as to a subject's character before the Casa de la Contratación in migratory application decision must respond, the standardized profession of Christian piety which precedes notarized wills witnesses. Although useful historical information can be extracted from the texts of such "boilerplate" standards and their usages, the appearance of irregularities from standardized language or procedure can be particularly revealing because they normally indicate matters historical subjects felt particularly compelled to modify in some way.[45] Although readers unfamiliar with the standardized templates that structure many legal texts will find it challenging to detect all modifications to individual documents, in some cases the modification of language, procedure, or intent is made apparent within the source entries themselves because, as occurs in the 1806 infanticide trial of María del Carmen Ventura, a subject within the record itself calls attention to the nonstandard legal procedure undertaken.

A third strategy, closely related to those of tracking for omissions and exceptions, involves closely reading texts for internal contradictions. Where do different voices or documents dating from different dates contain internal contradictions with one another? What do we make of it when two different witnesses provide contradictory evidence to a judge or notary? Which party do we believe and why, and why does it matter?

---

45. This is a strategy Burns advocates in *Into the Archive*, 125.

This strategy of searching for internal contradiction raises a final issue central to the task of interpreting historical documentation: the evaluation of reliable narrators and sources. One approach to trying to extract reliable information from judicial texts is to focus on the incidental rather than the intentional information such sources contain. When historians study judicial documents, particularly criminal trials, we are tempted to adopt the point of view of the judges who first collected and analyzed such materials. We read denunciations and defenses that recount stories of violent and dramatic crimes and it is hard not to form conclusions about the likelihood of defendants' guilt or innocence in these trials. However, approaching the examination of judicial documents from the same point of view as judges, with the objective of ascertaining the guilt or innocence of defendants and plaintiffs, is fraught with difficulties, including our forced reliance on that portion of materials and information that survives in the preserved archival record of a given case, complicated by our distance of several hundred years' removal from the events themselves. All parties, including the agents of the courts themselves, have agendas they are pursuing in court cases and especially as latter-day consumers of these records, we are likely to misunderstand or misapprehend all parties' undeclared objectives.

Rather than assuming that the central conclusions that can be drawn from judicial records concern the judgement of guilt or innocence of defendants, it may make more sense to focus on the incidental information contained in such records. Kathryn Burns discusses her use of this strategy in her discussion about a theft trial from late seventeenth-century Cuzco where instead of focusing on the "whodunit" aspect of the trial, she concentrated on incidental evidence about the social and economic lives of her historical subjects that details from the transcript allowed her to glimpse. Among these was her observation that the two Inca nobility allegedly robbed during a party they hosted had left Cuzco during the court's investigation into the case to pick potatoes. This surprising revelation was in no way germane to understanding who was responsible for the theft, but in Burns' terms, was one that "helps flesh out our sense of what it meant to belong to Cuzco's nobility at that time."[46]

Whereas three decades ago the history of colonial Latin American women was a tiny subfield, it is now a major field with a rich diversity of subjects and methods. This book offers an important selection of the sources that serve as the primary ingredients of historical analysis for this field. To study the primary source documents in systematic fashion, we highlight five salient points of this scholarship for scholars and students to use as a set of guiding concepts that interconnect these materials.

---

46. Burns, *Into the Archive*, 137.

First, how and where did women act with autonomy or access power within colonial patriarchy, defined here as the overarching set of institutions, values, and practices that privileged males of European descent over all others.[47] These documents encourage students to identify the deeper complexity of women's experiences and reveal how women negotiated their interactions with the institutions of crown and church in colonial society.[48]

Second, how and where is the law (or legal process) a tool for women? Rather than imagine the law to be a courtroom inhabited only by men, jurisdictional spaces—whether physical, like tribunals, or discursive, like legal arguments—were filled with women in the colonial era. In contrast to women's legal actions in the English colonies, Iberian legal codes and legal precedents gave important powers to women. How did women employ these strategies? And when did they need to use extralegal strategies?

Third, how did racial identity (African, indigenous, Spanish) mark women's experiences? To be sure, racial identity signified different legal status and tax burdens in colonial society. The enslavement of African women placed them in a precarious legal position vis à vis their owners while frequently exposing them to systematic abuse. For indigenous women, cultural, material, and social marginalization became dominant and was expressed in myriad ways, from their difficulty in securing access to credit to their physical removal from the geographical spaces of urban power, to the condemnation of their religious practices as heretical. Women of Spanish descent did not have these challenges, though they did face an inferior legal position to Spanish men. Moreover, constructions of identity fused gender and race; how certain people viewed certain women was based on race. Although excellent scholarship has demonstrated that identity was not fixed,[49] women's gender identity as defined in a given moment coded their daily experiences and shaped the strategies available to them.

Fourth, how did networks of women operate in colonial society? These documents give evidence of how women worked with other women to share knowledge and strategies in such realms as trade, health, and family care. But moments of tension also arose both within and between women from

---

47. For a helpful discussion of patriarchy in the colonial context, see Stern, *The Secret History of Gender*, 21–22.

48. The significance of women's voices in colonial texts is demonstrated in remarkable detail in the recent volume of Mónica Díaz and Rocío Quispe-Agnoli, eds., *Women's Negotiations and Textual Analysis in Latin America, 1500–1799* (New York: Routledge Press, 2017).

49. See, for example, Joanne Rappaport, *The Disappearing Mestizo: Configuring Difference in the Colonial New Kingdom of Granada* (Durham, NC: Duke University Press, 2014). In addition, the volume *Imperial Subjects*, eds. Andrew B. Fisher and Matthew D. O'Hara, offers a number of articles on this issue. See Fisher and O'Hara, *Imperial Subjects: Race and Identity in Colonial Latin America* (Durham, NC: Duke University Press, 2009).

different class and ethnic categories. Case studies in this volume allow readers to examine instances in which women acted as informers and witnesses against other women.

Fifth, how did women and men interact? A prominent characteristic of historical scholarship on women in colonial Latin America is that it frequently analyzes women in relationship with or in comparison to men. Therefore, readers will find that as much as they can identify about women within these documents, there is also much to be learned in them about men. Male figures are significant in each document, and this lets readers contemplate the kinds of relationships that existed between men and women who lived within a patriarchal society. Some relationships might conform to expectations, but we expect others might surprise readers. Use this as a tool, then, to examine how women and men related to one another within the different frameworks of kin, employment, state, and religious power that connected them. Ultimately, the contemplation of these primary sources allows for a deeper understanding of how women navigated the whole of colonial society, including their encounters and relations with men.

1

Grant of Tacuba by Hernán Cortés to Isabel Moctezuma, Firstborn Daughter of Moctezuma II and Her Last Will and Testament (Mexico City, 1526, 1550)

The Spanish conquest of the Aztec empire of south-central Mexico dramatically transformed the life of the woman whom the Spanish knew as Isabel Moctezuma. She was the eldest legitimate daughter of Moctezuma II, the reigning Aztec emperor at the time of Hernán Cortés' 1519 invasion of Mexico. In recognition of her status, his personal debt to her father, and the enormity of the pre-Columbian wealth controlled by her dynastic line, Cortés granted her the largest and wealthiest *encomienda* (grant of indigenous tribute and labor) in the Valley of Mexico in the mid-sixteenth century. His 1526 creation of this *encomienda* is reproduced in its entirety in the first document below. Isabel Moctezuma, like many other indigenous women of the conquest-era nobility, played a central role in the consolidation of Spanish power in the aftermath of conquest, but also demonstrated a remarkable capacity for adaptation to a dramatically new cultural and political landscape. Evidence of her generation's capacity for adaptation is apparent in the second document included here, her last will and testament, composed in 1550.

Isabel Moctezuma was born in 1509 or 1510. Before reaching the age of eleven, her parents had already arranged for her to marry her father's presumed successor, Atlixcatl, but this union never occurred. Subsequent to Cortés' imprisonment of the emperor Moctezuma, Isabel[1] had been married to the last two leaders of the Aztec empire, first to her uncle Cuitláhuac, who died from smallpox, and then to her cousin, Cuauhtémoc. The Spanish captured and later tortured the latter during their final assault on the Aztec capital on August 13, 1521. Cortés took Cuauhtémoc with him on his 1524 voyage of conquest into Honduras and ordered him executed there the following year. Upon his capture, Cuauhtémoc pleaded that the Spanish treat his wife and her female attendants with the respect due their station. His

---

1. Although the editors generally refer to all historical subjects by their surnames, in this chapter we use Isabel's Christian name in order to distinguish her from her more widely known father, the emperor Moctezuma II.

plea, and that of her father, may have influenced Cortés' treatment of Isabel.[2] Aside from partially honoring his promises to Moctezuma respecting Isabel's future finances, Cortés used Isabel for his own purposes. Willingly or not, she bore him a daughter; and subsequently, he arranged marriages for her to a succession of his political allies. When Cortés returned to Mexico City from Honduras, he moved Isabel to a house where his other concubines lived; she may have been living there at the moment he designated the *encomienda* of the town of Tacuba to her.

The *encomienda* of Tacuba (a community about five miles west of Tenochtitlan–Mexico City) that Cortés designated to Isabel on the eve of her wedding to Alonso de Grado, although a fraction of Moctezuma II's original holdings, was extensive. By the mid-sixteenth century, it had become the largest *encomienda* in the central valley because every other such grant originally of greater size had escheated to the crown.[3] Its wealth, and the Spanish crown's unusual continued acknowledgment of its legitimacy, ensured that the Spanish and eventually the republican Mexican state would continue to pay Isabel's descendants' benefits from the grant until 1933, the year the chief historian in Mexico's National Archive certified the transcribed copy of the original *encomienda* consulted for the present translation. During her lifetime, Isabel herself attempted to increase her own claim to wealth, and those of her heirs, particularly her female descendants. In one *probanza* (petition) that Isabel submitted to the Spanish state in an attempt to expand her claim to those lands she should have inherited from her father, historian Pedro Carrasco uncovered her assertion that "if there were no males who were close relations and most worthy, females could succeed to the rulership."[4]

In 1528, Isabel gave birth to her first child, a daughter, fathered by Cortés, whom she named Leonor Cortés Moctezuma. Cortés did not formally legitimize Leonor as he did Martín Cortés, the son borne him by Malintzín, the indigenous woman who served as his primary translator and advisor during the wars of conquest, but he did recognize Leonor as his daughter. Cortés arranged for Leonor to be raised in the home of Juan Gutiérrez de Altamirano, an aide and cousin by marriage of Cortés, whose household also undertook to

---

2. As acknowledgment for his capture of New Spain, King Charles V had awarded Cortés with the title *repartidor* (distributor of Indians as vassals), *capitán general* (supreme military commander), and governor of New Spain. It was in the former capacity that Cortés awarded Isabel her *encomienda*.

3. Donald E. Chipman, *Moctezuma's Children: Aztec Royalty under Spanish Rule, 1520–1700* (Austin: University of Texas Press, 2005), 65.

4. Pedro Carrasco, "Royal Marriages in Ancient Mexico," cited in Robert Haskett, "Activist or Adulteress? The Life and Struggle of *doña* Josefa María of Tepoztlan," in *Indian Women of Early Mexico*, ed. Susan Schroeder, Stephanie Wood, and Robert Haskett (Norman: University of Oklahoma Press, 1997), 160.

raise his son with Malintzín. Leonor and Martín both lived in the Altamirano household, located three blocks south of the main plaza in the capital city. Gutiérrez de Altamirano served subsequently as executor of Isabel's estate and administrator of the conqueror's estate as well.

We know little about the relationship Isabel might have had with her estranged daughter. As Anna Lanyon suggests may have been the case for Malintzín and her son Martín, Isabel might have occasionally glimpsed her daughter at public events or market days on Mexico's large central square.[5] By the time of Isabel's death, Leonor had already been married for nearly a year to *conquistador* (conqueror) Juan de Tolsá, an unsuccessful silver baron of the Zacatecas region. Isabel must have at least kept track of the development of her life, however. For although Isabel did not mention Leonor in her first articulation of her will, translated below, she did make some provision for her daughter in an unofficial supplement. Diego de Isla, the scribe who recorded Isabel's will, declared that she had testified to her three executors on her deathbed that Leonor was to receive one fifth of the monies remaining from a lump sum of six hundred pesos that she had set aside from her estate to pay for her funeral and masses.[6]

As Cortés discussed in the Tacuba grant, after Cuauhtémoc's execution, he arranged for a new marital alliance for Isabel in 1526 to one of his military followers, Alonso de Grado, who died of unknown causes six months later. And while she was pregnant with Leonor in 1527 or 1528, Cortés arranged for her marriage to her fourth spouse, Spaniard Pedro Gallego de Andrade, who died allegedly of poisoning shortly after their wedding. Isabel then spent nearly four years as a widow until 1530 when she married Juan Cano, a *conquistador* who had originally sailed to Mexico with Pánfilo de Narváez's defeated expedition against Cortés, but who later joined forces with Cortés and became a prosperous *encomendero* (holder of an *encomienda*). Isabel shared the remaining twenty years of her short life with Cano. Although she had borne no children to any of her first three spouses, she gave birth to one son, Juan Andrade Moctezuma, with Pedro Gallego de Andrade, and had an additional five children—Pedro, Gonzalo, Juan, Isabel, and Catalina Cano Moctezuma—with her last husband. Details of the fortunes of all her children, and some indication of the relationship she had with them, are indicated in her will and testament below.

Almost immediately after her death, Isabel's heirs, and, in particular, her widower, Juan Cano, along with Diego Arias de Sotelo, son-in-law of her

---

5. Anna Lanyon, *The New World of Martín Cortés* (Cambridge, MA: Da Capo Press, 2003), 12.

6. Chipman, *Moctezuma's Children*, 68.

illegitimate daughter,[7] Leonor Moctezuma Cortés, contested Isabel's designation in her will of her first-born son, Juan de Andrade, as the principal inheritor of the Tacuba *encomienda*. The lawsuit that itself endured for eighty years after her death, eventually designated Juan Cano, her widower, along with her first-born son, Juan de Andrade Moctezuma, and their heirs, as equal claimants to her wealth (rather than privileging Juan de Andrade as the principal recipient as she had originally indicated was her desire). The suit, however, dismissed the claims of descendants of Leonor, her illegitimate daughter by Hernán Córtes.[8]

No texts that women themselves authored survive from the first years of the Spanish conquest of Mexico, so historians are forced to draw conclusions about their experiences and perspectives from others' recordings, such as the 1526 *encomienda* grant in which Cortés characteristically presented his own and others' actions in terms chosen to reflect himself in the best possible light. Cortés presents his granting of the *encomienda* as an act of generous obligation. But in what ways did he and his class of allies stand to benefit from the creation of this grant? What might we observe from these texts about both the opportunities and the restrictions on indigenous women's personal, economic, and legal lives in this setting? We can assume Isabel's will embodied many of her own wishes and decisions. What evidence do we see of how she was able to exercise her will, and in what ways was she hindered from doing so? Our own era takes as sacrosanct the notion of amorous ties between spouses and between parents and offspring. Are there indications that Isabel's context afforded individuals opportunities for such personal affection? Both of Isabel's daughters, *doña* (lady) Isabel and *doña* Catalina eventually became nuns. Although she willed the bulk of her estate to her eldest son, what financial provision does Isabel try to make for her daughters? Should we conclude anything from this? Finally, how do the choices Isabel made in her will compare to those of other, non-elite, indigenous women made in the first century after conquest in the Andes presented in Chapter 3? Does Isabel, like Ana Copana, seem to have remained strongly connected to pre-Columbian material culture? Does she seem to have had the same relationship as Copana to Catholic spirituality? What might explain these similarities and differences?

---

7. Leonor, because she was born outside of wedlock and because her father did not acknowledge her, was classified as "illegitimate." Illegitimate children were distinct from "natural children," offspring born outside of marriage to fathers who recognized them and to parents of consensual relationships who were not legally impeded from marrying one another.

8. Juan Cano, her last husband, also launched a lawsuit four years prior to Isabel's death to recuperate land, houses, and other valuable assets that should have formed part of the patrimony she inherited from her father. See Anastasya Kalyuta, "La casa y hacienda de un señor mexica Un estudio analítico de la 'Información de *doña* Isabel de Moctezuma,'" *Anuario de Estudios Americanos* 65:2 (2008), 13–37.

1.1 Grant of Tacuba, Made by *don* Hernán Cortés to *doña* Isabel Moctezuma and Her Heirs (1526)[9]

"REAL CEDULA," certified copy of that which Hernán Cortés granted to Isabel Moctezuma. Luis Sierra Horcasitas

Mexico, 22 December 1933

> *[Luis Sierra Horcasitas, director of Mexico's Archivo General de la Nación wrote to Luis González Obregón, head of the institution's historians' division, to say he required a certified copy of the* Real Cédula *(Royal Decree) by Hernán Cortés granting the town of Tacuba and its surrounding area to* doña *Isabel de Moctezuma. The following is the certified copy González Obregón provided. The reference to the stamped paper that Obregón used indicates he based his version on an eighteenth-century transcription of the original sixteenth-century text.]*

[A seal at the top of the document reads] "Carolus IV. D, G, Hiapanier Rex" A cross. *Un quartillo.*[10] 1793 and 1794.

Whereas, at the time that I, *don* Hernán Cortés, Captain-General and Governor of this New Spain and its provinces for His Majesty, came to these lands with a number of ships and people to pacify and populate it and to bring its people under the dominion and service of the Imperial Crown of His Majesty, as has been done, I had news of a great *Señor* (Lord) called Moctezuma residing in the great City of Tenochtitlan, who was *Señor* of it and of all the surrounding provinces and lands. I made my arrival known to him through some messengers in order that he should obey me in the name of His Majesty so that he should offer himself as his vassal. He welcomed my arrival and to better demonstrate his great zeal and will to serve His Majesty and to obey that which through me in his Royal name was ordered, he showed me much love and commanded that in all places that the Spaniards would travel on their way to this city we should be very well received and be given all that was necessary for us, as was always done, and much more as well. And to this city we came and I and all in my company were well received.

---

9. GD 122 Archivo de Buscas y Traslado de Tierras, vol. 63, exp. 54, fs. 778–788. Año: 1933. Copia certificada de la real cédula que concedió Hernán Cortés a Isabel Moctezuma, expedida a Luis Sierra Horcasitas. The original reads *don* "Fernando" Cortés. Fernando and Hernando are both variants of the more commonly used name Hernán, which for consistency's sake has been used throughout this translation.

10. Like almost all legal documents, this one is written on sealed (stamped) paper, here with a cost of one *quartillo*, one fourth of a *real*, which, in turn, was worth one eighth of one *peso*.

[Cortés then explained that Moctezuma had consented to be imprisoned by Cortés whom Cortés claims he was anxious to obey. He described how, with Moctezuma's aid, he pacified the central territory of the Aztec empire, and maintained good relations with the indigenous population until Pánfilo de Narváez, emissary sent by Cuba's governor Diego Velázquez, arrived to arrest Cortés for his unauthorized invasion of Mexico. Narváez's arrest, so claimed Cortés, provoked a rebellion against the Spanish and against Moctezuma who died in the uprising. Having received a mortal wound, Cortés asserted that Moctezuma requested that he should settle his final affairs.]

He begged me and entreated me earnestly saying that if he died from this wound, out of respect for the depth of his love and desire to please me, I should take it as my duty to take charge of his three daughters, and that I should have them baptized and taught our doctrine, because he knew that it was very good. After I had conquered this city, I had [the three daughters] baptized and named. I named the one who is the eldest, his legitimate heir, *doña* Isabel, and the other two *doña* María and *doña* Mariana. And when he was dying from his head wound, he turned to me and called to me and begged me with great affection, saying that if he died, I should watch over his daughters, saying that they were the most valuable jewels that he was giving me, and that I should divide among them the property that he left, remembering especially the eldest one whom he loved very much, and that if by the will of God he escaped from the illness, and had victory in this siege, that he would show me even more fully his desire to serve His Majesty and give me stronger proofs of the love that he had for me. Besides this, he also wished me to relate to His Majesty how he had left his daughters in my care and to entreat him in Moctezuma's name to command me to watch over them and keep them in my protection and administration since he was such a great servant and vassal of His Majesty, and always had great favor for the Spaniards as I had seen and see, and because of the love that he had for them, he had been so badly treated, although he did not regret it. Even in his own tongue he said (among other reasons) that he charged me with conscience in this matter.

Wherefore, in acknowledgment of the many services that the *Señor* Moctezuma has performed for His Majesty, the good offices that during his life he performed for me, and for the good treatment he gave to the Spaniards in my company in His Royal name, and the goodwill that he showed in his Royal service since without a doubt he played no part in the uprising which his brother alone instigated in this city, and his hope that he would be a great help in keeping the land always very peaceful and that the *naturales* (natives) would learn to understand us and would voluntarily serve His Majesty with great sums of pesos of gold, jewels, and other things, which on account of the coming of Narváez and his own brother's insurrection had been lost, and considering also that God Our *Señor* and His Majesty are greatly served by the planting of our Holy Religion in these lands, which each day is growing in influence, and so that the daughters of Moctezuma and the other *señores* and *principales* (principal indigenous leaders), and other people native to this New Spain are shown the greatest demonstration of the doctrine as possible, so that they will desist from the idolatry that until now they have followed, and will be brought to the true knowledge of our Holy Catholic Faith, especially the children of the *principales* like *Señor* Moctezuma, and for all of this and so that the conscience of His Majesty and my own will be released in his Royal name, I judged it best to concede his plea. I took to my house his three daughters to ensure that they should receive the best treatment and accommodation possible, administering and teaching them the commandments of our Holy Catholic Faith, and the other good customs of Christians, so that with greater goodwill and love they would serve God Our *Señor*, and know the Articles of the faith, and so that the other *naturales* would take them as an example.

It seemed best to me, considering the rank of the person of *doña* Isabel, who is the legitimate heir of *Señor* Moctezuma, and the one with whom I had been most urgently charged, and whose age required that she would have a companion, to give her for a husband and spouse to a person of honor and nobility, who has served His Majesty in my company since the beginning of our journey to these lands, who has fulfilled for me and in the name of His Majesty highly honorable duties and offices such as treasurer and Lieutenant-Governor, and many others, and in these offices had been judged very capable, and in the present is serving in the office of Visitador General[11] of all the *indios* (indians) of this New Spain. His name is Alonso Grado; he is a native of Alcántara. To *doña* Isabel I promise and give in dowry and arras[12] and her descendants in the name of His Majesty and as his Governor and Captain General of these lands, and so that by right of her patrimony and legitimacy belongs to her, the Lordship and *naturales* of the town of Tacuba that has one hundred and twenty houses, and Yetebeque, its estate which has forty houses,[13] and Ixquiluca, another estate that has another one hundred

---

11. This was a crown-appointed inspector of a colonial jurisdiction.

12. An arras was a financial gift not larger than 10 percent of the husband's assets that a groom pledged to his bride to demonstrate her value to him. Its value was to be given to widows from their husbands' estates, and along with their dowries were also protected from claims by their husbands' financial creditors whether before or after death.

13. The AGN's 1933 transcription here reads "Esteveyules su estancia." William Prescott's transcription of the document reads "y Yetete, que es estancia." The AGN also produced a second transcription of this document, published in the *Boletín* in October 1995 in which the

and twenty houses, and Chimalpan another estate that has forty houses, and Chapulmoloyan that has another forty houses, and Aescapulaltongo that has twenty houses, and Jilotzingo with forty houses, and another estate that is called Ocoyacaque, and another called Caltepeque, and other called Jalasco, and another estate that is called Huatusco, and another called Duotepeque, and another that is called Tasalaque, all of which amounts in total to one thousand two hundred and forty houses. These estates and towns are subject to the town of Tacuba and to its *señor*. I give this property in the name of His Majesty in dowry and arras to *doña* Isabel so that she may have, hold, and enjoy it by right of inheritance, for now and forevermore, with the title of *Señora* (Lady) of the town and the rest herein contained. This I give in the name of His Majesty to fulfill his royal duty and my own in his name. By this order, I declare that this property will never be taken away from her by any means nor at any time. And as further guarantee of this, I promise and certify in the name of His Majesty and I beg that His Majesty will be pleased to confirm the grant to *doña* Isabel and her heirs and successors, of the town of Tacuba and the rest herein contained and the other estates and subject towns that are in the possession of some Spaniards; and they should not have been given them until His Majesty learned if he would be served by this.

I hereby declare to be null and void any *cédula* (decree) *de encomienda* or donation I may have given to any person granting them privileges in the town of Tacuba and the other properties herein contained and I declare that in the name of His Majesty I revoke them, and restore them to *doña* Isabel so that she may have them as her own, and so that by law they belong to her;[14] and I command to all people, residents and inhabitants of New Spain that all its occupants and citizens should understand and receive *doña* Isabel as Lady of the town of Tacuba with its estates, and that nothing should impede nor hinder her from this, under pain of [a fine of] five hundred pesos of gold for the Exchequer of His Majesty. Dated the 27th day of June, 1526. *Don* Hernando Cortés. By order of the Governor of my *Señor*, Alonso Valiente. This is a copy that I certify. Contadoria General de Retases de México 29 of May 1796.

Juan Ordoñez,[Signature]

---

property is described as "Yetebeque su estancia." The editors have adopted this most recent interpretation and the spellings used in the *Boletín*'s transcriptions of the other locales listed.
14. Donald Chipman notes that just a few years earlier, Cortés had granted Tacuba in *encomienda* to one of his officials, Pedro Almíndez de Chrino, inspector-overseer charged with securing the king's share of metals, *Moctezuma's Children*, 46, 49.

1.2 Last Will and Testament of Isabel Moctezuma (1551)[15]

In the name of the Holy Trinity, Father, Son, and Holy Spirit, three people in one true God who lives and reigns forever and ever, and in honor, glory, and praise of Our Lady the Virgin Mary who is my Lady and defender. To whomever may see this power of attorney know that I, *doña* Isabel Moctezuma, legitimate wife of Juan Cano my *señor* and husband, resident of this great city of Tenochtitlan-México of this New Spain, being sick in body with the illness that God our lord has seen fit to visit upon me, and in sound mind and judgement and natural understanding, with license and authority and express consent that I request of Juan Cano, my *señor* and husband, who if by this act the law allows consent in order that I, for myself, create and decree this power of attorney according to what it contains. And I, Juan Cano, who am present, grant and acknowledge that I give and concede license and authority to you *doña* Isabel, my wife, as you have asked me, and I promise and pledge to do this unwaveringly, and not to revoke, reclaim or contradict it either [when I am] with sound judgement or without it under explicit obligation that for it I make of my possessions, and I request that those present accept this, my license and authority of faith. And I, the present notary, attest that Juan Cano gave and granted authority to *doña* Isabel, his wife, to make and frame this document in my presence and in that of the witnesses signed below. And I, *doña* Isabel, accept and receive and declare this is so, and state that because I am very afflicted by the illness that I have, and by its severity, that I cannot specifically make and order my will and last wishes in their entirety and because I have communicated that it is my will that for my soul, my goods will be made and disposed with the *señores licenciado* (holder of a licentiate degree),[16] Juan Altamirano and Andrés de Tapia and Alonso de Bazán, residents of this city who are present. I grant and know that I freely give and grant all my power according to all that I have and by right all that I possess to you three together, *señores licenciado* Juan Altamirano and Andrés de Tapia and Alonso de Bazán, so that you can execute my will and last wishes according to and in the form and manner that they wish and judge to be good, that through them my will shall be executed. From this moment onward, I grant, approve and desire that [their judgement] will be validated and fulfilled as if I myself did ordain it. In this way, I give them such will and power that I have and as required by law in such matters, and this document

---

15. Reproduced in "Documentos inéditos," *Boletín del Archivo General de la Nación, México* Cuarta serie (Otoño, 1995), 197–202.

16. *Licenciado/licenciados* is inconsistently pluralized in the text—in both the AGN's transcription and the transcription reproduced in the *Boletín*. The inconsistencies are reproduced in this translation as well.

can be and must be recognized with its incidental and dependent annexes and clauses in its free and general administration.

I wish and it is my will that when it pleases God, our *Señor,* to take me from this present life that my body will be buried in the church and monastery of San Agustín in this city in the place where Juan Cano my *señor* judges best, and to fulfill and execute my testament, commands, clauses and bequests that the *señores licenciado* Juan Altamirano and Andrés Tapia and Alonso de Bazán for me and in the name and by right of this power [of attorney] will execute and order. I give, name and designate them as my executors and grant all three together and each one separately my power of attorney so that they can access and sell my goods as needed to pay for the bequests and pious works that are included in the will. I also declare and command that it is my will that all the slaves[17] and *Indios,* both male and female, *naturales* of this land, that Juan Cano my husband and I hold as our own, for the portion of them which is mine, should be freed from all service and duties and from captivity, and as free people they can do what they want and I order that they be freed. And I also wish and order and it is my will that the *señores licenciado* Juan Altamirano, and Andrés de Tapia, and Alonso de Bazán in this my testament in my name and by virtue of this power [of attorney] can arrange and dispose of my goods for the masses and good works, and alms and penances for my soul and conscience, according to manner and form and in other things that they judge to be good, because I have communicated and spoken with them about this, and they can spend and dispose of one fifth of the value of all my goods on the abovementioned matters, and can fulfill any other order or orders to any person or persons that they judge fit, because I have indicated my will to them in this matter.

I also declare that I wish and order that all that it appears that I owe in debts and in salaries to my servants and other things that they judge should be done for the discharge of my soul and conscience the *señores licenciados* Juan Altamirano, and Andrés de Tapia, and Alonso de Bazán, I order them through my testament that they do, pay and discharge. And I also declare that I confess that at the time that I married with Juan Cano my *señor* and husband I did not have personal property,[18] nor property nor any money, except the Indians and towns, and that *señor* Juan Cano at that time had some cows and money, I do not know how much. I also declare and order that I revoke and annul any bond given to any person for anything of any

---

17. Although there was a substantial population of African slaves in Mexico by the mid-sixteenth century, Donald Chipman, *Moctezuma's Children,* 64, assumes those to which Isabel referred here were all indigenous.

18. Isabel Moctezuma might have more specifically meant she did not possess any furniture; the phrase she uses is *bienes muebles* (movable property) as opposed to real estate.

value any other testaments or codicils, or clauses, or orders, or bequests that until now I have made and ordered, open or closed in any way and any clause contained in them, or outside them either written or spoken, or if I as here expressed in their clauses word for word,[19] and give power fulfilled to the *señores licenciados* Juan Altamirano and Andrés de Tapia and Alonso de Bazán so that they can revoke and will revoke any such testaments, codicils, clauses and bequests that they judge by my deeds and orders before this my power [of attorney], because I wish and it is my will that they are invalid and should be worth nothing in and of themselves and I wish and order that the testament that the *señores licenciados* Juan Altamirano and Andrés de Tapia and Alsonso se Bazán by virtue of this my power [of attorney] make and order and the clauses in it contained are validated by my testament and last wishes and will be complied with and kept according to what they order and command.

I also declare that insomuch as Juan Cano my *señor* and husband and I own some precious textiles and bed linens, and beds, from these lands and from Castile and rugs and carpets and cushions and embossed and engraved skins (*guademecíes*) and pillows and handkerchiefs (*paños de manos*), and work tools, and clothing for myself, all of which I wish and order should go to *doña* Isabel and *doña* Catalina, my legitimate daughters by Juan Cano my husband, and I wish that these goods not be sold in an auction as goods of mine at the time of my death, nor should these goods be divided but rather should only be for *doña* Isabel and *doña* Catalina, my daughters. And that if it appears to be a good idea to Juan Cano, my *señor*, to sell these goods either in or outside of a public auction as he wishes, he can sell them as he sees fit, and once he has sold them, I order that one third of the goods be given to *doña* Isabel and *doña* Catalina, my daughters to improve their situations. I also wish and declare that it is my will that the town of Tacuba should remain with me and I give it and order it given to Juan de Andrada, my legitimate son by Pedro Gallego, my legitimate husband, because it is mine, since I have had and have it, I wish and it is my will that Juan de Andrada, my legitimate son, should have and possess it and after him, his heirs and successors forevermore. I also declare that it should be understood that I leave the town of Tacuba and its subjects to Juan de Andrada, my son, except for the towns of Cuyoacaque and Capuluaque, y Cuapanoaya, and Tepebaxuca, because these four towns along with those that are subject to them, I give and order that it is my will that Gonzalo Cano, my legitimate son by Juan Cano, my husband, should have and inherit them, for himself and his successors forevermore, with the qualification that if either Juan de Andrada or Gonzalo Cano, my legitimate sons dies in this life without leaving legitimate children born of legitimate marriage, in this case my legitimate son with Juan Cano, Pedro

---

19. "*De verbo ad verbum*" in the original.

Cano, will inherit that which was given to Juan de Andrada. And if Gonzalo Cano should die in this way, that is without legitimate children born of legitimate marriage, Juan Cano my legitimate son by Juan Cano my husband should have and inherit the indicated towns that I order he should have for himself and for his heirs and successors forevermore.

And I pray that his majesty be served to confirm and approve and take as good that which I leave ordered in these two clauses and decrees to my children in remuneration for the great sum that is owed to me as the legitimate daughter and heir of Moctezuma my father, who was *señor* of this New Spain, and this was given to me in compensation for that which was owed, fulfilled, and paid to my father. This power [of attorney] and orders within it and the testament that by virtue of it are ordered the *señores el licenciado* Juan Altamirano and Andrés de Tapia and Alonso de Bazán with the remainder of my goods I leave and name and institute as my legitimate and universal heirs Pedro Cano and Gonzalo and Juan Cano and *doña* Isabel and *doña* Catalina, my legitimate children by Juan Cano my *señor* and husband and Juan de Andrade my legitimate son by Pedro Gallego my legitimate husband, to hold and inherit, save for the grant worth one third that is ordered to *doña* Isabel and *doña* Catalina my daughters; the rest to be divided among them equally. I also declare that inasmuch as I have begged his majesty to make me a grant of the lands that remain and were based on and owned by Moctezuma my father, I wish and order and it is my will that if his majesty sees fit to issue me the grant, *doña* Isabel and *doña* Catalina, my daughters with Juan Cano, will have and inherit them without any of my sons placing any embargo or impediment on them because I give to them and order by right of improvement *(por vía de mejora)* one third of all my goods, and I do this in their favor in the best legal way that I can and must, in testament of which I confer this document in the manner and form that I said before to the present notary and witnesses inscribed below, by which before them was read *de verbo ad verbum,*[20] that which is done and executed in the City of Mexico, which resides in the Royal Audience of his majesty, being inside its walls on the 11 of July the year of the birth of our *Señor* Jesus Christ 1550.

Witnesses who were present, and for this reason specially called and requested, were father *fray* Juan Cruzate, prior of the monastery of San Agustín and *fray* Gregorio de Salazar, and *fray* Luis de Esobaleda, and *fray* Luis de Carranza, professor friars in the monastery of San Agustín and Hernando Mateo Carillo and Juan Altamirano citizens and residents of this city, and because I do not know how to write myself on my behalf at my request signed *Fray* Juan Cruzate, *Fray* Gregorio de Salazar, *Fray* Luis de Cabeceda, *Fray* Luis de Carranza and Hernán Mateo Carillo and Juan Altamirano. One

---

20. Word for word.

copy was made and corrected and certified with the original residing in the City of Mexico on the 12 of December 1551. [This is followed by a list of other witnesses.]

———————————————

Suggested Reading

Chipman, Donald E. *Moctezuma's Children: Aztec Royalty under Spanish Rule, 1520–1700*. Austin: University of Texas Press, 2005.

Lanyon, Anna. *The New World of Martin Cortés*. Cambridge, MA: Da Capo Press, 2003.

Schroeder, Susan, Stephanie Wood, and Robert Haskett, eds. *Indian Women of Early Mexico*. Norman: University of Oklahoma Press, 1997.

Townsend, Camila. *Malintzin's Choices: An Indian Woman in the Conquest of Mexico*. Albuquerque: University of New Mexico Press, 2006.

Document Themes

- Family
- Law
- Property
- Race and ethnicity
- Religion

2

Beatríz, *India*'s, Lawsuit for Freedom from Slavery (Castile, Spain, 1558–1574)

Introduction and Translation by Nancy E. van Deusen

What might have motivated Beatríz, an *india* (indigenous woman), to appear in 1558 before the tribunal of the House of Trade (Casa de la Contratación), located in Seville, Spain, to petition for her own and her daughter's freedom from slavery? Perhaps it was the fact that her daughter, Catalina (b. 1540)—one of five children whose fathers were never mentioned in the court documents—had been branded recently by their owner, Juan Cansino, a *vecino* (resident) and magistrate of the town of Carmona.[1] One of the issues to be resolved in the lawsuit was why Beatríz had refrained from approaching royal authorities after the passage of the 1542 New Laws, which in principle granted freedom to those *indios* whose masters could not provide legal documentation to prove bondage. Unlike dozens of other litigants attempting to prove their status as free *indios* before Spanish legal tribunals, Beatríz had waited sixteen years.[2]

Born around 1496, Beatríz claimed she had been born in the Spanish-controlled territory of Mexico (which became part of the viceroyalty of New Spain in 1535) and had been brought illegally and involuntarily to Portugal and then to Spain where she entered the Cansino household around 1530. Her master, Juan Cansino, maintained that she was an *india* from Portuguese territories where, by law, *indios* were not free from slavery. At play was whether Beatríz was from a place, alternately referred to as Malagueta, Malaqueta, Manacata, or Malacata, depending on whether witnesses claimed that it was located in Mexico, South America, or Africa.[3] Although demonstrating the location of her place of origin was key to winning emancipation for Beatríz and other enslaved *indios*, witnesses could also rely on physical

---

1. Carmona is twenty-two miles east of Seville.
2. Spanish archival repositories include at least 127 lawsuits filed between 1530 and 1585 by men and women labeled as "indios" and their masters. This figure may be a false positive because we do not know about the dozens, if not hundreds of other *indios* who, for a variety of reasons, failed to sue for their freedom.
3. Because different witnesses spelled the location differently, these inconsistencies have been maintained in this translation.

descriptions and a knowledge of an indigenous language to bolster a case. The problem with claiming knowledge of indigenous languages, however, was that most slaves brought to Castile had come as children and could not recall their native tongue. It was also problematic because indigenous language experts interrogated litigants in the more common indigenous languages like "the Mexican language" (read: Nahuatl), or Guaraní (for the Rio de la Plata area), when, in fact, hundreds if not thousands of other languages and dialects were spoken throughout Spanish and Portuguese America in the sixteenth century.

During Beatríz's lifetime, the enslavement of people categorized as *indios* in Spanish and Portuguese America was ubiquitous. In many places, the numbers of *indio* slaves outnumbered Africans forced into bondage and transported to America. Indeed, the forced removal and sale of native American peoples, most of whom were children, was one of the mainstays of the colonial economy before 1550. Many were permanently relocated in places far from their homelands. One could find Taíno people from the Greater Antilles islands in Lima, Peru, or Brazilian Tupinambá Indians in Honduras. Several thousand *indio* slave children like Beatríz also crossed the Atlantic and lived their lives in Portugal or Spain. As scholars have shown, despite the passage of the New Laws, the enslavement of *indios* in the Spanish-claimed territories of the Western hemisphere continued, albeit in smaller numbers, well into the seventeenth, eighteenth, and some historians argue, into the nineteenth century.[4] It is a history that, until recently, has been forgotten. But the fragmented and circumscribed stories of upheaval and relocation found in court cases such as Beatríz's allow us to reconstitute that history of violence, loss, and survival.

In Spain, freedom lawsuits could be heard before authorities in the House of Trade or by the appellate body, the Council of the Indies.[5] The New Laws and subsequent legislation afforded *procuradores* (legal representatives) to *indio* complainants (those initiating lawsuits) or defendants (the parties against whom lawsuits were leveraged) and waived the court costs for *indios*. Generally, authorities of the House of Trade reviewed legal complaints filed by disgruntled slave owners who resented the fact that two Crown inspections in 1543 and 1549 had freed more than one hundred slaves because masters could not provide documents showing legal acquisition of their slaves in Spanish America. House of Trade officials also considered *relaciones* (legal accounts) filed by *indios* whose masters had refused to free them after the passage of the New Laws of 1542. More than fifty-five percent of litigants were

---

4. Andrés Reséndez, *The Other Slavery: The Uncovered Story of Indian Enslavement in America* (Boston: Houghton Mifflin Harcourt, 2016).
5. In the House of Trade, cases were reviewed by a presiding judge and three officials.

women like Beatríz or her daughter, Catalina, who were concerned that slave status not pass to their children. After authorities had interviewed witnesses on behalf of litigants and defendants, they determined whether a case could proceed. Because slave litigants were required to remain in masters' households for the duration of the lawsuit—unless they could prove severe mistreatment—they were sometimes beaten, illegally branded, or intimidated into making false statements that favored slave owners. Masters like Juan Cansino also punished litigious and "rebellious" female slaves by selling or branding their children. For these and other reasons, some slaves persisted, but others desisted. Many of the cases remained incomplete or ended abruptly. Of those cases that reached completion, however, 95 percent were freed. But, even then, slave owners might appeal the case before the appellate body, the Council of the Indies, although these appeals were generally unsuccessful. In light of these statistics, it is unusual that Beatríz and her daughter Catalina would lose both the initial lawsuit and appeal. In fact, it was only when the Council of the Indies decided to review the appeal that the matter was finally resolved in favor of Beatríz and her offspring.

Freedom lawsuits are valuable historical documents for several reasons. They provide insights into the hopes and experiences of little-known personages, especially women. But they can be tricky to analyze. We sometimes think that lawsuits reveal *the* truth but in fact, they tend to show how claimants and defendants, witnesses, lawyers, and magistrates all constructed believable and sometimes contradictory "truths" in a legal locus. What kinds of strategies, particularly involving gendered constructions, did litigants and witnesses utilize in this case? Where do we see inconsistencies contained in witness depositions that illustrate defendant and claimant efforts to manipulate laws or achieve desired judicial rulings? This case also presents telling evidence about contemporary constructions of indigenous identity. Witnesses' identification of *indios* as imperial subjects of either the Portuguese or Spanish territories was often a thorny and subjective process. How did defendants characterize *indios*? What sorts of physical, cultural, and geographical referents did they use and for what purpose? Witness depositions, as this case demonstrates, were active sites of power, which manifested in participants' choice of language and narrative construction. Evidence was deployed strategically, and sometimes incompatibly, to craft believable narratives about the identities of *indios* meant to influence the final ruling. Lawsuits are of interest to students and scholars not so much because they allow us to discern the truthfulness of the events they portray but because they provide us with an opportunity to analyze how and why litigants, defendants, and deponents employed particular gendered and discriminatory characterizations to invent or reinforce plausible truths about past and present experiences.

2.1 Demand of Beatríz, *India*, from the City of Mexico in New Spain, [before the House of Trade], 17 May, 1558[6]

I state that for more than twenty years, Juan Cansino, *vecino* (citizen and resident) and magistrate of the village of Carmona has had me and my six children captive in the said village, and he has sold one of them. As [Cansino is] the magistrate and favored [one] in the village of Carmona I have not been able to pursue justice, even though I and my children are free, in conformity with the royal provision of His Majesty [the New Laws of 1542]. He has and continues to treat me and my children poorly, [and has] branded one of them on the face as you can see because it is this young woman [Catalina] whom I have brought with me here. I beg that your majesty, in conformity with the royal decree [the New Laws of 1542] that addresses the freedom of the *indios*, order that I and my children be freed. One of them named Simón [was the one] the said Juan Cansino sold. I ask that your Majesty look for him and bring him here, as well as my other children so that they can all be freed. And may your lord order that Juan Cansino appear [before the judges]. For the crime he has committed of having hidden me and having kept me and my children captive when we are free and for having branded my daughter, [I request] that his lordship condemn him with the greatest and gravest penalties that must by law be done and that I and my children be paid for all the service we have rendered since the day His Majesty declared the *indios* to be free. I plead for justice.[7]

[In order for the judges to determine whether there were legal grounds to pursue the case, and more specifically, whether there was evidence that she was an india *from the global territories claimed by Spain, they asked Beatríz to bring in witnesses, one of whom was Beatríz, the wife of Juan Vázquez:]*

2.2 Testimony of Beatríz,[8] Wife of Juan Vázquez, *Indio* and Blind Man, 25 August 1558[9]

Witness, Beatríz, wife of Juan Vázquez, blind man, and *vecina* of Seville.[10]

I have known [the complainant, Beatríz] in Carmona and in Seville since the Empress died [May 1539], which was a long time ago—I do not know

---

6. Archive of the Indies (Seville, Spain), Justicia, 908, n. 1.

7. "Demand of Beatríz, *india*," 17/V/1558.

8. In a later deposition she was called "Ysabel," 23r [image 91].

9. "Deposition, Beatríz, wife of Juan Vázquez, blind *indio*," 10r–11r.

10. Beatríz's (the witness who was also called "Ysabel," not the complainant) husband, also testified.

how many years.[11] Because this witness is from Mexico, this witness takes Beatríz to be an *india, natural*[12] of Malacata, which is in the province of New Spain. Given that the language of Mexico is distinct from that of Malacata, they know very well who is from Mexico and who is from Malacata because they do not speak the same language, just as Castilians recognize Portuguese and Flemish and other *naciones*[13] by their aspects but do not speak the same language. And so it is the same for this witness. I do not speak the language of Malacata but recognize in the aspect and manner of Beatríz that she is an *india* from Malacata. It is the same with a Castilian who knows a Portuguese and because the husband of this witness knows the language of Malacata and he has said to this witness that she [Beatríz] is native of there [Malacata] and because a long time ago when this witness was speaking and conversing with Beatríz, she told her [the witness] that she is from Malacata that is in the province of New Spain. She told me this while we were in Carmona. [*The witness then explained that she had previously known Beatríz in Seville, and reiterated that Beatríz had always told her she was from Malacata. She confirmed that Beatríz had five children, including Catalina.*] She did not sign because she does not know how to write and she does not know her exact age except that it seems to her that when the Empress died she was a girl of around fifteen years old, more or less.

Francisco de Almonte, notary of his majesty.

2.3 Confession of Beatríz, *India*, 9 September 1558

Having seen the lawsuit, *Señor Licenciado* (licenciate) Salgado Correa ordered Beatríz to appear and she took the oath as required by law before God and the Holy Mary on the sign of the cross and under it she was asked and answered in the following way. Asked her name and where she is from: She said she was named Beatríz and that she is a *natural* (someone who belongs to or is an original inhabitant of a place or broader "culture") of Malaqueta in New Spain, in the province of Mexico. Asked when she came to this

---

11. Isabella of Portugal (1503–1539), was Holy Roman Empress and married to king Charles V of Spain.

12. As an adjective, *natural* could modify *india* as the "natural" state of the person; as a noun it could mean "originally from," or "place of origin." In this instance it means that Beatríz is from Malacata.

13. *Nación* was an abstract grouping based on place of origin (Flemish, Genoese, Castilian), "type" of group (Arab or Moor, black or *negro* and *indio*), residence, or imperial affinity.

land, and who brought her, she said that around twenty-seven or twenty-eight years ago [circa 1530] a Portuguese captain named Antonio Correa brought her and gave her to a merchant who bought her and came to sell her in Carmona to Juan Cansino, her master. The merchant was a Castilian and sold her when they brought her and she was [still] a girl who had only given birth one time in Portugal. It could be around twenty-four years ago that she was sold to Juan Cansino and [since then] has been in his household in the village of Carmona where she has raised her children. [It was] there [that] she gave birth to the ones she has had. Asked if she knows or can understand the Mexican tongue of the province of New Spain she said "no." Asked if she is from the land of Maligueta [sic] of the Indies of the king of Portugal she said, "no." Asked for what reason she did not demand her freedom [before], as [she is doing] now, she said that she did not know that she could demand her freedom until Juan Cansino [gave her a] certain mistreatment, a beating with a stick. Being informed that the king, our *Señor* ordered that the *indios* be freed, she came to demand [her freedom]. Asked which witnesses know her and know her place of origin she said the blind *indio* and his wife, [but that] she does not have more witnesses, and that this is the truth. She did not sign because she does not know how to write.

[On 10 September, the judges of the House of Trade determined that the case would proceed. Authorities notified Beatríz's owner, Juan Cansino in person on 19 September, and gave him six days to make a statement before the judges.]

2.4 Juan Cansino's Declaration, 30 September 1558[14]

Asked if he knows Beatríz, he said yes because he has [legally] possessed her as his captive slave for about twenty-eight or twenty-nine years. Asked how many children Beatríz has had since she has been in his *poder*, he says she has had and procreated four children; one named Catalina, and another called Tomás, and another called Isabel, and another called Juan and all of them are at present in his household and under his *poder*. Catalina is nineteen or twenty years old, Tomás sixteen, Isabel, fourteen or fifteen, Juan ten or twelve. In addition, when she came under this declarant's authority she had another son named Simón. This deponent bought Simón at the same time he bought Beatríz and five or six years ago Juan de la Vega, a *vecino* of this village of Carmona, a relative of mine, and on this declarant's behalf, sold

---

14. 14r–16v.

Simón to a *vecino* of Seville. [*Here Cansino provides further details about this sale, and then explained that his father-in-law, Hernán Peréz, since deceased, had bought Beatríz and Simón in Carmona and had given both slaves to him (Cansino) as part of the dowry of his wife, Peréz's daughter, at the time of their marriage.*] Asked about Beatríz's place of origin and of which *nación* (nation) he has understood her to be until now, [Cansino] said that he has always taken her to be an Arab, the daughter of a Moor (*moro;* Muslim inhabitants of the Mediterranean)*,* because Beatríz has always said that she was the daughter of a Moor and that she was raised in Portugal. And of this Portuguese nation they gave her and her son to this deponent and that is how I received her. I have never taken her to be an *india* from the Indies of his Majesty [the king of Spain], nor have I heard it said nor has Beatríz said that until now.

Asked if this witness ordered Catalina to be branded with the brands that she has on her face and what barber branded her, he said that it might be two years ago more or less that this witness ordered the branding of Catalina on her face. He does not know the name of the barber who branded her, except that he was a young man who lived near the slaughterhouse of this city and he does not know if he would know him now even if he saw him. He ordered [Catalina] to be branded because she ran away many times and because she robbed a sack of coins from him and a gold-plated silver necklace and much wheat and many other things and jewels and cheeses and wool and wine and everything she could get, she and her mother and her children and likewise the said Simon whom he sold had robbed this witness of many things. Because of this, and because he was very disobedient, he sold him. He did not brand any of her other children.

Asked if Beatríz has told Cansino while under his authority that she is free and that they should let her and her children be free because they are free, Cansino said that about a year ago, Beatríz started saying she was an *india* in his house, but that before she had always said she was an *india* from the Indies of Portugal and that she had been raised in Portugal. Now she says she is from the Indies of His Majesty [the king of Spain]. [*Cansino finished by reiterating the claims he had already made.*]

[*Next, during the questioning of witnesses, several* indios *and others testified on behalf of Beatríz. Among other questions, witnesses were asked whether Beatríz was an* india *natural of Malacata, which is next to Chusipila and in the province of New Spain of the Indies of his Majesty, which* indio *language was spoken in that province, and why they believed that Beatríz was an* india *of Malacata.*][15]

---

15. "Interrogatory of Beatríz," 9/XI/1558, 2 pieça, 21v–22r.

2.5 Deposition of Catalina Hernández, *India*[16]

The witness Catalina Hernández said she was an *india* and *natural* of the Rio de la Plata province and that she was raised in San Juan de Puerto Rico and Margarita until she was brought to Spain. She is the widow of Gonçalo Veles.

To the first question she said she has known Juan Cansino for around twenty-two years, and Beatríz, *india,* since her children Catalina, Simón, Ysabel, Tomas, Juan and Diego were born because this witness was in the village of Carmona with her husband the entire twenty-two years until her husband died, around three years ago. Then this witness went to Baeça and from there to this city [of Seville].

She said that she is approximately fifty-seven years old and that Beatríz is the cousin of this witness, the daughter of a sister of this witness's mother but that even this [fact], would not deter her from telling the truth and that no one has said or begged her to lie or given her money or promised her money and that she tells only the truth.

To the third question she said that she knows that Beatríz, on her father's side is from Margarita, and on her mother's side from Puerto Rico, so she is an *india* of the Indies of His majesty on both sides. Asked how she knows this, she said because when this witness was brought from the province of the Rio de la Plata, where she was born, to Puerto Rico, the mother of Beatríz (this witness's aunt) who was born and raised in Puerto Rico [was there], and this witness was there too from that time onward. And while being in Puerto Rico, Beatríz's father came from Margarita and then married [Beatríz's mother] and while in Puerto Rico, she became pregnant with Beatríz. And while pregnant, she then went with her husband to Margarita because that is where he was from. And they brought this witness with them. And while they were in Margarita, the mother of Beatríz gave birth to her and raised her until she was around fourteen, when she and this witness were taken to Spain. I was older [than she] and the Christians [had] killed Beatríz's father and when they brought us, Beatríz's mother, who was still alive, stayed there alive [in Margarita].

She was later asked where Margarita is and she said it is near Lima, in Peru.

Asked the names of Beatríz's father and mother, she said Santiago and Juana.

They were brought to Spain around twenty-seven years ago and at the time, Beatríz was about fourteen years old and this witness was about thirty years old.

Asked who brought her from Margarita to Spain, she said the barber, Diego Sánchez, who lives in this city [Seville] next to the House of Trade

---

16. 2 pieça, 24v–27v.

and his wife, Elvira Hernández, now deceased. And more than forty *india* women lived together [on the ship] and they were on Terceira Island [in the Azores] for three years. At the end of those three years, one night while embarking on a ship to come to Castile, they came and carried off Beatríz and a young brother of this witness. And they took them to who knows where, but it was said that the barber, Diego Sánchez, had sold them. And this witness was brought to this city. And because this witness cried when she saw Beatríz and her brother taken off the ship, her master Diego Sánchez whipped her.

Asked if Beatríz speaks or understands the Mexican language of the *indios,* she said that she speaks the language of Peru because this witness spoke [it] with her and they understood one another.

Asked how she can say that on her father's side Beatríz is from Margarita and on her mother's from Puerto Rico, when she [Beatríz] has said and confessed that she is from Malaqueta in the province of New Spain? She answered that God never wanted Beatríz to be from Malaqueta, but from where this witness says [she is from] and if she has said she is from Malaqueta it is because [Beatríz] does not know how to respond and does not understand anything.

Asked if Beatríz is from the Indies of Portugal, she said "no," from the Indies of our king.

She said that Diego Sánchez and his wife brought this witness and Beatríz as slaves because later this witness came to this house [of Trade] and asked for [her] freedom and they freed her and being free she married and for this reason she knows that all the *indios* and *indias* of the Indies of His Majesty are free and cannot be slaves.

2.6 Witness on Behalf of Juan Cansino: Juan Luis Calafate, Sailor and *Vecino* of Lisbon and Resident in Triana, a Neighborhood of Seville[17]

[*Having sworn an oath the witness was asked the following:*] The first question asked of this witness is if he knows about Malagueta, which is a land of the King of Portugal and is under his dominion and *señorio* (political domain) and the Portuguese govern it and the Mine of the Malagueta is there because this witness has been there traveling on Portuguese ships that left from Portugal and went to the said Malagueta. Malagueta is a land and on the coast of Guinea which begins at Sao Tomé, or nearby, and then follows

---

17. 31r–32r.

the land [southward] until reaching Brazil, the Indies of Portugal. The land and coast of Malagueta is inhabited by blacks and this is what [the witness] knows for having seen it. He did not sign because he does not know how to write and he is approximately thirty years old.

[Although a rare occurrence in the freedom lawsuits of indios *in the House of Trade or the Council of the Indies, Juan Cansino requested that Beatríz be called in for additional questioning and his legal representative drew up a set of questions for her to answer. Cansino and his lawyer's stated intention was to catch Beatríz lying.]*

2.7 Additional Depositions of Beatríz, 9–15 March 1559[18]

Beatríz responded to the questions posed by Francisco Aguilar [legal representative of Juan Cansino] in his name, and under advisement of the magnificent *Señor Licenciado* Salgado, judge of this Casa [Casa de la Contratación] by his majesty and in my presence, *señor* Yuso, notary. On 12 May 1559, she declared the following:

To the first question, she said that in her land of Margarita there are no animals of the kind mentioned in the deposition, and if there are this confessant has not seen them. Asked if there are horses, asses, and other service animals she said "no."

To the second question she said that in the land of this confessant they wear cotton [garments] worked with colors. Asked if there is velvet, brocade and different kinds of cloth, she said "no," they only dress in cotton, as she said.

To the third question she said that in her land they grow and eat herbs and that is how they live and that there they have pepper, cloves, cinnamon, ginger and other spices.[19]

Then, the same day [15 March 1559] she was asked some things in the presence of Juan García Hermosilla, someone who understands the Mexican language and who was sworn in, in order to see if she understands the language. Being asked by Hermosilla where she was from and who was her master Beatríz responded that she did not understand . . . *[Beatriz does not understand any of the questions and swears an oath accordingly]*.

[On 11 July 1559, the judges of the House of Trade issued a ruling that Beatríz and her children had not proved their intention and that they would

18. Depositions of Beatríz, 9/III/1559, 71v–73v.
19. These spices were not native to Mexico.

remain slaves and under the custody of their master, Juan Cansino.[20] *Fourteen years later, in 1572, the year after Beatríz had died, her daughter, Catalina appealed the sentence and issued a demand before the House of Trade, on 14 March 1572.]*

2.8 Demand for Appeal, Catalina Hernández on Behalf of Her Deceased Mother, Beatríz, and Her Siblings[21]

Most illustrious lords, I, Catalina Hernández, daughter of Beatríz Hernández, state that at the time New Spain was conquered, my mother was among the other *indios* from there who they brought [to Iberia]. By bad and illicit means, the man who brought her [also] sold her. Because my mother was a person of little understanding and judgment and was so oppressed, my brother and I have been unable to have recourse to your lordship in order that you [be able to] grant us our freedom since we cannot be captives, in conformity with the laws and royal ordinances of his majesty.

[Having reconsidered the merits of the case, the judges determined that the appeal could go forward. Both complainants and defendants called in witnesses.]

2.9 Witnesses on Behalf of [the Complainants] Catalina/Beatríz

On [March 15, 1572] witness, Marina Hernández, *india,* widow of Pedro Muñoz, *indio,* deceased, *vecina* of this city in San Julian in the *Corral* (yard) of the Knife Makers. [*Hernández was then sworn in with the accustomed oath and her questioning began.*] She said she has known Catalina Hernández and Beatríz Hernández, her mother, both *indias,* for twelve years, and that she met them in this city and that this witness knows that Beatríz Hernández *india,* mother of Catalina, was a *natural* of New Spain in the Indies of his majesty and that this witness knows this because [Beatríz] told her many times [as did] other *indios* called Juan Gonzáles and Juan Vázquez who were also *naturales* of New Spain where this witness is also from. And that Beatríz appears to be an *india* from New Spain in terms of her language and her [physical] aspect and this witness spoke to her many times in the language

---

20. 77r–v.
21. 82v.

of New Spain. When [other] *indios* spoke to her she understood, and that is why this witness understood her to be a *natural* of New Spain.

[In the intervening folios the court moved through the process of reopening the case. Five additional witnesses were called on behalf of Beatríz. Three had their testimony stricken from the record (through a tacha *or error correction), but the other two confirmed the above testimony by Marina Hernández which proved the merit of the case. In April and May, the* procurador general de los indios *(legal defender of indigenous people), Francisco Sarmiento repeatedly petitioned the judges of the Casa de la Contratación to remove Catalina and her siblings from Cansino's power during the trial and place them in* depósito. *Court officials relayed the news of the reopened legal process from Seville to Carmona where the decree was read at Cansino's house to his wife and servants (though he is not present). Juan Casino then presented to the court a power of attorney authorizing his son, Hernando Casino, to act on his behalf. Copies of the original legal demand and ruling from the 1559 case were entered into the record. Soon thereafter, the court received additional testimony.]*

After this, on 4 July 1572, before the *señor Licenciado* Salgado Correa, judge, Catalina Hernández presented as a witness in this case a woman called Marina Rodríguez,[22] *india natural* of the province of New Spain, a widow and *vecina* of this city who lives in the parish of San Julian in the *Corral* of the Knife Makers. [*Rodríguez swore an oath and promised to tell the truth in her testimony, and reaffirmed her earlier testimony that she had known both Catalina and Beatríz Hernández for about ten years. She affirmed she was over fifty years old and had no personal conflict of interest in the case.*]

To the second question she said that she has made a declaration on behalf of Catalina Hernández and asked [the court] that it be read and shown in front of me; the notary read it to her, and after having heard and understood the summary information, Marina Hernández said that the content is true and affirmed it. [*Rodriguez did note here, however, that the court had misrecorded her name as Hernández and asked that the error be noted.*]

[*To the third question, the witness affirmed that her earlier testimony regarding Beatríz's birth place was true.*] . . . the witness is certain and has no doubt that Beatríz was an *india natural* of the province of New Spain, and Pedro Nuñez, deceased *indio* and husband of this litigant, knew this for certain because he engaged and communicated with her and said that she had been born between Oaxaca and Teguantepeque[23] in a land called Manacata. If

---

22. Earlier in the text, the court recorded her name as Marina Hernández—and the record reverts to this name in the testimony below.

23. Tehuantepec is a municipality in the current state of Oaxaca, Mexico.

Beatríz had not been born in that land she would not speak the language of New Spain so well as this witness has seen her speak it and as such all the *indios* [in Seville and Carmona] treated her and took her to be an *india* from New Spain, without seeing or hearing anything to the contrary.

To the fifth [sic] question, this witness said that she takes Beatríz to be a person of little understanding and ability and she knows this for certain because Juan Vázquez, deceased *indio* and other persons knew that she got drunk on wine.

[Witnesses on behalf of Juan Cansino no longer contended that Beatríz came from "Malagueta," located along the western coast of Africa and connected to Brazil (see earlier testimony, above), but they did argue that she had been born in Portugal, and was the daughter of an Arab. Several witnesses maintained that because Beatríz was a Portuguese Moor, that Catalina was a morisca, a forced convert to Catholicism from Islam.]

2.10 Witnesses for Cansino

Witness, Gonzalo de la Vega, fifty years old more or less, councilman.[24]

When this witness was in the house of Juan Cansino [de la Vega's brother-in-law], Beatríz told this witness many times that she was an *india* from Portugal and that she had been in Portugal when she had a son with a Moor. While going to the fountain to fetch water [the Moor] impregnated her. The son was [still] in Portugal. He did not sign because he did not know how to write.

2.11 Questions to Discredit Witnesses

[Complainants and defendants had the opportunity to discredit witnesses for the opposing side (called the tacha*), which meant that their testimonies would be struck from the legal record. Witnesses were considered unreliable if they were related or proven to be biased in favor of the litigant. One could also discredit witnesses by attempting to malign their character. Questions for the* interrogatorio *often contained the desired answer in them, and were what we would now call "leading" questions. Juan Cansino and his son Hernando*

---

24. 172r–173r. The witness, Gonzalo de la Vega, was married to one of Juan Cansino's sisters. Witnesses who were relatives or close associates were supposed to be barred from testifying because of bias.

Cansino, acting on his father's behalf, resorted to this strategy and Catalina Hernández, Beatríz's daughter, followed suit.]

Questions for Witnesses on Behalf of Juan Cansino to Discredit Witnesses on Behalf of Catalina Hernández, 2 September 1572.

Does the witness know the witness presented on behalf of Catalina Hernández, Juan Topin, who said he was an *indio natural* of Santo Domingo? Does the witness know that [even] before Juan Topin testified in this lawsuit he was [known as being] vile and inferior and of loose opinions, old, decrepit and feeble and without capacity and understanding and that he is a very close and intimate friend of Catalina Hernández?

Do witnesses know Catalina Sánchez, who said she was a *natural* of New Spain, a *vecina* of Triana on the Street of Altilleza, and a witness in this lawsuit, is a foolish woman lacking in judgment. She said she was thirty and that she had known Beatríz in New Spain. Do witnesses know that this is false because when Beatríz, *india,* and mother of Catalina, died more or less a year ago, she was over seventy years of age and that villagers in Carmona knew she had been in these parts for over forty years?

Do witnesses know Marina Rodriguez, who said she was an *india natural* of New Spain, *vecina* of a parish in Seville in the *corral* of the knife makers . . . that she is a poor person, vile and inferior and of loose opinions, an old woman and decrepit and of little substance and a very close and intimate friend of Catalina Hernández.

Do witnesses know Isabel Nabarro and Juana Ponce, *vecinos* of Carmona? Nabarro was a captive slave of Quintanilla and Juana Ponce is a captive slave of the Vicar, *don* Lope Ponce and between the two of them and even before they testified they were vile and inferior and of loose opinions and not credible and very intimate friends of Catalina Hernández, who by offering them favors has gotten them to testify against the truth.

Do witnesses know Bartolomé López, worker and Ana, slave, and do they know that Bartolomé Lopez was Catalina's long-time "friend" who has had a daughter with her and who thinks she is free, and as such would passionately say what is contrary to the truth. [Do witnesses know that] he is an enemy of Juan Cansino's because Cansino caught him living illegally with Catalina and [do witnesses know that] Ana, a slave, who has been a captive and wanted all slaves to be free, besides being a liar and black, would say [things] contrary to the truth? The two are inferior people, vile and of low opinion and no one should give them any credit for what they say.

[On 10 September 1572, Catalina and her lawyer requested that her witnesses be allowed to stand, despite the claims that were made in the tacha.

She also called in new witnesses, all of whom were Spanish and vecinos *of Carmona to verify that her witnesses were reliable and that Juan Cansino's were not, and should be discredited mainly because they were all his close relatives or worked for him.]*

Questions for Witnesses on Behalf of Catalina Hernández

Are the witnesses on behalf of Catalina well known individuals, Christians and fearful of God? Do witnesses know that Juan Cansino and Hernando Cansino, his son, a current councilman of the village are powerful and rich persons and that they have many friends and relatives in the village of Carmona?

Do the witnesses know that when Catalina Hernández went about drawing up evidence in Carmona to support her case, that Hernando Cansino, son of Juan, went about letting the witnesses know what they had to say in his favor and that he confronted and insulted those witnesses who wanted to say what they thought?

Do witnesses know that Juan Cansino went about persuading many neighbors of the village that Beatríz, *india* mother of Catalina Hernández spoke Portuguese [and that she was a *morisca*] and he promised a bag of wheat if they would declare this [in their depositions]?

Do witnesses know that Diego Romy, public notary of the village of Carmona, who drew up the interrogatory evidence for Juan Cansino is an intimate friend of Hernando, his son, and that they always eat and go about together and that Hernando Cansino was present when Romy examined witnesses?

[On 21 November 1572, the judge and members of the tribunal of the House of Trade determined that Catalina had not proven her case, that she and her siblings and Catalina's daughter would remain slaves, and that Juan Cansino should not mistreat them. Within two years, the defender of the Indians, Francisco Sarmiento, appealed the decision before the Council of the Indies, the appellate court of the House of Trade. After reviewing the case, the Council members reversed the sentence, thus freeing Beatríz and her offspring from bondage.]

2.12 Appeal Sentence

Council of the Indies, Madrid, 22 January 1574

In the case between Catalina Hernández, her brothers and children of Beatríz, deceased *india*, and Ana, daughter of the said Catalina Hernández, and Juan de la Peña her legal advocate versus Juan Cansino Aragones, *vecino* and magistrate of the town of Carmona and Sebastian de Santander, his legal representative:

We find that the definitive sentence of this lawsuit given and pronounced by the official judges of the House of Trade in Seville on behalf of the said *indias* was appealed, judged and pronounced badly and that the said parties [Catalina, etc.] appealed well. As such we must revoke and we revoke their lawsuit and sentence[25] . . . We [the members of the tribunal of the Council of the Indies] declare the said Beatríz, deceased *india* to have been free and not subject to any servitude by her birthright, despite the sentence rendered against her by the said judges on 11 July 1559. We also declare as free by birth the said Catalina Hernández, her brothers, and Ana, Catalina's daughter as the children and grandchildren born of a free mother, as the said Beatríz *india* was, and we condemn Juan Cansino to not perturb or disturb them in their freedom in any way. . . . We condemn [Cansino] to give and pay the said *indios* a just and deserved salary for their service from the day on which this lawsuit [appeal] began, 30 April 1572.

Suggested Reading

Reséndez, Andrés. *The Other Slavery: The Uncovered Story of Indian Enslavement in America*. Boston: Houghton Mifflin Harcourt, 2016.

van Deusen, Nancy E. *Global Indios: The Indigenous Struggle for Justice in Sixteenth-Century Spain*. Duke, NC: Duke University Press, 2015.

———. "Indios on the Move in the Sixteenth-Century Iberian World," *Journal of Global History*, 10:3 (November 2015), 387–409.

———. "The Intimacies of Bondage: Female Indigenous Servants and Slaves and Their Spanish Masters, 1492–1555," *Journal of Women's History*, 24:1 (2012), 13–43.

Document Themes

- Family
- Labor
- Law
- Migration and mobility
- Sexuality and gender

---

25. Ellipses in this paragraph represent the omission of formulaic phrasing.

3

Women's Wills (Potosí, 1577 and 1601; La Plata, 1598 and 1658)

Wills written in anticipation of death provide extraordinary windows into lives lived as well as aspirations for the future of loved ones and kin. This chapter collects the wills of four women of color (two indigenous, one mestiza, and one Afro–Peruvian) from several Andean cities and spans the period from the late sixteenth to late seventeenth centuries. Potosí was a mining metropolis with a population of near one hundred thousand while La Plata, today known as Sucre, was a much smaller city that functioned as an administrative center for the Viceroyalty of Peru. The two cities were in relatively close proximity, so travel and interaction between the two was common. The propensity of non-Spaniards to leave wills in early Latin America has been well documented by historians.[1] In particular, indigenous women left wills in surprisingly large numbers in comparison to both Spanish women and indigenous men.[2] In cities, women had ties to market networks as well as *cofradías* (religious brotherhoods) and, thus, had extra reasons to make legal records when they feared death. Women also recognized that leaving instructions in a will could help to care for family members once they were gone. Thus, this chapter illuminates rich details about the lives of non-Spanish women who availed themselves of a Spanish legal tradition to settle scores, make their peace, or tie up loose ends within the complex colonial cities in which they lived.

Spanish inheritance law guided what women owned and what they could do with their property at death. First, women could separate property from their husbands (this might come from their dowry, for example). And, while women did not need their husbands' permission to bequeath such property, there were certain inheritance laws they had to follow. People could dispense one-fifth of their estate to whomever they wished. The other portion of the

---

1. See the collection edited by Susan Kellogg and Matt Restall, *Dead Giveaways: Indigenous Testaments of Colonial Mesoamerica and the Andes* (Salt Lake City: University of Utah Press, 1998).
2. Frank Salomon offered excellent insights into the testamentary practices of indigenous women in "Indian Women of Early Colonial Quito as Seen Through Their Testaments," *The Americas* 44:3 (1988), 325–41.

estate had to be given to legitimate (that is, born-in-wedlock) children in equal shares, regardless of sex.[3]

All wills follow a formula prescribed by Spanish notarial custom, and the basic outlines of that formula are evident in the documents in this chapter. Individuals began by identifying themselves and their state of mind; the will then proceeded to address burial plans, some of which were very elaborate; next, testators listed debts they owed or those owed to them; a will then listed assets, bequests, and lastly named both a universal heir (or heirs) and the executors of the will.[4] The will was completed with signatures by the witnesses and the notary public. Frequently, testators themselves did not sign these documents due to illiteracy. In this sample, none of the women signed their wills.

Even though all wills followed a formula, the individual documents reveal important differences. The wills collected here reveal four distinct female experiences. The details allow readers to trace how women of color experienced kin networks, material culture, religious devotion, and economic transactions. Moreover, these documents show women acting as agents in their own lives and in the lives of their descendants. Wills allowed people to collect debts, to make claims for property, and to carry out obligations to loved ones.

The 1577 will of the free *morena* (black woman) Luisa de Villalobos shows the remarkable migration of an Afro-descended woman from Nombre de Dios in Panama to Lima on the coast of Peru and finally to the highland mining city of Potosí in modern-day Bolivia. The section of her will excerpted here focuses on her belongings, her debts, and her bequests. While she does not list an occupation, the emphasis on clothing and cloth in her will suggests that she may have been a seamstress and a petty cloth merchant. By tracing her economic transactions, one can locate her multiracial network of indigenous, Afro-descended, and Spanish women and men. While Villalobos is careful to identify herself as a free person, her will also mentions a master. Is she referring to the man who was her former master from whom she retained the same title? Or was she perhaps still in debt to him for her freedom as she declared she owed him fifty *pesos*?[5]

---

3. See a longer discussion in Silvia Marina Arrom, *The Women of Mexico City, 1790–1857* (Stanford, CA: Stanford University Press, 1985), 67. Also, I discuss the ways in which, through the practice of writing wills, parents sometimes challenged inheritance law in Jane E. Mangan, *Transatlantic Obligations: Creating the Bonds of Family in Colonial Era Peru and Spain* (New York: Oxford University Press, 2016), 163–69.

4. In order to contextualize the *peso* values listed in the wills, readers may wish to know that in 1600, annual rent for a small urban property ran at about one hundred *pesos*, a bottle of wine cost ten *pesos*, and a loaf of bread was one *real* (or one-eighth of a *peso*).

5. On enslaved colonial women and strategies for freedom, see Michelle A. McKinley, *Fractional Freedoms: Slavery, Intimacy, and Legal Mobilization in Colonial Lima, 1600–1700* (Cambridge: Cambridge University Press, 2016).

Ana Copana made her will in 1598 and died soon thereafter, as the official inventory (not excerpted here) shows. She was an indigenous woman born outside the city of La Plata who eventually moved to the high Andean city where she had a family and became a property owner. Copana's will richly details the material culture of an urban indigenous woman, the examples of which remind us that colonial cities, often considered centers of Spanish culture, were also filled with people who walked around in indigenous-style clothing made of indigenous textiles. At the same time, Copana's religious devotion, an adaption to Catholicism introduced by the Spanish, is also evident. Her will reveals her equal commitment to both the material and spiritual realms. Note the provisions she made in her will respecting the eventuality that a man named Pedro González might appear on the scene to make a claim to her granddaughter or her property. Copana's example illustrates how indigenous women adapted to colonial life while maintaining distinct cultural and kin identities.

The indigenous woman *doña* (lady) Isabel del Benino dictated her will on a rural estate outside of the city of Potosí, where she lay dying.[6] It was later admitted into the notarial record in Potosí at the insistence of her daughter and heir, *doña* María del Benino, born to her former master when her mother was presumably working as his servant. Isabel Benino's only other immediate family member was her husband, who was not the father of her daughter. How do both her husband and her daughter appear in the will? Who does she favor and what might be her motivation? Further, what does her rural economic engagement suggest about the business possibilities for an indigenous woman who grew up alongside Spanish presence in the Andes? It is also instructive to compare Isabel Benino's will to that of Ana Copana in order to consider how indigenous women's lives might differ. Notice, for example, that both women paid special attention to religious devotion. The economic relationship Benino had with clerics (who bought agricultural goods from her) afforded her a power that Copana did not have.

Finally, the will of *doña* Ana de Barba y Talora reveals insight into the life and death of a *mestiza* (woman of indigenous and Spanish parentage) in seventeenth-century La Plata. Barba y Talora cannot be said to be typical, for she was divorced from her husband, only one of her children had survived early childhood, and that child, a daughter, was blind. Much of her will, then, can be read as the financial strategy adopted by a single mother. What

---

6. The use of the honorific *doña* by Isabel del Benino was indicative of her relative wealth and connection to a former Spanish boss as well as a Spanish son-in-law. In the colonial world, an expansive use of honorific titles occurred relative to Iberia, which led to contestation at times about social hierarchy. See James Lockhart, *Spanish Peru, 1532–1560: A Colonial Society* (Madison: The University of Wisconsin Press, 1968), 153–55.

specific steps did *doña* Ana take to prepare her daughter for life on her own? How did she address her mixed-race identity? Did she lead a life that suggests connections to indigenous culture, Spanish culture, or both?

All of these wills reveal women who led dynamic lives with complex social and economic networks and who strongly expressed how they wanted to be remembered. Moreover, they prompt some collective questions. Wills document particular moments in peoples' lives and thus provide snapshots of spiritual, social, and economic reckoning. How might this framework influence the details we can learn about women's lives through this type of document? What do women's debts reveal about their work and the role of money in their day-to-day existence? How did women use wills as strategies to plan for loved ones after death? And, if you think comparatively about the four wills, how did the *mestiza*, indigenous woman, and *morena* differ from each other in terms of social status or material culture?

Finally, keep in mind that these documents are equally informative about men in colonial society because all the women who left wills had connections to the men who were their spouses, sons, fathers, bosses, business partners, and priests. Thus, wills constitute a clear window into the gender makeup of women's networks and allow us to see how and when men's presence was most (and least) influential. Did women choose men to be their executors? Did they benefit from donations made by men? Did they provide for and receive financial and nonmonetary support from their husbands?

3.1 Will of Luisa de Villalobos (1577)[7]

In the name of the Holy Trinity, Father, Son and Holy Spirit, three persons and only one true God, and all the rest that the holy mother church of Rome holds and believes, and hoping to place my soul on the path to salvation and for that for my advocate the Holy Virgin Mary, that she beg her precious son, my Lord Jesus to grant me his grace and know that to his service and honor I make and order my testament in the following form and manner, I, Luisa de Villalobos, *color morena*, free and not subject to any servitude, native of the city of Nombre de Dios in the Kingdom of Tierra Firme, resident as I am in this Villa Imperial de Potosí.

First, I commend my soul to God [*the next half page is illegible due to damage.*]

---

7. Archivo Histórico de Potosí-Casa de la Moneda, Escrituras Notariales, Volumen 8, Fols 1204–1206v, July 24, 1577.

I declare that I owe fifty *pesos* of silver, assayed and marked, to my master who knows Juan de Aranbuco and Antono de Yllescas. I order that they pay him because I owe the money from five years ago.

Item,[8] I declare that in the City of Kings,[9] I have in the possession of María Fula *morena* 100 silver *pesos* that I gave her to keep for me. I order they be collected and delivered to Francisca Godines.

Item, I declare that to Francisca Godines or her closest heirs [you] pay the value of nine glass bottles of orange blossom water[10] and thirteen flasks of the said water.

Item, I declare that I owe Antonio Gutiérrez six *pesos*, and I order that he be paid from my estate.

Item, I declare that one yellow skirt with velvet trim, another trimmed with velvet, one doublet of fine wool[11] and one wool cloth in which is it wrapped belongs to Costanca, *morena*, of the falconer of the Villa Real, for which she owes fifty *pesos*. I order that it be collected and that the said clothing be returned to her. Once collected, the said *pesos* should be given to Andrés Sánchez because they are his.

Item, I declare that I have in my possession four *pesos* in *reales* at eight to the *peso* and two *pesos* plus a *tomyn* which are from Catalina *morena*, slave of Francisco Ruiz. I gave and loaned those said *pesos* and *reales* to Juan Díaz. I order that they be collected and returned to their owner.

Item, I declare that I sold two and-a-half *varas*[12] of table linen to a girl who is currently in the house of Juan Barba for two *pesos* per *vara*. I order that they be collected and given to the said Catalina because they are hers.

Item, pay four *pesos* to Gerónima de Contreras.

Item, I declare that I have pawned with Sancho Antón, shoemaker, a *piña*[13] worth six *pesos* and also eight pounds of silver mercury for the value of some shoes that I took from him. I order that the *piña* and mercury be collected and the *piña* be given to Domingo or to Catalina, his wife, slaves of the said Francisco Ruíz, or the person that Father Medina of the Jesuits says, and Sancho Antón be paid for the shoes. The mercury I declare to be mine.

Item, I declare that Jorge Cocana, slave of Andrés de Burgos, owes me thirty-four *pesos* of silver currency that I loaned him in front of Francisco Martín, who is in Tarapaya, and I have asked him for them in front of María

---

8. *Ytem* in the original, meaning next in an itemized list.

9. Lima was known as the City of Kings.

10. Orange blossom water was used as a perfume in the early modern era.

11. *Telilla* in the text; a fine, thin wool.

12. The *vara* was a common measurement used at the time and it is approximately equivalent to three feet.

13. The *piña* was the term used to refer to an unminted cone of refined silver.

de Herrera and the *negra* (black woman) of Jofre. I order they be collected and the twenty *pesos* given to Juan Díaz, my master.

Item, I declare that in the City of the Kings, I have in the possession of María Fula four shirts (two men's and two women's), three skirts (two of them of fur and the other of cotton), four sheets, two pairs of damask tablecloths, twelve napkins, three handkerchiefs, two doublets (one of blue damask and the other new), of fine wool with gold-plated silver buttons, two bedcovers (one scarlet and one embroidered), two scarlet pillows, two multicolored[14] blankets, two plates and two pewter platters, and one scarlet sash and one box in which are some handkerchiefs. I declare that these are mine and I order they be collected. I desire and it is my will that with all of this Father Medina does what he likes.

Item, I declare that in this Villa [Potosí] I have three mattresses and three sheets of linen and other blankets and five Rouen shirts, three handkerchiefs, three *tocas de mengalas*[15] and three embroidered headdresses, three blankets, two pillows, ten *varas* of Rouen cloth, one painting of Christ and another of Our Lady of the Rosary. This I order that it be given to the said Juan Díaz. Likewise, I have another sheet of linen and a small image of the Veronica, and an *acsu*[16] of *cumbe*,[17] a *chumbe*,[18] five skirts, one yellow, another blue, one black with its shawl, and two brown, and two blue silk blouses, and one fine black wool blouse and one black shawl and this I order to be given to Juan Díaz. Likewise, I have two paintings[19] of Cristo de Oro, both paintings cost seventy *pesos*. I order that the bigger of the two be given in the name of [illegible].

Item, I order that I have a small, delicate golden image of our Lady, five pairs of earrings, four of gold and the other of crystal and gold, plus two chests, one for letters and the other larger, and three old blankets.

Item, I order that my sister, a slave of Gerónimo Leto, be given two brown skirts that I have as well as a blanket and two shirts.

Item, I order that the new *cumbi acsu* which I have be given to Juana, *india* (indigenous woman), my *comadre*[20] whom Juan Bernal knows.

Item, I declare that Isabel, mother-in-law of Leonardo Cenapoles, be given a white cotton *acsu* and a *chumbe*.

---

14. *pintados.*
15. bonnets.
16. *Acsu* is the Quechua word for a woman's tunic, part of typical Andean female dress.
17. *Cumbe* or *cumbi* is the Quechua word for finely woven wool cloth.
18. A *chumbe* is the Quechua word for a woolen belt used to cinch the *acsu*, in Andean female dress.
19. *Hechuras* in the original.
20. Here *comadre* means a good female friend.

Item, I declare for my property two sashes, one new of scarlet and the other of blue wool and a headscarf with [illegible word], two rosaries, a silver *agnes dei*[21] with its silver chain, and six *varas* of Rouen cloth.

And to fulfill and satisfy this, my will, I leave as my executor Juan Díaz, my master, to whom I give my full power to administer my estate.

And I revoke, nullify, and declare void any other will or codicil that I have made.

And to fulfill and satisfy this my will, I order fifty *pesos* be given to my niece Isabel who is in Gerónimo Leto's house.

[signed] Sebastian de Vergara, scribe. 24 July 1577

3.2 Will of Ana Copana (1598)[22]

In the name of God, Amen. Know all who see this letter of testament, that I, Ana Copana, natural of Cayque,[23] being ill of body and sound of mind, that God, Our Lord saw fit to give me in order that I serve him, believing as I believe in the mystery of the Holy Trinity, Father, Son and Holy Spirit, three persons and only one true God, and all the rest that the holy mother church of Rome holds and believes, and hoping to place my soul on the path to salvation and for that for my advocate, the Holy Virgin Mary, to beg her precious son, my Lord Jesus to grant me his grace and know that to his service and honor I make and order my testament in the following form and manner:

First, I entrust my soul to God who created it and when I should leave this world, I order that my body be buried in the church of our Lord Saint Sebastian in the chapel of Our Lady of Copacabana and the customary alms be paid for the burial.

Item, I order that a requiem mass be sung over my body.

Item, I order that eight masses be said for my soul in the parish of Saint Sebastian.

Item, I order that another six masses be said for my soul and my executors pay the customary alms.

Item, I order that they say another six masses for my soul, by selling a little bit of corn that I leave in a *pirua* (corncrib).

---

21. Lamb of God: A figure of a lamb bearing a cross or flag, and symbolizing Jesus Christ.
22. Archivo General de Bolivia, Escrituras Publicas, Escribano Castro, Fols. 297–319, 20 de junio de 1598.
23. The original text reads, "native of Cayque," but the place-name is crossed out. Likely this referred to the highland community of Caque, just north of Arequipa.

Item, I order that the day of my burial the body of Saint Sebastian accompany me and my executors pay the customary alms.

Item, I declare my belongings:

Item, I order one *Xauxa*[24] *acsu* of *cumbi* and its *liclla*[25] be sold by my executors and with it they say the masses for me.

Item, I leave an *acsu* and its *liclla* of *cumbi* to my granddaughter, María, and a pair of *topos.*[26]

Item, I leave two *licllas* so that they say masses for me.

Item, I leave my granddaughter, María, a *cumbi nanaca.*[27]

Item, I leave my youngest granddaughter, named Ines Titivalla, a *cumbi acsu* and some silver *cocos.*[28]

Item, I leave my houses to my granddaughters María and Ínes Titivalla, to be shared in equal parts.

Item, I order that a large *solar* (lot) which I have that is connected to the said houses be sold and it is my will that my executors sell it. With that money, masses should be said for my soul and for my husband's soul, in all the monasteries of this city where my executors wish, and they pay the alms for them.

Item, I leave two pairs of large *topos*, I order they be sold.

Item, I leave a half-*pirua* of corn, I order that they make flour with it for the sustenance of my granddaughters.

Item, I leave a [illegible word] of trim. Also, I leave some small pieces of silver and some old broken, silver *tupus.*

Item, I leave red and blue wool.

Item, I leave sixteen chickens, I mean twenty, big and small.

Item, I leave a large trunk and also sixteen sheep, big and small, and also nine reddish cows.

Item, I leave an old silver bowl and some glass pitchers.

Item, I state and it is my will that *don* (sir) Juan Bayllanco and I have and raised my two granddaughters in the said houses and nobody should remove them from there because I have raised them with much work.

---

24. Xauxa, or Jauja, is a region of Peru, its usage here refers to a particular pattern in Copana's *acsu* that identifies that region.

25. *Liclla*, also spelled *liquilla*, is the Quechua word for the large shawl that was part of typical Andean female dress.

26. *Topos*, also spelled *tupus*, is the Quechua word for the dress pins use to attach the *liclla* (shawl) around the *acsu* (tunic). Typically, these pins are made from silver.

27. *Ñanaca* is the Quechua word for a woven head covering, part of typical Andean female dress.

28. *Cocos* are silver drinking vessels, typically used for drinking native corn beer and kept in pairs.

Item, I declare that my daughter who died left two outfits for her daughter. I order my executors to keep them for my granddaughter to give to her when she is bigger. Do not sell them. In case the girl whom they are for, who is Inés, should die, my executors can sell them and have masses said for me wherever they wish.

Item, I order that in case Pedro González should come to say that a girl that I have, who is my granddaughter, is his or is the daughter of his *yanacona*,[29] I state and confess that she is not because I have raised her since childhood and her mother left her to me when she died.

Item, Pedro González might also say that these houses are his. I state that my husband and I bought them with our own money and sweat and he does not have anything to do with them, because they are mine.

Item, I have three bushels[30] of corn in the *chacara* (farm) of *don* Juan; I order it be brought from there.

Item, I confess that my husband, may God bless him, and I bought a *solar* from an *indio* named Andrés to whom I gave ninety *pesos* in *reales*. He did not give us the title to the land and, because he was a known friend to my husband, we did not force him by law to give me the titles. I have sown [crops] in those lands as my own, and for three or four years I have not planted because I cannot do so anymore and I am old. I order that my executors collect the titles, paying nine *pesos* that I still owe and in collecting the titles. My executors should sell the land and with the money from it, they should have masses said for me in the monasteries of this city and in the principal church because it is my will.

Item, I leave six pairs of *queros* (wooden drinking vessels for corn beer).

Item, I declare that Juan Gambi owes me three and-a-half *pesos*.

Item, Inés, the wife of Diego Laco, owes me five *pesos* from a *birque* (large earthen vessel).

Item, Alonso Daque owes me fifteen and-a-half *pesos*.

Item, Lorenco Yunga, married to a Quillaca woman, owes me ten *pesos*.[31]

Item, C— [illegible word], shoemaker, owes me three *pesos*, plus an *india* owes me a yoke [for animals], and the chiriguana cantor[32] named Luymana owes me seven *pesos*; I order it be collected.

And an *india*, the sister-in-law of María Yanpara, owes me two *pesos*.

---

29. The term *yanacona*, in colonial usage, refers to an indigenous person (usually a man) responsible to a Spanish master and without kin ties to a specific *ayllu* (Andean kin-based community).

30. *Cargas* in the original. In fact, a *carga* was a load equivalent to 1.6 current bushels, but bushel is used throughout this text as a translation for *carga*.

31. Yunga identifies Lorenco as being from the Yungas region in Bolivia; his wife is a Quillaca native, which is in the Oruro region of Bolivia.

32. Chiriguana refers to an indigenous Guaraní ethnicity in the lowlands of Bolivia.

And the wife of Guarany owes me three *pesos*.

And Francisco Vila owes me twenty-two *pesos*, I order it be collected from him.

And to fulfill this will, I leave for my executors Lorenzo García Botetano and *don* Juan Bayllanco to whom and to each one individually I give my full power [of attorney] so that they may administer my estate, collect and pay and sell what must be done, and that my executors use the power for the best interest of the salvation of my soul.

I revoke, nullify and give for void any other will or codicil that I have made. I do not want any to be valid except for this one that is executed in the city of La Plata on May 28, 1598, being witnesses Juan Zambí and Diego de Eredía and Alonso Gui and because he did not know how to sign, the witness begged them to sign for him

[signatures]

Item, I declare for my estate nine bushels of salt.

Item, I declare eight bushels of corn, those eight are in some sacks in my pantry.

Item, I declare for my estate four *birques* and seven jugs and three pots and some painted cups.

Item, I declare that I owe for me and for my daughter, may God bless her, [illegible] to an *india guayra*[33] named Canco and her husband who is named Pedro. If they call, pay them from my estate what I owe.

Item, I declare that Elvira *india* owes me four *pesos*. I order it be collected.

Because this is all true I beg that a witness sign for me, witness Lorenzo García and Diego Heredia and Luis de Vera and Juan de Satas

[signatures]

3.3 Will and Codicil of *doña* Isabel del Benino, *India*[34] (1601)

In the Villa of Potosí, on August 23, 1601, before the *licenciado* (licenciate) Juan Ramírez de Salazar, *teniente corregidor* (deputy district governor) and senior justice in this jurisdiction, Pedro de Montalvo, senior *procurador* (legal

---

33. *Guayra* is the Quechua term for the native Andean smelting process using clay ovens, and the term is applied here to a woman who carried out the task of smelting ore.
34. Archivo Histórico de Potosí, Casa Nacional de la Moneda, Escrituras Notariales No. 32 Venegas. 23 August 1601.

representative) of the *encomienda* (landed estate), presents this petition with the will that is mentioned therein.

I, *doña* María del Benino for myself, say that *doña* Isabel del Benino, *india*, my mother, being in the Anti Valley, executed her will and codicil under which she died in which she named me as her universal heir and executor. This that I present she executed with all the solemnity possible for her on earth. It is in the interest of my right that [the will] be put in the record of this notary so that it does not get lost and from it I receive the authorized copies that are and will be necessary.

I ask and beg your lord incorporate the said testament in the register[35] and from it give me the authorized copies that will be necessary and so that there is faith I ask for justice.

From Pedro de Montalvo:

The said *teniente corregidor* having seen this petition and will, I order that so that this be kept and not lost, it be put in the register of my present scribe and a record made of its contents, so that this transfer move forward.

> *[Licenciado Ramírez de Salazar signed the document before Pedro Benegas, public notary. The will of* doña *Isabel follows.]*

In the name of the Holy Trinity, father, son and Holy Spirit, Amen. I, Isabel del Benino, *india*, native of Cajamarca,[36] being ill of body and sound of mind, state that if God, Our Lord, is served to take me from this life with this illness that at present I have, I order my soul to God who raised it from nothing in his image and who saved me and redeemed me through his precious blood, and the body to the earth from whence it came.

First, I order that if God is served to have me die from this illness, my body be rested in the chapel of this *chacara* of *doña* María del Benino, my daughter. After one year has passed, it is my will that my bones be taken to the Villa of Potosí where they will be buried in the monastery of our Lord San Francisco in the tomb of Nicolás del Benino, who was my master, where the masses declared below will be said for me.

Item, I declare for my goods owed to me by Pedro Holguin, 150 *pesos*; I order them collected.

Item, Cristóbal de Perales owes me one hundred *pesos*, for which I have a document; I order it collected.

Item, Francisco, servant, owes me fifteen *pesos* which I lent him in *reales*; I order it collected.

---

35. Here she refers to the official registry of the notary public.
36. Cajamarca is located in Peru's northern highlands and was the site of the battle between Francisco Pizarro and the Inka ruler Atahualpa.

Item, Gaspar de Miranda owes me ten bushels of corn that I sold him, six at four *pesos* and the other four at three *pesos* which totals thirty-six *pesos*; I order it collected.

Item, the Father Joseph de Llanos, priest and vicar of this valley, owes me a remainder of thirty *pesos* from some goats that I sold him; I order it collected.

Item, the Father Vicar owes me for twenty hand-picked goats that I recently sold him at two-and-a-half *pesos* that totals fifty *pesos*; I order it collected.

Item, Pedro Nuñez Vello owes me twenty-five *fanegas* of corn that he took from me on two occasions, fifteen of them at four *pesos* a load and ten at three *pesos* which totals ninety *pesos*; I order it collected.[37]

Item, Bautista del Benino owes me the remainder of an account of ten *pesos*; I order it collected or he gives me two lambs that I want and they can be counted against the debt.

Item, the heirs of Captain Luis Gomez de Chávez, deceased, owe me for the said deceased party, ten bushels of maiz at three *pesos*, thirty *pesos*,[38] and twenty hand-picked goats at twelve *pesos* and six *reales*, totaling from the corn and the goats eighty-five *pesos* and also ten *pesos* for a new large-sized *payla*[39] that they took from me [two illegible words] which amounts to ninety-seven *pesos*; I order it collected from the estate of the deceased.

Item, the *indios carboneros*[40] of Sillata, Carangas, owe me 280 *pesos* according to a written memo from *don* Juan *cacique* (hereditary indigenous chieftain) who came with an order to collect his *indios* and take them to their villages; I order it collected.

Item, Pedro Holguin owes me twenty bushels of corn at three *pesos* per bushel. I say and order that this totals seventy *pesos*; I order it be collected from him and this is apart from the 140 *pesos*.[41]

Item, I declare for my estate that I have 400 oxen that cost me 200 *pesos*.

Item, I have, at present, fifty bushels of corn for my estate.

Item, I have for my estate four pregnant mares, I mean large and small animals.

Item, I declare for my estate two pieces of clothing of *cumbi*.

Item, one article of *avasca*.[42]

Item, one woolen dress with its trim.

Item, a woolen *lliclla*.

---

37. Four *fanegas* constituted one *carga*.
38. This confusing notation is how it is written in the original.
39. Metal vat.
40. Refers to indigenous men who sold wood, llama dung, or other combustibles for fires.
41. Which *doña* Isabel already noted earlier in the will.
42. *Avasca* is the Quechua term for cloth made of a coarse weave of alpaca wool.

Two pairs of silver *tupus* with their bells. My dresses are in Potosí in the possession of my daughter, *doña* María del Benino.

Item, ten *llamas* I declare for my estate.

Item, I declare that I do not owe anything to anyone, unless I am charged with some restitution that has gone wrong.

Item, I order for the day of my burial a *misa cantata* (High Mass), with my body present with a vigil, and the customary alms be paid from my estate.

Item, I order that later in this chapel, they say six low masses for me and the customary alms be paid from my estate.

Item, I order that during the year that my body will be in this chapel in the *chacara*, the priest of the Valley say one monthly mass for me and the customary alms be paid from my estate, I mean these to be low masses.

I order for the day that my body is taken to Potosí, they say a High Mass over my body in the monastery with a deacon and sub-deacon and the customary alms be paid from my estate.

Item, I order for the day of my transfer they say ten low masses in the monastery at the will of my executors and the customary alms be paid from my estate.

Item, I order the necessary wax be spent on the day of my burial and transfer at the will of my executors and according to what they say, with simple oath, pay them whatever is spent on wax plus five *pesos* and other things necessary for my burial.

Item, I order that they give alms of ten *pesos* to have a mass said for me in each monastery of Potosí and in the principal church ten masses, and it be paid from my estate.

Item, I order that my executors, in auction or outside of it, sell the estate that I have left and declared in order to comply with the orders that I leave and by their oath they will profit from what they sell from my estate at good prices and with the understanding that most of my estate is in the countryside. They should not take more than what they are given.

Item, I order that they give twenty *pesos* in alms to the Hospital of the Natives in Potosi, given them from my estate.

Item, for my estate I have vestments for saying mass that is comprised of a missal, vestments, table cloths, little bell and large bell of two *arrobas*,[43] more or less that is in this *chacara*, I order that it be sold to comply with my record, last will and testament.

Item, I declare as my final wish that, as I have dictated in this will [with respect to] the masses to be said by Father Pedro de Llanos, priest of this Valley, if I die [he] should discount the masses that he says for my soul in accordance with that I have ordered and declared, and do not interpret that

---

43. *Arroba* is a measure equivalent to twenty-five pounds.

they are to give any money to the said vicar from my estate until he has complied with the burial and masses that are said for me or the quantity of money that he owes me. If any is lacking, I order he be paid from my estate what he is owed and it more is leftover, I order that it be collected from him and to comply with the other orders.

Item, to conclude my last will and testament so that is comes to a proper conclusion, I name as my executors and custodian *doña* María del Benino, my daughter, and Gonzalo Holguin *vecinos* (citizens) of this Valley of Anti, to both and or to each one.

Item, I declare and confess for my *hija natural* (daughter born out of wedlock),[44] *doña* María del Benino, whom I leave for my universal heir in all the remainder of my estate. Even though I am married in the law of the Holy Mother church with Domingo Quispe, my husband, who is present, in terms of our estate and goods, from the day I married him until today he has had and has what pertains to him knowingly, in his possession, insofar as half of the marital earnings so nothing pertains to him insofar as the half of the marital gains I have declared in my record and will. And thirty *pesos* that I have lent Domingo, my husband, and he owes me, should be collected from him. The said Domingo Quispe, before me, the present notary and below-signed witnesses, said and declared to be true what *doña* Isabel del Benino, his legitimate wife, said and declared in this clause. Because it is so, he [Quispe] asked Gonzalo Holguin to sign because he did not know how.

Item, I order that in addition to the masses I have ordered, if my estate can cover it to give twenty *pesos* to the Hospital of the Natives in the Villa of Potosí and if it does not cover it, do not give it to them, or if there is some other money left over from that which I have ordered in this, my will, say some masses for the souls of purgatory and this I leave to the will of my executors and I, the said notary, certify that I know the declarant of this will and record, all who were present: Diego Pérez Loreyro and Juan Holguin and Juan Suparara and Diego Quispe and Pedro Chincha *yanaconas* of the said *chacara*, that was dated on the 20th day of the month of December of 1597, In supplication and by witness.

[Signed by Goncalo Holguin before Joan Perez Loreyro Public and cabildo notary.]

Codicil of *doña* Isabel del Benino

After the aforementioned in the said *chacara* on March 1, 1598 *doña* Isabel del Benino said that she declared and declares for her estate a *solar* and

---

44. On the distinction between "natural" and "illegitimate" children, see Chapter 1, footnote 7.

run-down house in the parish of the Conception in the Villa of Potosí, I order them sold for my estate.

Item, [I] declare for [my] estate a *solar* that is next to the house of Alonso Torrejon in the parish of Saint Peter; I order it be sold.

Item, I declare that Domingo Asangato owes me twenty *pesos* of currency that I loaned him in *reales*; I order it collected.

Item, Damian *indio* of Caracoto owes twelve, I mean fifteen *llamas*. I order them collected from the *chacara* of Aguirre.

Item, Pablo Guanca owes me six *pesos* from a load of flour. I order it collected.

Item, Pedro Chichay *yanacona* of this *chacara* owes me ten *pesos*, I order them collected from him.

Item, Antonio Cornejo Morcano, ten *pesos* which he sent me to say that Christobál de Perales is supposed to pay me; I order that Christóbal de Perales swear by oath if he owes them and that they be collected for my estate.

Item, Diego Quispe my brother-in-law owes me twelve loads of corn; I order it collected.

Item, it is my last will that [illegible words] *doña* María del Benino my daughter and heir here in this her *chacara*, should alone be my executor and custodian and carry out and comply with the orders of this, my last will and testament as best as she perceives and the masses that I ordered to be said in Potosí should be said above all in a manner that all is done by her will as all is directed toward the good of my soul and in this way I declare before Gonzalo Holguin and Gerónimo Escudero, to whom I beg to sign here and witness before all who are here present to all of the above as stated: Juan Suchavara, Diego Quipse, Pedro Chincay, and Domingo Quispe, her husband. [*The codicil is signed by Gonzalo Holguin and Gerónimo Escudero.*]

3.4 Will of *doña* Ana de Barba y Talora[45] (1658)

In the name of the Holy Trinity, Father and Son and Holy Spirit, three people and one true God with whose grace all things have their beginning middle and praiseworthy end. Amen = Know all those who see this letter that I, *doña* Ana de Barba y Talora, native of the Villa Imperial of Potosí, (daughter of Luis de Barja, who is already deceased, and of Joana Colquema,)[46] resident

---

45. Archivo Nacional de Bolivia, Escrituras Publicas, Ortiz Gallo, Volume 186B. Fols. 1041–1045v.
46. Colquema is an indigenous name, which reveals the indigenous-Spanish ancestry of Barba y Talora.

of this City of La Plata and legitimate wife of Juan de Castro Samelvide, who is absent from [the city] through marital relief dictated by the ecclesiastical judge who ordered our divorce and separation from cohabitation. I find myself at present with the bodily illness that our Lord has seen fit to give me, but sane in my judgment and wisdom that his Holy Majesty granted me, and fearing death which is a natural thing for all creatures, ignorant of it and uncertain of the hour when it will arrive. I desire the serenity that befalls the unburdening of conscience, and choose for my advocate and intercessor in the Holy Royal Kingdom of the Angels, mother of god and our Lady, so that [she will] intercede with her preciousness and forgive me my sins and admit my soul on the road to Salvation, lighting for me the knowledge so that his majesty in his holy service is willing, I order my will in the following shape and form:

First, I entrust my soul to God, our *Señor* (Lord), who nourished and redeemed it with his precious blood, death, and passion, and I order it back to the land from which it was formed. Item, I order that my body be buried in the principal church of this city, in the location and place that my executors wish, and that the priest and sacristan accompany my body with a cross and a tolling of the bells, without further ostentation nor accompaniment, for which the customary alms will be paid from my property.

Item, I order that the day of my burial, if there is time, those gathered sing a mass for me with my body present, with a vigil and response, and the customary alms will be paid from my property.

Item, I order that one hundred low masses be said for my soul by the clergy that my executors wish and the customary alms be paid from my property.

Item, I order two *pesos* to the *mandas forzosas* (a bequest to the church) be distributed and I set them aside from my property.

Item, I declare that I owe Manuel Bel two *pesos* and six *reales*; I order he be paid.

Item, I declare that I owe Rafael García Ros nine-and-a-half *pesos*; I order he be paid.

Item, I declare that I owe Andrés de Orostegui four *pesos*; I order he be paid.

Item, I declare that I owe *doña* Inés de Obando, legitimate wife of Juan de Ortega, my *compadre* (close friend), five *pesos* for a silver candle snuffer, also some wax and some little things that I took from her store. I order that whatever she says I owe her should be paid to her.

Item, I declare that I am married and veiled by the order of the Holy Mother Church to Juan de Castro Samelvide, even though we have been separated as declared above, and only one of those children that we had during our cohabitation has survived, a daughter who is named Juana, who is blind. I declare her for the daughter of my husband and myself because all the others died in their childhood.

Item, I declare that at the time we married, I took in dowry for the possession of my husband, in different types of things, up to two thousand and five hundred *pesos*, all of which he spent and gambled, giving cause for which he mistreated me and obliged me to ask for the divorce. I declare it as such so that it is known for all time.

Item, I declare that my husband did not bring his own money to the marriage. I declare it so it is known.

Item, I declare that during the time that I lived with him, my husband did not have any financial gains because as I have said he used all of what I brought [to the marriage] to gamble. I declare so that it be known for all time.

Item, I declare for my property the following:

First, the Captain Diego Fernández de Vega, merchant, owes me six hundred *pesos* by a public document before the present scribe. I order it collected as part of my estate.

Item, I declare that the *Bachiller* (graduate) Juan Díaz de Nava, priest of Totora[47] owes me 330 *pesos* from simple decrees that are in a desk that I leave; I order it collected.

Item, I declare that Luis Altamirano owes me forty *pesos* for a fruit bowl that I sold him; I order it collected.

Item, I declare that Baltasar de Bocos owes me sixty *pesos* for a clavichord; I order that if he pays, it be returned to him.

Item, I declare that I own two altar cloths,[48] one in decorated blue cloth[49] and the other half laminated, with two statues of the Holy Christ.

Item, I leave a statue of the Virgin of the Immaculate Conception with its cloak of blue cloth and silver crown.

Item, I leave another small statue of the Virgin of Candelaria, which the statues and the dossal of blue cloth; I leave them for my daughter Juana.

Item, two pictures of the same size with their golden frames, one of Saint Gertrudis and the other of the Conversion of Saint Augustine.

Item, another picture of the Coronation of the Virgin with its golden frame.

Item, a canvas of Saint Gertrudis without frame.

Item, another small picture of Saint Francis of Paula without frame.

---

47. This appears to be a reference to the town of Totora in the province of Cochabamba, Bolivia.

48. Called dossals, or *doceles*.

49. *Tela quajada azul.* The term *tela de cuajada* could refer to cheesecloth but this seems unlikely. *Cuajada* can also mean "decorated."

Item, other pictures of little value, and a large box and a small box, which I bequeath to a girl who I have in my house, my niece named Juanita, daughter of my brother Manuel de Barja, for the love I have for her.

Item, I leave a mirror with its black frame.

Item, I leave a copper brazier that cost me fifty *pesos* and is in my house.

Item, a wooden bedframe, four mattresses, two blankets, a canopy, and a bedspread of blue and white cotton.

Item, a new *cumbe* bedspread and a new *cumbe* dressing gown.

Item, another bedspread of white taffeta.

Item, I leave a new lace cloth[50] that is five fingers in length.

Item, I declare that a clavichord in my house belongs to Luis Altamirano who has a small harp of mine; I order it be returned and the harp be collected.

Item, I leave a medium-sized wooden desk and another smaller desk, covered with black sheepskin, with its drawers.

Item, I leave a string of pearls that has the Virgin at the neck and bracelets of coral and pearls on her hands.

Item, two rings and a gold necklace with white stones.

Item, an Our Lady of the Immaculate Conception, garnished with some stones.

Item, a gold toothpick and another seven small brooches also of gold, for shirt fronts.

Item, a large harp.

Item, two trunks lined with Moscovia cloth, two large wooden boxes, one small and the other larger.

Item, a bench, two medium tables, one new and the other used.

Item, a small stone water filter and an old, common table.

Item, a monochord that I have loaned to Marcos Antonio Bautista.

Item, a small clavichord with two small tables on which it stands.

Item, one chamber pot, four candlesticks, two with their drip collars, two small censors, one bowl with its tray, a small drinking cup, a large bowl with its two small handles, eight spoons, four plates, two small pots with their lids, another somewhat bigger, another medium with its two-handled lid, a small pitcher, a chamber pot, four small plates, one platter, another medium, another small plate, a salt cellar without lid, all of silver that weighs sixty-four *marcos*.[51]

Item, a holy water font with a silver heart that weigh two *marcos*, more or less.

Item, I leave another bedframe, wooden and common.

Item, I leave two new blankets, one with a lace border and one without.

---

50. Specifically, a *corte* (cut); meaning sufficient cloth from which to make a woman's dress.
51. All these items were made of silver and the weight would determine the value. One *marco* weighed a half pound.

Item, I leave some sheets, pillowcases, shirts, new and used petticoats, head scarves, handkerchiefs, which are found in my trunks with six *varas* of new linen, two and-a-half of Rouen and four of Brittany, and other odds and ends.

Item, I leave some skirts and doublets in some boxes.

Item, I declare that in addition to the goods I have mentioned, that my daughter has her entire bed [and bedclothes] as well as some clothing and interior clothing for her personal use, I declare it so it is understood.

Item, I declare that I owe the *Bachiller* Eusebio de Armas for the rent of the house in which I live, which runs from the beginning of this year in which we are, at ten *pesos* each month, because all that prior I have paid him.

Item, I declare that Marcos Antonio Bautista teaches my blind daughter to play the harp at the rate of ten *pesos* per month; I order that this account be settled for the time that he has taught her and with what I have been paying him and that he be paid what he, in his conscience, says I still owe him.

Item, I declare that the Maestro Juan Candidato has taught my daughter to play the clavichord. For all the time that he has taught her, I do not owe him anything because I have paid him.

Item, I declare for my additional belongings a wooden platform, three *varas* long and two-and-a-half *varas* wide.

Item, two woolen runners of different colors that are for the platform.

Item, another three small runners of the same style that are for the tables and trunks.

Item, another small runner of *cumbe* of three *varas*, somewhat worn.

Item, I leave other odds and ends and household items of little value that are my belongings.

And to fulfill and satisfy this my will, requests, and bequests contained therein, I name as my executors and administrators of the estate the Captain *don* Eugenio del Olmo y Cabrera, *vecino* of this city, and the *licenciado* Estevan Feliz de Arron, lawyer of this Real Audiencia (Royal Court) to each one of whom I give power so that in time they may collect and gather, sell and auction (or outside of auction), all these goods, charging and taking them from whoever has them, appearing in court cases, making motions and all the necessary steps to finalize my estate by granting letters of payment, deeds, and all the other contracts that are necessary even after one year of the executorship has passed. I will prorate the appropriate time and I give you sufficient authority as the law requires.

And I name for tutor and guardian of the person and goods of my daughter Juana, the said *licenciado* Estevan Felix de Arron to whom I beg, for the love of God, that after my death, as an act of charity accept this guardianship and care of my daughter. And he should take her to his house so that *doña* María de Barros, his legitimate wife (to whom I make the same request that his divine majesty will pay them for the good and charity that they perform), can teach her virtue. It is my will that they accept the burden of this guardianship without payment. In the satisfaction that I have with *licenciado* Estevan Feliz de Arron, I charge him with continuing to teach music as he has begun with my daughter so that she is sufficiently skilled to procure her a place in a convent. There she can serve the choir, and be kept for this ministry. This is what I desire: that she apply herself in service to His divine majesty in His holy house.

And to complete and pay for this, my will, commands, and requests contained herein, the remainder of my belongings, rights and actions that in any way belong to me, I leave to and name as my universal heir my blind daughter Juana, because I declare that I have no other heir, ascending or descending, so that she can enjoy it with God's blessing and mine.

Item, I declare for my goods a new woman's chair with its adornments.

Item, I order that my mother, Juana Colquema, be given mourning clothes of *bayeta de la tierra* (locally woven cloth) and twenty *pesos* that I leave her.

With this I revoke and annul any other wills, codicils, powers to testate that are dated before this, executed in writing or verbally so that none of those are valid in court or outside of it except this that I now make and execute before the present scribe. Let this will be validated and executed as my last will and disposition in whose testimony I order it in the Registrar which is dated in the city of La Plata, April 9, 1658. I, the public scribe, grant that the testator is seemingly of sound mind but did not sign because she did not know how. At her request a witness signed being called and requested Christóbal de Salacar, Juan de Bonifaz, Lorenzo de Mayorga, y Diego Antonio de Villareal y Thomas Monrroz present and resident in this court at the request of the grantor

Diego de Villareal
Before me Diego Ortiz Gallo, Public Notary

Suggested Reading

Christensen, Mark, and Jonathan Truitt. *Native Wills from the Colonial Americas: Dead Giveaways in a New World.* Salt Lake City: University of Utah Press, 2015.

Jouve-Martin, José R. "Death, Gender, and Writing: Testaments of Women of African Origin in Seventeenth-Century Lima, 1651–1666," in *Afro-Latino Voices: Narratives from the Early Modern Ibero-Atlantic World, 1550–1812*, ed. Kathryn Joy McKnight and Leo J. Garofalo (pp. 105–25). Indianapolis, IN: Hackett Publishing Company, 2009.

Kellogg, Susan, and Matthew Restall, eds. *Dead Giveaways: Indigenous Testaments of Colonial Mesoamerica and the Andes.* Salt Lake City: University of Utah Press, 1998.

Document Themes

- Family
- Labor
- Law
- Religion
- Sexuality and gender

4

Midwife Francisca Díaz's Petition to Return to Mexico (Seville, 1566)

Francisca Díaz was an Iberian-born midwife who first sailed to Mexico in about 1560. She thus formed part of one of the first waves of Spanish women who traveled to the New World in the decades after the initial conquest of the Aztec and Inca capitals. The following text is the petition that she presented in Seville before *don* (sir) López de Armendáriz, an *alcalde mayor* (district judge) in the Real Audiencia (Royal Court) of that city for permission to return to New Spain along with her son, whom she planned to marry off there, and an enslaved woman called Ana whom she had acquired in Mexico.

Throughout much of the colonial period, Spain carefully monitored persons who wished to migrate to the Indies. In 1510, the Council of the Indies, the supreme advisory body to crown policy in the New World, decreed that "all people were prohibited to travel to the Indies without bringing with them licence to do so from the officials of the Contratación (Royal House of Trade)."[1] The Council subsequently relaxed its prohibitions on individuals and groups who might travel overseas, but scrutiny over migration persisted. The House of Trade kept records about all travelers, and the Council issued several subsequent proclamations governing the practice. These discouraged married men from traveling to the Indies without their wives, but also, at least in the first fifty years of the sixteenth century, discouraged most women from traveling to the New World.[2] Further, the Crown forbad members of various other groups from migrating, including Muslims, Jews, Gypsies, and Protestants, descendants of those "reconciled" by the Inquisition, non-Spaniards, vagrants, and delinquents. In 1554, the Council decreed that "the

---

1. Título XIII, I. De los pasajeros y personas prohibidas pasar a las Indias y estar en ellas, y de las licencias e informaciones de los pasajeros. Angel de Altolaguirre y Duvale, *Colección de documentos inéditos de ultramar* Series II, Tomo XXI (Nendeln: Kraus Reprint Limited, 1967), 61.

2. José Manuel Azcona Pastor, *Possible Paradises: Basque Emigration to Latin America* (Reno: University of Nevada Press, 2004), 125. Peter Boyd-Bowman's examination of Sevillian passenger registries documented that while women represented about 6 percent of all emigrants before 1540, for the next twenty years, that number grew to more than 16 percent and between 1550 and 1579, women constituted more than 28 percent the total population of Spanish emigrants. Peter Boyd-Bowman, "Patterns of Spanish Immigration to the Indies Until 1600," *The Hispanic American Historical Review* 56:4 (November 1976), 83.

officials of Seville would allow single women to travel to the Indies, as long as they were not prohibited from doing so [because of their membership in one of the afore-named groups], even if they did not carry a license to journey."[3] Shortly after the 1554 decree, however, likely for reasons of female safety as well as for perceptions of propriety, the crown mandated that single women might only travel when accompanied by close male relatives. Such restrictions notwithstanding the majority of women who traveled to the New World in the sixteenth century were unmarried.[4]

Díaz, as a married woman whose husband had remained in Spain when she first traveled alone to the New World, would certainly have required a license for her first journey. She was likely motivated to travel, as were many of her male Castilian contemporaries, for financial reasons. The Spanish economy was shrinking in the second half of the sixteenth century and this pushed individuals and households to seek more opportunities elsewhere. As a skilled midwife, Díaz observed she found a professional *niche* in the particular market of (likely Spanish) women who were her clients in New Spain. Other Spanish women, like the nuns discussed in Chapter 9, traveled to the New World because of their spiritual motivations; still others, like Ana de Anguiano whose story is treated in Chapter 5, accompanied husbands or other relatives who were merchants, skilled craftsmen, or administrators, and some of them joined their male relatives in these fields, either before or after the men's deaths. A final group likely traveled because they believed that the relative scarcity of Spanish women in the Indies would mean they might make more advantageous marital matches there.[5]

On her second voyage, even though she was widowed by then, Díaz evidently still required official license and applied for that permission, likely to a municipal-level judge or *alcalde ordinario*. The phrase "*no ha lugar*" (had no place in law) scrawled on the back of her first petition indicates that this official—doctor Vázquez—denied her plea. Undeterred, Díaz apparently resubmitted her permission before *alcalde* Armendáriz, referred to in the closing documents as an *alcalde mayor* (district judge), and therefore of greater authority than the initial judge who rejected her petition. The closing lines of Armendáriz's judgement and a *Real Cédula* (royal decree) dated 1567 which conceded royal license to Díaz to return to New Spain along with her son and the enslaved woman, Ana, indicate that her petition succeeded in the

---

3. Altolaguirre y Duvale, *Colección de documentos inéditos*, 63.
4. Boyd-Bowman, "Patterns of Spanish Immigration," 84, found that 60 percent of the female population who migrated to the New World were unmarried, including those who, as children, were too young for marriage.
5. Mary Elizabeth Perry, *Gender and Disorder in Early Modern Seville* (Princeton, NJ: Princeton University Press, 1990), 16.

end.[6] Because her son Andrés was ten years below the age of legal majority, he did not have to submit his own separate *probanza* (petition or proof) but could be included in her application. Francisca Díaz may have had to provide particular justification for her need to re-import Ana to Mexico because in the context of the more than five hundred African immigrants imported into New Spain annually in the mid-sixteenth century, New Spain's viceroy (royal governor), Luís de Velasco, had in 1553 requested that Spanish King Philip II limit their entry because "there are more than twenty thousand who are increasing and will eventually spread confusion in the land."[7]

Díaz sought a license that she could carry with her to legitimize her presence in the New World, and the officiating *alcalde* referred to her petition as a *probanza*. *Probanzas* were legal dossiers from which a variety of subgenres developed in the Spanish and Spanish American Early Modern World. Early colonizers and inhabitants of the Indies (including most famously one of Hernán Cortés' footmen, Bernal Díaz del Castillo) produced *probanzas de méritos y servicios* (proofs of worth and service), testifying to their military and administrative service to the crown, as arguments for the receipt of royal favors, while *probanzas de limpieza de sangre* documented petitioners' claims to blood cleanliness free of the taint of Jewish, Muslim, and eventually indigenous or African ancestry.

In this set of documents, Díaz's petition serves more explicitly to attest to the legitimacy and propriety of her passages between Iberia and the Indies, and her residency in the latter. The details of her experiences as revealed in her *probanza* complicate our notions of the practical, financial, and emotional conditions of women's sixteenth-century lives and help us to reconstruct a more nuanced picture of women's reproductive, social, and financial experiences in this setting. Apparently, her professional practice in New Spain brought Díaz considerable wealth; she amassed sufficient income, at any rate, to afford the purchase of a slave, and to finance two trans-Atlantic journeys. A document conceding license to other members of Díaz's kin who traveled from Talavera, Spain, to Mexico City to collect her belongings after her death, dating from 1581, suggests that Díaz continued to accrue substantial wealth after her return to Mexico.[8]

---

6. Archivo General de Indias, Indiferente, 1967, L. 16, F. 155R. "Real Cédula a los oficiales de la Casa de Contratación dando licencia a Francisca Díaz, comadre, para volver a Nueva España llevando una esclava llamada Ana y un hijo."

7. Luís de Velasco, quoted in Herman L. Bennett, *Africans in Colonial Mexico: Absolutism, Christianity, and Afro-Creole Consciousness, 1570–1640* (Bloomington: Indiana University Press, 2003), 21.

8. Archivo General de Indias, Indiferente, 2060, N. 149. "Expediente de concesión de licencia para pasar a México a favor de Francisco González, vecino de Talavera, con su mujer Isabel Núñez, vecina de Talavaera, hija de Juan Gutiérrez y de Francisca Díaz (murió en

Along with her financial success, Díaz's petition testifies to both her medical expertise and to her familiarity with legal practice, for much of this document is composed of the questions she herself apparently suggested that the *alcalde* should pose to the witnesses she had assembled to substantiate her right to a license; the court evidently concurred, agreeing that witnesses were to "*Digan lo que saben*" (They should say what they know) after each of her suggested queries.

What details can be extracted from Díaz's petition to fill in details about her life? What prompted her to travel to New Spain in the first place, what motivated her return journey to Iberia, and why might she have been ambiguous about her reasons for returning to Spain after her first journey to Mexico? What do details from the text allow us to conclude about Díaz's social and economic status? Because we know that midwifery practices, in the pre-conquest society of central Mexico were widespread and sophisticated, why might Díaz have commented that her services were so much in demand in that setting?[9] What can we learn from the material included and excluded from her *probanza*? Why might she have encouraged questions testifying to Ana's status as a slave? How does the evidence supplied by Díaz's various witnesses compare? What might explain any differences in their testimony?

4.1 Francisca Díaz Petitions the *Alcalde*[10]

Most powerful *Señor* (Lord),

I, Francisca Díaz, midwife, native of the town of Talavera de la Reina, declare that I have been in Mexico, which is in the Indies, and I came on the fleet led by Cristóbal de Eraso and I bring with me Ana, my slave. And while there, I practiced my profession of midwifery, in which I am very skilled, and I did much good for many people. And now I want to return to the city of Mexico and bring with me Ana, my slave, and also Andrés Gutiérrez, my son aged fifteen years, who is single, in order that he be married. I have

---

México), con sus hijos con una criada. Para ir a cobrar los bienes dejados por la dicha Francisca Díaz." Although the medical profession often denigrated midwives as poor and ignorant, recent research in the European context suggest midwives there often pertained to various social strata. See Samuel S. Thomas, "Early Modern Midwifery: Splitting the Profession, Connecting the History," *Journal of Social History* 43:1 (2009), 115–38.

9. For more on pre-Columbian and early post-conquest obstetrical history, see Nora E. Jaffary, *Reproduction and Its Discontents in Mexico: Childbirth and Contraception from 1750 to 1905* (Chapel Hill: University of North Carolina Press, 2016).

10. Archivo General de Indias, Indiferente 2051, no. 32. Thanks go to José Manuel Vázquez Ruiz for his transcription help with this document.

merchandise in the quantity of five hundred *pesos* to bring with me and I need to take with me three other people to serve me because I am old.[11] All this is supported in this report which I present. To your highness I beg for a license for this purpose, and in granting it, your highness, you show me great favor.

[illegible signature]

[The following summary of the text was written on the back of the preceding page. The positioning of the letters indicates the document would have originally been folded up, with its reverse side acting as an envelope.]

Francisca Díaz [three illegible words]

Begging license to return to New Spain from whence she came and requesting permission for other things contained in her petition.

To *Señor* Doctor Vásquez

So that she and the slave that she brought and her fifteen-year-old son, not being married, and with *pesos* and all the rest. But the petition is dismissed. (*Mas no ha lugar.*)

4.2 Second Petition

[On December 4, 1566, Díaz appeared before a different official, alcalde *Armendáriz, and presented her petition requesting permission to return to Mexico with her son and with the enslaved woman, Ana. She identified herself and the ship upon which she arrived from Mexico and requested that the* alcalde *carefully consider her petition and her witnesses' testimony, which would address the following questions:]*

First if they [the witnesses] know me, the said Francisca Díaz, and for how long and if they also know Ana, my *negra* (black) slave.

Item.[12] If they know and etc. that the said Francisca Díaz was in the city of Mexico, which is in the Indies, for the time of four years, more or less, and in all this time practiced her profession of midwifery in the said city of Mexico, where she was of great use and that it was necessary that she dwell there and practice her occupation because there was a lack of midwives who had

---

11. We do not know from this document how old Díaz was. One of her witnesses, aged fifty, says he has known her for more than forty years, so all we can know is that she is at least that old. She may be exaggerating her age as a means to justify traveling with the enslaved woman, Ana.

12. *Ytem* in the original, meaning next item in a list.

knowledge and experience in this profession, and this witness should say what he knows and saw as the question asks. They should say what they know.

Item. If they know and etc. that because of a certain need that presented itself to the said Francisca Díaz, she came to Spain to this city of Seville where she is at present, she came on the fleet that just arrived from New Spain, together with the fleet from *Tierra Firme*[13] under general *don* Cristóbal de Eraso, and she brought with her in her service a *negra* slave named Ana. This witness should say what he knows and has seen as the questions asks. They should say what they know.

Item. If they know and etc. that all that has been said is publicly known and stated (*de pública voz y fama*), the *licenciado* Santiago de Ugarte.

Item. If they know and etc. that Francisca Díaz has been and is sick, and is a woman of advanced years, for which reason it was necessary for her to bring with her the slave from Mexico to this city for her service and for this reason it will also be necessary for her to return with her to the city of Mexico for her service because her service is necessary for the reasons given. They should say what they know.

Having presented the petition and questions, as they are written, Francisca Díaz asked for the fulfillment of her petition and asked for justice. Witnessed by Hernando de Villarroel and Juan de Torres.

The *señor alcalde* said that he commanded that Francisca Díaz's *probanza* be taken and received and that it be examined according to the questions. Diego de Ojeda, notary.

Then, a short time later, Francisca Díaz presented witnesses Diego de Talavera, Hernando de Palma, Pascual de Sagobal, and Gabriel López, hosier, for the *probanza*. Each one of them took an oath according to form and law, by virtue of which they promised to tell the truth in this case in which they were presented as witnesses and what each of the witnesses said and deposed is as follows:

Witness: Diego de Talavera, dealer in the China of Talavera, *vecino* (citizen) of Seville in the street de la Sierpe. The witness was presented, sworn, questioned, and declared the following:

To the first question, he said that he has known Francisca Díaz the midwife for over twenty years, because they are both natives of the same village of Talavera,[14] and that he has known Ana, *negra* slave of the said Francisca Díaz, for two months, more or less, from the time when the fleet of ships came to this city because Francisca Díaz came on this fleet and brought with her Ana, her slave.

---

13. The mainland (as opposed to the Antilles) of Spain's New World possessions.
14. Talavera de la Reina is a city in the western province of Toledo, four hundred kilometers northwest of Seville.

Asked about his particulars,[15] he said that he is of about thirty years of age, more or less, and that he is not related to the said Francisca Díaz, and that he has no financial interest in this transaction.

To the second question, he said that what he knows is that six years ago, more or less, Francisca Díaz the midwife came from the said village of Talavera, where she was born, to this city [Seville] and that from here she left for the Indies, to New Spain, to practice her profession of midwifery and has been in the city of Mexico, according to what this witness knows, and recently came back to this city in the fleet that she arrived here two months ago, more or less, and that this witness knows that Francisca Díaz is a skillful woman with experience in her profession of midwifery, and that this is public and notorious among those who know her and that he has heard it said to others that in the city of Mexico, where she has been, she has practiced her profession of midwifery and has done much good in the city because of her ability and that, after she came on this fleet as he has said, he has seen her also practicing her profession of midwifery in this city of Seville. And this is what he knows of this question.

To the third question he says that, as he said in the previous question, this witness knows and has seen that Francisca Díaz came from the Indies to this city on the most recent fleet that arrived two months ago, more or less, under General *don* Cristóbal de Eraso, and that she brought with her Ana, her *negra* slave, and that regarding this slave the witness has seen that she belongs to Díaz and is for her service, according to what he has seen and what Francisca Díaz has said. And this is what he knows about this question.

To the fourth question, he says he has already answered this.

To the fifth question, he says that this witness has seen that the said Francisca Díaz is very old and requires assistance and it seems to this witness that it was necessary for her to bring Ana her slave with her on this voyage from Mexico to this city for her service and in the same way it will be necessary to return with her, if she goes back to the Indies, for the reasons already given. And this is what he knows about this question. And this is the truth under oath that he took and he signs. Diego de Talavera. Diego de Ojeda, notary. . . .

[The second witness, Hernando de Palma, a spice merchant, fifty years old, and resident of Seville, supplied virtually identical testimony to the court as the first witness, indicating that he had known Díaz because they were both natives of the same village of Talavera. He expanded only on the following details in reply to the second question:]

---

15. *Las generales* in the original. Normally, "*las generales de la ley*" refers to a person's basic personal information.

. . . that Francisca Díaz came to this city [Seville] on this most recent fleet and it is said that she comes to fetch certain children, and that since she has returned she has been seen practicing her profession of midwifery in this city. And this is what he knows about this question.

To the third question he said as has been said that Francisca Díaz the midwife came to this city on the fleet that came about three months ago, and he says that she came to fetch her children and she brought the *negra* slave Ana with her for her service and the witness believes that it was necessary for her to bring her with her for her service, and this witness takes [Ana] to be her slave because she has seen her possessing her as a slave and the slave serves Francisca Díaz.

To the fourth question, he said that he has already said what he has to say about this.

To the fifth question, this witness said that he knows that Francisca Díaz is very old, because he has known her for more than forty years as he has said, and she arrived here ill and it appears to this witness that it was necessary for her to bring with her the said Ana her slave for her service and company and that even here in Seville he has seen that the said slave, since her owner is old and sick, helps undress her, and readies her for bed, and serves her in all that is necessary and that in this way it appears to this witness that if Francisca Díaz returns to the Indies, it would also be necessary for her slave to return with her for these reasons. And this is the truth according to the judgement that he has made and he signs. Hernando de la Palma. Diego de Ojeda, notary.

[The third witness, Pascual de Sabogal, a surgeon barber, aged thirty, declared he had known Francisca Díaz on the voyage that had brought her back from Mexico to Spain three months earlier. He declared that he did not know the enslaved woman, Ana, but provided no other evidence supplementing that which the other witnesses had provided. The fourth witness was Gabriel López, a hosier, and vecino *of Talavera de la Reina, age twenty-five. López said he had known Francisca Díaz for more than fourteen years, and had known Ana for three months. His answers to several of the questions merely corroborated the evidence of the other witnesses, but in answer to the second question, he elaborated on the reasons for Díaz's return journey from Mexico to Spain:]*

. . . To the second question, he said that what he knows about this question is that six years ago, more or less, when this witness, who, like Francisca Díaz, is from the town of Talavera, he saw Diaz depart from the village of Talavera to come to this city of Seville to embark from here to New Spain, and that afterwards this witness heard that she went on a voyage and was living in the city of Mexico, practicing her art of midwifery and this is public and notorious and for this reason this witness believes that in the city of Mexico, she did great service with her profession and that Francisca Díaz returned on this most recent fleet and he has heard it said that that she came because there were objections there that she had been married in Talavera and that she should come and to live as husband and wife, and after she came she learned that her husband had died and that since she returned here, Francisca Díaz was at the childbirth of the wife of this witness and from what he saw, she was very skilled in her art. And this is what he knows about the question.

And so, having submitted an authenticated copy of the *probanza*, Francisca Díaz said that she requests that the said *señor alcalde mayor* grant her the *probanza* in public form to keep her rights and she asks for justice.

The *señor alcalde* said that he commands that Francisca Díaz be given two or more—as many as she wants—copies of the authenticated copy of the said *probanza* and that his authority and judicial decree should be interpolated into each one so they will be validated, to which he gives faith and he signs his name, doctor *don* Lope de Armendáriz, Diego de Ojeda, notary.

[signs] Doctor *don* Lope de Armendáriz

And I, the said Diego de Ojeda, scribe and public notary of his majesty, transcribes it and make my sign in testimony of its truth.

[signs] Diego de Ojeda, notary.

Suggested Reading

Altman, Ida. *Transatlantic Ties in the Spanish Empire: Brihuega, Spain and Puebla, Mexico, 1560–1620.* Stanford, CA: Stanford University Press, 2000.

Mangan, Jane E. *Transatlantic Obligations: Creating the Bonds of Family in Conquest-Era Peru and Spain.* New York: Oxford University Press, 2016.

Owens, Sarah E., and Jane E. Mangan. *Women of the Iberian Atlantic.* Baton Rouge: Louisiana State University Press, 2012.

Poska, Allyson M. *Gendered Crossings: Women and Migration in the Spanish Empire.* Albuquerque: University of New Mexico Press, 2016.

Document Themes

- Family
- Labor
- Law
- Migration and mobility

5

Life and Love in Women's Letters to Spouses (Spain and Mexico, 1567–1576)[1]

Letters showcase women's voices and experiences in a distinct manner from court records and notarial documents. When women took ink to paper, they revealed unique aspects of married life and the challenges of living apart in the era of Spanish expansion and New World domination. The letters in this chapter highlight two distinct experiences; the first four letters are from women in Spain writing to men in Mexico and the latter five letters are between a husband and wife who both lived in the New World but were separated by the obligations of work. These letters, with a geographical trajectory depicted in Map 3, come from a larger collection of letters sent between Spain and the Indies, most of which were archived in Seville in the Archivo de Indias as part of a Crown inquiry.

Sending a letter in the 1500s constituted an undertaking that is representative of that time and place. First of all, literacy rates were not very high in Spain or in the New World at this time.[2] Thus, many letters were not necessarily written by the hand of the sender. Rather, men and women hired scribes or used trusted acquaintances to write letters for them. In addition, to safeguard the contents of a letter, it was necessary to use networks of friends, relatives, and kin to help with their delivery from one location to another. Royal documents of the Spanish empire had their own system of transport with crown officials, but for personal letters, other arrangements had to be made. Francisca Hernández's letter makes the most of the issue of needing to have a trusted representative to carry letters. Finally, once scribes wrote letters and senders entrusted them to carriers, it took months for a letter traveling between Spain and Mexico to reach its intended recipient. Thus, while letter writing was an important outlet for separated couples to send messages, the communication was precarious and slow.

---

1. The editors thank Ana Fasold-Berges for her translation assistance in this chapter.
2. In her study of sixteenth-century Spain, Sarah Nalle, for example, discovered rates of literacy for women ranging from 2 percent (rural Toledo) to 16 percent (urban Valencia). Sarah Nalle, "Literacy and Culture in Early Modern Castile," *Past and Present* 125 (November 1989), 68. On educated women's culture of literacy, see Anne J. Cruz and Rosilie Hernández, eds., *Women's Literacy in Early Modern Spain and the New World* (London: Routledge, 2011).

In addition to letters, news from the Indies was a commodity, and the best place to find it was Seville. As the launching point for passengers and the arrival point for returnees, Seville was the hub. The official House of Trade, or the Casa de la Contratación was founded in 1503 in order to track licenses for passengers and inventories for property passing between the metropole and the colonies. Note that in her letter, María Goméz states she heard from a scribe who arrived on the latest fleet from Mexico that there were inquiries as to whether she was alive or dead. This news prompted Goméz to travel from her city of Ronda to Seville (roughly eighty miles) with her son in order to follow up on these inquiries. Other letter-writers have a general idea of the whereabouts of their husbands, thanks in part to hearsay.

Thus, previous letters and hearsay inform the content of letters by María Gómez, Francisca Hernández de los Arcos, and Leonor Gil de Molina. All communicated with men who had been in the New World for years, even though their tone suggests they write as if they had just seen each other. This tone derives from the immediacy of purpose that prompted them to write. All the women asked for money, for additional communication, and for the return of the men to whom they wrote. What we see anecdotally is borne out in the scholarship on the era;[3] women whose husbands or sons left Iberia for the New World often supported themselves by taking menial jobs, such as sewing or selling food, or apprenticed their children, and relied heavily on relatives for help to provide housing and food. The letters reveal a common experience: women whose spouses and children left them in Spain while they sought New World endeavors suffered hardships.

Women's efforts to contact their departed husbands often revolved around the issue of men's responsibilities to their children. Sometimes, the children were newborns or not yet born when husbands boarded ships for the New World. The task of raising the children fell to the women. While the needs of children were constant—they required food, shelter, clothing, care in times of illness—some women found it more urgent to write their husbands around times of crisis or when the child was nearing adulthood. For daughters, the approach of adulthood meant that it was time to amass a dowry to ensure a suitable marriage. The networks of a father could help sons find work and, as we see in the case of María Gómez, the hope that a son could join his father in Mexico. Overall, we see that children figure prominently in these letters as the bond between men and women who have been separated for years on

---

3. Mary Elizabeth Perry, *Gender and Disorder in Early Modern Seville* (Princeton, NJ: Princeton University Press, 1990).

end. And women viewed paternal contributions to the future of these children as a cultural obligation on the part of their husbands.[4]

The responsibility of a father to his children as well as of husband to his wife was also considered within a religious framework. The letters frame notions of obligation in terms of Christian duty. Women's language here served as both reminder and threat. Francisca Hernández, for instance, claimed that if her husband did not pay her in this life, he would pay in the next. Whether by making direct pleas for economic assistance or relying on religious discourse to shame men into action, these women used their letters for direct messages.

Some of these letters surely went unanswered. In that case, women might continue to write or they might decide to file a complaint with the crown to bring their husbands back to them. As strange as this might seem, the crown, in keeping with religious models of family, but also in the interest of modeling family units for its empire, supported some women in their attempts to find their husbands. According to royal legal code for the Indies, married men were only allowed to stay in the Indies for three years without returning to Spain or bringing their wives to the New World. Moreover, had a women's husband married again in the New World, that would have been a crime of bigamy and led to further investigation. While many women remained unsatisfied in their searches, a lucky few were reunited with husbands or received some financial support from them after Crown intervention.[5]

The letter writers from Spain have much in common in this context, but they are also separated by an important distinction: María Gómez and Leonor Gil de Molina were both legitimately married to the men to whom they wrote while Francisca Hernández de los Arcos was not. It was not uncommon for men and women to have children outside of marriage in early modern Spain.[6] Moreover, the medieval tradition of *barraganía* had written into law a series of guidelines to practice with regard to lovers and illegitimate children born to, for example, merchants who were away for long periods of time. Despite the fact that Hernández de los Arcos's situation was not unique, her letter reveals important strategies that she used to protect the identity of her lover. Also, her recourse to support from the Crown or from family was diminished

---

4. On women seeking assistance from spouses in the Indies, see Jane E. Mangan, *Transatlantic Obligations: Creating the Bonds of Family in Conquest-Era Peru and Spain* (New York: Oxford University Press, 2016), especially Chapter 3.

5. See Mangan, *Transatlantic Obligations*, Chapter 4.

6. Allyson M. Poska analyzes practices of family formation, women's sexuality, and out-of-wedlock births in Poska, *Women and Authority in Early Modern Spain: The Peasants of Galicia* (New York: Oxford University Press, 2006).

Map 3: Letters Sent between Spouses and Lovers

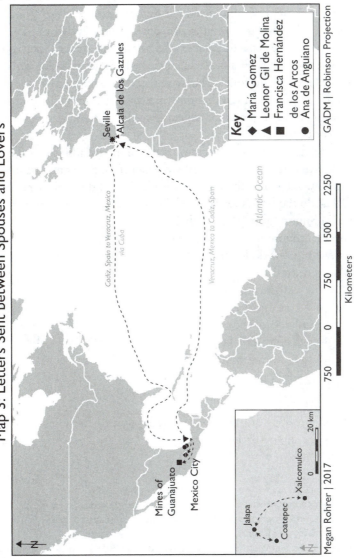

Megan Rohrer | 2017

GADM | Robinson Projection

Key
- ◆ María Gomez
- ▲ Leonor Gil de Molina
- ■ Francisca Hernández de los Arcos
- ● Ana de Anguiano

Seville
Alcala de los Gazules

Mines of Guanajuato
Mexico City

Cadiz, Spain to Veracruz, Mexico via Cuba

Veracruz, Mexico to Cadiz, Spain

Atlantic Ocean

Kilometers
750 0 750 1500 2250

Jalapa
Coatepec
Xalcomulco

0 20 km

in comparison to women like Gómez and Gil de Molina because of the illegitimate status of her children.[7]

While the first four letters highlight the challenges of couples separated by an ocean, in the final five letters, the back-and-forth correspondence between Ana de Anguiano and Francisco de Barbosa suggests the possibilities of married life for a woman who followed her husband to the New World. Anguiano was part of a growing number of women who traveled to the Indies by the latter half of the sixteenth century.[8] Despite making the long journey to Mexico, she found herself alone while her husband traveled for work. Nonetheless, the content and tone of her letters with her husband are quite different from those of her contemporaries who remained in Spain and reveal the experience this couple shared of adjusting to the culture, local economy, and local networks in Mexico.

As you read the letters, locate points of comparison between the transatlantic letters and the Mexican ones. Consider, too, the comparison between the married women and the unmarried one; how did marriage create difference? What do the letters reveal about how family was defined in this era—what was common for mothers, fathers, and children? What do the letters tell us about the economics of family life or daily life in the 1500s? And, finally, how many emotions do letter writers express in these letters and what words reveal the emotions?

5.1 María Gómez Writes to Her Husband (1567)[9]

Letter 13

María Gómez (*vecina* of [the city of] Ronda) writing from Seville to her husband Juan Escudero (barber and surgeon)[10] in the City of Mexico. 1567. Vol. 91, fols. 157–157v.

---

7. On the distinction between "natural" and "illegitimate" children, see Chapter 1, footnote 7.
8. For an example of a woman who traveled without her husband to the New World, see the case of Francisca Díaz in Chapter 4.
9. This and all the following letters are translated from Rocío Sánchez Rubio and Isabel Testón Núñez, *El hilo que une: Las relaciones epistolares en el viejo y el nuevo mundo. (Siglos XVI–XVIII)* (Mérida: Universidad de Extremadura, 1999). Sánchez Rubio and Testón Núñez located these letters among bigamy cases in the Ramo de Inquisición of the Archivo General de la Nación de México.
10. Barbers, in addition to grooming-related work, acted as low-level medical practitioners who performed such services as bloodletting, surgery, and dental extraction. Surgeons operated

Señor (Sir) Husband,

It would be reasonable after these nineteen years since you moved away from me and left me pregnant, or rather newly delivered, one day before you left for those parts [Mexico] and with two children, that you would have corresponded with me and with them. But I saw that you had left me no means of raising even the one I was nursing. Still I raised these two sons, and one of them died at age four, and Juan, the eldest I have with me alive and he has a great desire to meet his father, and he, already a man, seeing the scarce means that I have, wants to leave me to find you.

Therefore, I beg you, for the love of God, to pity me and the great travails that I have suffered and continue to suffer to raise him; do not permit him to leave while I remain here without a husband and without a son; instead you should come with all haste possible to live with me and with your son like the Christian that you are. And it is certain that if you would see and know him, he would rejoice and have great happiness in this.

His name, as I say, and according to your wish, is Juan and he is now named after you: Juan Escudero, and this is his surname. He is a very good young man and virtuous, and with the little that I earned as a woman with my hands, I put him to work as an apprenticed tailor. And it is certain that with what he earns, we are both able to eat and if it were not for him, as I am old and tired and am near the end of my days, I would already be dead.

And *señor*, with this fleet that came from New Spain, a scribe says that he received a letter from which he took a memo and sent it to Ronda, asking for news of me, about if I was dead or alive, and if I was married and for how long, and about how many children I have and if they were alive or dead. And the report came to my hands and after I took the necessary steps, and came to this city of Seville following the letter and with the great desire we had, I and your son, to learn about you. We went to la Contratación (the House of Trade) and we spoke with the scribe that sent the letter and when he saw me and your son, he said it was from you, and that a *perulero* (native of Peru) who had come on this armada had given him a letter, but he had lost it and did not know where it was. And I did this in vain, and we spent some money (*unas blancas*) on this that your son had not yet earned.

At the time that I write this, we are in Seville and although we know how to ask for it, for the love of God, we have to complain to the *señores* of the House of Trade in order that they tell us which scribe that it was the reason why he sent us the letter and cost us so much work.

---

at a slightly higher level on the medical hierarchy, and though they often had no formal education, they learned how to set bones, perform amputations, and do bloodletting as apprentices.

And so *señor*, for the one God, we pray very much that you pity us and remember that we all *habíais de morir* (must die) and that you are captive.[11] I say this in truth and because if it were not for people telling me, I would do you much harm even if good people were to see it. For the love of God, send a letter that you have written; it is not just that such an honorable man, as they tell me you are, which I take to be true, should be so long in mortal sin and separated from his wife. And because I have faith in God and that you will make things much better than I find them, I trust in this end.

And I tell you that I and your son, Juan Escudero, are alive and well, and my sisters kiss your hand. Your brother-in-law Luis Real died six years ago and left one son who has a great desire to see you. May my God, Our *Señor* (Lord), keep you and give you the grace to agree to come to Spain so that my eyes may look upon you before I die.

From Seville, 13 September, 1567. From your desiring and very loving wife.

María Gómez.

Señor: if by chance you, have a post in that city such that you cannot come, for the Love of God your son Juan Escudero begs you to send us some secure funds for him to leave to see you and see you, because he has great desire, as I say, to meet his father, but that I would not come because, for my sins, I am old and sick and am afraid if I were to undertake such a long journey, I would die.

To my very desired and beloved Juan Escudero, barber and surgeon, in the City of Mexico, in New Spain, my *señor*.

5.2 Francisca Hernández de los Arcos Writes to Her Lover (1574)

Letter 26

Francisca Hernández de los Arcos, from Seville to her lover Cosme Sánchez de Bilbao (merchant), in the mines of Guadajate, close to the City of Mexico. 1574. Vol. 105. s/f.

---

11. Both María Gómez in this letter and Francisca Hernández, in the subsequent one, repeatedly wrote that their estranged menfolk *habíais de morir*. They were surely attempting to prompt the charity of the men by reminding them of the Christian notion of the last judgment that at death all humans must face God's judgment of their deeds on earth.

Señor Hermano (brother):[12]

I am frightened by your great stubbornness in not writing me through a trusted person, since I had found such a person, who was the innkeeper of Santa Catalina, where your son died on the day of San Juan. He told me he had been with you and spent fifteen days in your home. The reason was that since he spoke to you in person and he told you that you should come to see your children and especially to see the one that had been born, and whether it was a son or daughter, whoever had this information with him, a letter would be greater comfort to me since you know that you are at least obliged to write that, even if you do no more than leave me with two children and five months pregnant. From this pregnancy, I gave birth to a son whose name is Juan Sancho de Bilbao, like your father, and I have raised the children with great effort. Juan and Diego are alive. Rodrigo was killed; for this I have remained inconsolable.

You have not done that which you promised as a Christian, but rather have shown that you undertake these tasks as if you had no conscience and were on the point of death. You well know that because of you I lost my land, my estate, my husband, my children, and that I am hated by my siblings and my mother, and that after you left, I was cut off from the relatives of my husband; if it had not been for *don* (sir) Rodrigo Ponce, they would have one come to kill me one night.

All these hardships I have suffered because of you and not only for you now but also for your children. It was not enough to make me lose my house but also the house of *don* Rodrigo. I beg you for the love of God to remember me and your sons since you know that I would not make it known that they are yours.

I do not have Diego de Bilbao, your son, with me because out of pity a cousin of mine took him with him to Las Palmas so I would not lose him, because he is now a man, and I, as a mother, can hardly provide for them. The one whom you left me with pregnant is already a man, and the other will become one as well. Many times, I have wanted to do this [i.e., write to you] but because I believed you would not answer me, I thought it would always be this way. This man has such little conscience, does he think he will never die? I wish you would have remembered me more, even if it was only for having led you where I did; even if you had no other relative, you would be obliged to repay me for this.

Señor Gonzalo de Peralta, your friend, has told me how well and rich you are. That richness God has given you, so that it will be seen that you are a Christian and since you have to die, you have to restore something of your

---

12. Rather than actually referring to her brother, Hernández de los Arcos called Sánchez de Bilbao "her brother" as a term of endearment and intimacy.

conscience. Speak with him [Peralta] when you see him as you did when you were friends, because you know each other, and he will inform you of my hardships and of how I am living. They tell me it is a shame to see me in such hardships as are seen here, and he took care to take some of them up in his own hands and [said he would] make sure that you would send me some money to help me with my hardship. If you saw fit to send for your son Juan and for me, I am ready for anything you might send because I have been many times [ready] to go there but I have not done it because I understood you to be a better Christian than you have shown you are.

For the love of God, I beg you to write me and send me some money to help me because I am tired of working because the little you send me will be worth much to me. And if you send it, let it be to the House of Trade, so that it will not be like those of the Sarmiento family who never give me anything, not even a power [of attorney] because they told me you had never left it with them. For this reason, send it to me now because if you send something I can get it; and even if you write through the House of Trade, write to me at the house of the bonnet maker on Gradas Street. Write to *doña* María Grillo; you must have the greatest care in writing to me since I was the mother of your sons. You must by now understand the pain that I have in my heart and such is the health of *doña* María Grillo, that it affected the pay that she gives me and your sons.

I am in the company of a *señora* from my region who is very honorable; I do not have anything else you may have sent me but you must see that I am a Christian and you must die some day and my health gets worse each day. Your sons have a great desire to see you, both the one that has left and the one I have with me; they ask me every day about you and, as your sons, they wish to see you and they pray to God for you. If you are married, this should not prevent you from repaying me what you owe me and from remembering your sons because if in this world you do not pay me, you will pay it in the next.

Look carefully at what you do because for you I suffer *derrostrada* (shame-faced) and go about in *tierras ajenas* (foreign lands) because however much hardship I face in this world, you will endure in the next since you are the cause of it all. There is not enough paper to write you all that I feel, and these letters are written with drops of blood from my heart.

Mateo Jorge came from the Indies and I did not ask him anything about the shoes that you said you had sent with him, I did not say anything to him, nor has he given me anything, nor do I think to ask for them.

I will not say more, except to wish that God and his blessed mother should have you before them and in Christianity.

From Seville, the last day of May 1574. At your service,
Francisca Hernández de los Arcos

Letter 27

Francisca Hernández de los Arcos, from Seville, to her lover Cosme Sánchez de Bilbao (merchant), in the mines of Guadajate, close to the City of Mexico. 1575. Vol 105, s/f.

Señor Brother,

I have done this [written you] many times, and I have been more careful in it than he.[13] You have not answered any letter, for I do not know what reason although it cannot be because of me. That you had children with me should give you sufficient cause to remember, for you left me with two [children] and another one in the belly. The one you left in the belly is as big as the others and is put to work as a *colchero* (mattress maker) because of your absence. And the boy desires to meet and know his father, and he asks me every day for him. And since you had the mouth to speak to the innkeeper of Santa Catalina and two others that came to speak to me, it would be good if you also had the hands to send me some money for your children and for me as a gift. Just because you are married you cannot forget about me or them, because you have obligations since you know that for all the hardship I suffer and have suffered you must ask forgiveness from God, since I suffer on your account; look to God in heaven and ask him for it.

With what nerve do you send me to ask me for Dieguito?[14] Do you think me as foolish as before? And since you sent everything to Dieguito, you should also send [support] to Juan since you know they are [both] yours and you should not blame them as you know. And when you send for them, you should send for them as *hijos de padres*[15] so that there is knowledge that they should have something [from you], because they have not been deprived on my side, and you know me and who I am, and that they were not made by somebody else. Remember you must die [one day] so do not regret not doing right by them; it would be good if you had sent some support ever since you got there. A man that has not taken care to send me a letter does not deserve to forget the rest. May it please God that just as you remember me, God will remember you; and I leave it to Him that which is in his possession. And you know well that I am right, since you took away the peace that I could have had. I have not written you recently because I have had some brief jobs and

---

13. Here, she presumably means that she has taken more care than Cosme Sánchez de Bilbao.
14. Likely her son, Diego de Bilbao.
15. Hernández de los Arcos is trying to distinguish between orphans, or unrecognized children here.

I inform you since they tell me my husband is alive and wants to go there[16] with wine.

My mother and my brothers are coming to where I am; I have taken all these assaults because of you, you should pay me by gifting me from there. To the carrier of this letter, would you do me the favor of gifting him something and doing for him that which is necessary. So that he will hold you in greater friendship you should give him something that he can bring, and take care because until now I have not had nothing to thank you for but a jug of water that you sent me from there. And if you send him with something, send a *poder* (power of attorney) so that I can collect what you are sending, and do it with this messenger because he is a trusted and known person and will return. And he will tell you about the hardship I have and where I am and whom I serve, since I wanted my fortune to come from you, for better or worse[17] look to the responsibility you have, when you ran from duty. And with this, may Our *Señor* give you better judgment that you have had until now, and health so you can take up some of that for which you are responsible. If you write me put it . . .[18] in them in Gradas [street] in the house of the bonnet maker, and I will get the letters there.

From Sevilla, the 20th of May 1575. I remain at your service, as always,

Francisca de los Arcos

To my *señor* brother Cosme Sánchez de Bilbao, merchant, in the mines of Guadajate in New Spain, near the City of Mexico. This is my *señor*. Guadajate, to the messenger four *reales*.[19]

5.3 Leonor Gil de Molina Writes to Her Husband (1576)

Letter 30

Leonor Gil de Molina, from Alcalá de los Gazules, to her husband, *licenciado* Juan Chávez de Vargas (instructor in grammar), in Mexico. 1576. Vol. 106, s/f.

---

16. Presumably, to Mexico.
17. This idiomatic phrase is "*Mi ventura que por vos viniese yo a ser más y a ser menos*" in the original.
18. Ellipses in the original.
19. One *real* was a piece of currency worth one eighth of a *peso*.

My much desired *señor*,

If I had understood how much I would feel your departure, I would have understood dying since I have not experienced anything before in so much pain, because when I have previously been apart from, I did not feel it to the point that I do now, because the pain my heart feels is so much because I have so much hardship and the remedy for it is so far away. Many times, if God had not been with me, I would have already made a terrible mistake, because I am an inconsolable woman who is so little favored by him who has a duty to oblige me. But since God is such a great *señor*, he makes a space in my heart and gives me patience to live this trying life. If I tell you what I felt when I sent you the mattress and the books and they were sent back; I felt so much pain that I tell you truthfully that I began to have *cisuras* (wounds), for more than a month; and after they gave me the letters, it pleased God to make them heal and restore my health for the time being, which I pray God will not take away from me until we see each other.

What you wrote to my uncle Mateo Sánchez in your letter did not come into effect because they understood that in order to keep me in his home, they had to give me his estate and this is why they said that there was no house for him until his daughter left. And I have seen the lack of love from my aunt and the little help of my brothers; my sister left her house and came to live with me. And one month after we began living together, on the Saturday of Carnestolendas,[20] she had a pain on the side, which took her life after twenty-one days and we buried her on the day of the Incarnation. Her death has affected me so much that I know if you saw me now, you would not recognize me. It was a lot that I lost when losing Miguel Pérez. I should not have bored you with this, because you already know how bad things got, and for the love of God, I hope that you feel this and will bear it with patience because these are the acts of our *Señor*, and because I understand where you must go, I tell you this.

For the love of God, remember the hardships we both have, and if it is possible to send some money to pay for the house in which we live and the other one that my uncle is renting to us next year, for us and for my brother, the widower, who will be with us. We are going to live in the house Juan Lobo bought, next to my uncle's house, which belonged to his mother from Silleros. We go there to keep the favor of my uncle and because in our hardship we have had not had any other house. That is why he wanted to bring us close to his home where we can be cared for until God brings you back to Spain.

For the love of God, may you perceive what little fortune we have and as soon as possible, determine to come back here to live or take us with you whether by sea or by land, because ever since Miguel Pérez left us, we should

---

20. Three days before Ash Wednesday.

have been with you, but since it is a path we cannot walk, we will be praying to God to let us see you with him for the good of serving him. And so I have nothing more to say except that I pray God listens to our prayers.

From Alcalá, April 28, 1576. I love you more than anything I love you, your wife,

Leonor Gil de Molina

To the very magnificent *señor,* the *licenciado* Juan de Chávez in the City of Mexico, in the home of *señor* doctor Miranda, *oidor* to His Majesty. He is my *señor.*

5.4 The Married Couple Francisco de Barbosa and Ana de Anguiano Write One Another (1573)

Letter 254

Francisco de Barbosa from Xalcomulco to his wife Ana de Anguiano, in Jalapa. 1573. Vol. 184, s/f

My Señora (lady),

I arrived in this town of Xalcomulco with Juan López and we came upon these *indios* (indigenous people), and because of their great affection in matters of money, they gave us two *amantecas* (featherwork pieces), of the best kind that there are. To the governor, we sent a half *arroba* of wine,[21] which the messenger went looking for. Do me this favor, my *señora,* send word to Lerna's house so that Lerna gives the wine to the messenger, because he should not fail to do this. And if there is none, tell Tomás de Herrera to give it, I will pay for it; and whatever way it is done, the *indio* cannot come without wine.

To my son-in-law, who brings this himself; give the 200 pesos.

I have not sent you fish because we did not even find one to eat.

Receive my goodwill. Juan López kisses your hands; and it should not be known by any means that from here we bring *indios,* for the love of Alonso de Orta, because this is advisable. We have very good news from *el* Río, and that is why the *indios* go willingly.

---

21. One *arroba* was equivalent to 4.26 gallons of wine.

Give the letters to Juan de Sahagun. May Our *Señor* permit me to return to see you in the peace that I desire for you and may he give us his good blessing.

From Xalcomulco, today Wednesday afternoon, February 14th, 1573.

Yours Until Death.
Francisco de Barbosa.

To my *señora* Ana de Anguiano, in Jalapa, my *señora*.

Letter 255

Francisco de Barbosa, from the inn of Cuatepec, to his *señora*, Ana de Anguiano, in Jalapa. 1573, Vol. 184, s/f.

My *Señora*,

Today, Friday morning, I received your letter, and with it great pleasure in knowing about your health, which Our Lord will always give you.

I received the mattress, and the *indio* took the other, and inside it a shirt of mine, and a *cofia* (cap), a pillow and two *bobos*[22] that I bought here and I wanted to send them before eating them.

I received the letter from Hernando Alonso and saw what it said. I have already told you what Córdoba wants to do with Alonso Gallego, and I wrote you a long letter, and I also wrote to your honorable son-in-law about how much good he has done. They are trying to kill me with this sale[23] and Pero [sic] Hernández is the one that wants to form the debt, and your brother is taking steps against me so that I will be thrown out of this. I do not know where it will end; I have not seen any other letter other than the one the *indio* brought.

I cannot go out on the way to meet the *alcade mayor* (district judge and governor) because I do not know when he will come. I will go there Thursday or Friday without fail, that is why you have fodder and do not tell anyone I am coming. And tell Alonso Gallego in secret not to go anywhere, because we will go where he knows, that I will be there soon. You will ask for the money as a favor, and if they give it to you keep it very safe, because it is of great need.

Today, Friday, we finished stoning the well, which in truth costs me more than fifty *pesos*; but it is fixed for as long as the world exists. Work on the

---

22. *Bobo* has many meanings, including simpletons, but here it likely refers to a fish found in rivers in Mexico and Guatemala.
23. *Ejecutarme en esta venta* in the original.

fountain will carry on until Monday and they will work on it until Monday all day, because then the *indios* will finish and after I will go see you with the help of God.

I sent Bartolomé yesterday to Tecamachalco to straighten the chair and buy me boots, already these ones can no longer bring me anywhere. Tell Mariquilla that I am alive and that I will pay her for the love she shows you. Kiss the hands of the *alcade mayor* for me because since I do not have paper, I cannot write him. Kiss also the hands of *señor* Horta and *doña* María.

I do not have anything else to tell you. May Our *Señor* keep you in his holy hand, Amen.

From the inn of Cuatepec, today Friday at 10 o'clock. Yours until death.

Francisco de Barbosa

To my *señora* wife Ana de Anguiano, in Jalapa, my *señora*.

Letter 256

Ana de Anguiano, from Jalapa, to her husband Francisco Barbosa. 1573, Vol. 184, s/f.

My *señor*,

I have been, and am, with so much distress that you cannot imagine in not knowing the state of your health, or even what you have been doing. On your life, you must send word to us about what has happened to you, for in the sixteen days since you left here you, you seem to have forgotten where your house is. My children and I kiss the hands of the one to whom we do not speak. I ask you to what end you have left. On your life, make haste.

I do not say more, only that Ines Núñez has not given me money, I will tell you that she says she does not have it.

From Jalapa, today, Wednesday, where I remain. Your wife.

Ana de Anguiano.

The *señor alcade* is scared because you did not write to him with the information about the land. I have a friend that would send them there without the three pesos, but he did not send them, since I believe you are on your way.

Letter 257

Ana de Anguiano, from Jalapa, to her husband Francisco Barbosa. 1573. Vol. 184, s/f.

My *señor* and all my consolation:

You know I have been very lonely without you and that I do not know what will become of me. On your life, my soul, hurry as quickly as you can.

They bring the adze[24] and two axes—one for cutting because we found none among the tools—and they bring the *barreta* (crowbar) and the *cantarita* (copper pot) canteen and three *bateas* (kneading troughs). They bring two shirts and *zaragüelles* (trousers), and a hand cloth and a cap, that the *urca*[25] has not appeared. . . .[26]

From here, there is nothing you need to know. On your life, my soul, do what you can to avoid sending me Bartolomillo; do not send him, because he is wicked, and he is of no use to me, because God knows what it took to get him out of town, and he is so childish. If you can, send a little bacon with an *indio*; you know I cannot eat.

I do not have anything else to tell you about, only that we are all well. May our *Señor* let me see you. With my soul I leave you.

From Jalapa, today, Friday, where I remain. Yours until death.

Ana de Anguiano.

Reina says to collect the *cal*[27] that is in San Juan.

To my *señor* Francisco de Barbosa, wherever he may be, my *señor*.

Letter 258

Ana de Anguiano, from Jalapa, to her husband Francisco Barbosa. 1573. Vol. 184, s/f.

My *señor*,

Because the messenger is trusted, I write you. My children are well, except that Reina is very unhappy over her ceramics, and a lot of it broke, and I do not know what will become of it. And it does not stop raining day and night; our *Señor* will stop it here.

So, on your life, write me a little because I am very sad and lonely. I have nothing more to say. May our Lord give you health.

From Jalapa, on the day of San Pedro and San Pablo, I remain.

Your wife.
Ana de Anguiano.

---

24. A carpentry tool.

25. Possibly an alpaca. One Andean term for alpaca is *urco*. The *Diccionario de Autoridades* (1739) defines *urca* as a large boat, which obviously cannot be its meaning here.

26. The final line of the paragraph reads: *Mira si las llevastes en las calzas*. The editors have not succeeded in translating the phrase in a way that makes sense in the context of the paragraph.

27. *Cal* has several meanings including a white wood, quicklime, and white wash.

Reina and her woman kiss your hands; they say hurry up and that we all have to go up.[28]

To my *señor* Francisco de Barbosa, my *señor*.

Suggested Reading

Altman, Ida. *Transatlantic Ties in the Spanish Empire: Brihuega, Spain and Puebla, Mexico, 1560–1620.* Stanford, CA: Stanford University Press, 2000.

Cook, Alexandra Parma, and Noble David Cook. *Good Faith and Truthful Ignorance: A Case of Transatlantic Bigamy.* Durham, NC: Duke University Press, 1991.

Perry, Mary Elizabeth. *Gender and Disorder in Early Modern Seville.* Princeton, NJ: Princeton University Press, 1990.

Document Themes

- Family
- Labor
- Migration and mobility
- Property
- Religion

---

28. *Ir arriba* in the original.

6

Mothers and Wives in Labor Agreements (Arequipa, 1590; La Plata, 1602; and Potosí, 1571 and 1659)

In the latter quarter of the sixteenth century, indigenous and occasionally Afro–Peruvian women began to appear before notaries to sign work contracts. In such acts, women agreed to perform a particular type of labor, during a specific period of time, for a specific person, and at a specific wage, all formalized in front of a notary public. Women also came before notaries in this period as mothers who signed up their children for apprenticeships. Generally speaking, non-Spaniards most often signed contracts to work for Spaniards, but there were occasional exceptions to this rule. The collection of documents in this chapter highlights how colonial-era wives and mothers made labor agreements. While historians take it for granted that indigenous and Afro–Peruvian women worked as servants for Spaniards, the details of those arrangements are revealed in very few documents. The texts that follow provide an official record of such agreements. They were written according to a formula that demanded certain things of the worker *and* of the employer. We can learn about the supposed nature of these jobs because these formulas were repeated over and over in different cities of colonial Peru. However, because each contract varied slightly, this chapter allows the reader to consider individual women as historical, social, and economic actors.

As many of our chapters demonstrate, women worked throughout the colonial era. They worked as market vendors, seamstresses, laundresses, wet nurses, servants, sex workers, midwives, and in houses, shops, and taverns, in textile mills, and on farms. In the corporate setting of the convent, they also ran agricultural estates, acted as landlords, and served as lenders of capital. Generally speaking, women worked in jobs closer to home than did men (so men might be long-distance merchants whereas women were urban merchants) and most physically taxing jobs such as mining were predominantly performed by male workers while women did jobs considered less physically demanding. Indigenous men were designated as tribute payers by the Spanish colonial system and thus their labor (for example, as mine laborers) was often forcibly required by Spanish officials. Enslaved women worked doing whatever they were told (for instance, as domestic workers, street vendors, bakers, or plantation workers). The only women who did not work were elite Spanish women whose economic situation allowed them to engage servants or purchase slaves who performed all domestic chores. Many non-elite Spanish women, however, worked in order to support household economies.[1]

Women's negotiations around labor often involved their roles within families as well. Mothers who approved or initiated apprenticeship contracts for children sought training for their sons. Wives who signed labor agreements often did so in the presence of their husbands so that, as heads of households, these men could give permission for their wives to enter into labor agreements. Some of these women entered into not only the household of another family when they worked, but also new kin networks associated with these. The presence of relatives who appear in the following work agreements suggests that women did not work in isolation from their husbands and families but often sought contract work as part of a household strategy or responsibility.

Any strategy relative to work in the colonial era revolved around earning money. The contracts reveal important economic shifts that occurred as indigenous people became drawn into a *peso* economy, as indigenous women began to labor away from their homes and families, and as forms of exploitative labor occurred beyond those imposed by the colonial state in "individual" relationships that relied on paternalism. Notice that in more than one case, women received wages in advance to pay off debts. In such cases, their future labor earnings had already been spent before they even started working.

As you read, you will notice that these work and apprenticeship agreements are brief. Imagine that hundreds of such contracts might be signed in the space of one month in any given city. Examine these examples closely. What do women's jobs suggest about the roles they fulfilled in colonial society? What kinds of wages did the women and children receive? How is racial identity reflected in the form of payment? What does the format of the work contract suggest about the obligations of employer to worker? What do the contracts tell us not just about women, but about families in colonial society? Finally, would the female laborers benefit from agreeing to these notarized contracts? Why or why not?

---

1. On women and urban work, see Jane E. Mangan, *Trading Roles: Gender, Ethnicity and the Urban Economy in Colonial Potosí* (Durham, NC: Duke University Press, 2005).

6.1 Work Contract of Catalina Caima[2]

In the city of Arequipa of Peru on January 13, 1590 before Francisco Fernández Tarifeno, *alcalde ordinario* (judge) of this city, and in presence of me, the public scribe and notary, appeared Catalina Caima, *india* (indigenous woman), native she said of the city of Cuzco. She said that of her good will she agreed by document to service and stipend with Hernando Alvárez de la Serda, to serve him and *doña* (lady) Isabel de Castro, his wife, for the period of one year counting from today, the date of this document. She is to be given for this service twelve *pesos* of eight *reales* each and two dresses of *avasca*[3] or cotton; it is understood that one *acsu* (tunic) and one *lliclla* (a shawl) [should go with] each dress. [She will also have] to eat and drink and [she will] be cured if she is ill. She is obliged during the said time period not to leave, nor be absent from the said service. If she should do this, she will lose the time served and begin to serve anew. Hernando Alvárez de la Serda, who was present, agreed to the payment of what is said above and to not dismiss the *india* from his service during the said time period under penalty that he would pay for the entire year. To comply as such, each one of the parties for themselves gave power to your majesty's justices and renounced the laws in their favor and the general law. I, *licenciado* (licenciate) Alvárez, the public scribe, testify that Juan López Mancano signed this and because the *india* did not know how to write, the notary of this document signed for her. Witnesses were Juan López Mancano and Juan Vejarano and Sebastián de Encinas Cañizares

[signatures]: Francisco López Tarifeno, *Licenciado* Alvárez de la Serda.

Witnessed by Juan López Mancano and signed before me, in the name of this public and *cabildo* (municipal council), scribe Afrian de Ufelde.

6.2 Work Contract of Inés Quispe[4]

In the City of Arequipa on February 7, 1590 before me, Francisco Hernández Tarifeno, *alcalde ordinario* of this city appeared Inés Quispe *india*, native she said of the community of Tiayvaya, in the jurisdiction of this city, *encomienda* (landed estate) of Alonso Picado, *vecino* (citizen) of this city. Of her good will she said she agreed to service and stipend with Fernando Hernández

---

2. Archivo Regional de Arequipa, Adrian de Ufelde 1590, folio 21.
3. *Avasca* is the Quechua term for cloth made of a coarse weave of alpaca wool.
4. Archivo Regional de Arequipa, Adrian de Ufelde 1590, folio 69.

Retamoso, *vecino* of this city to serve him and *doña* Mariana de Mercado his wife for the period of one year, counting from today, the date of this document. She is to be given for the said service twelve *pesos* of eight *reales* each and two dresses of *avasca* or cotton; it is understood that one *acsu* and one *lliclla* [should go with] each dress. [She will also have] to eat and drink and a home and will be taught the Christian doctrine and be cured if she is ill. She agrees to having received the two dresses and ten *pesos* toward her said salary for which she was satisfied. [Hernández] agreed to pay the said *india* the remainder of her salary and to not dismiss the said *india* from his service during the said time period under penalty that he would pay for the entire year. Each party, in obligation of goods received and to receive, gave power to the justices and renounced the laws in their favor. The said *alcalde* signed and executed this and I, Fernando Hernández, testified to this. For the *india* who did not know how [to sign], witness Mateo de Funes [signed]. Blas Velasco and Graviel de Larra, *alcaldes* of this city.

Signed Francisco Fernández Tarijeno and Francisco Retamasso

As witness, Mateo de Funes

Before me, Adrian de Ufelde, public notary.

6.3 Luisa de la Cerda Signs Apprenticeship for Her Son[5]

In La Plata August 14, 1602 in presence of me, the scribe and witnesses, I swear, recognize and grant that Luisa de la Cerda free *morena* (black woman) appeared and agreed that her son, Fernando de la Cerda *mulato* (person of African and Spanish parentage),[6] serve with Gonzalo Hernández, master tailor, for the period of two years counting from today, the date of this document until completed. During this time, [Hernández] must teach [de la Cerda] the trade of tailor and [the latter] shall serve him in all that he is ordered and is reasonable. For this service, [Hernández] is to give him after one year an outfit of Quito wool in whatever color he wishes; this is understood as pants and jacket and cape and a hat and two Rouen shirts and two Dutch ruffs[7] and all the shoes that he needs. And at the end of this time, he is to give him another outfit of good wool and two more Rouen shirts and two Dutch cuffs and a hat and shoes. Gonzalo Hernández is to assume the cost of the outfits, and he is to teach her son all that he can learn and know

---

5. Archivo Nacional de Bolivia, Escrituras Publicas, Michel 1602, Tomo 71, f. 606v.

6. He is described as a minor later in the document.

7. *Cuellos de olanda*, pieces of cloth worn at the neck to be laundered separately from the jacket, thus keeping the jacket clean.

about the trade of tailor without any dishonesty or fraud. And, he is to give him food, housing, and clean clothing during this time and cure him of his illness and teach him good customs in conformity with Christian obligations. In turn, her son is obliged not to leave this service during the two years. If he should leave during that time, Francisco de la Cerda shall be taken from any location and place where he is and compelled by the rigor of law and justice to finish the owed time, and that he should lose any time he shall have served and restart the two-year service again. Gonzalo Hernández [*Hernández agrees to the conditions and the document is signed by Hernández and the notary.*]

6.4 Work Contract of Isabel Guayra[8]

Isabel Guayra, *india,* native of Checasupa, and wife of *don* Juan Pariguana, agreed to serve Juan de Xexas for one year. Juan de Xexas is to give her one hundred silver *pesos* plus the rent of a store for Isabel.[9] Isabel said that she agrees to serve with the said Juan de Xexas for the year to serve him by selling coca in a store.[10] And, for doing this service and renting the store, he is to give her [a quantity of] silver which is 146 *pesos* and she is to take her clothing and shoes and food from those *pesos*. And Isabel, *india,* agreed to keep good accounts for the said Juan de Xexas of all the coca that he delivers to her so that nothing is unaccounted for. And, during this time, Isabel agreed not to sell any other person's coca apart from the said Juan de Xexas. Signed by Martin de Barrientos (public notary).

6.5 Work Contract for Luisa Sisa[11]

In the Imperial Villa (city) of Potosí, on October 17th, 1659, some *indios* appeared before me, Juan Pérez de Goynativia, public notary of this Villa. One is named Luisa Sisa, a *yanacaona* (personal retainer) of the principal church of this Villa, and with express license and agreement of Francisco Saes, *indio,* who said he is her legitimate husband. [Sisa] agreed with Francisco Yanguren, *vecino,* of this Villa that she would serve him as a wet nurse to raise a son of

---

8. AHP-CNM.EN 4 Cuadernillo #11, Fol. 1, Potosi, 23 may 1571.

9. Here there is an omission of the formulaic language that outlines the obligations of the employer to the worker, as spelled out in the contracts of Inés Quispe and Catalina Caima.

10. On the trade of coca in Potosí, see Paulina Numhauser, *Mujeres indias y señores de la coca: Potosí y Cuzco en el siglo XVI* (Madrid: Ediciones Catedra, 2005).

11. AHP-CNM.EN 118 Fol. 573–573v, 17 octubre 1659 JPdG.

his and breastfeed him and do all that is necessary that she can do insofar as raising the son as well as what she can do in the house of Francisco Yanguren. Further, she is obliged to never be absent during a year-and-a-half. Yanguren agrees that he is to give her five *pesos* every month. At the end of the stated year-and-a-half, he is to give her a basic dress and a custom dress for which he will reserve ten *pesos*. And, likewise, it is a condition that on any occasion when Francisco Saes would like to see Luisa Sisa, his wife, or sleep with her, it must be with the consent of Francisco Yanguren because of the risk this could have for the baby. Signed Juan Pérez de Goynativia.

6.6 Work Contract of María Cangua and Juana de Torres[12]

In the Imperial Villa of Potosí on March 24th, 1659, some *indias* appeared before me, Juan Pérez de Goynativia, public notary of the Villa. Through interpretation, they said they are named María Cangua and Juana de Torres, mother and daughter, *naturales* (natives) of the Province of Copacabana. They said that inasmuch as they owe María de la Barrera, who is present, ninety-two *pesos* and four *reales*, and because they have no way to be able to pay her, they have begged and pleaded with Graviela de Toro, who is present, that she pay the said quantity for them. In exchange, they will make *chicha* (corn beer) for her and discount the *pesos* as they make it, with María de la Barrera. To be fair they want to make and offer as their guarantor Cristobal Tito of the *pueblo* of [illegible] and Ysabel Yuscama of the *ayllu* (Andean kin unit) of Copacabana, who are present.[13] The said María Cangua and Juana de Torres will repay in this way: they are to make *chicha* during the whole year and for the work, with each trip (of *chicha*) their debt to Graviela de Toro will be discounted by four *reales* and one *real* for food which is a total of five *reales* per trip.[14] Signed by Juan Pérez de Goynativia.

---

12. AHP-CNM.EN 118 Fol. 779–780, 24 marco 1659, JPdG.
13. Here there is an omission of the formulaic language that outlines the obligations of the employer to the worker, as spelled out in the contracts of Inés Quispe and Catalina Caima.
14. It is unclear how much corn beer constitutes a trip. Given that other contracts for *chicha* are notarized around this time, there was probably an understanding of a standard amount based on the typical size of the vats in which it was brewed. Still, this debt will not be paid until these women have brewed 185 "trips" of *chicha*, which sounds like a lot.

Suggested Reading

Mangan, Jane E. *Trading Roles: Gender, Ethnicity and the Urban Economy in Colonial Potosí.* Durham, NC: Duke University Press, 2005.

Stern, Steve J. *Peru's Indian Peoples and the Challenge of Spanish Conquest: Huamanga to 1640.* Madison: University of Wisconsin Press, 1982. See especially Chapter 6, "The Political Economy of Dependence."

Vergara, Teresa. "Growing Up Indian: Migration, Labor, and Life in Lima (1570–1640)," in *Raising an Empire: Children in Early Modern Iberia and Colonial Latin America,* ed. Ondina E. González and Bianca Premo. Albuquerque: University of New Mexico, 2007.

Document Themes

- Family
- Labor
- Race and ethnicity

7

Criminal Complaint by Angela de Palacios on Behalf of Her Daughter, Leonor Arias (Potosí, 1584)

In February of 1584 in the populous silver-mining city of Potosí, Angela de Palacios filed a criminal complaint against a man and a woman for allowing her daughter, the fourteen-year-old Leonor Arias, to be deflowered. As with many accusations of sexual assault, the testimony by the mother and daughter differed from that provided by both the accused and by several witnesses. Sadly, the extant document does not reveal the final outcome of the case.[1] Once the relevant complaint by Palacios was acknowledged and testimony was taken, the case turned to focus primarily on property, specifically an enslaved man and a horse belonging to *doña* (lady) Isabel de Chávez, the original accused in the judicial case of first instance. This chapter focuses on the excerpt pertaining to the allegation of Leonor Arias' sexual assault to study colonial society's culture of gendered honor, the mobility of women within colonial Peru, and gender roles within urban social networks.

Witness testimony highlights a young woman's sexual behavior and the potential of sexual assault as the main themes in this case. In colonial Peru, a young woman's family and household protected and guarded the significant asset of her virginity until marriage. The practice of *recogimiento* (seclusion) was a social tool that served to protect women who might be at risk of losing their honor.[2] So, too, was the convent a place where young women might be placed prior to marriage to protect their honor by keeping them in relative isolation from men.[3] However, great variability often existed between the theory and the practice of chastity. Women of various racial backgrounds and social statuses had sex outside of marriage, both with and without their consent.[4] In this late sixteenth-century case, Angela de Palacios brought suit against Ortiz de Velasco

---

1. This is not uncommon in colonial archives where a case file may have been partially destroyed or misplaced over the course of several hundred years.

2. *Recogimiento* here refers to the virtue of enclosure and quiescent conduct for females; is also treated in Chapters 8, 12, and 13.

3. See Lyman L. Johnson and Sonya Lipsett-Rivera, *The Faces of Honor: Sex, Shame, and Violence in Colonial Latin America* (Albuquerque: University of New Mexico Press, 1998).

4. For Peru, see Bernard Lavallé, *Amor y opresión en los Andes coloniales* (Lima: IEP, 1999), 67–84. See an empire-wide discussion in Ann Twinam, *Public Lives, Private Secrets: Gender,*

for having sex with her unmarried daughter and also charged one *doña* Isabel de Chávez as an accomplice for allowing the alleged rape to occur in her home.

When colonial women traveled, as Palacios and her daughter had done, they ran a greater risk of assault or aggression because they were moving outside of the networks that protected them best. In fact, when women traveled in this era, husbands, fathers, and brothers frequently hired or appointed trusted men to look out for their wives, sisters, or daughters.[5] In young Leonor Arias' case, her mother charged that she had fallen prey to aggressive men first while she traveled from her original home of Lima, the administrative center of the Viceroyalty of Peru, to the provincial city of Arequipa, and from there to Potosí, and next while living in Potosí. According to her mother's account, Arias was the victim of a crime, and this may well have been the case. Once she arrived in Potosí, Leonor Arias would presumably have had limited mobility. Most young women of Spanish descent were expected to be in the company of their relatives and servants at all times to ensure their exclusion from dangerous or compromising situations. As a new arrival in Potosí, however, Arias likely had weaker social networks of relatives and kin than young women who had grown up in the city and this may help account for what befell her. Alternately, it is possible that Arias had chosen to engage in premarital sexual relations. Women whose suitors did not have their parents' approval sometimes resorted to establishing a sexual relationship with these men in order to pressure their families into allowing them to marry their co-conspirators to avoid scandal and preserve familial honor.[6]

The houses and streets of Potosí come alive in the testimony of this case. We can try to imagine the newly arrived Leonor Arias making her way in a city of approximately one hundred thousand people, where a massive indigenous population mined silver and a large mixed-race population processed that silver. How would the size and complexity of this city have helped Ortiz de Velasco to make an impression on the young Arias? Several domestic servants were called as witnesses in this case. Their comments highlight the extraordinary access all members of a colonial household had to one another's

Honor, Sexuality, and Illegitimacy in Colonial Spanish America (Stanford, CA: Stanford University Press, 1999).

5. See Jane E. Mangan, *Transatlantic Obligations: Creating the Bonds of Family in Conquest-Era Peru and Spain* (New York: Oxford University Press, 2016), 112–18.

6. For a discussion of sexuality and marriage focused on non-elites in seventeenth-century Lima, see María Emma Mannarelli, *Private Passions and Public Sins: Men and Women in Seventeenth-Century Lima,* trans. Sidney Evans and Meredith D. Dodge (Albuquerque: University of New Mexico Press, 2007). Allyson Poska's work on women in early modern Spain suggests that notions of honor did not drive female sexual behavior for non-elite women in the era. See Poska, "Elusive Virtue: Rethinking the Role of Female Chastity in Early Modern Spain," *Journal of Early Modern History* 8, 1:2 (2004), 136–46.

business, whether or not they were master or servant, Spanish or people of color. Servants could be helpmates to subterfuge, yet they could also reveal transgressions. Which appears to have been the case here?

That Leonor Arias had lost her virginity was not in question; the issue, rather, was whether anyone might be blamed for it. In some instances, parents looked for some form of payment for the loss of virginity.[7] The case brought by Palacios, however, never reached that stage. Moreover, the defendant's accusation that her daughter had sexual relations with more than one man made it less likely that Palacios could sue for loss of her daughter's virginity. What might Angela de Palacios have hoped to gain from bringing this suit and drawing additional public attention to her daughter's loss of virginity? No mention is made of Leonor's father; how might the absence of a male head of household affect this case or the standing of Angela and Leonor in the first place? What does witness testimony about Ortiz de Velasco suggest about expectations of men in colonial society? What might have happened to Leonor Arias after the tales of her sexual encounters were spread widely through social networks?

Unworthy / Abandoned by the husband

7.1 Criminal Complaint against Juan Ortiz for the Rape of Leonor Arias (Potosí, 1584)[8]

In the Imperial Villa of Potosí on February 8, 1584 before *señor* (lord) *don* (sir) Alonso Ortíz de Levya, *corregidor y justicia mayor* (district administrator and senior judge) in this province of Charcas[9] for his majesty, appeared Angela de Palacios, resident of this said Villa and said that she had a criminal complaint to make, according to law (*como mejor de derecho y aya lugar de derecho*) against Juan Ortiz de Velasco, resident of this Villa and against *doña* Isabel de Chávez, her [daughter's] guardian[10] and against the other persons who by information appeared guilty. In recounting the case, she said that she

---

7. For parents suing for reparations over loss of honor, see Patricia Seed, *To Love, Honor, and Obey in Colonial Mexico: Conflicts over Marriage Choice, 1574–1821* (Stanford, CA: Stanford University Press, 1988) as well as Twinam, *Public Lives, Private Secrets.*

8. Archivo Nacional de Bolivia, Sucre. Expediente 1584.2. *Doña Isabel de Chávez e doña Angela Palacios sobre violentacion de la hija de esta Leonor Arias, por Juan Ortiz e devolución de un negrillo esclavo*, Potosí, 23 folios.

9. The province of Charcas is located in modern-day Bolivia.

10. The term in the original is "*deuda*"; the editors use the word *guardian* to imply a form of protection for Leonor that *doña* Angela imagined she would provide, although no legal guardianship is implied by this relationship. Isabel de Chávez's loyalty was possibly divided. She was to act as Leonor's guardian, but later testimony suggests she was also the biological aunt of Leonor's aggressor, Juan Ortiz de Velasco.

has a daughter, Leonor Arias, a girl of thirteen or fourteen years, more or less, whom she brought, still a maiden, from the City of Kings (Lima) in the company of *doña* Inés Ramirez de Cartagena, wife of Diego Bravo *vecino* (citizen) of this Villa. While on the road, Juan Ortiz de Velasco and other people solicited [Leonor] and persuaded her to know them carnally and with flattery and pleas, as well as with force and against her will. They lay with her carnally and they corrupted her and took her virginity. Once [Leonor] had arrived at this Villa and was living in seclusion in houses that are on Juan Baron Street, where they play ball, Juan Ortiz de Velasco entered through the walls of these houses that border on the houses of Felipa, a *negra* (a black woman), and, by force, lay with Leonor Arias, her daughter. And what is worse is that by the same force, he took her out of her house and had her, taking advantage of her for several days while staying in the house of *doña* Isabel de Chávez, her guardian, who concealed that this was happening in the house. In all this, the named person and the other guilty parties committed grave and dreadful crimes worthy of punishment and penalty. I ask that your mercy order that there be an inquiry and arrest the guilty parties and put them in the public jail of this Villa because these acts beg for justice in whatever form is convenient. The *Señor Corregidor* orders an investigation of the content of this complaint that relates what happened in order that justice be served.

Before me, Fernando de Medina, public notary, in Potosí on February 8, 1584 Leonor Arias, daughter of Angela de Palacios and resident of this Villa, swore an oath before God our *Señor* (Lord) and made the sign of the cross, according to the law swore to tell what she knows respecting the investigation of the aforementioned. She said under oath that a month ago, more or less, she and her mother entered this Villa. They came to it in the company of *doña* Inés Ramírez de Cartagena, wife of Diego Bravo,[11] and they lived in this period in a house that is in the street of the *Juego de la Pelota* (the ball game). After arriving, *doña* Inés was in the city of Arequipa, more or less, for two months waiting for Diego Bravo, her husband. When he arrived to Arequipa, he solicited [Leonor] and persuaded her to lie carnally with him. And Leonor told him that she did not want to do the aforementioned because she was a *doncella* (virgin). Bravo persuaded her to do it. Leonor always repeated these words even though she was not a *doncella* because *don* Fernando de Cartagena, son of *licenciado* (licenciate) Ramírez de Cartagena, had already had her on the road from Lima to the city of Arequipa, but she said it so Bravo would stop harassing her. Arriving at a town in the provinces, although she does not remember which one it was, other than that she stayed there in the Inn de

---

11. A man by the same name worked as a public notary in the city of La Plata in this period, which would signify an important role in colonial society. However, it is not clear if the two were one and the same.

Vergara, Juan Ortiz de Velasco sent her to a soldier named Tomás de Castañeda who traveled with them so that he could persuade her to lie with him. Also, Castañeda took Leonor from the door of a room in the said inn and carried her to the lodgings of Juan Ortiz de Velasco. There he had her in his bed that night, lying carnally with her as many times as he wanted. Once they had arrived at this Villa, and were living in the house in the *Juego de la Pelota*, Ortiz de Velasco solicited her many times so that he could lie with her carnally. When Leonor's mother left her at the guest house, Ortiz de Velasco entered it through the house of Felipa Velázquez, *negra,* jumping the walls of the pens[12] and lay carnally with Leonor more by force and against her will than by her choice. And last Wednesday on the fifth day of this present month, Leonor's mother was absent from the house because she had gone for food and to see about a lawsuit that she has. Ortiz de Velasco came into the house through the pens of Felipa Velázquez, and he told Leonor that the following night they would be together and that she should wait for him in the breezeway of the house of Felipa Velázquez.[13] From there, he would remove Leonor from the house of her mother and take her to the house of *doña* Isabel de Chávez, his relative. From there he would take her to another *pueblo* (town), saying also that he did not have much to give and use to serve Leonor. That night Leonor did not go to the breezeway of Felipa Velázquez's house as he had told her, but Juan Ortiz de Velasco jumped the walls of the pens of Felipa Velázquez's house, as he had already done, and took her in his arms from her mother's house over the walls of the house of Felipa, *negra*. He took her through the settlement toward San Pedro and from there he took her to the house of *doña* Isabel de Chávez, his aunt, where he slept with her. Then *doña* Ana de Valderrama, wife of Juan Ochobueita, and *doña* Luisa Riquelme and other people took her from there on Friday night, the seventh of this present month. *Doña* Angela de Palacios went to the house [of his aunt Chávez] while she was there to ask if she [Leonor] had been seen and *doña* Isabel denied this, saying that she did not know of that woman. And the deponent [Leonor] was behind *doña* Isabel's bed because she ordered her [Leonor] there. And that night that her mother looked for her, Juan Ortiz de Velasco accompanied her [mother] to her house, saying that he had never heard nor seen her [Leonor].

She was ordered, under oath, to respond as follows.

---

12. Animal pens.

13. *Zaguán* in the original. *Zaguanes* or breezeways were entryway spaces located adjacent to exterior doorways; they often served as passageways between buildings' interior and exterior spaces. Sonya Lipsett-Rivera found that these spaces served as liminal areas between private and public spaces in late colonial and nineteenth-century homes; *Gender and the Negotiation of Daily Life in Mexico, 1750–1856* (Lincoln: University of Nebraska Press, 2012), 87–88.

She was asked if Felipa, the *negra,* knew or understood that Juan Ortiz entered through her house to the house of Leonor's mother and if she (or any other person) consented to it. She said she does not know, and that what she has said is the truth. She said that had no personal conflict of interest with any party in the case. She was asked her age and she said she is fourteen years old and she did not sign because she does not know how to write.

Order

On this day, month, and year the *señor corregidor* reviewed the declaration of Leonor Arias, and I order that Juan de Velasco be arrested and placed in the jail of this Villa before the investigation of this case proceeds. Because if we proceed without arresting him, he might flee and remain without punishment for the crime that he appears to have committed. This I declare and order, before me, Fernando de Medina public scribe, witness.

7.2 Testimony of Catalina Valero

Potosí, February 24, 1584

Witness, Catalina Valero, resident of this Villa of Potosí, wife of Francisco de Herrera swore an oath before God our *Señor* and made the sign of the cross, according to the law swore to tell what she knows respecting the investigation of the aforementioned. Valero said that she has known Angela de Palacios for more than eight years and her daughter Leonor for the last twenty days, more or less, she has known Ortiz de Velasco and *doña* Isabel de Chávez for the past two years, more or less. And, she says that twenty days ago, Catalina was in her house asleep in her bed one morning at dawn, and Margarita, a female slave of *doña* Isabel de Chávez, knocked on her door. Catalina ordered her to open the door and she came in to where Catalina was lying in her bed. She had with her Leonor Arias, daughter of Angela de Palacios, and the slave told Catalina, "*Señora,* my *señora doña* Isabel de Chávez does not want to have this girl in her house. I beg your mercy that she may stay here for a day or two while she finds a place to stay." The slave did not tell Catalina who sent [Leonor] to her house, nor did this witness ask her. That same day at 10 o'clock, more or less, Ortiz de Velasco came. He brought Leonor food for lunch and at that time that he came to the house Catalina did not see Ortiz de Velasco because she was out of the house in the stream of the Villa watching how they processed some bits of ore. When Catalina came home about 11 o'clock, Ortiz de Velasco had already gone. When this witness entered her house, they told her that Ortiz de Velasco had come to Catalina's house and he had brought food for lunch to Leonor Arias. The same day around vespers,[14] Leonor took her shawl and she wanted to go out. This deponent said to Leonor, "Why do you want to go? Do not go until Ortiz de Velasco comes." So Leonor took her shawl off and after it got dark, Leonor again took her shawl and wanted to go. And this witness made her stay and sent for Ortiz de Velasco, who came later to her house. And since she knew that Leonor wanted to go he told her, "Don't go because you are in a good house," and with this, Ortiz de Velasco left and one hour later, more or less, Ortiz de Velasco returned to the house of this witness. He took Leonor and Simon de Herrera, Catalina's son, went with them. When Simon de Herrera returned, this witness asked him where they took that girl. Simon de Herrera responded that they had taken her to the house of Felipa Velázquez *morena* (a black woman) who lives on the [street of the] *Juego de la Pelota*. Likewise he said that Leonor was the daughter of Angela de Palacios, the witness's *comadre*,[15] and this is the truth. She said that she had no personal conflict of interest with any party in the case. She is forty years old, and she did not sign because she does not know how.

7.3 Testimony of Simón de Herrera

Potosí, February 24, 1584

Simon de Herrera, resident of this Villa, said that he has known Angela de Palacios for eight years and Leonor Arias, her daughter, for twenty days, more or less. Likewise, he has known Ortiz de Velasco and *doña* Isabel de Chávez for more or less two years. And, twenty days ago, this witness was asleep in the house of his mother, Catalina Valero, one morning. It was already dawn and he heard a knock on the door. He sent to open it and to find out who it was and in came a slave named Margarita who belongs to *doña* Isabel de Chávez, and with her, another girl named Leonor de Arias. Once inside, they went to talk with Catalina Valero, his mother, who was sleeping in her bed where this witness was likewise sleeping in another small room next to his mother. After entering, the slave said to his mother, "*Señora*, my *señora*, *doña* Isabel de Chávez sent me. *Señora*, my *señora*, *doña* Isabel de Chávez does not want to have this girl in her house. I beg your mercy that she may stay here for a day or two while she finds a [permanent] place to stay." His mother responded to the slave that she did not want to have her in this house. Margarita, *negra*, begged the mother of this witness on behalf of Leonor de Arias that she take her for the day because

---

14. Vespers were prayers in the evening, usually at dusk.
15. In this context, the term translates as "close friend."

she was *chapetona*[16] and had come from the city of Lima. And when Catalina Valero, mother of this witness, learned that the girl was from Lima, she said she could gladly stay. With this Margarita, *negra*, left. Leonor stayed, and at around 11 o'clock that day, this witness came back to his house to eat because he had gone out to see his ore washed in the stream of this Villa. And when this witness came in to eat they told him how Ortiz de Velasco had come to the house and had brought food for lunch for the girl: peach, grapes, and a stew, then he had gone. Having finished eating, this witness Simon turned to go to his house and when he came, he found the said girl covered with her shawl. Catalina Valero, mother of this witness, said, "Why are you covered with that shawl?" The girl responded that she wanted to go. The mother of this witness said, "Do not go. Wait. We will send word to Ortiz de Velasco." And so this witness, by order of his mother, went to find him and he found him in the house of the said Isabel de Chávez. He said to Ortiz de Velasco that Catalina Valero, mother of this witness, called him. Then Ortiz de Velasco came with him and having arrived at his house, Ortiz de Velasco called to the young girl. He said, "*Señora* Leonor, where do you want to go? You are in a good house, and if you leave here, what?" And after he had spoken with Leonor, Ortiz de Velasco left. Half an hour later, Ortiz de Velasco returned to the house of this witness. He said that the *señor corregidor* had gone to his house in search of Leonor and they had taken what was in his house. And since he was in the house, Ortiz de Velasco called for this witness and told him that he wanted to have a word with him. This witness distanced himself from Ortiz de Velasco, who asked if he would do him the favor of going with him and with this girl [Leonor] because he wanted to take her to a house. And he asked if he [Simon] would lend him [Ortiz de Velasco] a large cape so they would not be recognized. This witness gave him the cape, and he took the cape that Ortiz de Velasco was wearing. Ortiz de Velasco asked this witness if he had heard the curfew,[17] because it if had rung, he did not want to carry his sword. When this witness said yes [that the curfew bell had rung], he left the sword. He and Ortiz de Velasco left this witness's house with the girl walking by the stream that runs above the Villa and arriving at the refinery of Juan Gómez. But they could not cross because there was a lot of water, so they changed course and went higher up. They turned to enter the ravine in order to avoid law [officers]. From there they left the stream and went to the street of the *pelota* and this witness said to Leonor, "Angela de Palacios lives here," not knowing that Leonor was her daughter. And the girl responded, "I know the *Juego de la Pelota* very well." And halfway up the block, Ortiz de Velasco knocked on a door of the house where a *morena* called Felipa Velázquez lives. An indigenous woman answered and Ortiz de

---

16. Meaning a person who had recently arrived, usually from Europe to America.
17. *Queda* for *toque de queda*. Literally a bell tolling to signify the curfew.

Velasco said to her in indigenous tongue, "Tell Felipa Velázquez that Ortiz de Velasco is here." Then the indigenous woman opened the door for him and Ortiz de Velasco entered inside the house. He said "*Señor*, stay at the door with this girl," and this witness stayed with her at the door, waiting. He asked the girl "does Felipa Velázquez live here?" To this question Leonor said "Oh, take care of me. What am I doing. Let's go, Simon de Herrera, to your house." And when Leonor said this, the witness started to go with her down the street. Then Ortiz de Velasco came outside and when he didn't find them at the doorway, he came running until he caught up with them. The girl asked him, "Where are you taking me, your mercy?" Ortiz de Velasco said, "Here, I am taking you to the house of a *morena*," and the said girl responded, "It is possible *señor* Velasco that your mercy is taking me to where they will kill me? Leave me, for the love of God. I want to go by myself to Chuquisaca."[18] Ortiz de Velasco said, "I swear on my mother who gave birth to me and the milk that I suckled! Do you want to cut off my head?[19] Let's get out of here so *la ronda* (the patrol) doesn't come because if they catch us, they will take you to jail." And with this, Leonor returned and all three of us entered the house of Felipa Velázquez, *morena*. This witness stayed on the patio of the house and Ortiz de Velasco entered with the girl into a room where Felipa Velázquez was and this witness was in the patio more than half an hour watching for Ortiz de Velasco to come out. He heard certain words by which he understood that Leonor was the daughter of Angela de Palacios because from the patio he heard those inside say: "Your mother Palacios is looking for you." Since Ortiz de Velasco did not come out [of the room], this witness went to his house and Ortiz de Velasco stayed at the house. This is the truth. The witness said that he had no personal conflict of interest with any party in the case. Then the witness signed and when asked his age he said he is twenty-one years of age.

7.4 Witness Juana Pérez

Potosí, February 24, 1584

Juana Pérez, wife of Simon de Herrera, [*witness takes oath*] she has known Angela de Palacios for five years, more or less, and her daughter Leonor for the last twenty days. She has known *doña* Isabel de Chávez and Ortiz de Velasco for the last two years. She said that one morning at dawn, twenty

---

18. Chuquisaca refers to the Bolivian department that is in the central south of the country where La Plata (mentioned herein) is located. It borders the region where the Villa of Potosí is located.

19. This is a literal translation of the testimony; the phrase is akin to asking "do you want to sell me out?"

days ago, they knocked on the door of her house and that of Catalina Valero, her mother-in-law. Valero said to a *muchacha* (female servant) that she should see who was knocking and open the door. In came a *negra* named Margarita, slave of *doña* Isabel de Chávez, with another girl. Entering into the room of Catalina Valero, mother-in-law of this witness, the *negra* told her "*Señora*, my *señora, doña* Isabel de Chávez does not want to have this girl in her house. I beg your mercy that she may stay here for a day or two while she finds a place to stay." Margarita the *negra* told her, "*Señora*, just for today if you like, could your mercy have her in your house? At night they will come back for her." Catalina Valero told this witness that if it would only be for today, [then she could be there]. Valero asked the girl if she had a mother, and she responded, "yes," and said later she would tell her who. With this the *negra* left and the girl stayed. After a while, this witness asked the said girl what her name was and she responded that her name was Francisca. At around ten o'clock on that day, Ortiz de Velasco came to the house of Catalina Valero, mother-in-law of this witness. He spoke with the girl and then he turned to go. Ortiz de Velasco sent a boy [servant] with lunch, a cake and peaches, grapes and bread. Around nightfall, the girl took her shawl and said that she wanted to go and seeing this, her mother-in-law asked Leonor, "Why do you want to go? Do not go until Ortiz de Velasco comes." So Leonor took her shawl off and after it got dark, Leonor again took her shawl and wanted to go. Her mother-in-law made her stay and sent for Ortiz de Velasco, who came later. Knowing that Leonor wanted to go he told her, "Do not go because you are in a good house," and with this, Ortiz de Velasco left. One hour later, more or less, Ortiz de Velasco returned to the house. Before he took her [Leonor], this witness heard her say that evening, "How bad is Ortiz de Velasco. Because of him I go around in this manner because he took me from my house." This witness did not speak to him. This is what she knows. She said she had no personal conflict of interest with any party in the case. She did not sign. When asked her age, she said she is thirteen years old, more or less.

7.5 Witness Madame[20] Isabel Bisconte

Potosi, February 24, 1584

Madame Isabel Bisconte, wife of Juan Varón, resident in this said Villa. [*Witness swore oath*] said that she knows Angela de Palacios and her daughter, Leonor Arias, and has known Ortiz de Velasco for more than two years. She does not know *doña* Isabel de Chávez. About one month ago, more or less,

---

20. The original includes the term *Madame*, though it is unclear why.

this witness saw that Angela Palacios was living across from her house in the street of the *Juego de la Pelota*. She had seen Leonor Arias, her daughter, with her because at that time [Leonor] had communicated with her, and this witness had entered the house of Angela de Palacios and had spoken to Leonor Arias, her daughter, many times. In the time that she has known them, she has often seen Ortiz de Velasco walking past their door and standing in their doorway. About fifteen or twenty days ago, this witness heard tell that Ortiz de Velasco had taken the daughter from the house of her mother, Leonor Arias. When she was in the house of *maestro* Juan, surgeon, Ortiz de Velasco entered the house and said to this witness and to others there that they should be alert because the daughter of Leonor Arias had been taken from the house of Angela de Palacios. This witness and the others who were there responded that this was true and that he must have taken her and Ortiz de Velasco responded that this was not true and with this, he left. She did not hear more and this is the truth. She did not sign because she did not know how. Asked her age, she said she is thirty-three years old.

> *[The remaining extant folios in the case treat the appellate court's handling of the case but refer only with the matter of the legal ownership by* doña Isabel de Chávez *of a horse and a slave. There is no additional mention of the alleged abduction of Leonor Arias.]*

Suggested Reading

Boyer, Richard. "Catarina María Complains That Juan Teioa Forcibly Deflowered Her," in *Colonial Lives, Documents on Latin American History, 1550–1850*, ed. Richard Boyer and Geoffrey Spurling. New York: Oxford University Press, 2000.

Mannerelli, María Emma. *Private Passions and Public Sins: Men and Women in Seventeenth-Century Lima*. Trans. Sidney Evans and Meredith D. Dodge. Albuquerque: University of New Mexico Press, 2007.

Twinam, Ann. *Public Lives, Private Secrets: Gender, Honor, Sexuality and Illegitimacy in Colonial Spanish America*. Stanford, CA: Stanford University Press, 1999.

von Germeten, Nicole. *Violent Delights, Violent Ends: Sex, Race, and Honor in Colonial Cartagena de Indias*. Albuquerque: University of New Mexico Press, 2013.

Document Themes

- Family
- Migration and mobility
- Race and ethnicity
- Sexuality and gender

8

Bárbara López, *India*, Accuses Her Husband of Abuse (Santa Fe, 1612)

Local authorities in Santa Fe, Colombia took it seriously when the indigenous woman Bárbara López appeared before them with bloody bandages on her head and blamed her husband, Salvador López, for her injury. Under Iberian legal codes, which served as the foundation for law in the Indies throughout the colonial period, men had power over their wives and their households, but there were limits to this power. If a man abused his wife, she could file a criminal complaint against him as we see in this case. Spousal abuse was common in colonial Latin America and at times resulted in the death of a wife at the hands of her husband. While we do not have good quantitative data on how often this occurred, we know that sometimes husbands were charged for the crime of abuse and served time in jail.[1] The testimony and outcome of the following case illustrate some of the legal protections afforded to women in instances of alleged abuse as well as the difficulty courts faced in investigating and prosecuting cases of spousal abuse. Given the universality of domestic violence, we may also use this case to consider how Bárbara López's actions reflect the context in which she lived.

Incidents of violence sometimes stemmed from a man's perception that his wife was not living up to her role in the marriage. Expectations of marriage roles were heavily gendered in this era. Theoretically, men provided for families and households that women managed while providing meals, and giving loyalty and obedience to their husbands. In practical terms, overwhelming evidence shows that many women contributed to households in material ways and that an important portion of households were female-headed.[2] In the case of Bárbara López, however, her marriage to Salvador López brought with it an expectation that the couple enjoy *vida maridable*, or making married life, including sexual relations. Because men, as husbands or fathers, held legal authority over wives and daughters, the law did allow men certain leeway in terms of how they enforced their role as heads of household. In many instances, courts and communities permitted men's physical abuse of their

1. Steve J. Stern, *The Secret History of Gender, Women, Men, and Power in Late Colonial Mexico* (Chapel Hill: University of North Carolina Press, 1995).
2. See, for example, Jane E. Mangan, *Trading Roles: Gender, Ethnicity, and the Urban Economy in Colonial Potosí* (Durham, NC: Duke University Press, 2005).

wives as a reasonable method to assert spousal power. However, families and neighborhoods also upheld a moral code that kept such abuse in check; in other words, people knew when a man in their community was beating his wife and could step in if they viewed his actions as excessive.

Cases against men for spousal abuse could be brought to courts by wives or by state officials. Both secular and ecclesiastical courts tried such cases because colonial populations understood abuse within marriage as an offense against the church. Elite women were often housed for protection or surveillance by means of what was known as the practice of *recogimiento* (seclusion).[3] Women could establish reputations of virtue for themselves by practicing seclusion on their own and would then be known as "*mujeres recogidas.*" But *recogimiento* was sometimes accomplished when families or courts placed women in forced seclusion and scrutiny either in convents; private houses; or in some cities, formal institutions called *recogimientos* whose purpose was to reform and occasionally to protect women who had fallen into danger, legal limbo, or moral lassitude. While women were in the process of a legal case against their husbands, they were subject to potential physical attack as well as moral suspicion if not secluded in a supervised and enclosed household or institution known as *depósito.* While court officials in Santa Fe acted quickly in López's case, they made no move to place her *en depósito* or in a *recogimiento,* likely due to her non-elite status.

In the case studied here, Bárbara López's judge ordered that her wounds be examined and further that her husband be apprehended and jailed. Both López, her husband, and other witnesses presented evidence to the court. The nature of the witness testimony creates a "he said, she said" story structure and readers should be aware that not all witnesses were forthcoming in their statements. While some pieces of the narrative remain consistent throughout the transcript, many parts do not. This leaves us to wonder what actually happened. Did Salvador López hit his wife? Or did she hit him? Was the provocation because he was having an affair or because Bárbara was boisterously socializing independently of her husband?

Bárbara López's initiation of the case, as well as her withdrawal of her complaint, must also be considered from the perspective of both parties' status as indigenous peoples. The case dates from 1612, less than a century from the time that the Spanish entered the region of Santa Fe. Bárbara is identified by the court as an *india ladina,* which indicates that she has acculturated toward Spanish culture at least in terms of language and was able to present testimony

---

3. This institution and practice is also discussed in Chapters 7, 12, and 13. For an analysis of *recogimiento* in colonial Peru, see Nancy E. van Deusen, *Between the Sacred and the Worldly: The Institutional and Cultural practice of Recogimiento in Colonial Lima* (Stanford, CA: Stanford University Press, 2001).

to the judge without a translator. Prior to the existence of Spanish courts and even some decades after they opened, spousal relations and breaches in the code of marital conduct would have been handled through families, kin networks, and community leaders. But by 1612, the indigenous woman Bárbara López looked to the colonial judicial system to handle her claim. This may indicate either that by this period the indigenous kin network system had weakened so dramatically it was unable to support her, or it may reveal that Spanish courts introduced a legal practice into Andean life to which indigenous women readily responded when they perceived it might serve their interests.[4] López's petition to withdraw the case toward its close suggests, however, that she operating from a position of weakness rather than strength. Without her husband's income, apparently, Bárbara was unable to support herself.

This brief case opens up a window onto how men and women experienced marital discord in early seventeenth-century society as well as how their peers and the authorities in their midst responded to it. What do witnesses' testimonies reveal about acceptable contemporary behavior for men and for women? Notice that Bárbara López is identified as indigenous and as socializing with "Indians." What is the significance of this? What does it suggest about the legal system and about colonial society that the court judged that Salvador López could be released from prison? How does this court case reveal emotional states of people in the deep past?

8.1 Criminal Complaint against Salvador López, *Indio,* for Mistreatment of His Wife Bárbara[5]

Complaint

In the city of Santa Fe on November 26, 1612 before the *señor* (sir) *licenciado* (licenticate) Alonso Vázquez de Cisneros of the council of his Majesty and mayor of the court of this Real Audiencia (Royal Court) appeared a *ladina* Indian who said she was named Bárbara López, and she was a native of the *pueblo* of Bogotá. She made a criminal complaint against her husband, Salvador López, because yesterday on the 25th of the current month and year around five o'clock in the

---

4. For further discussion of this interesting topic, see Bianca Premo, *The Enlightenment on Trial: Ordinary Litigants and Colonialism in the Spanish Empire* (Oxford: University of Oxford Press, 2017).

5. Archivo General de la Nación, Colombia. Sección Colonia, Fondo Caciques e Indios, Legajo Indios de Chivatá . . . India demanda a su marido por maltratos Caciques Indios, 64, D. 16 1612.

afternoon, Salvador López, with no fear of God and disparaging the law, took a stick and hit her many times in the head from which he gave her two wounds that broke the skin and bone and which bled profusely. He did this without her giving him any reason to do so other than that she had told him "do not be having an affair; come make married life with me as your wife that I am." Bárbara López, *india* (indigenous woman), appeared in front of the judge by [reason of] her face and some bloody bandages that she had on her head, along with his mercy, the judge accepted her complaint and ordered that information be given as to the content of the complaint including about the wounds, all of which the *señor* judge conveyed to the present receptor who decreed and ordered that Salvador López be jailed by one of the bailiffs of the court.

[Signed by] Luis de Palma R.

[Next, Bárbara was examined by a court official to create an official account of her injuries.]

8.2 Evidence of Wounds

Later this day, month, and year above stated the 26th of November, 1612, I the receptor, in compliance with the order by the *señor* judge, say that Bárbara López removed the bloodied bandages that she had tied to her head. I saw that she had a head-wound one finger-length long that appeared to be a knife wound, and going across her forehead close to her hairline she had another deep wound two fingers long that seemed deep enough that it had been made by a stick because around the edges it is somewhat bruised.

[Luis de la Palma signed for the court record and the bloodied bandages were preserved as evidence.]

8.3 Recommendation

In the city of Santa Fe on the 26th of November 1612, Blas Fernández, bailiff of the court, in compliance with the orders of the *señor* judge arrested Salvador López and put him in the royal jail of this court. He handed the prisoner over to Diego Serrano, *alcalde* (judge) of the jail, who signed and took responsibility for him.

[signed by] Diego Serrano
Before me Luis de Palma R.

8.4 Witness Testimony

In the city of Santa Fe on the 29th of November of 1612, Bárbara López, *india ladina,* for the investigation of her complaint presented as a witness who was an *indio ladino* who said he is named Francisco López and he is a master chair-maker and native of this city. I, the receptor, recorded his Holy oath and he made the sign of the cross in the form of God, and he promised by these to tell the truth. Questioned as to the tenor of the case and complaint, he said that he knows Salvador López and Bárbara López, his wife, *indios,* and what he knows about this quarrel is that this past Sunday, the 25th of November, at around five in the afternoon, this witness was near the tile workshop[6] of San Agustín where Bárbara López and her husband were as well. He saw how Salvador López had fighting words[7] with his wife and this witness went into a hut[8] with other Indians who were inside and from there he heard tell that some indigenous women who were there, though he does not remember who they were, how Salvador and his wife were fighting. Then this witness left the hut and saw how Bárbara and her husband were fighting. This witness went up to Bárbara and saw that she had a head wound that was bleeding heavily. This witness did not see nor hear who gave [the injury] to Bárbara nor does he know more than what he has said, which is the truth and what he knows, under the oath that he made in this decree. Having read it, he affirmed and ratified it. He said he was of the age of forty-two years and that had no personal conflict of interest with any party in the case.[9] He did not sign because he said he did not know how.

Before me, Luis de Palma R

[On December 7, 1612 Bárbara López presented another petition before the Real Audiencia in which she asked that her husband be released from jail.]

I state that I have had my husband Salvador López jailed before the royal judge *señor licenciado* Cisneros, for having wounded me in the head. Because I have healed and because with my husband's imprisonment, I lack many

---

6. *Tejar* in the original.

7. *Pesadumbre de palabras* in the original.

8. The term is difficult to decipher in the original, but appears to be *bugio* in the original; which might be an alternate spelling of *bohio* or hut.

9. The text reads *"no le tocan las generales de la lei que le fueron fechas."* Normally, *"las generales de la ley"* refers to a person's basic personal information: name, surname, marital status, age, address, and sometimes immediate personal relationships, for example, of parentage. The phrase can also be used, as it appears to be here, to indicate whether a witness was in a position of personal conflict of interest with an implicated party in a lawsuit, for instance because of a familial relationship. The same phrase is also used by a witness in Chapter 20.

necessities, I withdraw my complaint. I do not want to ask for anything now nor anytime [from the court] which I do for the service of God Our Lord and for the above reasons. To your highness I ask and plead that you withdraw the complaint for me and free Diego Salvador López, my husband, from prison because it is justice that I seek for him.

[signed] Bárbara López

[Next Salvador López presented a petition to the judge.]

Very powerful Lord:

I, Salvador López, have been imprisoned in this royal jail many days now due to a complaint that my wife made in which she said that I had beaten her. Now she is better and has withdrawn the complaint. I suffer in this jail because I am a poor artisan and have nothing to eat. For this reason, I beg and plead your highness that you free me from this prison owing to the aforementioned for which I hope to receive mercy with justice.

Salvador López

[On the same day, December 7, the Count Luis de Palma sends a surgeon to evaluate Bárbara López and señor licenciado don *Francisco de Herrera goes along as a witness.]*

Declaration

In Santa Fe on December 7, 1612, I, the receptor, in compliance with the orders of the *señores*, presidents, and judges, received an oath by God our Lord as well as a sign of the cross in the form of God, from García Brabo, surgeon, who swore to tell the truth. Under the oath he said that he has cured Bárbara López, *india*, of a wound in her head and another in the forehead, wounds from which she is much improved. At present, she has no fever and is out of danger, even though the wounds have not completely closed. He said this is the truth under the oath, and he signed García Barbo, before me, Luis de Palma R.

[Three days later, Salvador López was brought before señor licenciado don *Francisco de Herrera Canpucano, magistrate of the court of the Real Audiencia to give his confession.]*

8.5 Confession of Salvador López

In the city of Santa Fe on December 10, 1612. I, the receptor, received the oath to God and a cross in the form of God from Salvador López, imprisoned in this royal jail to hear his confession in compliance with the orders of the *señor* judge. López took the oath and under it promised to tell the truth about what he knew about whatever he was asked. He was asked the following questions:

Asked his name and where he is from and what age and job he has = He said his name is Salvador López, and that he is native to the city and a shoemaker and thirty years old, more or less and thus he responds.

Asked if it is true that on November 25 just past five o'clock in the evening next to the tile workshop of San Agustín, this witness in the company of Bárbara López, his wife, had fighting words with her. And asked if, as a result, this witness gave her two head wounds which cut skin and bone from which she lost much blood. And whether he gave her these blows in the head without [his wife] having given him reason [for them] other than that she said that he should not be cohabitating and should live with her like his wife that she was.[10]

He said he denies the question. What happened is that the day and at the hour that he has been asked about, this witness was near the tile workshop and found Bárbara López, his wife in a hut with other Indians having a good time. This witness told her to leave the said party, and go to their house because it was time. She responded that she did not want to go home, but wanted to stay on. This witness told her to stay, then, and that he would also stay on to relax. And the witness and his wife had words about this from which it resulted that she gave [him] a push with which he landed on the ground and from there he got back up [*three illegible words*]. This which he has said is the truth in this confession having it read to him he confirmed. He did not sign because he did not know how.

Before me, Luis de Palma R.

[Magistrate Herrera Canpucano ordered that Salvador López should pay four gold pesos, two of them for the discalced nuns and two for the prisoners in the jail. After paying his debt, he would be freed on bail from the prison where he is, not being jailed for anything else. Shortly thereafter, after paying only one gold coin, López was freed on bail.]

Suggested Reading

Abercrombie, Thomas A. "Affairs of the Courtroom: Fernando de Medina Confesses to Killing His Wife," in *Colonial Lives, Documents on Latin American History,*

---

10. The question here implies that Salvador López was living with another woman and not "*hacienda vida*" or carrying out married life with Bárbara, a charge he denies.

1550–1850, ed. Richard Boyer and Geoffrey Spurling. New York: Oxford University Press, 2000.

Boyer, Richard. "Women, *La Mala Vida,* and the Politics of Marriage," in *Sexuality and Marriage in Colonial Latin America,* ed. Asunción Lavrin. Lincoln: University of Nebraska Press, 1989, 252–86.

Johnson, Lyman, and Sonia Lipsett-Rivera, eds. *The Faces of Honor: Sex, Shame, and Violence in Colonial Latin America.* Albuquerque: University of New Mexico Press, 1998.

von Germeten, Nicole. *Violent Delights, Violent Ends: Sex, Race, and Honor in Colonial Cartagena de Indias.* Albuquerque: University of New Mexico Press, 2013.

Document Themes

- Family
- Law

9

Sor Ana's Travel Excerpt from Mexico to Manila (Mexico and Manila, 1620)

Introduction and Translation by Sarah E. Owens

Sor (Sister) Ana de Cristo's "Travel Excerpt from Mexico to Manila" provides the modern-day reader a unique opportunity to view travel, evangelization, and empire through the eyes of a seventeenth-century Franciscan nun. From 1620 to 1621, a group of Franciscan nuns made an incredible journey to found the first female convent in the Far East. Led by their mother abbess *Sor* Jerónima de la Asunción (1556–1630), the small group of nuns and novices traveled from Toledo, Spain, to Mexico and then on to Manila, Philippines.

Of the ten religious women who formed the group (two joined them in Mexico City), only nine nuns would survive the journey. Surprisingly, it was not *Sor* Jerónima, who was sixty-four when she left Spain and almost continuously ill during the entire trip, who died, but another nun from the town of Belalcázar, Córdoba. Death loomed large on long oceanic voyages, and the nuns, although saddened by their loss, continued on to Manila to found a convent under the strict First Rule of Saint Clare. The descendants from that community still exist today, although the original building was destroyed during Allied bombing at the end of World War II.

The main purpose of *Sor* Ana's manuscript was to record the life story of the mother abbess, *Sor* Jerónima de la Asunción.[1] The genre of *vidas* (spiritual biographies) was quite common in early modern convents. Nuns wrote about themselves or about other nuns, but normally these accounts did not follow a linear story. Instead, they included many hagiographic details that exalted the religious life of the subject. *Sor* Ana's account also follows this traditional pattern. She often describes *Sor* Jerónima's extreme penance, fasting, and daily prayer schedule, but her text is also unique because she illustrates their remarkable transoceanic journey, often interjecting her own observations of their travels. *Sor* Ana had been ordered by other accompanying nuns and the father confessor to write this account, ultimately with the hope that their mother abbess might become a saint. During her lifetime, *Sor* Jerónima

---

1. The original 450-folio manuscript can be found in the convent of Santa Isabel de los Reyes, Toledo, Spain.

had accumulated a substantial following of devotees who viewed the austere nun from Toledo as a living saint.

Unlike *Sor* Jerónima, who was immortalized by the painter Diego Velázquez in at least two full-length portraits when the nuns stopped in Seville on their way to the coast of Spain, we know very little about *Sor* Ana de Cristo (1565–1636). She does, however, include first-person observations in her account and explains how she had known *Sor* Jerónima for more than forty years. The abbess, only ten years older than *Sor* Ana, had been her novice mistress back in Toledo and had taught her how to read. *Sor* Ana had not known how to write, but a friar taught her to do so during the journey so that she could take up the task of biography. Although this might sound like a trope of humility, this scenario was quite common in early modern Spain, where the skills of reading and writing were taught separately. Indeed, many nuns and other laypersons alike knew how to read but did not know how to put pen to paper.

As was common in the early modern time period, *Sor* Ana was exposed to an extensive aural culture in her convent community. She heard many sermons, learned rote prayers in Latin, and listened to other nuns read about the lives of saints and other religious texts. The fact that *Sor* Ana was able to write the biography with such advanced language structure is not far-fetched, but readers should note that the section of the journey reproduced here is much more polished than other parts of her account. Most likely friars, or even other nuns, helped her with the retelling of their transoceanic travels as they portray many extreme obstacles and highlight the courage of the mother abbess and her travel companions.

Their foresister Spanish nun Mother Juana de la Cruz (1481–1534) exerted a direct spiritual influence on the nuns described in this account. Juana de la Cruz had joined a *beaterio*, a house for third-order Franciscan laywomen, in a small town called Cubas, near Madrid, as a young woman. She later became abbess when the community was dedicated as a convent in 1509. During her lifetime, Mother Juana became renowned for her weekly "sermons," a type of trance-like rapture when supposedly she became the mouthpiece of Christ himself. Her contemporaries also believed that the Lord and the Virgin Mary had blessed a large number of her rosary beads, infusing them with miraculous powers. According to later biographers, including Antonio Daza, those beads had the power to cast out demons, calm stormy waters, and cure illnesses, among other uses. In addition, other beads that were *tocadas* or touched as contact relics to the original beads also contained those powers. Two of the nuns that joined *Sor* Jerónima hailed from Madre Juana's convent of Santa María de la Cruz, in Cubas. Most likely, they had been chosen for their close connection to their spiritual foremother and for the beads that they brought with them on the journey. The nuns frequently referred to "Saint" Juana, even though she was never officially canonized a saint. They firmly believed in the miraculous powers of the beads and they encountered many people of Spanish, indigenous, and African descent who venerated Juana as a saint.

In this portion of her account, *Sor* Ana describes the journey from Mexico City to the port of Manila. The group had just spent about five months in Mexico City awaiting news of the arrival of the Manila Galleon, the generic term for the yearly crossing of the Pacific Ocean to the Philippines by one or two ships. This was not the nuns' first oceanic voyage; they had already earned their sea legs on the voyage from Cadiz, Spain, to the port of Veracruz. The nuns had also had some exposure to life on the trail. Upon arrival in Veracruz, they mounted mules as they made their way along the Path of Inns, even stopping at the now-iconic shrine of the Virgin of Guadalupe on the outskirts of Mexico City. Without a doubt, however, the China Trail southward from the capital to Acapulco and then three-and-a-half months on the Manila Galleon would be the most arduous part of the journey.

Relatively few travelers, let alone women, have described life on the China Trail, aptly named for the transport of goods between Asia and Mexico City. *Sor* Ana's text offers a picture of feisty, spirited nuns who were willing to rough it physically to bring the order of Poor Clares to the Philippines. Myriads of mosquitos assaulted the pilgrims as they trekked past the town of Cuernavaca on their way to the port of Acapulco. The nuns, two friars, servants, and others who escorted the group fell ill to intermittent fevers and severe diarrhea. It is difficult to diagnose their ailments, but a combination of a malaria-like illness and dysentery are probable, exacerbated by unsanitary conditions with the women's insistence on "enclosing" themselves as if in a cloister. To remedy their sickness the women used some of their miraculous beads from Saint Juana, ingesting them as a type of ground-up medicine.

The three-and-a-half month sea voyage across the Pacific tested the true grit of the nuns. They were not afraid to die as martyrs if their galleon drifted off course to Japan or to die at sea if a storm wrecked their ship. The women enclosed themselves cheek to jowl in a small cabin as they did their best to care for the ailing *Sor* Jerónima and *Sor* María de la Trinidad. The tragic death of *Sor* María did not deter *Sor* Jerónima and she rallied once the galleon arrived at the port of Bolinao, a peninsula on the southwestern side of the island of Luzon. During their final trek across the island to Manila *Sor* Ana's account offers a bird's-eye view of native bearers who carried the women on hammocks and a colorful depiction of a devout pious indigenous woman in a remote village.

Sor Ana's travel account is a rare lens to follow the path of religious women in the early 1620s to a far-flung corner of the Spanish Empire. *Sor* Jerónima and her co-founders were the first Spanish nuns to board a Manila galleon and travel to the Philippines. Up until recently scholars of colonial Latin America have only been exposed to the first-hand accounts of male missionaries, soldiers, and noblemen. Documents such as this one by *Sor* Ana add a layer of information to our growing knowledge of the Spanish Empire and its diverse inhabitants. Her writings raise several interesting questions about the lives of female religious and their representation in the early modern Spanish Empire.

In this account, how did *Sor* Ana's membership in a strict Franciscan order influence the way she portrayed life on the journey? How did *Sor* Ana depict *Sor* Jerónima? Do you think that even from her sickbed she controlled the nuns and friars who accompanied her? How does this help to explain the role of nuns in Spanish Catholic culture of the 1600s; one that is commonly thought to be dominated by men? How and why did the Spanish men and nuns described here treat the enslaved woman, María? *Sor* Ana exaggerates certain events and leaves others out of this manuscript. If you were able to interview her, what specific questions would you ask her and why?

9.1 Chapter 47: Of the Trail from Mexico City to Embarkation[2]

We were traveling with much joy on rough trails along very high cliffs. We climbed upwards and then downwards in such a way that those above could barely see the others below and some paths were so tight that if a mule were to trip, it would fall as if it came from a very high tower; we traveled this extreme route for more than seventy leagues.

There were many rivers and streams with lovely water and wooded springs; there were fruit trees, coconut palms, orange groves, banana plants, and a type of plant that they use to make pita thread.[3] There were cemetery caretakers

---

2. Ana de Cristo, Sor. *Historia de nuestra santa madre Jerónima de la Asunción* 1623–29. Archivo del Monasterio de Santa Isabel de los Reyes (AMSIRT), Toledo, Spain.
History of Our Blessed Mother Jerónima de la Asunción: Travel Excerpt from Mexico to Manila, fols. 92–96v. I would like to thank Asunción Lavrin, Maricela Villalobos, and Edward Chauca for helping me with some of the difficult parts of this translation.
3. Pita thread (*hilo de pita*) is generally made from the inner part of the agave plant. For this definition of pita, see the online version of the *Real Academia Española Diccionario de Autoridades*—Tomo V (1737): http://web.frl.es/DA.html, accessed February 12, 2017.

like in Spain.[4] There were vineyards, and trees where cotton grows;[5] reeds so tall and thick that they are used to build houses and churches; sturdy pines and solid hardwoods, and such pleasant fields, flowers, fruits, and trees that it seemed like we were in paradise. Indeed, we were told that we were very close to it and to the River Jordan.

[In the short paragraph that is omitted here Sor *Ana continues the theme of the River Jordan. She describes the kingdom of Cambodia and she encourages Franciscan missionaries to travel to that region to convert infidels of the Muslim faith.]*

We arrived at a settlement of *indios* (indigenous people) where there were only two *españoles* (Spaniards): a priest and the governor. The governor's wife sent us a very well-prepared meal. We went visiting in the company of the priest's sister who was called *doña* Juana. When she saw Mother Leonor de San Buenaventura suffering from hemorrhoids and fearful of stomach cramps, she said she wanted her to be given a ground-up bead from Saint Juana with a sip of water and once this was done, she was completely cured. She said that the place is so poor that it could not support a doctor so she cured everyone with that relic [a bead from Saint Juana] and in particular, she had cured two *indias* who had been given Extreme Unction and had carried dead fetuses in their bodies for several days. Upon receiving the relic, they expelled out the rotting fetuses.

[The short paragraph that is omitted here describes the acclaim of Mother Juana de la Cruz's rosary beads. Many friars wanted to touch their rosaries to the original beads to obtain their miraculous powers.]

Some of the *doctrinas* (indigenous parishes) run by clergy that we encountered along the route showed us much hospitality housing us in their churches or in their homes. In some places, there were inns, while others were deserted. Some nights we camped by the side of rivers with such joy that it almost felt like we were in heaven because in no place along the way did we have any misfortune and we wanted for nothing in the *doctrinas* of the fathers of the [Franciscan] order where we were treated very well.

Nearing Cuernavaca, a group of *indios* met us dressed in white linen and carrying a crimson standard [*three words of illegible text*]. They came out of the friary of our fathers and the *corregidor* (district judge and administrator) who was from Toledo along with other *españoles* on horseback. We dismounted from [our mules] at an inn belonging to the friars, which was prepared for

---

4. This phrase about cemetery caretakers seems a bit out of place with *Sor* Ana's list of plants and trees, but this is also a good example of her prose, which is not always polished or linear.
5. Perhaps she was referring to cottonwood trees.

us by the head friar. We had three days' rest there after the roughest part of the trail. He treated us very well and then accompanied us for a few leagues, covering all our costs, and if we had let him he would have done so for the rest of the trip right up to the port. He bid us farewell, shedding many tears as if he were the confessor of each one of us. We received the same treatment from the Dominican friars in a place just after this one.

We arrived at another place where a priest was saying mass with two sacristans at his sides fanning away mosquitos because there were an infinite number of them. We made confession, received communion, and right there in the church he gave us food, and went with us as far as the River Balsas, which we crossed in *calabazas* (dugout canoes) each one tied to the other and rowed by *indios*. We then traveled along the River Papagayo, which was the roughest part of the journey due to its ups and downs and rocky cliffs. God saved us from great dangers because there were *tigres* (jaguars) and other wild beasts in this area.

The Father Commissary[6] had been to Acapulco two months earlier and a priest there had a house and everything necessary for us for when we went there. When we came in sight of the port, a salvo was fired from the fort. Some of our friars along with other gentlemen met us on the beach. As we entered the town we were greeted with a solemn procession. Dismounting from the mules, we joined the procession until we arrived at the high altar of the friary of Saint Francis and in our honor, they exposed the Blessed Sacrament and left it that way during the whole time we were in the church.[7] They said mass and we received communion. Everything was so decorated with banners on the alters as if it were a Corpus Christi procession, and with this, they brought us right up to the inn, which was closed like a cloister and they said mass for us every day and they made a room into a visiting parlor with a cane grille and a door for our doorkeepers.[8] While there, we all had some fevers; our mother [*Sor* Jerónima] was in great danger, and our Father Commissary had a bad tertian fever[9] and when he recovered, he ordered *Sor* Jerónima to stay behind with one nun and for the rest of us to continue our journey, but God put things right by giving *Sor* Jerónima such energy that one day they gave her the Viaticum[10] and the next she boarded the ship on

6. The "Father Commissary" refers to the position of commissary in charge of Franciscan friars. In this case *Sor* Ana was most likely referring to Fray Pedro Bautista who traveled with them on the galleon to Manila.

7. To expose the Blessed Sacrament meant that the consecrated host was displayed in an ornate monstrance for adoration.

8. This entire sentence is somewhat vague in Spanish. It appears that *Sor* Ana is saying that they brought the host with them to the inn.

9. "Tertian" literally means a fever that repeats itself every three days.

10. Holy Communion or Eucharist given to a person who is in imminent danger of dying.

her own two feet. The ship set sail on Holy Tuesday and the head friar sent her [*Sor* Jerónima] to sea with about one hundred hens and the mother of our sister María de los Angeles sent more than two hundred more with many other gifts. And during the month, more or less, that we spent there [in Acapulco], the neighboring Guardians continuously visited us.

9.2 Chapter 49. All the Things That Happened during Navigation from the Port of Acapulco to Manila

We set sail on Holy Tuesday and if the Lord had provided good comfort for the first ship [on the trip from Spain to Mexico], then it was at least as good on the second ship, which was very large with a larger cabin [for us] on the poop deck that had a beautiful corridor and a small toilet.[11] At last we traveled as if in a cloistered cell with doorkeepers. The Mother Vicaress and Mother Luisa de Jesús received messages there, and visitors who could not be denied, entered. Mother Magdalena de Cristo served as *provisora* (food provisioner) and worked like a man preparing the food, and servants then took it to the communal stove made of brick and lime, which was the designated place for everyone's food preparation. The friars had their lodging next to the door. The general of the ship, *don* Jerónimo de Valenzuela, looked after our every comfort as if it were his only duty. And since our mother was so thin, we put her in a bed and she did not leave it, suffering incredible discomfort, until we disembarked.

On Holy Thursday, Father Friar Pedro Bautista, Commissary of our friars, sang the gospel and the *señor* Bishop of Nueva Segovia preached a lofty sermon.[12] We had many sermons on Sundays and feast [days] because there were many great preachers. Everyday, the young and old sang the Hail Mary to Our Lady, the priests said the prayer, and they also sang the litany responsively in four voices in the choir. In the morning and at night there was doctrine for the boys and everyone said the prayer of the Immaculate Conception. Everything was so well orchestrated as if in a convent and if someone neglected a task, later he would pay for it. On Easter eve, the friars said very solemn vespers. On Easter day, they blessed the water and sang the Gospel because mass was never said. On the Octave of Ascension, Mother María de la Trinidad was afflicted with the illness that so quickly caused her death that the pain of losing such a

---

11. *Sor* Ana uses the word "*secretilla*" for small toilet. Nuns referred to their toilets as *secretas* and most likely she is using the diminutive to be polite.

12. Nueva Segovia refers to a diocese in the Philippines erected in 1595. For more information, see Catholic Encyclopedia, http://www.newadvent.org/cathen/11149b.htm

great nun whom we loved very much for her virtues caused us horrible pain. She was from the Convent of Belalcázar de Santa Clara. She had diarrhea and a high fever and did not respond to any remedies given to her. On the fifth day, the friars handed her soul over to God. We understood how the sorrow of this trial might cost our blessed mother her life since she also suffered from the same terminal illness and we understood that she might not wake up the next day, and the general kept inquiring about her and everybody from our fathers to everyone else prayed together and reflected at every instant who we would be if we found her lifeless. According to some of the words some of us heard from her, she said that she had seen God there in the purgatory of the deceased [María de la Trinidad] and later she told us that as the illness progressed at sea, she received great favors from the Lord because he had exposed her soul to a type of death or passage that often passed through her when she received God, His Majesty who left her here with us, blessed be His name.

The bishop and our friars celebrated the [funeral] service [of María de la Trinidad] very solemnly and instead of the funeral toll, three shots were fired from the artillery. They sang *responsos* (prayers for the dead) as she was thrown into the sea, dropped into the current at the bow, dressed in her habit and holding a crucifix in her hands; may her soul receive its prize. During the whole day our mother abbess suffered acute bouts of illness. Sixty attacks of the deadly diarrhea left her weak and only a shell of herself. Seeing that she was dying the Father Commissary was so upset that he said, "Watch her face very carefully so that she does not expire without you all seeing it." At this point, the bishop entered very teary-eyed and with the general on his knees and they asked for her blessing and from there they went to a secret meeting with our Father Commissary about what to do with her body. The bishop responded that there was no reason for her to be fish food and she would be brought to Manila in a box. The general conveyed this decision to the mother vicaress. She was so upset that she cried out to Saint Juana saying, "my mother, what about those pacts we made in San Juan del Hoyo;[13] when with many tears I asked you to take her to Manila in your hands. How can you leave us now with this affliction?" We gave her one of [Saint Juana's] ground-up beads and she started to get better. Now when we tell her that we used two of the originals: one for this occasion and the other for when we were in the port of Acapulco, she responded: "to touch the beads would have done the same, and the originals would have been more valuable to cure two kingdoms." She soon began to eat and we tried to treat her as if we were in the convent. We gave her broth made from a very good hen, and at night a chicken breast ground up with starch, which was heated up with a candle since no other fire was allowed for fear of fire in our wooden cabin. At the hour of the Hail Mary it [the common stove] is extinguished and then it is lit at dawn.

---

13. Possibly a variant of San Juan de Ulloa, an island off the port of Veracuz in Mexico.

The general ordered all-hands on deck; and it was shouted from above [the mast] that enemy Dutch ships had been sighted. There was a great commotion and the captains and soldiers began to ready their arms and ammunition with gunpowder. They put a big loaded canon next to our door. This was done to encourage the soldiers and to warn them about what might happen. Three years earlier, God had saved them miraculously when the Dutch had surrounded the ships even though they told us some of our men had died. They said they would put us in the hatchway, which is like a cave because it's very dark, below water. Our blessed mother, seeing the friars tending to us, sat up in her bed, even though she was so thin, saying: "Me, in the hatchway? I will do no such thing. Before that I'll help throw *piezas* (cannonballs) if necessary and I'll tell those heretics a thousand things." Since the drill lasted the whole day, no fire could be lit and the patient became very weak; but because the crew was so dedicated, God boosted our spirits greatly.

Another night when heavy winds whipped up, those who controlled the rudder made a mistake causing the ship to list and all the cabins filled with water. People said confessions very quickly and there were those who until that moment had not confessed in ten years and in all of that turmoil, they took refuge with our blessed mother. She ordered one of Saint Juana's beads to be thrown into the sea and the fair weather began. At the worst of the storm, the mother vicaress took a touched rosary[14] and wrapped it around the neck of a crucifix, beseeching her [Santa Juana] to show the virtue of her promise and liberate us with the holy beads. At that moment they [the beads] all broke off into crosses and after a short while they all turned back again around the same Christ [crucifix]. One of the sailors said that on a similar occasion, when all of the masts had snapped and everyone was giving their confessions to each other, he remembered that he had a "touched" bead. He shouted loudly for everyone to commend themselves to the Saint [Juana] and when he put the bead on the base of the mast, the tempest stopped suddenly and that after the successful voyage, they found the bead on top of the wood but without any fasteners and everyone gave thanks to God. Many similar cases like this one could be told about other sea voyages.

A desperate *negra* (black woman) named María threw herself into the sea and those that witnessed it grabbed her by the hem of her skirt. The captain ordered her tied to the mast and punished. Hearing her screams and knowing of her case, our mother sent the Father Fray Miguel de San Francisco with a bead so he could bless her; and she stood there in tears, commending herself to the saint [Juana]. And, as the *negra* being very angry said she was going to

---

14. The original Spanish is *"rosario tocado,"* literally "touched rosary." This is one of the rosaries that was considered a contact relic since it had touched one of Madre Juana's original rosary beads.

throw herself into the sea, the priest approached her and touched her with a bead, at which point she fainted with great trembling and sweating at his feet. When she came round she said that when she was touched by the bead, a *negro* who wanted to take her to hell was cast out of her. Then our blessed mother said to her: "Did you know, my daughter, that you were going to him?" She responded that yes, that she had been robbed of some *cuartos* (copper coins) and beads and the *negro* had told her: "You have no other alternative than to throw yourself into the sea." And she consoled her and dressed her, giving her many beads.

A period of calm set in for ten days. The priests went back and forth over whether we were going to land in Japan. They did not want to let their beards grow so they could slip onto the island as laymen, and as for us, they were going to build a hut with branches in the countryside until they could inform Manila to send a ship. God enabled us to respond to all of this with good spirits. The general said to our mother: "*Señora*, do you not see that we are lost and the ship is like a toothpick in the sea. Did you not tell me that on the other sea voyage when you threw a bead [overboard], you would get wind in the sails, but now no matter how many beads we toss the calm increases." She consoled him saying: "The Saint is so affable that I am convinced that this instance is a greater miracle than the other one, so we shall see." After this affliction, a wind blew in that brought us to safety. Then a frigate appeared in the distance, from which they shouted to us: "Praise be to Jesus Christ. What type of prayer did you say that you avoided fourteen Dutch ships that had just left port? They were waiting to rob you as they are wont to do." We gave thanks to God who saved us and that the men who spoke to us were Christians and for being close to land since we were so lacking food and drink that the friars said there were soldiers who would give a peso for a jug of water. Upset by their suffering, our blessed mother asked the general to remedy the situation. He responded that the officers were already receiving a half ration of water and it would be even worse to take it all away at once. She told the general, "trust God's mercy and in the name of Saint Juana you will be returned the entire ration." He said, "so be it," and with this, the outcry subsided and everyone was saying joyously that the Saint has ordered water be given to us.

Once the breezes began, not a lot happened and soon thereafter the ship dropped anchor. The men constructed a small skiff from some boards and a steward with four sailors was sent to receive a blessing from the blessed abbess. They asked her to commend them to God and to touch their rosaries. After receiving precautionary advice, they were given letters for the city of Manila. They encountered so much wind [on the skiff] that they found themselves in great danger, but God favored them with the power He gave to the beads. Afterwards, the men said they put a rosary around the mast and the never-ending waves that looked like mountains parted . . .[15] and it could not have been anything but a miracle that they arrived so quickly to Manila. The men gave tidings of the successful trip and they were congratulated.

When we dropped anchor, Father Fray Miguel de San Francisco was dispatched with all of the clothing in sampans[16] and from there, he went to Manila and we stayed three days in the port at the house of the regional magistrate who treated us very well and with much kindness since he had invited us while we were on the ship. From the port we had another five-day journey. It was not any easier than before since we had to ride on what they call *hamacas* (hammocks), which are carried on the shoulders of four *indios*.[17] It was like a funeral bier, and the only thing missing was the pall [cloth covering a coffin]; when it rained we made a kind of tarp with our veils. These trails close to Manila are very dangerous because there are pagan *negrillos* who take refuge in the mountains.[18] From their perches in trees, they shoot arrows and kill people when small groups travel together. We were well guarded because our blessed Commissary saw to our protection. There were harquebusiers shooting every now and again. God has given these people [*negrillos*] control of mountains of gold, which was amazing to see. Only they and the native *indios* know how to mine the gold, but they are good for very little and very humble and see no use for it.

After this segment of the journey, we arrived at a parish of Augustinian friars who treated us with much kindness. From there we went to a good town called Pampanga where there is also an Augustinian friary. The prior and the townspeople went out in a procession to receive us and the streets were decorated with branches. They had a good church where we confessed and took communion and from there we were brought to the chapter house, which is part of the friary. We spent three days resting there and we were showered with the indescribable charity of many [visitors]. The prior was the brother of the *señor* Archbishop of Manila who told us that he was from the Villa de Chinchos. The Dominican friars gave us such good lodging in their parishes as if we were from their same order. In one town before arriving at Pampanga, we stayed at the house of a very devout and very elite *india* who wore a habit. We spent two or three days and nights there during which she always rose at midnight with all her servants for matins and to say the catechism and to pray like a nun. She showed us great affection and gave us gifts even though we did not understand a word she said nor she us.

---

15. The phrase following this is illegible in the original.
16. A small boat with a flat bottom used in the Far East.
17. Most likely *Sor* Ana is using the generic term *indios* to refer to native people of the Philippines.
18. She is referring to the Negritos, an indigenous group of Australoid descent.

After finishing the journey of the *hamacas*, we rode in a sampan the rest of the way to Manila. We saw several leagues of beautiful greenery as we traveled on the river and the countryside is a mangrove that leads to the sea. As such, the river narrows in an area that enters the city and it wraps around the wall. Our convent is next to the sea and the river, with only one street between it and the wall. A day's journey before our arrival, our father provincial, who at the time was Fray Pedro de San Pablo, sent his secretary and other religious to welcome us with some gifts, and closer to Manila he, himself, came in his boat. He was accompanied by the blessed Father Fray Luis Sotelo, other religious, two judges with their wives, and other devout persons; all pleased to finally see nuns in their city. At the entrance, *señor* Govenor *don* Alonso Fajardo greeted us along with many people. The *maestre de campo*[19] with his captains and soldiers at his side, ordered the firing of the artillery. He [the governor] was lamenting that no one had notified him so that all the religious orders could have come with him to greet the new Order of Santa Clara. Our Provincial Father apologized, saying that it was the mother abbess's fault because she had asked him for a quiet entry. The governor responded that it was his humble responsibility to welcome her in the way she deserved so that the infidels could see the glory of these devote ceremonies for our holy Catholic faith.

Suggested Reading

Arenal, Electa, and Stacey Schlau, eds. *Untold Sisters: Hispanic Nuns in Their Own Works*. Albuquerque: University of New Mexico, Press, 1989.

Lavrin, Asunción. *Brides of Christ: Conventual Life in Colonial Mexico*. Stanford, CA: Stanford University Press, 2008.

Owens, Sarah E. *Nuns Navigating the Spanish Empire*. Albuquerque: University of New Mexico Press, 2017.

———. "Transatlantic Religious," in *The Routledge Research Companion for Early Modern Spanish Women Writers*, ed. Nieves Baranda and Anne J. Cruz. New York: Routledge, 2018.

Document Themes

- Migration and mobility
- Religion

---

19. *Maestre de campo* was the rank just below captain-general.

10

The Spiritual Diary of an Afro–Peruvian Mystic, Úrsula de Jesús (Lima, 1647–1661)

Translation by Nancy E. van Deusen

Úrsula de Jesús was a devout *donada,* a convent servant who professed simple religious vows, in the Limeño convent of Santa Clara in 1645.[1] She had been born into slavery in 1604, the legitimate child of an enslaved African woman who served a wealthy Spanish household. From age eight to twelve, Úrsula was sent to work in the household of one of Lima's most prominent lay holy women, the celebrated mystic Luisa Melgarejo Sotomayor. In Melgarejo's household, Úrsula had her first exposure to the spiritual climate that would eventually inform her own religious expression: the physical representations of baroque religious devotion constructed in the artwork and ornamentation of the Melgarejo home's personal altar; the celebration of Catholic devotion in the sermons, saints' lives, and confessional guides that Úrsula may have learned to read, and certainly would have heard read aloud; exposure to the circle of the city's religious luminaries, including the *beata* (lay religious woman) Rosa de Lima (later canonized as Latin America's first saint). Finally, Úrsula would doubtless herself have witnessed *doña* Melgarejo's bouts of religious ecstasies—visions, physical mortifications, and prophecies—which, following in the tradition of affective female religious practice established by the sixteenth-century Avilan nun Teresa de Jesús, represented the most orthodox means for spiritual women to expression their religious vocations in the Early Modern period.

At about age twelve, Úrsula left the Melgarejo household to work for the niece of Úrsula's mother's owner, sixteen-year-old Inés del Pulgar, who became a novice in the Santa Clara convent in 1617. For the next twenty-eight years, Úrsula served del Pulgar, attending to her mistress's needs for food and clothing in her private cell, and working alongside other servants

---

1. This introduction summarizes many of the salient features of the life and spiritual writings of Úrsula de Jesús that Nancy E. van Deusen provides in her introduction to *The Souls of Purgatory: The Spiritual Diary of a Seventeenth-Century Afro-Peruvian Mystic, Ursula de Jesús* (Albuquerque: University of New Mexico Press, 2004), 1–77. This introduction adopts van Deusen's practice of referring to the *donada* by her Christian name.

and Afro–Peruvian slaves in Santa Clara's kitchen and infirmary for long hours each day. Úrsula was one of between 100 and 130 Afro–Peruvians (both African- and New-World born) who worked in the convent of Santa Clara in this period. In the year 1637, when the convent housed a total of 446 women, Afro–Peruvian enslaved women constituted between 22 and 33 percent of the convent's total population.[2] The Afro–Peruvian enslaved population was even more concentrated in the city of Lima beyond the convent's walls. By the late sixteenth century and through most of the seventeenth, half of the population of Lima was black, although this number represented a growing population of free as opposed to enslaved Afro–Peruvians.[3]

As a slave, Úrsula occupied the lowliest rung of the highly stratified (and prominently displayed) social hierarchy that existed within the convent, where members of each successive social strata (slaves, servants, *donadas*, White Veil novices, White Veil nuns, and the prestigious nuns of the Black Veil) sometimes gave in to the temptation to lord their position over those on lower levels. One of Úrsula's peers, for example, an enslaved woman called María Malamba, served a *donada* in the convent for decades. Upon Malamba's death, her mistress seized the enslaved woman's few belongings to which her bereaved husband had previously laid claim.[4] The intensely stratified atmosphere of the convent, illustrated in such instances, may have contributed to Úrsula's initial decision to leave the convent rather than remain there as a *donada* once she had obtained her liberty.

Although she had not manifest any great spiritual devotion in her first decades at Santa Clara, Úrsula's contemporary biographer, an anonymous Franciscan, recorded that a few years before her manumission, God intervened to save Úrsula from physical peril and that it was this act that motivated her to embark on a life of intense spiritual devotion. This in turn, perhaps in combination with gratitude for Úrsula's gifts as a physical healer, prompted one of the convent's sisters to purchase Úrsula's liberty in 1645. Later that year, Úrsula decided to return to Santa Clara as a *donada,* professing formally eighteen months later. She lived for a further twenty-one years as a *donada* in the convent and during this time, generated a reputation as a mystic. She began to experience frequent visions, to communicate with God, and to develop her cherished spiritual gift: the ability to intercede on behalf of souls

---

2. van Deusen, *The Souls of Purgatory,* 26.

3. Herbert S. Klein and Ben Vinson III, *African Slavery in Latin America and the Caribbean,* 2nd Edition (New York: Oxford University Press, 2007), 25. See also Michelle A. McKinley, *Fractional Freedoms: Slavery, Intimacy, and Legal Mobilization in Colonial Lima, 1600–1700* (Cambridge: Cambridge University Press, 2016), 32.

4. van Deusen, *The Souls of Purgatory,* 4.

trapped in purgatory in order to alleviate their suffering and in some cases to assist them to ascend to heaven.

The selections below contain passages from Úrsula's spiritual journal, a standard literary *genre* of Counter-Reformation female religious, composed between 1647 and 1661. The fact that a spiritual biography, or *vida*, of Úrsula exists is both extraordinary and representative. It is unusual in the sense that it is one of the very few such existing texts detailing the spiritual lives of non-Spaniards. It is representative in the sense that it follows the literary conventions that colonial nuns frequently used in composing their spiritual biographies following in the tradition of celebrated medieval and early modern mystics. Because it was potentially heterodox for nuns to claim authorship of their writing, they often justified their writing by claiming, as Úrsula did, that they produced them at the behest of God or of their confessors.[5] Although the entries are recorded in the first person, we do not know if Úrsula recorded any of them herself; she acknowledges dictating some parts of them to at least one sister, and it is likely this is what she did for all the entries. Nancy E. van Deusen observes that the diary "was probably uncensored because it contains very few scratched out words or phrases and shows no evidence of editing."[6] Readers will observe that the writing style is less polished and less formal than *Sor* Ana's excerpts in Chapter 9. Are there other important distinctions between the spiritual experiences described in *Sor* Ana's letters and those Úrsula recorded? It is worth considering how Úrsula's experiences as an enslaved woman within the social hierarchy of both the city of Lima and the convent of Santa Clara informed her religious visions. What influences and preoccupations from her secular life are manifest in the particular kinds of spirituality Úrsula expressed? Students might also consider how Úrsula's navigation of contemporary attitudes toward non-Spaniard religious professants compares to those depicted in Chapter 13 with its discussion of early eighteenth-century attitudes toward indigenous nuns in Mexico. How did Úrsula respond, spiritually, to Spanish attitudes about non-Spaniard spiritual inferiority—or inadequacy—for religious perfection? Finally, as an Afro–Latin American, how did her experiences and outlook, as a *donada* who operated within one of the key institutions of colonial society, compare with those of secular Afro–Latin Americans, like the free black women, Luisa de Villalobos (Chapter 3), and Luisa de la Cerda (Chapter 6), or the enslaved eighteenth-century women whose legal and social experiences are treated in Chapters 14, 15, 17, 19, and 20?

---

5. Ibid., 50.
6. Ibid., 60.

10.1 Excerpt One from Úrsula's *Vida*[7]

On the day of the Epiphany,[8] I was in a state of recollection after having taken communion. I do not know whether these are tricks of the big-footed one,[9] or from my head, but I recalled María Bran, a slave of the convent who had died suddenly some fourteen years ago: one of the things most forgotten for me in this world. At the same time, I saw her in a priest's alb,[10] the whitest of whites, beautifully embellished and gathered together with a short cord with elegant tassels. She also wore a crown of flowers on her head. The celestial beings arranged for me to see her from the back, although I could still see her face and she was quite lovely, and her face a resplendent black. I said, "How is it that such a good black woman, who had been neither a thief nor liar, had spent so much time in purgatory?" She said she had gone there because of her character, and because she slept and ate at the improper time. Although she had been there a long time, her punishment had been mild. She was very thankful to God, who with His divine providence had taken her from her land and brought her down such difficult and rugged roads in order to become a Christian and be saved. I asked whether black women went to heaven and she said if they were thankful (8v)[11] and heeded His beneficence, and thanked Him for it. They were saved because of His great mercy. When I ask these questions I do not do so because I want to but, just as I soon as I see them, they speak to me without my wishing it to happen, and they make me speak without wanting to. I need for them to commend me to God because all this torments me. She also told me that I should thank God for the gifts He had given her, and although I thought she went to heaven, I could not be certain.

I am burdened by a terrible temptation. When I run into the nuns, I want to bury myself so that they do not see me. On my way to the choir, I encountered a circle of nuns standing there, and so-and-so among them.[12] As I passed by, she said, "Is there anyone in this house who performs miracles?" I felt like dropping dead on the spot. Distraught, I went to God, as He knows. "Why did you allow this to happen, my Lord—what is it in me that they say

---

7. Reproduced by permission from Ursula de Jesús, *The Souls of Purgatory*, edited by Nancy E. van Deusen: 80, 82–85, 87–88, 90–92. The editors have preserved the capitalization, punctuation, and translation rules of the original published text and notes in this selection.
8. 6 January.
9. This is a reference to Satan and is used throughout the text.
10. The alb is the vestment priests wore to say mass. (*DA*, 1: 161). (Real Academia Española. *Diccionario de autoridades*. Vol. 1. Facsimile, Madrid: Gredos, 1963, henceforth *DA* —Eds.)
11. These page numbers, which van Deusen includes in her translation, refer to the pages from Úrsula's diary (—Eds.)
12. So-and-so is a translation of the term, *fulana*, often used to avoid naming someone.

such things?" I was so bereft that my heart would not stop pounding in my chest. *Pay no attention to this, leave it to Me. They called Me a trickster and imposter, and they did not believe me, even when I was afflicted. And there, at the end when I was dying, they said it again. What you now ask is more difficult than if two hundred men wished to move a mountain from one place to another by their own might, without it being my will.* Later, I had the opportunity to climb up to a lofty cell and from there I saw a mountain. What the voices had said to me, here inside myself, now happened. *Even if they were one thousand, or even more.* I looked again at the other side, and there I saw the San Cristóbal Mountain.[13] Within myself, the voices explained that even if they were many, without the will of God, they could do nothing. I forgot to mention that Christ told me not to fear this deceiver; he had no more power than that which they wished to give him.

10.2 Excerpt Two

Monday, as soon as I had gone to the choir and prostrated myself before the Lord, I saw two black women below the earth. In an instant, they were beside me. One of them said to me, "I am Lusia, the one who served Ana de San Joseph, and I have been in purgatory for this long, only because the great merciful God showed compassion toward me.[14] No one remembers me." Very slowly, she spoke of God's goodness, power, and mercy, and how we should love and serve Him. Lusia had served this community in good faith, but sometimes they had accused her of certain things, and at times she suffered her penance where she tended to cook. For the love of God, would Ursula please commend her spirit to God. Before Lusia died, she had endured awful hardships, and because of them they had discounted much of the punishment. This is all mixed up, as I remember it. She spoke at length, and her appearance corresponded to the way she looked while living. I did not know who the other dead black woman was. On another day, in the morning, Lusia returned with the same demand and requested the same for doña Polonia de Moya.[15] She said doña Polonia had endured terrible suffering and had no one who would remember her, and I thought I saw her there. I said to God

---

13. San Cristóbal Mountain is visible from the convent of Santa Clara.

14. Ana de San Joseph was elected interim *vicaria* (assistant abbess) in 1650, while the conventual election was pending. See "Auto Arzobispal," 1650. (Archivo Arzobispal de Lima [AAL], Convent of Santa Clara [SC], 9: 6, —Eds.) The word *caridad* can be translated as "love," "compassion," or "charity" (*DA*, 2: 309.)

15. Doña Apolonia de Moya appears in two documents related to a dispute over the sale of her cell. It is probably the same person (see "Autos que sigue Francisca de Aliaga . . . contra

that if He sent the suffering, I would commend them to Him and offer whatever I could for them and for that friar, who almost always appears before me. On one of these days, the friar told me that what a community did together for a soul was great, and worth more than when it was done for many souls, because then, only a little went for each one. I see that the flames do not come out of the top of her head as they did before, now they only reach to the middle of her forehead. I do not know whether this is the chicanery of that trickster.[16]

Another time, the *morena* [black woman] Lusia returned with the nun, doña Polonia saying that I should ask the Father in the name of the Incarnation of his Son on their behalf—I said, "In the name of the Incarnation?" and the Angolan woman said, "Yes, in the name of the Incarnation." She explained, "Had He not become flesh, been born, suffered, and died for our redemption?" I saw the nun with that peculiar eye that looked as though it would burst.

Thursday, at times I would like to know how the nun, doña Mariana Machuca, is.[17] While having this temptation, I asked my Lord Jesus to guide me so that I would no longer have it and would do only what He wished. Today, while I was where I usually am, a desire swept over me. I resisted it as much as possible, because I do not know whether these are contrivances of that one [the devil]. I saw her in purgatory, in the same way as she was here: seated on her chair with her cane held close to her. I wondered, "In purgatory? How can such a saintly person be there?" The voices said that she was there, purging herself, and that *it is worthwhile for the living to mortify themselves in many ways, although they live as though they had not done that. They see and hear as though they cannot hear or see, and in this manner, many things are not the way they really are.* The voices said, *that in order not to sin they avoided certain things, so as not to be punished when they deserved it, or they let obligatory matters slide. All these were the devil's tricks. No matter what, one should never stop fulfilling one's duties. God's creatures will not be left without receiving the proper discipline, because that might be the cause of their perdition. They are redeemed with the blood of our Lord, Jesus Christ.* I do not know how to describe what happened there. The punishment doña Mariana experienced was minimal, and that children also pass through the fire, and that on the day

---

Apolonia de Moya," 1639–44, AAL, SC, 6:41; and "Autos que sigue Francisca de Aliaga," 1642–44, SC, 7:20.)

16. Another reference to the devil.

17. Mariana de Machuca spent thirty years as a nun in Santa Clara and died on 8 September 1630 (Córdova y Salinas, *Crónica*, 904) [Diego de Córdova y Salinas, *Crónica franciscana de las Provincias del Perú*, 1651. Reprint, Lino G. Canedo, ed. (Washington, DC: Academy of American Franciscan History, 1957), 904. —Eds.]

of the Incarnation she will go to heaven. This is written the way I remember it, in bits and pieces. God only knows what it is; I pay no heed.

Friday, I have the nerve to say, "My Lord Jesus, and there, have they heeded this?" Because I said this, the voices repeated what they had said before, saying *My good Jesus.* I said, "I should say, 'My Lord, Jesus Christ.'" They said it is important for a child to treat his parent with love and reverence. Later, near the end, I see her[18] on her deathbed, with large candles, and all the other things they place on the dead. This must be a trick of that devil.

Later, in the evening, while in my bed and praying to God with my eyes closed, Cecilia appeared in front of me. I was so terribly frightened that I began shaking like someone poisoned by mercury. Wherever I turned she appeared before me, in the same way and dressed in the same manner as when she was alive. She was an Indian donada who had died some years ago.

Saturday afternoon, on the day of San Marcelo,[19] I was praying the entire rosary, and the voices told me to meditate upon when they took my Lord down from the cross and the intolerable pain and agony He suffered there. I should consider that the Lord had suffered all He had suffered from the moment He entered this world solely for our salvation and redemption, and He had done it all because of His eternal Father's (10r) will. If His Father willed Him to be born, He said, "Thy will be done"; if He willed Him to suffer, "Thy will be done"; if He willed Him to die, "Thy will be done," all in such a way that He followed the will of God in everything. I said I did not wish to see or hear anything. I want to get up now and leave here. My Lord Jesus was our teacher from whom we should learn obedience, humility, and all the other virtues. I should recognize that I am nothing, a worm, and deserved only hell. Only because of God's goodness and love did I receive his beneficence. I should be extremely grateful for these gifts and worship my Lord with the same reverence and love with which the angels adored Him in the manger, on the cross, and in the tomb. I should also ponder how, because of God's will, He had moved that tremendous slab away from the tomb. At that moment, within myself I had the desire to understand how they had carried my Lord to the sepulcher. They explained that, it happened in the same way that I see them carry the most Holy Body in the procession on the Friday of Holy Week, and in the same manner that the venerable men, accompanied by angels, went along singing. I do not know how to describe what happened there. Afterward, I offered three

---

18. I was unable to understand what *la sid* referred to in the document.
19. 16 January.

decades of my rosary for each soul,[20] most of them clerics and friars outside the convent. In a chastising tone, the voices said, that with so many in the house for whom I could plead or offer prayers, why did I look for those outside, naming so-and-so, whom I had named in my prayers. While saying this, a throng of nuns came out from under the earth, and two by two they came by way of that deep place from the area near the kitchen. First, there was doña Teresa, looking very well, with her wimple beneath the habit very white. I recognized some of the nuns who had died more than twenty-four years ago. They all came with their veils covering their faces; only Teresa was unveiled. I recognized a Beatris, two Juanas, and another named Mensia. I was astonished that they had been in purgatory for such a long time. They said, "Does that frighten you? We have been there since the days of Saldaña."[21] I asked after a few nuns, particularly doña Ana Delgado.[22] The voices told me that she was in heaven. I asked after another whom I won't name, and they responded that from the moment she died, terribly burdened, she had descended into hell. They awaited her there, with terrible cauldrons, where she will remain forever. They named the sins she had committed that condemned her and for which she had never asked forgiveness. Although she was always taking pleasure from her vices, she suffered from some of them. If, as she lay dying, she had asked for forgiveness, God, in His goodness would have pardoned her. She did not do that, though, and I should see the harm caused by living carelessly and allowing oneself to be carried away by the appetite. This taught me a lot about the importance of spiritual exercises and that in this house the one sin that displeases God, our father Saint Francis, and our mother Saint Clare greatly, are the friendships. What happened there I am unable to say, but I was dumbstruck by it all, and for having asked after the one who is so far beyond my (10v) recall. They make me ask against my will, and I do not even know who speaks to me, and I afraid that someone undesirable will respond. If it were up to me, I would ask after other, very different dead souls. In that same procession I also saw a black woman named Lusia off to one side. I asked if black women also went there, and they responded, *Yes, they remain separated to one side, and everything there occurs in great concord.* On Sunday, while in

---

20. The rosary was divided into three groups of ten beads each.

21. Francisco de Saldaña was a wealthy Portuguese man who donated his estate to the foundation of the convent of Santa Clara. The four foundresses were Justina de Guevara, Ana de Illescas, Barbola (or Bartola) de la Vega, and Isabel de la Fuente.

22. In 1620, Ana Delgado, (in the convent, Ana de Jesús), an aristocratic married woman, decided, along with two of her daughters to become nuns. Popular among the community, she was known for her humility, ecstatic raptures, and rigorous disciplines. After fifteen years as a *clarisa* (a nun of the order of Saint Clare —Eds.), she died on 29 November 1635, Córdova y Salinas, *Crónica*, 900.

a meditative trance pondering what had happened, I saw doña Teresa in a very well lit place. She looked happy, and her face was well covered with a pristine wimple; her veil was very long. It seemed that she only suffered now because she could not see God. I asked myself, "Does purgatory have cavities?" The voices said, *Yes, and that specific sins brought specific punishments. Those punished in the cavities received the same torture as those in hell. That well where I saw Alfonsa was where they went when they had committed a mortal sin. Although they asked for forgiveness, confessed their sins, and were forgiven, they still went there to be purged. In order to go to heaven they had to be purer than one thousand crystals. Those wishing to please God were fearful and careful not to offend Him and asked forgiveness. Those are the ones who are like doña Teresa. If they are miserable, wretched, and fall into mortal sin, they should ask God for forgiveness: if they are truly remorseful for having offended Him. They can then be certain that this is what the blood of our Lord Jesus Christ is for and offer it to the eternal Father for all He suffered.* This was an important lesson. I do not know how to describe what happened there. May God be with me and free me from all evil. Everything torments me.

On Tuesday while doing my spiritual exercises, I saw that wretched one they told me about the other day, a thousand depths below. She was in that wretched place, lying flat on her back on something like a barbecue, surrounded by many demons who tormented her. Flames came out her mouth, eyes, and ears, just as when flames burst from a firework that is not allowed to leave the ground. She had that noise in her head, and they touched her head, using a thousand different methods of torture. Others came and placed horrible pieces of iron around her feet. The voices said, *See, this is how the indulgent and lazy ones live. They turn their backs on everything and pay attention to nothing. They do not fear God, but only feed their appetites, spending their time jeering and causing a ruckus. God offers them the help they need.* In speaking of the woman who was standing there, God said that He had provided her with memory, understanding and will so that she could make the appropriate choice. She had chosen that life, in spite of the confessors, preachers, the inspirations, and books. Our Lord Jesus Christ said, *Be vigilant and pray in order to avoid temptation. She had made that choice and fallen into temptation.* Everything goes to bits and pieces as I recall it. It is amazing how everything there is said harmoniously, (11r) and in such an orderly manner. When I leave that place I feel so confused, wondering why they come to me with such things, me, a poor little woman who means nothing, what use am I? Sometimes I want to get up and run from there. I already told God that He knows very well I want nothing more than to please Him. I do not come here because I want them to speak to me, and the same with the visions. The voices also told me that when I see someone in that way, I should counsel her gently for her good.

10.3 Excerpt Three

Another evening, I went to the choir. I was so tired I could not help but fall asleep. I said to my Lord, "I am going to go now because I cannot go on." It must have been divine providence, because I chanced upon a very sick woman who called me and asked me to light a candle and the charcoal and do a few other things and to summon a nun to help cure her, which is something the sister usually did. The nun responded to me very disagreeably, saying she was too tired, that the sick woman was too much trouble, and that she had already fulfilled her duties. I returned to the sick woman saying I had already called the sister. She took so long in coming that the sick woman asked me to summon her again, but once again the nun told me she did not wish to go. I told the sick woman that she was not going to come and that she should order me to do what I could. For better or worse, I would take care of her needs as best I could. When it was very late, and the night nearly over, the sister said, "I have been unable to sleep all night out of guilt because I did not help the sick woman." I went to the choir, and I don't know who it was who started speaking about how she was enjoying Christ's glory and how He left it for us and He came and suffered terribly throughout his life to redeem us and set a good example. For all that, we never failed to forget His kindness, and that He raised and redeemed us with such great effort. In this way she referred to the favors He had done and continues to do. Afterward, the voices told me to say, "I thank you, my Lord, because you made me a Christian. I thank you a thousand times over for bringing me to your house, one hundred million times for the blessed sacraments you sent for our benefit, one hundred million times because you wanted us to receive them today." In this way they referred to the many favors and how we should give thanks for them. They told me how often for each of them and how much evil they have saved me from, how much I deserved to be in hell, and how I should give thanks to God for this.

(12v) Another time, after I had taken communion the voices told me to commend the spirit of a black woman to God. She had been in the convent, and had been taken out to be cured because she was gravely ill, but died a few days later. This had happened more than thirty years ago, and I had forgotten about her as if she had never existed. I was frightened and thought to myself, "So long in purgatory?" The voices responded, *For the things she did.* Here, the voices led me to understand that she had illicitly loved a nun and the entire convent knew about it, but that my father, Saint Francis, and my mother, Saint Clare had gotten down on their knees and prayed to our Lady to secure the salvation of that soul from her Son. That is because she had served his house in good faith. Later, almost in front of me, I saw a crown of large thorns being lowered from heaven, suspended by a ribbon. I could not tell how many there were, maybe sixty or so. Within two days, I saw the morena again in that same corner, somewhat distant, like the first time I had seen her there. Then the voices told me that she did her penance in the old dormitory, and I now saw her in her human form, wearing a green skirt and a head scarf. The morena explained that she was there because of the tremendous mercy God had shown her and that our father, Saint Francis, and our mother, Saint Clare, had gotten down on their knees on her behalf. I asked her, not because I wanted to, but because they make me. Within myself, I asked, "How, and why so much time in purgatory?" She told me that God loves his wives[23] so much that when He sees them fail to carry out their duties, He feels it deeply, just as husbands do when their wives are unfaithful. God, who raised and redeemed us, is so beneficent. So much happened there that is incomprehensible.

10.4 Excerpt Four

On Holy Wednesday, I awakened before dawn at three with such a terrible fright that the bed and I both shook uncontrollably. God was very merciful toward me so that my screams did not knock down that room. I had begun feeling the same fear the day before because of a black woman from the convent who had died without receiving confession. Because she was sick they had taken her to a farm to see whether she might recover in a different climate, but as I said, she died. She told me that at that time of night she had so much to do because when she was a cook and baker she was made to work very hard, and the señora abbess could have corrected that problem. Later, I went to the choir during the hour when everyone went to the kitchen. When I prostrated myself I saw a crucified Christ. From the wound on his side a stream of the purest blood poured out, which then merged with the blood from the wounds on his feet. A thicker, more powerful stream was created from them. When some arrived, the blood fell on them, and when they left, others appeared. The voices explained that *This was a sea that would never run dry and it would last until the end of the world. Consider this: if everyone in the world took water from the sea would it run dry? In the same way, this sea would never run dry.* Who can say what happened there? I was in a state of shock, crossing myself again and again.

---

23. When a novice took her vows and became a nun, she literally became a bride of Christ.

(14r) On Thursday of Holy Week, I had spent the entire night in front of the holy altar without being able to do anything but sleep. At dawn, I said to the Lord, "Hello. I have been lazy all night long." The voices said that I would see what I could do and a weak nature needs to rest. The entire night before I had prepared the food for this day in the convent. The voices said, *Why does that cooking matter to you? What matters is that you should look toward God. What matters is whether He looks or does not look at us. Look at what you accomplished during the night.* Then the celestial being repeated, *If I had a friend and I saw him working* [det][24] *and in danger of dying and then he recovered, I could leave him, but if he did not and I left, the friend would have reason to complain for the rest of his life.* I have forgotten much of what happened because a long time has passed and I am not going to write it down. I am not being conscientious.

On the second day of Easter, while pondering the wounds of my Lord, I told Him to take away these illusions. I asked the Father, and the voices told me that I should confide in Him and to ponder the glory of His resurrection and that all that He as God had done to enter paradise. What was it for? He did not need it, save to teach others what they should do to enjoy his Father's paradise. What would become of us if He had not suffered? Something came over me, and it felt like my heart would burst in my body. They taught me so many beneficial things, and I said to myself, "Would the enemy say such good things to me?" Then I turned back to God and said, "How can I believe it is you speaking to me, Lord? My God, I am nothing, of no use, do not allow me to have illusions from the devil. I come directly to you with the desire to please and love you. I have no other father, god, or teacher." Here he told me—after other things I do not recall—*Have you heard it said, when people affirm something, "By the Royal Crown"? So He says, "By His wounds."* I do not know how to recount what happened there. In the afternoon I left the kitchen for a short time. When I returned, I chanced upon a companion who was angry that another cook, whom they assigned to work for a month, ate too much. I simply said to her, "One pot of food at midday and another in the evening." Still, she remained angry. Each time I see her do it I have to stop her. In the evening, I went to the choir and just as I prostrated myself before the Lord, the voices said, "Why had I said that about so-and-so, mentioning her by name. Would I want them to say that about me?" I said to myself, "The nuns were saying it," but the voices said, *Let them say it, but you confirm it by repeating it. This came from the devil because it was gossip. You know that you must speak to her in a kind manner and use words that do not anger her. If she does not correct her behavior, do not torture yourself, leave it to*

---

24. The text is deteriorated here. (—Eds.)

me. For my part, when I was in the world they said many things to me, and I remained silent. I was frightened. These are just bits.

On the third day of Easter a mulata entered the kitchen. She was upset because each time her owner's mother came she mistreated and chastised her, lying to her daughter about her. On the contrary, she felt she did all she could to please them. During the siesta, I went to the choir and said to my Lord God, "Are you not God, the Father of mercy? Why do you not alleviate the suffering of this poor, disconsolate woman?" The voices said to me, *I am pleased when some suffer from what others do to them.* With this response, I desisted.

Suggested Reading

Bristol, Joan Cameron. *Christians, Blasphemers, and Witches: Afro-Mexican Ritual Practice in the Seventeenth Century.* Albuquerque: University of New Mexico Press, 2007.

Jaffary, Nora E. *False Mystics: Deviant Orthodoxy in Colonial Mexico.* Lincoln: University of Nebraska Press, 2004.

Jesús, Ursula de, and Nancy E. van Deusen, *The Souls of Purgatory: The Spiritual Diary of a Seventeenth-Century Afro-Peruvian Mystic, Ursula de Jesús.* Albuquerque: University of New Mexico Press, 2004.

Myers, Kathleen Ann. *Neither Saints nor Sinners: Writing the Lives of Women in Spanish America.* New York: Oxford University Press, 2003.

Document Themes

- Race and ethnicity
- Religion

11

Isabel Hernández, Midwife and Healer, Appears before the Inquisition (Mexico, 1652)

Isabel Hernández, a *mestiza* (person of indigenous and European parentage) midwife and *curandera* (healer) of humble means appeared before Mexico City's inquisitorial tribunal in the spring of 1652 to answer to allegations that she was a *hechicera* or witch. This charge, although not considered a heresy, was one the Mexican tribunal of the Holy Office investigated with considerable frequency.[1] Along with helping their clients with medical problems, *hechiceras* were often accused of using "love magic" to secure the exclusive devotion of an existent lover or to attract the interest of a new one.[2] As was the case with Hernández, many of the practices that both colonial populations and the Inquisition associated with witchcraft were linked to indigenous religious or medical practices, even though the practitioners themselves were not always indigenous. At the time of the foundation of the three New World courts of the Inquisition in Mexico City and Lima (1570), and in Cartagena (1610), the Habsburg king Philip II removed Latin America's indigenous population from the jurisdiction of the tribunal, in part as a response to the wave of popular protests that swept through Mexico following the brutal execution by public burning that the Franciscan Order had sentenced a Nahua *cacique* (hereditary indigenous chieftain) in Texcoco, *don* (sir) Carlos Ometochtzin, in 1539. As a *mestiza,* Hernández was a colonial subject who, like all Spaniards, mixed-race people, and Africans, fell within the jurisdiction of the Inquisition.

Her trial followed the standard process by which the inquisition operated: a denunciation, the defendant's imprisonment, the court's seizure of the defendant's possessions, and his or her initial interrogation before the court. The

---

1. Solange Alberro, *Inquisición y sociedad en México, 1571–1700* (México: Fondo de Cultura Económica, 1988), 205, found that 18.8 percent of the cases opened by the court for the period between 1571 and 1700 were for charges of "magic and witchcraft."
2. Although courts of the Inquisition sometimes charged men with witchcraft, the majority of the accused were women. For example, of sixty accused witches in Lima between 1650 and 1700, 82 percent were women. Lee M. Penyak and Walter J. Petry, eds., *Religion and Society in Latin America: Interpretive Essays from Conquest to Present* (New York: Orbis Books, 2009), 129–30.

court then urged the defendant to tell the truth in three formal admonishments. This was followed by the collection of testimony from relevant witnesses, a formal accusation (sometimes preceded by the considered written assessment by the court's theological qualifiers), and the defendant's responses to these charges. Witnesses' testimony was then communicated in an anonymous fashion to the defendant, who again responded to any new evidence presented. Cases concluded with the inquisitors' judgment and sentence.

Hernández's five-month-long inquisition trial, several passages of which are excerpted here, includes fascinating details about several matters: her work as a health-care provider, the community networks that existed between different residents of city of Tlaxcala where she lived, and elements of the operation of the court of the Holy Office itself. While many of her denouncers focused on allegations of her engagement in "love magic," in Hernández's own confessions, as the following passages indicate, she focused more on descriptions of her work as a midwife.[3] She provided a detailed confession to the court, for instance, of her assistance to one woman pregnant with an undesired (and unacknowledged) child. Hernández does not explicitly indicate in her testimony if the baby was stillborn or whether she played a role in ensuring its demise. The newborn simply disappears from her description. It is likely that she had facilitated the woman's miscarriage by giving her a dose of *cihuapatli* (the aster flower), identified by Francisco Hernández, the celebrated sixteenth-century naturalist, as an effective producer of contractions either at or before the full term of pregnancy.[4] This was one of the many plants the inquisitors' officers found in Hernández's lodgings, which when asked to identify, she merely acknowledged that it was "to give to women in labor." Interestingly, the court did not pursue the discussion of the details of the pregnant woman's experience, or the outcome of the fetus she was carrying, beyond Hernández's vague description. Charges of inducing a miscarriage did not appear among the list of formal charges that the court included in its formal accusation against Hernández.

Two witnesses had originally denounced Hernández to the tribunal two years before the court pursued its investigation of her for having offered to provide them with powders that they might use to control the *rigida condición* (strict or controlling nature) of their husbands. We cannot discern definitively from the documents if by employing this phrase, Hernández's denouncers

---

3. For a discussion of inquisitorial accusations of women's engagement in "love magic" see Ruth Behar, "Sexual Witchcraft, Colonialism, and Women's Powers: Views from the Mexican Inquisition," in *Sexuality and Marriage in Colonial Latin America,* ed. Asunción Lavrin (Lincoln: University of Nebraska Press, 1989), 178–206.

4. For more on *cihuapatli*'s usage in colonial Mexico, see Nora E. Jaffary, *Reproduction and Its Discontents in Mexico: Childbirth and Contraception from 1750 to 1905* (Chapel Hill: University of North Carolina Press, 2016), 80–84, 179.

were using a euphemism for physical abuse or if they were instead describing either the jealousy or perhaps emotional aloofness of their husbands. Women who appeared before colonial tribunals (including in Bárbara López's case found in Chapter 8), often used explicit language to describe the violent acts of their husbands, so it is possible the women who denounced Hernández were referring to the emotional rather than the physical behavior of their husbands.

Besides the occasionally perplexing language, readers will be confronted with various other curious elements of Hernández's trial. The first two witnesses who denounced the midwife in 1650 both declared that they were prompted to act only after a delay of twenty years.[5] Neither witness provided plausible explanations for the lengthy delay, nor did the court's officials question them about it. The first witness, Inés de Herrera, opened her statement by asserting that she had been prompted to come forward having heard the Inquisition's "Edict of the Faith," a text describing the heretical practices about which Catholic subjects should be vigilant against, read aloud one month earlier in her parish church. By the seventeenth century, the Mexican Inquisition had ordered that the general edict of the faith should be read out publicly on one of the Sundays of Lent each year in New Spain's cities and towns.[6] Herrera claimed that upon hearing the Edict, she had recalled Hernández's offers, twenty years earlier, to provide Herrera and some companions with powders and medicines they might use to attract and repel men's romantic attention. The second witness, Catalina de Herrera, presumably the mother of Inés, provided much the same information.[7]

We cannot know whether the *comisario* (inquisitorial agent and acting judge) in Tlaxcala or the women's parish priest had simply neglected, in contravention of the Holy Office's requirements, to regularly publish the Edict of Faith to their communities for two decades. Possibly, this is what happened, and that it was only upon first hearing the Edict—two decades after the fact—that both women immediately recalled Hernández's suspicious acts. It is also possible, and perhaps more probable, that the Herrera women, had sat through several annual readings of the Edict but had not had any motive to denounce Hernández until some other (unacknowledged) incident, prompted them to act. This seems a likely scenario because using the courts for "paying off old scores" was a practice that Henry Kamen describes as the rule rather than the exception in the generation of inquisitorial cases.[8]

---

5. This type of delay was not unusual in Inquisition trials where denouncers and witnesses often gave evidence about events that had occurred decades earlier.

6. John F. Chuchiak IV, ed., *The Inquisition in New Spain, 1536–1820: A Documentary History* (Baltimore, MD: Johns Hopkins University Press, 2012), 107.

7. AGN, Inquisición, vol. 561, exp. 6, fol. 530.

8. Henry Kamen, *The Spanish Inquisition: A Historical Revision* (New Haven, CT: Yale University Press, 2014), 229.

It is certainly an interpretation that Hernández herself supported, possibly having been prompted to do so by her appointed legal counsel.

Beyond considering the motivations for Hernández's initial two denouncers, details of the timing of Hernández's trial also allow readers to draw conclusions about the motivations of many of the witnesses who appeared before the Inquisition to denounce accused parties. The Inquisition prided itself on the secrecy of its proceedings; defendants were placed in its "secret cells" during their trials, and were enjoined to maintain absolute secrecy about their cases during and after their hearings. All identifying information was struck from denouncers' testimony before it was read to defendants so that they would be, theoretically, unable to decipher who had testified against them. In Hernández's case, how secretly does the court appear to have actually operated? Why might the witnesses who appeared in her case have been prompted to detail their interactions with the *curandera* and midwife to the court? Inquisition trials, when read carefully, can provide us with evidence about the religious and social lives of those whom the court investigated, but they are even more revealing of the preoccupations and anxieties of denouncers, witnesses, and the prosecuting bodies themselves. How do Hernández's peers and clients of various class positions seem to have viewed her? What acts or ideas with which she was charged does the court seem to have been most and least concerned with in its investigation of Hernández? We know that indigenous people existed beyond the institutional jurisdiction of the Inquisition, yet do you see evidence of how indigenous people nevertheless figured in inquisition trials?

11.1 The Trial of Isabel Hernández[9]

[Isabel Hernández's case opens with a title page indicating that in 1652, the court of the Holy Office charged Isabel Hernández with hechicería. *The court identified Hernández as a midwife and* curandera, *a widow, native of the town of Gueichiapa, but resident in Tlaxcala. The title page also indicates that Hernández's defense lawyer was one don* Juan García de Palacios *and that the trial had reached a conclusion after moving through the standard stages of an inquisitorial investigation. The following ecclesiastical personnel conducted Hernández's investigation. Inquisitors: Doctor don* Francisco de Estrada y Escovedo, *don* Juan Saenz de Mañozca, *and don* Bernabe de la Higuera y Amarilla; *the acting* fiscal *(prosecutor) was señor (sir)* licenciado *(licentiate)* Thomas López de Erenchum.]*

---

9. Archivo General de la Nación, México, Inquisición, vol. 561, exp. 6, fols. 525–82.

11.2 Denunciation of Isabel Hernández by Inés de Herrera

[*Left margin:* Inés de Herrera, forty-five years old against Isabel Hernández, widow, *vecina* (citizen) of the city of Tlaxcala, midwife and healer concerning spells.]

In the city of Tlaxcala on Monday June 20, 1650 at three in the afternoon more or less, before the *Señor licenciado* Antonio González Lasso, *cura beneficiado* (ordained priest) of His Majesty for this city and *juez comisario* (judge) of the Holy Office of this kingdom for the illustrious inquisitors, appeared Inés Herrera, widow of Hernando Alonso Cardoso, deceased, *vecina* of this city and owner of a *hacienda* (estate) in Hueyotlipan in this province.[10] She said she is aged forty-five and stated that on the day of the Incarnation, May 25 of this year, she entered the parochial church of the Glorious Saint Joseph in this city at the time of the publication of the Edict of the Holy Faith, and having heard in it that which concerns heresies and sinful states, she came to give an account of a certain declaration that she had attempted to make but then suspended because of the activities of Lent and Holy Week and she was ordered to appear today in fulfillment of which order she appears to make her declaration. The *señor comisario* made her swear the oath and Inés de Herrera swore to God our Lord and made the sign of the Holy Cross and promised to tell the truth.

She said that that twenty years ago, more or less, she was at the *hacienda* of Hueyotlipan with Hernando Alonso, her husband, and she had communication and friendship with Isabel Hernández who then was married and is now a widow and lives in this city where she practices the office of midwifery and healer. And this declarant told [Hernández] in friendship, about how Hernando Alonso was a person *de rigida condición* (with a controlling nature) and that she was considering accepting the favors of another man who was interested in her but that she did not dare to do so because of her husband because she was very afraid of him. Isabel Hernández responded that she should not worry about her husband, that she would give her something to remove the *mala condición* (undesirable nature) of her husband and that she should accept the favors of this man. To this she replied that if this man had another woman how would it be possible to accept this? To which Isabel Hernández replied that she would give her some powders which she did, and they were white and she told her to sprinkle them on his cloak, shirt, and other clothing and that after this he would die only for this declarant and for no other person. And then she received the powders and kept them, and eight days later she went to take confession and she was dissuaded from confessing

---

10. The text reads "*hacienda de lavor en el partido de Gueyotlipa*," a working estate in the region of Hueyotlipan, a municipality in the present-day state of Tlaxcala.

about them but she had not used them in any way on this man or on any other person although many times Isabel Hernández asked her if she had used the powders. And that about a year after this happened, this declarant was bathing with Isabel Hernández and another woman in a *temascal*[11] on the estate and Isabel Hernández saw a frog jumping and she secretly said to this declarant: "*If you grab that frog and strangle it I will make you some powders so that any man you like will die for you.*" To which this declarant replied that [Isabel] should strangle the frog herself and Isabel replied that for the spell to work, she would have to do it which she did not want to do and never tried it. She does not know if Isabel Hernández has used these things on anybody else and she never spoken one word about them nor has she had any further communication with her. And she says this is the truth under oath, and having read the declaration to her she said it was well written and that she had not said it for malice and since she does not know how to write she does not sign it and the *comisario* signed it for her.

[signature] Antonio Gonzales Lazo

Before me, Christobal de Ordaniuis notary. [*Herrera ratified her testimony two days later.*]

[*Catalina de Herrera, sixty-year old mother of Inés de Herrera also denounced Hernández to the court. Like her daughter, she, too claimed to have been prompted to do so by her recent hearing of the Edict of the Faith, and, like her daughter, testified that Isabel Hernández had offered to provide herbal cures to help women ameliorate the severe nature of their husbands.*

On February 22, 1652, nearly two years after both women had given their testimony, Inquisitors don Francisco de Estrada y Escobedo, don Juan Saenz de Mañorca, and licenciado don Bernave de la Higuera y Amarilla ordered Hernández imprisoned in the secret cells of the Inquisition and her case pursued.

The court's comisario and bailiff seized Hernández's personal goods from her residence and sold them in a public auction to pay for the expenses of housing and feeding Hernández while she was in the court's custody. Her belongings included clothing and textiles, dishes, religious items, and medicinal substances, the latter two which were submitted to the central court of the Inquisition for further examination.

The comisario then named a guard, Pedro Álvarez, a barber who was a resident of Tlaxcala, to accompany Hernández on her journey to the Mexican]

---

11. Mexican midwives and healers used *temascales*, "houses of heat," or sweathouses since the pre-Columbian period to cure various illnesses and maintain good health.

capital. The comisario *used the money from the sale of Hernández's goods to pay for the rent of a mule needed for the transport, for the labor of the Indian who accompanied them, and for Hernández's food.]*

11.3 A Further Denunciation

[Comisario González Lasio wrote the Mexico City Inquisitors shortly after sending Isabel Hernández in to the Inquisition's secret prison.]

After having remitted Isabel Hernández to the Holy Tribunal, a principal *doncella* (respectable lady) of this town called *doña* Beatriz de Nara y de la Mota called me in church and told me that it had caused her great scruples that she had forgotten to declare that Isabel Hernández, having shrouded her mother for burial had taken her teeth from her mouth telling two boys and a woman who accompanied her that she wanted them because they were relics because the deceased was a saint.[12] I advise you so that your orders can be served. The carrier brings the mattress or pallet of Isabel Hernández. May our lord keep you joyful for the good of Christianity. Tlaxcala May 20 1652.

[The court ordered González Lasio to formally interrogate Nara y de la Mota, and the comisario *also reported that he was sending in some objects for their examination including some bones, powders, hairs, and a monkey's hand. He also informed the court that after Hernández's imprisonment, he had overhead a conversation of three men, one of whom had commented that when* don *Diego de Villegas was governor of the district of Tlaxcala, Isabel Hernández had acted as his bawd, and that she had supplied powders to Villegas that he could use to make women enamored of him. Finally,* comisario *González Lasio reported that several other witnesses had come forward to denounce Hernández. One, Antonio de Lepe had informed the* comisario *that Hernández had supplied women in labor with the "egg of the Ascension" to aid their deliveries; another declared that Hernández had supplied her with powders to rid her husband's "mala condición" which had made him very ill. Others recounted the story of Hernández removing the teeth from the corpse of a dead woman whom she believed was a saint. As instructed by the court, the* comisario *interviewed all these witnesses. What follows is one of these interviews.]*

---

12. Underlining in the original.

11.4 Mariana de Alfaro Denounces Isabel Hernández

In the city of Tlaxcala on May 25, 1652 at 10 a.m. before the *comisario* appeared Mariana de Alfaro, without being called, the legitimate wife of Joseph de Riguen, age thirty-one, and *vecina* of this city and she swore to tell the truth and said that to unburden her conscience she denounced Isabel Hernández, widow, midwife, and *curandera* who lives in this city. Two-and-a-half years ago the declarant told Isabel Hernández about the hardships she suffered because of the *mala condición* of her husband when the two of them were alone, and then she learned that her husband was having an affair, which was the reason why she was enduring a *mala vida*. Isabel Hernández said that she should arrange to keep her eye on the woman [with whom her husband was involved] who was called Úrsula, who was of the *mulata* (person of mixed African and Spanish parentage) nation, and that when she went to the *corral* (farmyard) to perform her necessities, that [Alfaro] should collect some of her excrement or filth and put it to dry in the sun. And when it was dry, she should mix it up with some yellow worms that appeared when it was damp and mix it with a little fragrant water and all this mixed up she should give to her husband to drink in his chocolate and that with this, she would get rid of his lover, and that she had seen this done to a woman in Mexico, although she did not say the name of this woman. The declarant said to Isabel Hernández that she would not do this because it must be a great sin to which Isabel Hernández replied that it was not a sin because its purpose was to secure her husband and this is where the conversation ended. And later, on different occasions, Isabel Hernández asked her why did she not use the remedy and that she was to blame for her *mala vida* since she had the remedy available, but she never wanted to use it because she understood it to be a grave sin and she forgot about it. And although she heard the Edict of the Faith read, she never remembered this and now and when she learned that Isabel Hernández had been imprisoned by the Holy Tribunal it came to her memory and she declares it so. She does this to unburden her conscience and this is the truth by virtue of the oath that she has made. And when it was read to her, she said it was well written and said that she did not act out of malice. She promised secrecy and did not sign because she did not know how to do so. The *comisario* signed for her.

[signature] Antonio Gonzáles Laso
Before me, Christobal de Ordaniuis, notary

11.5 Isabel Hernández's First Appearance before the Inquisition

In the city of Mexico, on Wednesday May 22, 1652 in the afternoon audience before inquisitors doctors *don* Francisco de Estrada y Escovedo, *don* Juan Saenz de Mañorca, and *licenciado don* Bernabe de la Higuera y Amarillo. They commanded to be brought before them a woman who has been imprisoned in the secret cells of the Holy Office and she received the oath in the manner required by law under which she promised to tell the truth in this audience and in all subsequent ones that should occur until the determination of her case and she promised to keep secret in all that she might believe or see or understand that happened concerning her case. She was asked for her name, and from where she came, and her age and her occupation and about when she was imprisoned.

[*Left margin:* Isabel Hernández de Guichiapa, *vecina* of Tlaxcala.]

She is called Isabel Hernández, *mestiza*, native of Guichiapa in this Archbishopric, and did not definitively know her age, but she appeared to be over forty years old, and that her occupation is that of midwife, and she is now a widow, and a *vecina* of the city of Tlaxcala where she was taken prisoner this morning.

[*Hernández declared that her parents were both deceased. Her father was a Spaniard from Castile and a manual worker. Her mother, a* mestiza, *was her father's "mujer natural."*[13] *She knew nothing of her paternal grandparents and only that her maternal grandparents were thought to be descendants of the Tobar family of Guichiapa, nor had she any knowledge about her parents' siblings. She told the court that she had a deceased brother who had married an indigenous woman, who was also deceased. She provided the court with biographical details about her own brother and sister's lives and those of their descendants but they are not germane to her case. She then detailed her own marital history:*]

She said that she has been married and widowed four times. The first with Pablo Martínez blacksmith, native of Almendralejo in Castile and who died in Guichiapa and by whom she did not have any children. The second time she was married to Pedro García from the same place, by trade a blacksmith, and who died in Esmiquilpa[14] and by whom she had three children who are living today: one in Tlaxcala called Andrés García, married to Cathalina de Guzmán and who has three young children, two boys called Juan and Joseph and a girl called María Rita and he [Andrés García] is a silk weaver. Her second son is called Juan López and he lives in Atrisco and is by trade a

---

13. His woman, but not his formally married wife.
14. Possibly Ixmiquilpan, Hidalgo.

basket weaver and is married to María de Jaén and they do not have children. And the third is called Nicolás Hernández and he lives in Tlaxcala and he is also a basket weaver. And the third time, she married Juan Asencio, a native of Estremadura, by trade a butcher in Esmiquilpa where he died and with him she had a daughter called Juana who died in Puebla, where she married Melchor de Robles, Spaniard, by occupation a tailor who is in Parral, and they had a son called Pedro. And the fourth and last time she married Francisco de la Parra, a shopkeeper, and it was in this city in the barrio of Santa Anta and he died in Tlaxcala and he was a Spaniard and she does not know from where and they did not have children.

She was asked about the caste and parentage of her parents and grandparents and if they or any of them was a confessant or prisoner or penitent of the Holy Office of the Inquisition.

She said that she has understood and understands them to have been old Christians according to what her parents said. And that on her mother's side, she descended from the natives of this kingdom, from principal Indians of the Kings of Tlaxcala and that none in her lineage have been imprisoned by or penitent before the Holy Office, nor has she, before the present occasion.

[Hernández next confirmed that she was a baptized and confirmed Christian who regularly heard mass and took communion and possessed a Bull of the Holy Cross.[15] She named her godparents. She made a sign of the cross before the court and recited the four prayers but did not know more of the Christian doctrine and admitted she had forgotten the commandments and the articles of faith and the confession because of "a terrible illness" that had devastated Tlaxcala.[16] She also confirmed that she could neither read nor write. The interrogation then continued:]

[*Left margin:* account of her life.]

Asked for the account of her life. She said that having been married the second time to Pedro García, he took her from the town of Guichiapa to Esmiquilpa where they were for five or six years, and where she was widowed again and she married for the third time to Juan Asencio by whom she was widowed and she came to this city and lived in the district of Santa Anna where she had a store that sold things to eat and she married for the fourth time to Francisco de la Parra and over fifteen years ago they moved to the city of Tlaxcala because of flooding. She has left this city some four times since

---

15. *La bula de la Santa Cruzada* was a series of indulgences originating in the Middle Ages with papal concessions to crusaders. In the sixteenth century, the *bula* was converted to indulgences given in return for service to the Spanish crown.

16. Literally, she says *"un tabardillo grande,"* a high fever.

They are all
doñas → Significant of their class

then to perform midwifery in Guachinango[17] for *doña* Isabel de Cervantes and *doña* Anna de Castillo and *doña* María de Guzmán and she has not travelled anywhere else.

She was asked if she knows or presumes the reason why she has been imprisoned and brought to the secret cells of the Holy Office.

[*Left margin*: Presumes the reasons for her imprisonment, that she relate and declare them.]

She said she presumes it is because about a year ago María de Chávez, *vecina* of the city of Tlaxcala, came to see her one day in the company of one of her daughters, called Michaela, and both of them begged her to give them some powders to soothe Michaela's husband who had a *rigida y mala condición* (strict and bad nature) and for this [Chávez] gave a coin[18] to this confessant and she told them that she did not have the powders that they wanted; and the next day she collected some dried herbs from her pots and rubbed them in her hands and made the powders and gave them to Michaela who came for them [*Left margin*: she gave some powders made from dried herbs from her pots and said that Michaela, who is the one who asked for them, should give them in chocolate to her husband] and she told her that she should give them to her husband in chocolate or however she liked and that with this, he would be soothed. And this confessant does not know what herbs they were except that they were the first that she came across, although she did know that they could not harm him; and that the reason why she played this trick was that she is a poor woman and that on that day she did not have anything to eat and she needed to earn the four *reales*.[19]

And she also remembers that *don* Diego de Ulloa, being the governor of Tlaxcala, begged this confessant to bring to his house a woman of this city called Cathalina de Ortigossa, married to Juan Alonso, who is a pork butcher by trade because he was in love with her and so she brought her one night and leaving her by the back door of the house of the governor, she left to do some business [*Left margin*: The pimping she did and what happened] and she returned to wait for [Ortigossa] to come out and when she came out of the governor's house, she said that she came out feeling very afflicted, without saying why, and asked her [Hernández] to take her to her house and a short while later the governor arrived and he was very angry and bad-tempered and he grabbed on to Cathalina de Ortigossa and said he wanted to throw her in the river [*Left margin*: Cathalina de Ortigossa] saying to her what was it that he had done to her, and she responded that he had done nothing, and seeing this

---

17. A district in current-day northern Veracruz and Puebla states.
18. A *tostón,* a coin worth one half peso.
19. *Reales* were a unit of currency representing one-eighth of one *peso.*

fight, the confessant asked Cathalina de Ortigossa why they were having this fight, and [Ortigossa] implored this confessant to say that she had given her some powders and to free [Ortigossa] from this danger. She said to *don* Diego de Ulloa that she had given to Cathalina de Ortigossa some powders without actually having given any to her, and with this *don* Diego de Ulloa calmed down and said that Cathalina de Ortigossa had put some powders on his neck that had stung him but this confessant did not know what powders they were and Cathalina de Ortigossa never told her, but she knows only that, to help [Ortigossa] from this danger, she claimed to have done this act herself, and she ended her discussion of Cathalina de Ortigossa.

And she remembers that when a woman in Tlaxcala was pregnant who was understood to be a virgin, when the time of her childbirth drew near, because she could not be in the house or proximity to her father and sister who were honorable people, she gave them to understand that [the medical situation of the woman] was the detention of the blood, and that she would cure her with some powders and that it would be more convenient to bring the woman to her house, and having taken her there, the woman gave birth that night, and word ran [*Left margin*: opinion that ran that she cured the sick one with some powders] in Tlaxcala that this confessant had healed her with some powders and that although many friends asked her what powders she had used, she answered them that they were some powders that she knew and that she did not want to say, when the truth was that she said this to prevent them from learning about the frailty of the woman because of her good reputation. And that these three cases that she has described could be the reasons why the idea has spread that she gives powders and uses them and having added some other things, this being the truth that she confessed because in God and in her conscience, there is no sin in anything against our Holy Faith because she is a faithful Catholic Christian.

[The court then warned Hernández in three formulaic monitions, or warning notices, that she was admonished to tell the truth in all aspects of her testimony. After the second monition, Hernández described some of the rituals with which she greeted newborn infants, and also described some other powders she had once sold to women to clean their faces.

The court next produced its formal accusation of Hernández. The fiscal *charged her with being a witch, one who engages in superstition, and a deceiver* (supersticiosa *and* embustera) *for having used herbs and powders and taken money from people and deceiving them with tricks. As was standard, in the formal accusation, the* fiscal *repeated the substance of what each witness had described as Hernández's religious crimes, listing a total of ten acts and concluding that Hernández should be judged harshly because she showed no remorse and because her actions meant that "it might be presumed that she had a pact with the devil whom she invoked in her prayers and spells," a notion none of the witnesses had discussed.*

Hernández then responded to each charge in turn. For the most part, she denied the truth of the charges brought against her, including the accusations of her first two denouncers, Inés and Catalina de Herrera, although she occasionally substantiated a witness's testimony, as she did in the case of one witness, Antonio de Lepe, who declared that Hernández had used a treatment involving an "egg of the Ascension" on his enslaved negra *when the latter was in labor. To this charge, (#6) Hernández replied:]*

. . . She says that only this is true, and that she has heard it said but does not remember by whom, that keeping an egg from the day of the Ascension of the Lord until the next day of the Ascension when you cut it [*Left margin*: that she did that with the egg of Ascension and she did what it says in the charge] was a good medicine and she did it, and she found the egg was hard and she dissolved it in wine, a part of which she gave to a black slave of Antonio de Lepe who could not give birth and that after she had given it, she gave birth and that if she had known that it was prohibited, she would not have given it.

11.6 Hernández Responds to the Charges against Her

[In the ninth chapter of the accusation, the court asked Hernández to identify various items that the comisario *and bailiff had seized from her residence:]*

She said to put them before her so she could tell the truth. [*Left margin*: asked to be shown the powders and other things so she can identify them]. And having unwrapped in her presence a cloth, they found in them the tail of a little animal that she said was *tlacuache*,[20] and that she had it to give to women who were in labor, and to those with urinary illnesses. These powders, she put in hot *pulque*,[21] or mixed with fried onion, or with almond oil. [*Left margin*: She identified the things and described each]

---

20. Bernardino de Sahagún recorded in the early post-conquest era that dried and powdered tail of the *tlaquatzin* (an alternative spelling of *tlacuache*), an opossum, was believed to have powerful expulsive properties.

21. *Pulque* is an alcoholic drink made from the fermented sap of the maguey cactus.

Item.[22] She was shown a paper wrapped up in a rag in which she said was a root called *chichilpatle*[23] that she gave to *criaturas* (babies) when they had indigestion.

Item. She was shown another cloth in which was wrapped some colored items which she said were *axí* (chili pepper), to give to women who were feverish after childbirth mixed with *ule* (rubber), and that this was made by Indians from some worms.

Item. She was shown some other cloths that had some herbs in them that she said were *suapatle*[24] to give to women in labor.

Item. She was shown another cloth and it was wrapped around a stone fragment that she said was a bezoar stone and that for this purpose she had been given it.[25]

Item. She was shown another rag in which was a root that she said was *contrayerba* to make cures.[26]

Item. She was shown another paper which had some white powders in it and she said it was to wash the faces of women. And then they showed her some other papers with some venetian glass in it that she said were used to make *agua de rostro* (water for washing faces) along with limes. [*Left margin*: That the white powders that were in this cloth are of the shells of the egg used for the Ascension and are used to make water for faces]

Item. She was shown another cloth that had some white powders in it and she said it was the shells of egg of Ascension and was for making face water.

Item. She was shown a little blue cloth which had a little black round ball in it and she said it was a *coyol* (a type of palm) that the children ate.

Item. She was shown a paper that was wrapped around some cloth with some colored powders inside that she said were of *ilacastli* that the Indians sold that were good for the baths of women who experienced *escocicas* (stinging).[27] [*Left margin*: that she does not know what is in this cloth.]

Item. She was shown a little brown cloth in which there was a seed and she said that she did not know what it was that but that the children played with it.

---

22. *Item* in the original, meaning next in a series of elements.

23. Nahuatl for "bitter medicine"; *chichiliá* (verb—to make bitter), *pah-tli* (medicine).

24. This is an alternative spelling for *cihuapatli*.

25. One early seventeenth-century medical tract described using a *piedra becar* in this way: "Water which can be drunk at meals is heated with *escorconera* (garden viper-grass), and into it is put in the pitcher a *piedra becar*, and a little *contrayerba*, and between meals and at meals is given this syrup." Andrés de Mamayo, *Tratados breves de algebra y garrotillo* (Valencia: Por Juan Chrysostomo Garriz, 1621), 46.

26. Plants with this name may refer to a number of species used for medicinal purposes.

27. We have been unable to translate *ilacastli*, although Frances Karttunen translates the closely related *ilacatztic* as "something twisted."

Item. She was shown a little idol of stone that she said was something the children played with.

[*Left margin*: that the dried hand that appeared to belong to a monkey was found by a nephew of hers] Item. She was shown a dried hand that appeared to be that of a monkey and she said that a nephew of hers called Juan found it in the *plaza* (main square) and then she had given it to father Antonio Gonzáles when they took her so that she would not keep anything.

[*Left margin*: that she did not know what these feathers were] Next. She was shown a small paper with two colored feathers in it and she said she did not know what they were or if they were of some woodpecker or of some parakeet.

Item. She was shown a cloth wrapped around some white powders that she said were the teeth of a dog to give to children who had indigestion.

Item. She was shown a white fang hanging on a cord that she said was of a *pejemulier*[28] and was for rheumatism and that one of her sons had given it to her.

[*Left margin*: that that which looked like meat and was shown her was not but was a chili pepper.] And that that which looked like meat was not but rather was a red chili pepper which is what she identified at the beginning.

Item. She was shown another little paper which had in it some white shavings or rinds that she said were for a medicine that she got from Macote, a *erbolario* (herbalist) in Tlaxcala for a woman who had a swollen mouth. And then was found a paper on which was written in poor letters a psalm that she said her godmother *doña* Juana de Arizaga, deceased, gave her to learn how to recite the psalm and that since she does not know how to read she did not learn it.

[*Hernández then declared that she had already told the truth about the tenth accusation against her and resumed her defense as follows:*]

. . . And to the conclusion of her accusation, she said that she has not done any of things that they accuse her of, nor does she know of any person who has done them and that she has already confessed and in her audiences, she has told the truth, and that in Tlaxcala there are people who want to do her ill, because of the skill she has had at [aiding in], and for this reason they have brought testimony against her. And that if they tortured her she would die in it because she did not owe anything and God could condemn her if this was all a lie, and that this is the truth by the oath she had sworn.

[*The Inquisition appointed a* letrado (*lawyer*), don *Juan García de Palacios, to defend Hernández with whom she consulted briefly. The court*

---

28. A *pejemulier* is also known as a *dujong*, a large marine mammal.

*then proceeded with the "*publicación de testigos*" (publication of witnesses' testimony) in which the Inquisitors read aloud an anonymous summary of all the evidence accumulated against Hernández from each individual witness who had testified against her, omitting any details which indicated the identity of all witnesses. In Hernández's case, as was standard, the information contained in the* publicación de testigos *segment of her trial did not differ from the material presented to her in the court's formal accusation against her, and Hernández replied to the evidence consistently with her first responses; that is, she denied almost every charge made against her. She confirmed only the testimony provided by Antonio de Lepe, who had described Hernández's provision of an "egg of the Ascencion" to aid his slave during a difficult labor. In an appearance before the court on July 5, after having consulted with her defender, Hernández made the final last plea of innocence to the court.]*

11.7 Isabel Hernández's Final Plea of Innocence

[In her final appearance, Hernández reiterated that she had spoken truthfully in all her testimony and she questioned the unsubstantiated nature of many of the witnesses' testimonies. She ended her plea as follows:]

. . . And all or some of [the witnesses] could have been incited to testify by Blas Estevan, a doctor who is the rival and enemy of this confessant and who may have initiated this testimony against her because he often threatened her when he found her visiting some sick person. And there is not the smallest word of truth in the whole case. And for this reason, faith and credit should be extended to her because she is a good Christian, fearful of God. And with this, she has no more to say in her defense but instead puts herself in the mercy of this Holy Court, contesting that she is suffering in innocence and that she will be found innocent and she begs and pleads to be absolved and put in liberty and here she concludes her case.

[Six weeks after Hernández presented her final defense, the court called her before them to render judgment. Her inquisitors sentenced her in a standard fashion for this crime at this time: she was to serve in the convent of the oidor *(judge) don* Gaspar Fernández de Castro *for the time that the tribunal judged appropriate and also exiled her from the city of Tlaxcala for two years. Hernández pledged that she would never repeat the crimes for which she had been accused, and she thanked the Inquisitors for the mercy they had shown her. She also affirmed that she had not heard anything against the Holy Faith while being held in the cells of the Inquisition. The court acknowledged receipt*

of a summary of the costs of feeding Hernández and providing her with linen, and eating utensils during her 105-day imprisonment totaling forty pesos.]

Suggested Reading

Behar, Ruth. "Sexual Witchcraft, Colonialism, and Women's Powers: Views from the Mexican Inquisition," in *Sexuality and Marriage in Colonial Latin America,* ed. Asunción Lavrin (pp. 178–206). Lincoln: University of Nebraska Press, 1989.

Few, Martha. *Women Who Live Evil Lives: Gender, Religion, and the Politics of Power in Colonial Guatemala.* Austin: University of Texas Press, 2002.

Jaffary, Nora E. *Reproduction and Its Discontents in Mexico: Childbirth and Contraception from 1750 to 1905.* Chapel Hill: University of North Carolina Press, 2016.

Lewis, Laura A. *Hall of Mirrors: Power, Witchcraft, and Caste in Colonial Mexico.* Durham, NC: Duke University Press, 2003.

Sousa, Lisa. *The Woman Who Turned into a Jaguar, and Other Narratives of Native Women in Archives of Colonial Mexico.* Stanford, CA: Stanford University Press, 2017.

Document Themes

- Labor
- Law
- Race and ethnicity
- Religion
- Sexuality and gender

12

Don Juan de Vargas y Orellana Accuses His Wife *doña* Francisca de Marquina of Abortion (Potosí, 1703)

In the absence of personal letters, it is difficult to apprehend the details of family life in the 1700s except when a court case brings them before the historian's eye. Though this judicial file is truncated before a decision is rendered, the excerpt of the legal proceeding is rich in detail as it reveals a couple, *doña* (lady) Francisca de Marquina and *don* (sir) Juan de Vargas y Orellana, in crisis over in-law tensions and concern about reproduction. The precise judicial rationale for the case is that a Spanish woman sought a divorce from her husband, which then spurred counter-accusations on his part about her having aborted her pregnancy. The accusation of abortion warranted witness testimony. It is clear from the trial transcript that *doña* Francisca's mother, *doña* Petronilla, was heavily involved in her daughter's affairs. There is no mention in the case, though, of *doña* Petronilla's husband, which is important because it suggests that no powerful male figure emerged as a protector of these two women (which may have made it easier for *don* Juan de Vargas y Orellana to mount the charges against them).

The notion of a woman seeking a divorce within Spain's eighteenth-century Catholic empire deserves explanation.[1] Divorce in this context was unusual. However, the possibility of an ecclesiastical divorce did exist. Such cases were much like civil trials with attorneys, motions, and witnesses, but would be heard before ecclesiastical judges who had the final say in judging the case. Though marriage was a sacred vow, certain situations could invalidate a marriage. For instance, where one party was unable to consummate the marriage (and thus procreation was impossible), a divorce could be granted. In cases of extreme spousal abuse, some women gained a divorce. Divorce in the 1700s signified that the couple was no longer expected to live together nor pool their economic resources. However, divorce did not signify that either party (man or woman) could marry again unless their spouse died.

---

1. Asunción Lavrin, *Sexuality and Marriage in Colonial Latin America* (Lincoln: University of Nebraska Press, 1989). On divorce in colonial Peru, see Bernard Lavalle, *Amor y Opresión en los andes coloniales* (Lima: IEP, 1999), 19–66.

In colonial Latin America, if a woman found herself in a difficult position with her spouse, she might choose to enter what was known as a *recogimiento* (a safe house). The *recogimiento* allowed women physical separation from their spouses while at the same time it provided institutional supervision (and hence respectability) to protect women's honor.[2] Notice that *doña* Francisca de Marquina entered the *recogida* of Orphan Girls in the city of Potosí during the period when her divorce to *don* Juan de Vargas y Orellana was pending. Ironically, as the witness testimony suggests, although this institution was meant to serve as a space of protection and respectability, it was also the place in which Marquina sought to end her pregnancy.

The details presented here seem to offer us at least two narratives. Was Marquina being manipulated by her mother to leave her husband and abort her pregnancy? Or was Marquina's mother helping her to leave an unhappy and/or dangerous marriage? This case prompts us to evaluate what is being examined and how it is being examined in order to decide if a woman was pregnant, if she aborted the fetus, and if her mother helped or forced her. Witness testimony, in particular, allows us to elaborate on how women and men in this time period thought about pregnancy and abortion. As you read the witness testimony, consider what kind of women were called to give evidence. How did men and women in this era determine pregnancy? What methods did they understand might provoke abortion or clues about whether an abortion had occurred? Who were the medical experts in the case? Why was this case of alleged abortion so important in the context of an ecclesiastical divorce?

12.1 Proceedings in the Ecclesiastical Divorce of *doña* Francisca Marquina[3]

The Doctor *don* Fernando Ignacio de Arango Queipo, father and most senior rector of this Holy Metropolitan Church on behalf of the excellent *Señor* Doctor *don* Juan Queipo de Llano y Valdéz, my senior Archbishop of this Archbishopric of the Council of your Majesty, Vicar and Ecclesiastical judge of the Imperial Villa (city) of Potosí, to whom I give commission for what will be heard and will give salutations in the name of our Lord, Jesus Christ, who is the true one. I make known that before me and in this Archbishop's Audience that a petition was presented and whose decrees have the following

---

2. Nancy E. van Deusen, *Between the Sacred and the Worldly: The Institutional and Cultural Practice of* Recogimiento *in Colonial Lima* (Stanford, CA: Stanford University Press, 2001).
3. Archivo Arzobispal de Sucre, Divorcios, Legajo 3, No. 5332. 1703 Potosi. 32 fols.

tenor: Juan de Artega, [submits] as attorney for and in name of *don* Juan de Vargas y Orellana, in the lawsuit and demand for divorce and separation that has been placed upon my party by *doña* Francisca de Marquina, his wife, and the rest that is known. I declare that *doña* Petronilla Fernández, mother-in-law of my party and mother of the said [Francisca], it seems for hatred and ill-will that she has toward my party has disposed her daughter to seek separation. While carrying out married life with my party, she used cunning to take Francisca to the *recogida* of Orphan Girls. On this occasion, *doña* Francisca was pregnant. The mother-in-law of my party has had such audacity[4] that in order that she [*doña* Francisca] not remain pregnant by her husband as under the order of Holy Matrimony, she [*doña* Petronilla] arranged to give her daughter a concoction so she would abort.[5] She committed the gravest offense possible against the highest Pontifical order. Consequently, my party is appealing to the superior judgment of your Grace to file my complaint with the Vicar of the Villa of Potosí so that before him I can make a secret report about the content of this demand. It will be proven by remarkable witnesses and by different acts and circumstances that led up to it, as well as that whoever is proven guilty in the case of abortion will be punished. Therefore, to Your Grace I beg and plead that you see fit to send me the necessary order[6] to begin discovery and to send information to the Vicar [so he can] proceed for censure against the witnesses who refused to make a declaration on the truth of the matter with respect to the mother-in-law of my party who has instigated the abortion as well as the divorce lawsuit. Given the information the Vicar will submit secretly, in the original to the power of Your Grace so that you may order that justice be served. I request costs and swear on the soul of my party.

[With this, don Juan de Vargas y Orellana's attorney officially asked the court that his case be heard. The next several folios admit the case to court and then witness testimony begins.]

Potosí, July 31, 1703
Witness

Don Juan de Vargas, for the secret investigation that has been offered before the Monsignor *don* Joseph de Sotomayor y Herrera, head priest of the Parish of San Roque of this Villa, Vicar Ecclesiastical Judge. I present as a witness a cloaked Spanish[7] woman who said she was a native of the city of

---

4. *Ardimiento* in the original.
5. The words used are *abortarse/aborto*.
6. The word used is *recado*.
7. The document notes that the witness is cloaked, indicating an attempt at anonymity or attempt to preserve honor while testifying in this case.

La Plata and is married to Miguel de Vargas. She said that she has been in this Villa for about seven months. Also, she said that she lived in same house as *doña* Petronilla and her daughter, *doña* Francisca de Marquina, for about six months, with the said women in their rooms. Speaking about various things that came up on one occasion, *doña* Francisca Marquina asked her what thing would be good to [use to] abort,[8] to which she responded that she did not know about that because she had never tried to abort. On another occasion, Francisca asked her if an herb that they call *sacha*[9] would be good to abort. This witness responded to her that she did not know, but said that the *indias* (indigenous women) used it to make those foolish [potions]. And this witness knew that *doña* Francisca de Marquina was pregnant because of what she showed in the toilet and in her actions [illegible phrase]. When she asked [Marquina] if she was pregnant, she denied it. Therefore, *don* Juan, husband of the said woman, sent her the urine of his wife one morning, and having seen it, she knew by it that she was pregnant. This is what she said and she declared that it is what she knows. She said that she had no personal conflict of interest with any party in the case. She is thirty years old, and she did not sign because she does not know how.

Potosí, July 30, 1703
Witness

Pasquala de Savala, free *negra* (black woman) who carries out the trade of midwife in this Villa, swore an oath before God our *Señor* (Lord) and made the sign of the cross, according to the law swore to tell what she knows respecting the investigation of the aforementioned. This witness said that what she knows and can say is that *don* Juan de Vargas, husband of *doña* Francisca de Marquina, who presents her as a witness, went one day to the house of this witness and he told her that his wife was unwell and that she should go to see her. And with that, she went, and feeling her belly, she found that [Marquina] was a few months pregnant. And some days having gone by, *don* Juan called on her again about the same matter. He told her that his wife's pregnancy was advancing and that after she was in the *recogimiento* and that *doña* Francisca sent *don* Juan to send this witness to the *recogimiento* where she was afflicted in her belly, according to what [Marquina] said. And she [Savala] went back another time to settle her and on these three occasions that she visited her as a midwife, she always found that Marquina was pregnant and further along each day, and according to her trusted knowledge and understanding, the bulge [Marquina] had in her abdomen was a baby and not her belly as has been said. This is the truth. She said that she had

---

8. *Mal parir* in the original.
9. This is probably a reference to *sacha inchi*, a plant native to the rainforest in Bolivia/Peru.

no personal conflict of interest with any party in the case. She did not sign because she was blind.

Potosí, August 2, 1703
Witness

An *indiecita* (young indigenous) girl [who through an interpreter] said she was named Rosa and she did not know her last name, native of this Villa, parishioner of the Parish of San Pedro in it, original of the Pueblo of Pichigua. She swore an oath before God our *Señor* and made the sign of the cross, according to the law swore to tell what she knows respecting the investigation of the aforementioned. This witness said that what she knows is that on March 2 until July of this present year, she served *don* Juan de Vargas and his wife, *doña* Francisca de Medina, with whom she was in the *recogida*. There [Marquina], two months ago, more or less, told her that she should go to where her mother was and tell her that she [Marquina] was hurting in her belly and that she should send her some remedy. And this witness carried out the order and *doña* Petronila Fernandez, mother of *doña* Francisca, gave this witness a wrapped paper saying to her that you tell my daughter that she should drink this, and having taken without knowing even what it was, she gave it to *doña* Francisca who put it in a *mate de yerba* (herbal tea) and drank it the next day.

Doña Francisca gave this witness a *basija de barro* (clay basin) as the *indios* call it, but one well wrapped with a blanket, ordering her firmly not to untie it and that she should take it to her mother and so she took it and she gave it to her and she does not know nor did this witness see what the basin held because *doña* Francisca's mother did not show anything to this witness. This is the truth. She said that she had no personal conflict of interest with any party in the case. She is around thirteen or fourteen years old, and she did not sign because she does not know how.

Potosí, August 3, 1703
Witness

Doña Thomasa de Soria, *vecina* (citizen) of this said Villa swore an oath before God our *Señor* and made the sign of the cross, according to the law swore to tell what she knows respecting the investigation of the aforementioned. This witness said that what she knows and can say is that about six months ago, more or less, *don* Juan de Vargas, husband of *doña* Francisca de Marquina, called her saying that his wife was sick and that she should see her and she give her some remedy and having seen *doña* Francisca de Marquina, this witness recognized that she did not suffer from any accident and asked what it was that she was feeling. She responded to her that a woman had told her that she [*doña* Francisca de Marquina] was pregnant, to which this witness said she did not believe that and only knew that her uterus had fallen down low and that it should be corrected[10] and she applied some remedies. This is the truth. She said that she had no personal conflict of interest with any party in the case. She is sixty-three years old and she did not sign because she does not know how.

Potosí, August 3, 1703
Witness

Doña Michaela Guerrero who said she was the widow of Gaspar de Roxas, resident in this Villa swore an oath before God our *Señor* and made the sign of the cross, according to the law swore to tell what she knows respecting the investigation of the aforementioned. This witness said that what she knows is that about six months ago, more or less, *don* Juan de Vargas solicited her as a person who practices midwifery and asked her if she would see his wife, *doña* Francisca Marquina, and so this witness went and saw her and recognized that [she] was two months pregnant, more or less, by her estimate, which she told [her] and she responded that Pasquala, who is also a midwife in this Villa, had told her that she had "*la madre mui baja*" even though she was pregnant and, after applying some remedies and settling her abdomen, she left her in this state. This is the truth. She said that she had no personal conflict of interest with any party in the case. She is sixty-eight years old and she did not sign because she does not know how.

Potosí, August 3, 1703
Witness

Domingo de Arse y Cueto, natural of the city of Ica, at present residing in this Villa, swore an oath before God our *Señor* and made the sign of the cross, according to the law swore to tell what he knows respecting the investigation of the aforementioned. This witness said that what he knows is that about three months ago, more or less, he met with Doctor *don* de las Casas, clergy of the minor orders, in the house of *don* Juan de Vargas. And conversing with him in the presence of *doña* Francisca de Marquina, about women giving birth and godparent networks, *don* de las Casas said that if he was in this Villa at the time of *doña* Francisca's childbirth, he would be the godfather. And this witness did not dispute that *doña* Francisca de Marquina, wife of *don* Juan de Vargas, was at this time pregnant, as he heard it said to her repeated times and in different occasions. And that this is what he has said and this is

---

10. *Que le abia bajado la madre que se la compuso* in the original. "*La madre*," literally "the mother," was used to refer to the uterus in the colonial era. The condition of having a uterus *muy bajada* may refer to a uterine prolapse.

the truth. He said that he had no personal conflict of interest with any party in the case. He is twenty-five years old, and he signed.

Potosí, August 3, 1703
Witness

Doctor *don* Diego Thesillos, doctor in this Villa, swore an oath before God our *Señor* and made the sign of the cross, according to the law swore to tell what he knows respecting the investigation of the aforementioned. This witness said that what he knows and can say is that at the beginning of her pregnancy, he assisted *doña* Francisca Marquina, wife of *don* Juan de Vargas who is presenting him as a witness and in the visits that he made, he recognized that [she] was pregnant as was indicated by the lack of menses and other incidents that pregnant women regularly have and in order to better ascertain the truth he called some midwives so that they could see and touch the abdomen and they said it was clear she was pregnant. This is what he knows and this is the truth. He said that he had no personal conflict of interest with any party in the case. He is forty years old, and he signed.

[At this point in the case, don *Juan de Vargas y Orellana and his lawyers admit the testimony of their witnesses and suggest that this testimony proves that an abortion was committed.]*

Juan de Artiaga as empowered by *don* Juan de Vargas, state that as justice demands, Your Grace should send notice of imprisonment against *doña* Francisca de Marquina and her mother *doña* Petronilla Fernández on account that the abortion has been proven.

The Vicar General of this Archbishopric of the City of La Plata: by this notice, the Vicar and Ecclesiastical Judge of the Villa Imperial of Potosí should deliver as prisoners to this city the persons of *doña* Francisca de Marquina and *doña* Petronilla Fernández.

[The court orders that both women should be sent to the Casa de Recogidas *of Orphan Girls in Potosí.]*

On October 11th, 1703, the *señor* Vicar went to the house of *doña* Petronilla Fernández, mother of *doña* Francisca de Marquina, in order to remove her and take her to the *Recogidas*. Having arrived at the house, his mercy [the Vicar] found *doña* Petronilla Fernández sick, in bed, and bleeding from her ankle. Because of this, her imprisonment was halted. The Vicar proceeded to embargo her belongings which were the following: six old, small canvases of different pictures, two broken stools, one old wooden bowl with some sold earthen mugs, and an [*illegible word*] an old trunk of cow's leather with some rags inside, [*illegible phrase*], a bed—old wooden frame, blanket, sheet, canopy, old *Cajamarca*-style[11] bedspread. And because her goods were so few and of little value, she was allowed to keep an old shawl and an old skirt even though they had been entered in the inventory of goods. She agreed to relinquish those if she were asked. Later they went to the Casa de Recogidas where *doña* Francisca de Marquina had been put *en depósito* (surveilled custody). Going to the room where she was and has been, the following goods were inventoried: First, an old wooden bedspread, without a canopy, an old blanket, an old mattress, an old bedspread like a blanket without sheets nor pillows, a small trunk without a key, and she was wearing a worn patterned Rouen blouse, a striped bodice, an old shawl, a wool skirt of *piel de febre*[12] and she did not have anything else. She swore to God and a cross that she did not have any more belongings because when she entered the said *Recogidas*, and had left all her clothing in the possession of her husband. [*The Vicar signed the inventory.*]

Marcos de Bracamonte presents a petition on behalf of *doña* Francisca de Marquina.

I declare that my party has been placed in the *recogimiento* of Orphan Girls of this Villa [Potosí] for many days owing to the demand that *don* Juan de Vargas has filed for marriage annulment. Those proceedings have been sent to the *señor* Vicar General of this Archbishopric. Meanwhile my party is experiencing extreme poverty in the *recogimiento* without which to feed herself thanks to the impiety of Juan de Vargas. He has not sent her even a half-*real* of relief. She is surviving each week really through ten *pesos* from *doña* Francisca de Barea and another ten *pesos* from Joseph Ortiz de Uribe, from the quantity that those two owe my party and though it is hers [*doña* Francisca's], *don* Juan de Vargas is spending it without my party having any hope that it be returned to her. And, to avoid similar prejudice and the little regard that *don* Juan de Vargas has for my party, if your mercy would serve with Christian and pious zeal, help by sending notice to the debtors that they do not give anything to him and that they contribute to my party with the ten *pesos* weekly for her food. They can [also] remit some *pesos* to the City of La Plata for the cost of the lawsuit, the reason why she is detained.

[*Marcos de Bracamente insists that his client is innocent and held in the* recogimiento *unjustly. Here the extant case file ends.*]

---

11. Reference to a style produced in the city of Cajamarca, Peru.
12. French textile, very fashionable in Spain in early modern Spain.

Suggested Reading

Jaffary, Nora E. *Reproduction and Its Discontents in Mexico: Childbirth and Contraception from 1750 to 1905.* Chapel Hill, NC: University of Chapel Hill Press, 2016.

Lavrin, Asunción, ed. *Sexuality and Marriage in Colonial Latin America.* Lincoln: University of Nebraska Press, 1989.

van Deusen, Nancy E. "'Wife of My Soul and Heart, and All My Solace,' Annulment Suit between Diego Andrés de Arenas and Ysabel Allay Suyo," in *Colonial Lives, Documents on Latin American History, 1550–1850,* ed. Richard Boyer and Geoffrey Spurling. New York: Oxford University Press, 2000.

Document Themes

- Family
- Labor
- Law
- Sexuality and gender

13

Founding Corpus Christi, a Convent for Indigenous Women (Mexico City, 1723)

The question of whether indigenous women possessed the intellectual aptitude and spiritual mettle to become nuns divided ecclesiastics in Latin America throughout the colonial period. Some, like Mexico's first bishop, Juan de Zumárraga, remarked as early as the late 1520s on the receptiveness of the daughters of Aztec nobility to Christian instruction. Similarly, sixteenth-century Franciscan Bernardino de Sahagún judged that indigenous women had the "aptitude to be nuns and keep perpetual chastity."[1] As also occurred in Peru, a small number of *mestiza* (person of mixed Spanish and indigenous parentage) women were admitted to Mexican convents shortly after the conquest; these included Isabel Moctezuma's two daughters, who entered the first convent for women, Nuestra Señora de la Concepción, founded around 1540.[2] By 1585, however, Mexico's Third Provincial Council, which produced the formal ecclesiastical regulations governing the Viceroyalty for the following two centuries, legislated against the openness to indigenous subjects' religious profession, deeming indigenous men unfit for ordination and omitting any discussion of indigenous women's religious vocation. By this period, most *mestizas* (women of indigenous and Spanish parentage) found in convents in New Spain worked there as servants rather than professing as nuns,[3] and for the following century and a half, strong opposition to the notion of allowing indigenous women to take the veil remained the dominant position in Mexico until spiritual debates and social attitudes had changed sufficiently within at least some sectors of the institutional church that the question of *indias'* (indigenous women's) formal profession could be reopened.[4] Indigenous populations' popular devotion to localized Catholic saints and the

---

1. Bernardino de Sahagún, as quoted in Asunción Lavrin, "Indian Brides of Christ: Creating New Spaces for Indigenous Women in New Spain," *Mexican Studies/Estudios Mexicanos* 15:2 (Summer 1999), 227.
2. On Isabel Moctezuma's descendants, see Chapter 1. On the creation of convents admitting *mestiza* and some indigenous nuns in sixteenth- and seventeenth-century Peru, see Kathryn Burns, *Colonial Habits: Convents and the Spiritual Economy of Cuzco, Peru* (Durham, NC: Duke University Press, 1999).
3. Lavrin, "Indian Brides of Christ," 229.
4. Ibid.

growth of a small body of spiritual biographies of devout *indias* and *indios* in the seventeenth century both contributed to the church's growing openness to the idea of the profession of indigenous nuns.

Contemporary experts' arguments both for and against indigenous women's capacity to profess are reproduced below in the reports generated for an inquiry Mexico's Real Audiencia (Royal Court) launched in 1722 into the question of establishing Mexico's first convent for indigenous women. The administrative initiative to found the convent originated with Mexican viceroy Baltasar de Zúñiga, marquis of Valero, who in 1719 proposed the foundation of a convent of Franciscan nuns to which only noble indigenous women *(cacicas* or *principales)* of legitimate birth would be eligible for admission. King Philip IV issued a *real cédula* (royal letter) in September 1722 supporting the initiative and requesting that the Real Audiencia initiate a formal report—an *informe*—into the matter. The *informe* called for the consultation of principal administrators and ecclesiastical authorities, including the directors of several convents, to render their assessments of the capacity of indigenous women to profess, and as the following responses illustrate, it elicited both positive and negative reactions from spiritual authorities. Initially disposed to reject the foundation of the convent, its receipt of a second *Real Cédula* approving the foundation in March of 1724 compelled the *Audiencia* to support the intellectually revolutionary establishment of the convent of Corpus Christi later that year.

As well as excluding commoners, aspirant nuns whose ancestors the Inquisition had accused of idolatry were prohibited from admission to Corpus Christi, as were women who had performed "vile occupations" such as slaughtering animals or selling *pulque* (a popular alcoholic drink made from fermented cactus nectar), or whose ancestors had performed such labors.[5] Several aspirant nuns were either excluded from admission or ejected from the convent at mid-century for having failed to demonstrate the purity of their indigenous blood from intermixture with Spaniards in an ironic reversal of Spaniards' preoccupation with demonstrating their own *limpieza de sangre* (blood purity).[6] Its founding documents decreed that the new convent would be run by several nuns of Spanish descent drawn from the Viceroyalty's other convents, but allowed that indigenous nuns would take over the administration of Corpus Christi after twenty years if they were judged capable of self-government. Corpus Christi, which followed the strict Order of the Clares of First Rule, required no dowries of its members who

---

5. Ibid., 242; Ann Miriam Gallagher, R.S.M. "The Indian Nuns of Mexico City's *Monasterio* of Corpus Christi, 1724–1821," in *Latin American Women: Historical Perspectives*, ed. Asunción Lavrin (Westport, CT: Greenwood Press, 1978), 153.
6. Gallagher, "Indian Nuns," 155.

numbered between eighteen and thirty-three throughout the eighteenth and early nineteenth centuries.[7] Although animosity to the admission of indigenous women to the status of nuns continued after its foundation, the church founded two additional convents for indigenous women in New Spain later in the eighteenth century: Nuestra Señora de la Pursíma Concepción de Cosamalopan in Valladolid and Nuestra Señora de los Angeles in Oaxaca.

One letter supporting and one opposing the foundation of a convent for noble indigenous women generated at the behest of the Audiencia's *informe* are reproduced below. What do they demonstrate about contemporary attitudes to indigenous populations? What were the specifically gendered attitudes toward indigenous women's spiritual potential that ecclesiastics held? In comparison to the excerpts concerning the Afro–Peruvian nun Úrsula de Jesús (Chapter 10), can we detect differences between ecclesiastical attitudes toward Afro–Latin American and indigenous female religious?

The sources excerpted here challenge the attempt to access indigenous women's own views of formal profession because women feature only as the subjects rather than the agents of these texts. Can they still be used to try accessing women's own attitudes toward formal religious profession? Rather than conceiving of convents as places where wealthy families could stow unloved and unmarriageable daughters, many scholars have shown that participation in formal religious orders and life within the convent would have attracted women in the colonial world because life within the convent afforded women considerably more intellectual, social, and even financial autonomy than they would have had access to in secular life.[8]

The very last pages of the excerpts chosen here give us a more direct glimpse of three of the indigenous women who were meant to profess in Corpus Christi themselves but who had recently made other choices. What do these excerpts reveal about their motivations and attitudes toward entering the convent and about those whom the church saw as eligible to profess? If women's voices *per se* are muted, what do these documents reveal about the perspective of indigenous women in colonial society? Given the unavailability of these women, the scribe of the Real Acuerdo learned from Madre Petra de San Francisco of Mexico City's convent on San Juana de la Penitencia that she knew of thirteen other able *cacicas*, several of whom worked as servants in the convent and others who had been educated in it from a young age

---

7. Gallagher, "Indian Nuns," 153.

8. Burns, *Colonial Habits;* Margaret Chowning, *Rebellious Nuns: The Troubled History of a Mexican Convent, 1752–1863* (New York: Oxford University Press, 2005); Ellen Gunnarsdóttir, *Mexican Karismata: The Baroque Vocation of Francisca de Los Ángeles, 1674–1744* (Lincoln: University of Nebraska Press, 2004); Kathleen Ann Myers, *Neither Saints nor Sinners: Writing the Lives of Women in Spanish America* (New York: Oxford University Press, 2003).

whom she attested would make able candidates for profession. Another six candidates for profession originated in the capital's Santa Clara convent. The *fiscal* (prosecutor) considered several nuns' supporting testimony sufficient evidence of their merit to concede license to found the convent, admitting these women as its founding cohort.

13.1 *Fray* Ignacio García de Figueroa Opines about the Qualities of Potential Indian Nuns[9]

Fray (brother) Ignacio García de Figueroa of the order of Our Father of San Francisco, *Predicador General* (official preacher to indigenous subjects) of the Archbishopric, curate of the parish of San Joseph de Naturales, which is in the convent of Our Lord of San Francisco in Mexico, this original city of America, obeying the command of Your Highness in which I am ordered to provide information about the advisability and inadvisability that may follow from Law I, Title 3, of Book 1 of the *Recopilación de las Reales Leyes de Indias*[10] regarding the foundation of a convent of discalced Franciscan nuns for principal and noble *Indias* in this kingdom, I state: There is just cause and urgent need, as defined by the cited law, for such a foundation because there are many *Indias* of known virtue and some, even the majority, do not enjoy the perfection of virtue that they might because of a lack of religious *recogimiento* (seclusion) that the spiritual and mystical life requires. The foundation of this convent is urgently required for the advancement of the spiritual life so that many souls will not be lost and so that the situation which the reverend father *Fray* Juan Bautista related from the past in the seventh of his *Advertencias* on folio 12 will not come to pass in our time.[11] There, he wrote of a priest who complained that the *Indios* were not good Christians. To this, an *Indio* replied that if the fathers took even half as much care to make the *Indios* good Christians, as the ministers of the idols had done in teaching their rites and ceremonies, the *Indios* would be good Christians since the law of Christ is better. And in the absence of anyone to teach them the law with patience, the *Indios* would not take to it.

---

9. All documents in this chapter are taken from Archivo General de la Nacíon (México), Historia, Vol. 109, exp. 2.

10. The *Recopilación de las leyes de los reinos de Indias,* first published in 1680, was an indexed collection of all the Royal and Viceregal directives pertaining to Spanish America. The passage cited here governed the regulation of convents and *recogmientos* for women.

11. *Fray* Juan Bautista was a Franciscan missionary and scholar of Nahuatl who taught at the Franciscan seminary in Santiago Talatelolco in the late sixteenth century. His tract, *Advertencias para los confesores de los naturales,* was published in 1600.

These words are certainly very worthy of consideration if the absence of somebody to teach them explained why *Indios* did not become good Christians. Today we say and we are told that the absence of convents where *Indias* may enter without dowries (due to their poverty) means that they are not nor can become good mystics who develop their virtue. And proof of this is that *señor* (sir) Juan Diego and his wife María Luisa, on hearing a sermon by the venerable father *Fray* Toribio Motolonia on the subject of virginity (as recounts *bachiller* Luis Lazo de la Vega in his history of Our Lady of Guadalupe), became so enamored of chastity that they decided together to remain in perpetual chastity.[12]

In the town of Guaxosingo,[13] the venerable father *Fray* Miguel de Estibales, compelled by obedience to his guardian who was then of that convent, declared before the public scribe of that place with the assistance of witnesses that in the town of Sinsonsa[14] his Guardian *Fray* Pedro de Reyna was attending mass with a candle in his hand and he saw after the consecration, that a form [a communion host] flew from the altar and into the mouth of an *India* who was behind the door of the church listening to the mass. And there is no doubt that if there had then been a convent of those *recogidas* and indoctrinated in the religious doctrine, this blessed *India,* María Luisa, would have passed to greater perfection, and that from this to highest sanctity for the greater glory of God.

Neither, *Señor,* can we deny that presently there are among the *Indias* some spirits that are as pure as those described, but these are not improved and cannot expand because of the absence of religious *recogimiento* in a convent since although they have sufficient cultivation by holy reverend fathers, they are distracted in many matters of the secular world from which they would not suffer if they achieved the *recogida* peace of a convent because there they could leave all secular concerns and could devote themselves exclusively to God. And although it is true, *Señor,* that there are many spirits so valiant

---

12. García de Figueroa here refers to a history by seventeenth-century priest Laso de la Vega who published a 1649 account of the Virgin of Guadalupe's reputed apparition to *Indio* Juan Diego in 1531. Vega reported that when Diego heard a sermon by Franciscan missionary Fray Toribio de Motolonía on how celibacy pleased God, he and his wife both resolved to remain chaste for the rest of their lives. See Stafford Poole, *The Guadalupan Controversies in Mexico* (Stanford, CA: Stanford University Press, 2006), 200. A *bachiller* was a person who had earned the degree of *bachillerato,* or baccalaureate.

13. Alternative spellings include Huejotzingo, Huexocingo, Guaxozingo, Bexosinco. The town is located in western Puebla state.

14. Sinsonsa does not appear in Peter Gerhard's *A Guide to the Historical Geography of New Spain,* Revised Edition (Norman: University of Oklahoma Press, 1993). However, Thomas Gage, does mention the town of Sinsonsa in his *Nueva relación que contiene los viages de Tomas Gage in la Nueva España,* and locates it in Michoacán.

and expansive that they do not suffer from the thorns of the secular world but rather are roses of virtue and fruits of sanctity among them. There are also other spirits that are so delicate, prim, and proper that the mere air of the secular world withers them, and these require the refuge and solitude of the cloister for their preservation and improvement especially because virginity and chastity is a virtue so delicate that it is always soiled by the corrupting airs of an impure conversation, which they lack in the secular world, and even more when without safe-keeping they . . .[15] since most times fathers leave their *doncellas* (virginal daughters) to mind their houses on their own, without company, about which their wives complain pitifully because when they are left as guards of the house, they cannot guard the vineyard of their own virginity. We have daily mourned this shameful state in our confessionaries, since in thirty-two years of administering to them, and of these, twenty-six as a priest, I have heard much of this. And many spirits that could be progressing have been kept behind with many crosses because of the lack of *recogimiento*.

[García de Figueroa then spends a paragraph flattering the Spanish king in an effort to convince him that supporting the foundation of the convent for indigenous women, he would please God.]

It is ordered in law 19 title 3 book 1 of the *Nueva Recopilación* that the maintenance of houses in which girls are taught not only the spiritual life, but also *la política* (decorum) should be ensured since it appears to His Majesty that their maintenance is necessary because it is a pious work and important to the service of God and the well-being of these lands for which reason His Majesty orders that where no such houses exist, they should be founded, and once founded, preserved. The foundation of the discalced convent for noble *Indias* will be seen not only as devotedly Catholic, but also as necessary and important to the service of God and the well-being of these lands since it will help remedy many harms about which the *Provinciales* (district governors) complain because of the absence of convents for the improvement of their daughters.

[García de Figueroa's report continues for another two paragraphs in which he repeats his support for the crown's legal and moral obligation to found the proposed convent. He signs his letter May 11, 1723, from the parish of San Joseph. Several other priests whom the Real Audiencia consulted expressed much more critical views of the idea of the convent's foundation, as illustrated in the following report.]

---

15. Two words are illegible here.

13.2 Priest Alessandro Romano Objects to the Foundation of a Convent for Noble *Indias*

Most powerful *Señor*

I am commanded by Your Highness through an order of Your *Real Acuerdo*[16] to express my views with respect to an establishment for *cacique* nuns that is proposed in this imperial city of Mexico. And obeying as I must this command, I declare that there is no disposition among the *Indias,* but rather positive ineptitude among them to become nuns for the following reasons.

Nuns are Christian women, who desiring the perfection of all virtue profess to live communally and in perpetual cloister under the obedience of a prelate who obliges them to keep the three vows common to all nuns as well as to the other rules and statutes that they judge to be the most efficacious means to obtain their goals.[17] In no way do I see the *Indias* disposed to any of this.

First, they do not possess the natural inclination to live communally, as is evident in their ancient and present way of living. Since before the arrival of our Holy Faith in these lands (except for those who lived in the company of their great grandparents), they lived either in the hills or in small towns as gentiles are still accustomed to do, even those who, after having holy baptism at the cost of much work by their ministers, found themselves reduced or were reduced to towns,[18] but still in large measure maintain their natural opposition to sociable and civil life, since each one builds his house distant from others. They do this for one of these two reasons: either because they do not have the patience and prudence to endure or conceal some inconvenience by their neighbors, or, which is more likely, from themselves. And if it is natural for the *Indios* to not tolerate living right next to one another, how could the *Indias* be expected to accustom themselves to living together in one house, each one exposed to the view of all those who would take note of their actions so that their prelates could correct them and so that they would be obliged to conceal and tolerate everyone else's inconveniences?

They lack, as well, speaking of *Indios* in general, the constancy of the soul in their good purposes, as experience teaches us. And although this is lacking in them, they have shown us the reason, because the facility to change the mind and their will originates, as Saint Thomas teaches, in the imperfection of the mind to know purposes. For this reason, the angels who clearly and

---

16. An official body composed of the Viceroy and officers of the Real Audiencia.

17. The three common vows are poverty, chastity, and obedience.

18. The author refers here to missionary orders' practice of "*reducciones*" by which they reorganized the indigenous population of rural Spanish America into concentrated towns, thus facilitating their conversion to Christianity.

perfectly know things are very tenacious in their judgments and affections. And for the same reason we see in men that those with *cortedad de entendimiento* (limited minds) are also more likely to change their minds and wills. Since the limited mental capacity of the *Indios* is notorious, their tendency toward inconstancy follows from this. Who does not see the unsuitability of the *cacicas* for the religious state, which is said to be the perpetual exercise of very arduous virtues, repugnant to human nature?

This discourse is confirmed by experience because there is no doubt that it is easier and less repugnant to human frailty to fulfill the obligations of marriage than those of religion, and even then, there is scarcely a married *India* who has not repented marrying, and many of them repent for good and leave forever their husbands. For which reason, I do not see how prudence can teach that such inconstant woman could profess the religious state, and that of perpetual cloister which requires much constancy of the spirit and not a little strength, which is generally also lacking in the *Indias* for which reason they are unsuited to the religious state. Since this is the state of the mortification of all the passions and of a continuous longing for the abnegation of self will which cannot be achieved without great strength of spirit, the effect, in large part of the mind that uncovers to the will the honesty of the virtues, hides the senses, and in this way, the encouragement and force to mortify the disorderly appetites. For this reason, all priests and spiritual directors require so greatly the meditation on the eternal truths by those they have under their care because without this they cannot fortify the soul. Without fortification, there can be no mortification, and without mortification it is illogical to presume to reach any virtuous state at all. The very limited mental capacity of the *Indias* is, after all, notorious and it is also clear that they are incapable of meditating on their own about the eternal truths and since they lack the force of the spirit so necessary to mortify the passions and to arrive not only to the cross that the *Señor* commands all Christians to carry as the necessary means of arriving at heaven, but also the heaviest and most difficult to arrive and for this reason I do not make it obligatory but rather a counsel which is that of the *religiosos* (male members of religious orders) that to most please the *Señor* they take a vow of various arduous and things that are difficult to achieve. The experience of thirty years has taught me that the *Indias* are of such limited understanding that they cannot meditate or seriously reflect on the virtues of our faith in which they are directed since by steps that I take to teach them the way to meditate, all of them have left, fruitless and in vain.

The doctors doubt whether the vow of chastity that those who are summarily inclined to a lack of restraint is valid and many of them . . .[19] affirm that it is not, based on the fact that this vow respective to a given person is not

---

19. Two words are illegible here.

of the greater good,[20] nor can it be a sacrifice agreeable to the *Señor* because it lacks the salt of prudence. I do not want that these reasons count to prove the *Indias* incapable of being nuns because of the great difficulty that must be spoken about of fulfilling all the obligations of this state. But who can deny that these reasons at least convince them that they should not be permitted to profess this state which could be the occasion more of setbacks than of spiritual benefits?

Nor is this satisfied in saying that divine grace and not the law of our discourse is that which checks and subdues our passions. Because grace does not only work in us, but also with us and ordinarily it accommodates itself to nature the doctors teach us who also affirm that the natural talents that the *Señor* has given some person can gather the use of this doctrine in his church. It costs us then the short achievement of the *Indias* to understand the honesty of the virtues proper to religious people, we must not assume that the *Señor* knows their false nature with extraordinary illumination, but rather judge that he does not want them for this state since he gave them the talent and understanding and discourse necessary for the order of their ordinary providence to achieve religious virtues.

But above all, I do not see in the *Indias* even one trace of this great and good sense that is required in a superior to govern a community of incapable women, and in the inferiors to obey a prelate of the same *calidad* (class and caste) because the governor of an incapable people needs great knowledge of the inclinations and dispositions of the soul of each one of her inferiors as well as much concealed patience and skill, bringing to each one in her path and suffering many faults without prejudice to the common good, qualities that cannot be hoped to be found except miraculously in a superior *India* of very little potential. And even less can one hope to find in the inferior ones who are incapacitated this heroic humility, patience, and blind obedience that is required to . . . to an ignorant, and consequently . . . superior.[21]

This, then, my powerful *Señor* is my opinion with respect to the new foundation that is intended. And I believe that this same opinion that many religious superiors have had until now, and continue to have in this immense Kingdom because even though *Indios* were capable of taking religious orders, because they are naturally so humble, nevertheless no religious superior has wanted them nor wants now to admit them even as lay members to their orders because of their great incapacity, inconstancy, and weakness of the soul. These reasons must have even greater force when speaking of *Indias* because they are of the more imperfect sex.

---

20. The phrase here is Latin: "*non este de meliori bono.*"
21. Two words are illegible in this sentence.

[Romano concludes by reiterating his main points, and dates his submission May 25, 1723. The fiscal of the Real Acuerdo, having weighted the opinions of the religious authorities consulted, judged that it would be helpful to create an inventory of the possible women who might be prepared to enter the proposed convent. He noted that such a list might begin with two cacicas originally considered for the convent, Luisa de Rivera who owned a business selling enaguas (petticoats) from Xilotepec (a community in the current state of Mexico) and a second woman who could be found in the company of a nun of the convent of San Juan de la Penitencia. However, both of these women, he learned, had recently married. The following excerpts describe the circumstances of three of the women who had been considered possible novitiates for the convent, but whose lives had turned in other directions.]

13.3 Biographical Details of Possible Novices for the Corpus Christi Convent

Account of the marriage of *doña* Luisa de Riviera

June 16, 1723: Having looked in the main square of this city for *doña* Luisa de Riviera, *India cacique,* she was found in a stall selling petticoats from Xilotepeq and in her company was one Francisco Xavier Chavazpado, a Spaniard, her husband. I spoke to both of them and they told me that they married on the fourth of October, the day of San Francisco, in the year 1722 and to validate this account I include witnesses Francisco Xavier Durán and Nicolas Rodríguez Moreno, Spaniards, *bachilleres* (graduates) and of this, I attest.

Joseph Manuel de Paz

Account of the marriage of Michaela de Candia

I certify and attest that having taken steps from Damiana Michaela de Candia, *India cacique* who notified me that she had a decree to enter as a nun in the new foundation and that she married. It occurred to her to look for me accompanied by her husband, Manuel *Indio* Sacristan[22] of the Hermitage of Nuestra Señora de Piedad, located at the opening of the roadway, and they told me they had contracted marriage in the month of May of this year and to validate this I include (in present in Mexico on the 17th of June of 1723) as witnesses *licenciado* Phelipe de Salazar, clerk of the Real Audiencia and *don* Diego de Arpuello, gatekeeper.

Joseph Manuel de Paz

---

22. A sacristan was a lay officer of the church who was responsible for the care of the sacristy and church.

Account of the marriage of Josepha de Solis

On September 14, 1723 *doña* Luisa de Riviera informed me that Josepha de Solis, *India cacique* who had been named to enter as a nun married Francisco Bermudes, servant of father *fray* Sandoval, *vicario* of the convent of San Juan de la Penitencia and the marriage took place on August 30, the day of Santa Rosa, of this year. And having asked *don* Miguel Moreno Vezarez, *mayordomo* of the convent about this, he told me it is true which and to verify it I make this account.

Joseph Manuel de Paz

Suggested Reading

Burns, Kathryn. *Colonial Habits: Convents and the Spiritual Economy of Cuzco, Peru.* Durham, NC: Duke University Press, 1999.

Díaz, Mónica. "The Indigenous Nuns of Corpus Christi: Race and Spirituality," in *Religion in New Spain*, ed. Susan Schroeder and Stafford Poole. Albuquerque: University of New Mexico Press, 2007, 179–192.

Gallagher, Ann Miriam, R.S.M. "The Indian Nuns of Mexico City's *Monasterio* of Corpus Christi, 1724–1821," in *Latin American Women: Historical Perspectives*, ed. Asunción Lavrin (pp. 150–72). Westport, CT: Greenwood Press, 1978.

Lavrin, Asunción. *Brides of Christ: Conventual Life in Colonial Mexico.* Stanford, CA: Stanford University Press, 2008.

van Deusen, Nancy E. *Between the Sacred and the Worldly: The Institutional and Cultural Practice of* Recogimiento *in Colonial Lima.* Stanford, CA: Stanford University Press, 2002.

Villella, Peter B. *Indigenous Elites and Creole Identity in Colonial Mexico, 1500–1800.* New York: Cambridge University Press, 2016.

Document Themes

- Race and ethnicity
- Religion
- Sexuality and gender

14

An African Woman Petitions for
Freedom in a Colonial Brazilian
Mining Town (Vila Rica, 1766)

Introduction and Translation by Mariana Dantas

Rita de Souza Lobo, the main protagonist of this chapter, was an enslaved African woman in early eighteenth-century Brazil. She successfully negotiated her freedom in 1743, but later had to prove her freed status and that of her Brazilian-born daughters to avoid re-enslavement. Lobo's story is appealing because, unlike so many other enslaved Africans and African descendants in Brazil, she managed to become free. Her struggles reveal, nevertheless, the vulnerability of freed people, particularly women, in a society organized around slavery and patriarchy.

In the early eighteenth century, Rita de Souza Lobo was taken from West Africa, most likely present-day Ghana, to the Brazilian port city of Rio de Janeiro. Slaves who were embarked in that region of Africa were commonly described as "Mina" or of the "Mina nation," a general term that ignored and erased their geographical or ethnic origins and collective identity.[1] Lobo experienced the traumatic Atlantic crossing as a young woman, or girl, a fact that would not have spared her from being sexually harassed or raped by ship crewmembers, a common practice on transatlantic slave ships. After arriving in Rio de Janeiro, she still had to endure the rough trek inland to the captaincy of Minas Gerais. The captaincy's rich mining sites had attracted tens of thousands of people and created an intense demand for slave labor.[2] Once near the town of Vila Rica, the seat of the captaincy, Lobo was purchased by a freed black couple. Her owners were former slaves who, after obtaining

---

1. The term *Mina* derived from the Castle of São Jorge da Mina, a Portuguese trading fort and the first European trading post established in the Gulf of Guinea, in West Africa. James H. Sweet, *Recreating Africa: Culture, Kinship, and Religion in the African-Portuguese World, 1441–1770* (Chapel Hill: University of North Carolina Press, 2003), 13–30.

2. Gold was first discovered in the interior of Brazil in the late seventeenth century. The region, named Minas Gerais, quickly became the economic center and most densely populated captaincy of colonial Brazil. Laird W. Bergad, *Slavery and the Demographic and Economic History of Minas Gerais, 1720–1888* (Cambridge: Cambridge University Press, 1999).

their freedom, sought their own prosperity through gold mining and slave ownership.

Rita de Souza Lobo became a wage earner for her owners, João de Souza Lobo and his wife, Francisca Nunes do Rosário. Enslaved women were rarely forced to work in gold mining. Their owners expected them to earn money as peddlers of food and drink, domestic workers, and sex workers. They enjoyed some autonomy and were often allowed to keep part of their earnings after surrendering the amount demanded of them. Occasionally they managed to save enough gold to purchase their freedom. Because African women were frequently employed as wage earners, they were more successful than male slaves at negotiating their manumission (the process by which slaves were legally freed). Rita de Souza Lobo, for instance, accumulated sufficient gold by 1743 to pay for her freedom.

Access to manumission also depended on a slave owner's goodwill. João de Souza Lobo, inspired perhaps by a sense of obligation toward the enslaved woman he pursued sexually and impregnated, offered Lobo her freedom with the condition that she remain in his company while he lived. Lobo, in turn, offered her owners a payment of one pound of gold to secure her freedom immediately.[3]

As a former slave, Rita de Souza Lobo would face new challenges. While enslaved, she had become sexually involved with a *branco* (white man), Francisco Martins Castellano. It was Castellano, it seems, who had advised Lobo to renegotiate the terms of her freedom. He had even tried to pay for Lobo's immediate manumission with credits that were owed to him—a common form of payment in colonial Minas Gerais, where the shortage of currency was notorious. But gold was ultimately preferable to credit, and thanks to her savings Lobo secured her freedom without becoming indebted to another man. She was unable, however, to avoid altogether Castellano's attempts to claim some authority over her. In order to hide the illicit nature of their relationship, she agreed to pass for his slave in public.

Despite their domestic arrangement, Rita de Souza Lobo worked hard to become independent from Castellano. She took up different economic activities, contracting purchases and sales, moving credit, and collecting wages as a washerwoman. She eventually acquired her own house in the town of Vila Rica and, according to witnesses, always conducted herself as a free person.

---

3. Manumission was relatively widespread in colonial Brazil, even though the number of freed slaves was relatively small compared to the overall size of the slave population; the majority of manumissions resulted from slaves' own efforts to purchase their freedom. Stuart B. Schwartz, "The Manumission of Slaves in Colonial Brazil: Bahia, 1684–1745," *The Hispanic American Historical Review* 54:4 (November 1974), 603–35.

Lobo's standing in Brazil's patriarchal and slave society remained vulnerable, however. When Castellano died in the mid-1750s, his son and executor of his will, Manuel Martins, claimed that Lobo and three of her five daughters were his father's slaves. Maria, Efigênia, and Escolástica, were born of sexual encounters Lobo had outside of her relationship with Castellano. All three were described as *crioulas*. Lobo's middle daughters, Anna and Francisca, had been fathered by Castellano and, because of their mixed descent, were described as *pardas*.[4] Martins recognized Anna and Francisca as his half-sisters and did not try to enslave them. But he took advantage of the domestic fiction Castellano had fabricated to list Lobo and her *crioula* daughters as part of the family estate and his own inheritance. Faced with the potential enslavement of her daughters and her own re-enslavement, Lobo appealed to local government officials and to the King of Portugal himself to defend their right to freedom.

The documents in this chapter illustrate Rita de Souza Lobo's legal efforts to prove her and her daughters' free status. Lobo initiated legal proceedings in 1766, most likely with someone's help; very few former slaves were literate in colonial Minas Gerais. At that time, she procured witness testimonies and documents that proved her manumission and the free-born status of her daughters (document 14.2). Her file, however, remained forgotten in the archives of the secretariat for several years. In 1774, with the help of an acquaintance on his way to Lisbon, Lobo tried again to argue her freedom by appealing directly to the King. Her plea gained the sympathy of the Overseas Council, the King's advisers in matters pertaining to Portugal's colonial possessions (document 14.1). Armed with an order from the King, Lobo petitioned the governor of Minas Gerais once more in 1775 to confirm her freedom. An official from the secretariat reviewed Lobo's earlier file, interviewed new witnesses, and pronounced that his findings corroborated Lobo's claims (document 14.2).

Rita de Souza Lobo's story reveals the many challenges slave women had to face in colonial Brazil: from sexual subjugation, to forced social submission, to potential re-enslavement after achieving freedom. But it also reveals these women's resilience and persistence as they sought their autonomy in a slave and patriarchal society. In the end, Lobo successfully proved her freedom on paper. Unfortunately, we lack information about whether or not those

---

4. The terms *pardo(a)* and *crioulo(a)* were used in colonial Brazil as descriptive terms to distinguish, respectively, a person of mixed African and European descent, or perceived to have a lighter skin tone, from someone of sole African descent born in the colonies. Douglas Libby, "A Culture of Colors: Representational Identities and Afro-Brazilians in Minas Gerais in the 18th and 19th Centuries," *Luso-Brazilian Review* 50:1 (June 2013), 26–52.

involved in her and her daughters' illegal enslavement were subsequently ordered to release them and complied.

Rita de Souza Lobo blamed her willingness to pursue an illicit relationship with Francisco Martins Castellano on her fragility; she may have meant her moral fragility. Yet, in what ways does Lobo's story of enslavement and transition to freedom reveal other, social and economic fragilities or vulnerabilities of black women in colonial Brazil? How did Lobo attempt to strengthen her standing in Minas Gerais's slave and patriarchal society? Did the fact that Lobo chose to live in an urban center influence the outcome of her story? While her relationship to Castellano became the source of her later troubles, what other relationships proved helpful to her? Overall, how did the social and economic behavior of African descending people in colonial Brazil influence people's perception of what it meant to be a slave or a free person?

14.1 Petition for Confirmation of Freedom Presented by Rita de Souza Lobo to the Portuguese Overseas Council in Lisbon, 1774[5]

Rita de Souza Lobo, freed *preta* (black woman), resident in Vila Rica do Ouro Preto, declares that, being a slave of João de Souza Lobo and his wife Francisca Nunes, they granted her a letter of manumission and liberty in the year of 1743 not just for the love they had for her but also because they received from the petitioner the amount of one pound of gold, that was then worth 192$000 *réis*.[6] And since then she began to behave as the freed person she had become, going wherever she wanted and living wherever she could afford without contestation or impediment from anyone. However, the petitioner, because of her fragility, got together with Francisco Martins Castelhado, in whose house and company she lived for many years in illicit union. But since he did not want the parish priest to know about their concubinage, he said and showed externally that the petitioner was his slave, and as such she was reputed to be by the neighbors and the same priest, something the petitioner did not deny, not just because of her ignorance and rusticity, but also because she believed she was safe because of the letter of freedom she possessed. And

---

5. This petition can be found among the Loose Documents from the Portuguese Overseas Council Archive—Collection for Minas Gerais (microfilmed and digitized), box 115, document 60, May 13, 1774.

6. The *real* (pl. *réis*) was the currency of colonial Brazil. But the absence of printed money and shortage of minted coins meant that transactions mostly relied on gold powder or small gold bars. In 1743, one-eighth of an ounce of gold (a unit called the *oitava*) was worth fifteen hundred *réis*.

during that time, she had five daughters, two *pardas*, Anna and Francisca, whom her said lover recognized as his and sent to a convent in this kingdom, and three *crioulas*, Maria, Efigênia, and Escolástica. And supposing that the priest has declared them captives of the said Francisco Martins in their baptismal records it is not because in truth they were, but because he believed that the petitioner was a slave. But the said Francisco Martins always treated her as a freed woman because he knew her to be one and, consequently, her aforementioned three daughters. In fact, when he passed away leaving his will he did not mention one word in reference to the petitioner or the said *crioulas*. However, Manuel Martins, son and heir of the said Martins Castelhado, knowing this indisputable truth, nevertheless declared the three *crioulas* in the inventory as captives of his father, and as a result they have been suffering under the yoke of slavery for more than thirteen years, because being rustic, poor, and miserable[7] they do not have someone to help and speak for them. She, the petitioner, as their mother, wanted to request that since she was free, and since birth follows the womb, [8] the said *crioulas* should not be subjected to captivity, for they had been born after the petitioner was freed. But when she looked for her letter of freedom she did not find it, either having lost it or having had it stolen, but she made up for the lacking document with a justification from five witnesses she produced through the citation of her masters João de Souza Lobo and his wife which they had not opposed as is judicially evident in the indubitably substantiated papers contained in the attached documents. But she has not filed any legal proceedings because of the rightful fear that justice will require a bribe. In light of these circumstances, she resorts to Your Majesty so that you, as a father and lord of your vassals may free the petitioner's miserable daughters from the unjust captivity in which they find themselves, since only the venerable and paternal providence of Your Majesty can help them, offering them justice without the bribes that are so common in that land. And may you order the Judge of the Royal Exchequer of Minas Gerais, and in his absence or impediment the Judge Intendant

---

7. "Miserable" was a rhetorical term often used in colonial petitions. It implied that a group or an individual's vulnerability made them deserving of the legal protection of the crown or to be favored by the king. R. Jovita Baber, "Law, Land, and Legal Rhetoric in Colonial New Spain: A Look at the Changing Rhetoric of Indigenous Americans in the Sixteenth Century," in *Native Claims: Indigenous Law against Empire, 1500–1920*, ed. Saliha Belmessous (New York: Oxford University Press, 2012), 41–62.

8. In the Portuguese Empire, as well as elsewhere in the Americas where Africans and their descendants were enslaved, the children of enslaved women were considered to be legal slaves. Conversely, the children of free mothers could not be legally claimed as slaves. Margarida Seixas, "Slave Women's Children in the Portuguese Empire: Legal Status and Its Enforcement," in *Women in the Portuguese Empire: The Theatre of Shadows*, ed. Clara Sarmento (Newcastle, UK: Cambridge Scholars Publishing, 2008), 63–80.

of Vila Rica or the Local Judge of Marianna (since she is suspicious of the District Judge for personal reasons), that given the judicial documents the petitioner has presented, he soon free her said three *crioula* daughters Maria, Efigênia, and Escolástica, ordering that the said Manuel Martins pay them promptly the wages determined by two arbitrators of good conscience who shall take into account the time in which they have been unjustly enslaved. And all shall be granted by the said Martins summarily and soon without the involvement of another official in order to avoid further delays which is what the defendant [Martins] wants, so that he may eternalize this dependency. And since the petitioner and her daughters are poor, miserable, and rustic, and he more powerful and with friends, he will easily corrupt your justice and will seek the means to satisfy his malice.

I ask Your Majesty that by your greatness you will see it fit to grant the mercy requested.

[There is an annotation on the margin of the petition, possibly from one of the Overseas Councilors, which reads, "The mercy the petitioner requests can only be obtained by the immediate greatness of Your Majesty." A second annotation, dated from November 22, 1774, orders the governor of Minas Gerais to ascertain with all exactness the claims Rita de Souza Lobo has made and then to issue a decision.[9]]

14.2 Lobo's Legal File[10]

[This file includes: a) A petition by Rita de Souza Lobo regarding the freedom of her daughters, presented to the governor of the captaincy of Minas Gerais in 1775. b) The opinion of an officer of the secretariat of the government of the captaincy, whose name is illegible. c) Record of the testimonies of witnesses interviewed by the officer of the secretariat in 1775. d) The Instrument of Justification, or claims proceedings, that Rita de Souza Lobo initiated in 1766 and filed with the local courts in 1767; it includes: (i) a list of Lobo's claims, (ii) witness testimonies, (iii) information about the content of Francisco Martins Castellano's last will and testament, (iv) copies of her daughters' baptismal records, and (v) a letter from Lobo's former owner.]

9. This petition can be found among the Loose Documents from the Overseas Council Archive—Collection for Minas Gerais (microfilmed and digitized), box 115, document 60, May 13, 1774.
10. Public Archive of Minas Gerais, Collection Secretariat of the Government of the Captaincy—Colonial Section, box 8, document 14, July 24, 1775.

a) Illustrious and Most Excellent Sir,

Rita de Souza Lobo, freed *preta*, resident of this town for many years, declares that she had petitioned his Royal Majesty, deceased, with a very just request about the five daughters that the petitioner bore after being free of slavery, and who are serving a perpetual enslavement, except one who has already died. The said petition was taken to the court by the hand of Sargent Major Francisco Sanxas Brandão, who has returned it to this capital with a statement sent from the Monarch to Your Excellency's predecessor ordering that it be investigated and, if in fact [her daughters] were in captivity, that they be released and paid the wages they were due during their enslavement.

[The rest of this document states that the response Lobo received from the Crown was an order to investigate her claims, and requests that the current governor of Minas Gerais search for the documents she had filed in 1767.]

b) Illustrious, Excellent Sir

Through documents, which I now share with you, and witnesses that I extra-judicially interviewed, I have come into the knowledge that Rita de Souza Lobo, mentioned in the enclosed petition, was the slave of João de Souza Lobo and of his wife Francisca Nunes do Rosário. The two, because of the good services she provided and a pound of gold they received from her, gave her a letter of manumission and freedom. Under that condition she came to this hamlet of Inficcionado from the Hill of Agua Quente [in the captaincy of Minas Gerais] to live with Francisco Martins Castellano. He, to disguise the illicit communication he had with her, called her his slave, and declared her as such in the Roster of Confessed during their first years [together].[11] She nevertheless had with him the two *mulata* (person of African and European parentage) daughters that she declared in her petition, of whom I know one to be deceased and the other in Rio de Janeiro and willing to be placed under the authority of Manuel Martins, son and heir of the aforementioned [Castellano].[12] However, after a few years, because [Castellano] was jealous that she had given birth to two *crioula* daughters, as well as of her first daughter who was born as soon as she had arrived in that hamlet, he left her. From then on, she began to live by herself, buying a house, exchanging credit, selling and contracting as a free person with no objections from the said Francisco Martins or any other person. And once

---

11. The Roster of the Confessed was a list of parishioners who had complied with their annual obligations of confession. It was organized by household and therefore identified members of the family unit as well as household dependents, such as slaves or members of the extended family.

12. It appears that Lobo's surviving *mulata* daughter was willing to live under Manuel Martin's patriarchal authority as his dependent.

he died, it is known that he did not bequeath the petitioner or her daughters in his will; even so, the said Manuel Martins listed them in the inventory as slaves and sold the mother and two *crioula* daughters, the youngest ones, to the Priest Pedro Machado, who resides near Serro Frio [a district in northern Minas Gerais]. After concluding a judicial inquiry through the summation of the testimonies I include here, its findings were:

Having heard the accused Manuel Martins, he only presented me with a torn note of credit passed by his father Francisco Martins to João de Souza Lobo, former owner of the petitioner, according to which [Francisco Martins] committed to satisfying the amount of 249 *oitavas* of gold for which amount the note stated he had bought [Rita de Souza Lobo] in the year of 1743. However, without witnesses who had observed the said purchase and contract of credit, and only [Martins's] signature, and there being no deed of sale or any other document that could prove that alleged sale, he only brought to my presence some witnesses who had heard say, most of them from [Castellano], that he had bought [Rita] from her owner. Still in no other way was I given evidence that the said purchase had been real and that the credit agreement had been verified.

Given the terms of this case I am persuaded that both the petitioner and her daughters are freed; she because of the freedom she obtained from the only owners she recognizes, and those because they were born of a free womb as was that of their mother at the time of their birth. The request of the petitioner is worthy of the paternal providence to which she has appealed. [*The officer asks that the governor proceed as he judges best and signs the document with his initials.*] City of Mariana, July 24, 1775.

c) [*The first pages of the recorded testimonies of witnesses interviewed by the officer of the Secretariat of the Government of the Captaincy are missing. The first available folio of the document begins in the middle of a witness statement.*]

Rita de Souza Lobo was never the slave of said Francisco Martins but instead lived under the authority of the aforementioned with this title to better disguise the illicit communication she had with him and so that testimonies given to the priest of that parish not cause the priest to separate them. Therefore, he was completely certain that her only owners had been João de Souza Lobo and his wife Francisca Nunes, from the Hill of Agua Quente in the parish of Catas Altas, who in the past had given [Lobo] her letter of freedom. And in the security of her freedom she lived and moved around and at this time she had the daughters she had mentioned in her petition, and who he, the witness, is informed are being held or were sold by Manuel Martins, son of the aforementioned Francisco Martins, with the exception of the two *mulatas* who [Manuel Martins] recognized as daughters and, as such, were sent to one of the convents in the kingdom of Portugal, as is the current practice of all in that hamlet. And this, with some specificities provided by witnesses, he made known through a letter from September 2, 1770 to captain Bernardo Vasco Cardoso, who per order of the then governor of this captaincy had informed himself of this matter having thus, both at present and since that time, recognized as free the aforementioned *preta* and her daughters and the fraud that the aforementioned Manuel Martins perpetrated against them. And no more did he say about the petition [*the statement is signed by the public notary Joaquim José de Oliveira*]. [Witness signature:] Jeronimo Barros Souza.

[The second witness was Captain Bernardo Vasco Cardoso, a forty-four-year-old resident of the city of Mariana, whose occupation was described as miner. Cardoso confirms that he had been asked in 1770 by the governor of the captaincy to seek information about Rita de Souza Lobo. He states that she was the slave of João de Souza Lobo and his wife, from whom she purchased her manumission. Cardoso repeats much of the information shared by the first witness about Lobo's relationship with Castellano, adding only that after the relationship ended "she lived in her own house, selling and contracting as a freed person and paying the cost of her head tax." He also acknowledges that Manuel Martins had held or sold Lobo and her crioula *daughters despite their free status.*

The third witness was captain Pedro Gonçalves Chaves, a sixty-two-year-old farmer, and resident of the parish of Inficcionado, where Rita de Souza Lobo once lived. His testimony added the following information to the previous two testimonies:]

[Rita de Souza Lobo] was the slave of João de Souza Lobo of the Hill of Agua Quente, who because he was intimate with her he took her away from his house for the sake of his wife and he placed her in the hamlet of Inficcionado in another house he had bought or rented for that purpose. And while in that situation, it is said that Francisco Martins Castellano bought [Rita de Souza Lobo] from [João de Souza Lobo], but the witness is not sure. [*Chaves describes in the same terms as the other witnesses Lobo's relationship to Castellano, but he adds that:*] In the beginning [Lobo] demonstrated submission and obedience to the said Francisco Martins just like a slave. But it was not like this towards the end, because she bought, sold, and contracted on her own as a freed person and on terms such as those of the purchase of a house that he, the witness, had sold to Antônio da Costa Pena, who in turn sold it to the said *preta* woman for credit. [Lobo] had then become indebted to him, the witness, and as a result of that obligation he, the witness, received in payments [from] the said *preta* woman seventy-six thousand and so many *réis.* [*Chaves testifies further to Lobo's commercial dealings and financial solvency by stating that:*] [She] has bought several shipments of goods in her name and commits to satisfying their price, paying others in the same way she paid him the witness.

d) Civil Instrument of Freedom and Justification issued by petition from Rita de Souza Lobo, freed *preta*

Know all who view this public instrument of justification and citation of witnesses given and issued by judicial order and authority in the office of me, notary public named below, that in my possession and notary office there are certain acts of justification between the parties Rita de Souza Lobo and João de Souza Lobo and Francisca Nunes do Rosário, his wife, which were *de verbo ad verbum* [word by word] as follows:

(i) [*The first part of the Instrument of Justification is the summary of the claims made by Rita de Souza Lobo in a petition that had been issued by, or with the help of, local town judge Captain Antônio João Bellas. Lobo appeared in person to file the summary with the office of the governor of the captaincy, in the town of Vila Rica, on July 17, 1766.*]

Rita de Souza Lobo, freed *preta* of the Mina nation, resident in this town, declared that she, the claimant, proposes in this court to prove the following items, and requests that once that is done, she receive her instrument of proof:

Item 1: That the claimant was the slave of João de Souza Lobo and his wife Francisca Nunes do Rosário, freed *pretos* and residents in the parish of Our Lady of Catas Altas do Matto Dentro, a precinct of the city of Mariana.

Item 2: That the said owners of the petitioner gave her a letter of freedom written in the year of 1743 because the claimant had for that purpose given them one pound of gold, which they received from her hand, and because of the great love her said owners had for her in return for the service the claimant had provided to them.

Item 3: That since that time and year of 1743 until now the claimant has always been on her own.

[*The document is missing the folio in which the rest of item 3 and items 4 and 5 are listed. We can assume from the witness statements that these items reflected Lobo's claims that she behaved as a free woman after obtaining her manumission; that she never had another owner; that she had lost her letter of manumission; and that her children were born after she had been freed. The existing pages of the document pick up again with the testimonies of Rita de Souza Lobo's former owners.*]

(ii) [*On the same day, July 17, 1766, the witnesses were called to the office of the notary public of the town of Vila Rica and questioned by the inquisitor of the court, João Rodrigues Martins.*] 1st Witness: Francisca Nunes do Rosário, freed *preta*, resident in the Catas Altas, parish of Our Lady of Conceição, precinct of the City of Mariana, who lives with her husband João de Souza Lobo, said to be sixty years of age more or less. Witness to whom the said inquisitor administered the oath of the holy gospels by putting her right hand over the holy book and charging her to say and swear on the truth of all she knew and was asked, and having received the oath, she promised to do as instructed.

And asked of her the witness about the content of the first item presented by the claimant she said that she is the very Francisca Nunes do Rosário named in this article and that there is no doubt, and she knows firsthand, that the claimant Rita de Souza Lobo had been hers and her husband's slave and she said no more about this.

Of the second item she said that she knows first-hand, having witnessed it, that the claimant had given them one pound of gold for her freedom in the year of 1743, and that they gave her a letter of manumission and freedom signed by her, the witness, and her husband, it being certain that she and her husband had loved the said claimant because of her good services; and she said no more about this.

Of the third item she said that after she and her husband had given the claimant her letter of manumission she immediately left from under their authority and dominion, moving to wherever she wanted since she was her own master and because the said letter of freedom was granted without any onus or condition, all with no objection by any person still to this day; and she said no more about this.

Of the fourth item, she said that she knows first-hand that the said claimant after being freed lived several years in the parish of Our Lady of Nazareth of the Inficcionado and that nine or ten years ago the said claimant moved to the parish of Ouro Preto of this town [of Vila Rica] where she was still living without going to another part, without objection of any person, and it is certain that the said claimant did not have another owner in these mines aside from her the witness and her husband since they had bought her from a shipment coming to these mines from Rio de Janeiro; and she said no more about this.

Of the fifth item, she said that there is no doubt that the said claimant complained to her, the witness, that she had lost the letter of her freedom that she the witness and her husband had given her; and she also knows first-hand that the same claimant never during the time she was her slave had any children, and only since some time back did she start having the children she declared in this item; and she said no more about this last and final item of the petition, which had been read and declared to her by the said inquisitor. [*After the deposition was read back to the witness, who agreed it was accurate, the inquisitor signed it for her because the witness "does not know how to read or write."*]

[*Francisca Nunes do Rosário's testimony was followed by the testimony of four more witnesses. The second witness was João de Souza Lobo, Rita de Souza Lobo's former master. He was described as eighty-seven or eighty-eight years old, a freed* preto, *resident in Catas Altas, a town of the city of Mariana, and a miner by occupation. The third witness was Antônio Luis da Costa, also a freed* preto, *who appeared to be seventy years old. Costa resided at the base of the hill of Antônio Dias, adjacent to the town of Vila Rica, and was a miner by occupation. The fourth witness was Estácio Ferras Sampaio, a* branco *of approximately fifty-one years of age, and a resident of the town of Vila Rica; he was a solicitor of causes in the town courts. The fifth and final witness was Joana Coelho de Oliveira Coimbra, a freed* preta *whose age appeared to be seventy years, a resident on the New Street of the town of Vila Rica, and an innkeeper by occupation. Costa, Sampaio, and Coimbra all stated that they were acquainted with Lobo, and therefore knew information about her firsthand. They noted that Lobo had moved from her owner's house after purchasing her manumission and settled in the parish of Inficcionado for a few years. She had then moved to the town of Vila Rica where, some added, she earned a living as a washerwoman. Finally, they all testified to the veracity of Lobo's claims and to her and her daughter's right to freedom.*]

(iii) Rita de Souza Lobo, freed *preta*, declares that for the benefit of a petition she has she needs a certificate containing the content of the disposition or dispositions from the last will and testament of the deceased Francisco Martins, resident in Inficcionado, in which he mentions the petitioner and her three *crioula* daughters named Efigênia, Escolástica, and Maria. And if no such dispositions are found in the last will and testament she needs this fact noted in the certificate. Additionally, that the same notary public, when examining the inventory that was drawn after the death of the said Martins, declare who listed the property that was inventoried, and for what price were the said *crioulas* evaluated; and if such information is not in the inventory, that it be noted in the certificate.

[*On September 11, 1767, the notary public of the exchequer of the City of Mariana submitted a certificate declaring that in a book of last wills and testaments that was kept at his notary office he located the last will and testament of Francisco Martins Castellano. In that document, he found no mention of the claimant Rita de Souza Lobo, or of her daughters, as slaves or the manumitted slaves of Castellano's. Finally, he noted that he had no information about the inventory of the deceased's property because that document had not been registered with his notary office.]*

(iv) Rita de Souza Lobo, *preta* of the Mina nation, declares that having been the slave of João de Souza Lobo and his wife Francisca Nunes Rosário, freed *pretos* and residents in the parish of Conceição das Catas Altas do Mato Dentro, she achieved her letter of freedom for a price that she satisfied in the year of 1743. With that freedom, she moved to the parish of Inficcionado where she lived in the house of Francisco Martins, a white man and today deceased. In those circumstances the petitioner had during the following years five daughters, two by the name of Ana and Francisca, and three *crioulas* by the names: Maria, Efigênia, and Escolástica. And because she needs the baptismal record of each one of the three *crioula* daughters: it is requested that you be asked to order the reverend vicar of the said parish of Inficcionado, or who in that capacity may serve, to report from the books of baptismal records the content of the record for each one of the said crioulas: Maria, Efigênia, and Escolástica, daughters of the petitioner.

Antônio Dias Delgado de Carvalho, vicar of Inficcionado and graduate in the Canons from the University of Coimbra

I certify that reviewing the second book of baptisms of this parish, in it, on the back of folio 30 there was a record with the following content: "On the sixteenth day of the month of November of one thousand and seven hundred and forty-three in this mother church of Our Lady of Nazareth of Inficcionado I baptized and put the holy oils on Maria, daughter of Rita slave of Francisco Martins. The godparents were José Ferreira Fialho and Anna *mulata*. And this being the truth I made this record, signed it and affirmed it under oath. Parish of Inficcionado, day, month, and year above, the vicar Luis Jayme de Magalhães Coutinho." And nothing else was found in the said record.

I also certify that on folio 83 of the same book there is another record with the following content: "On the twenty-first of September of one thousand seven hundred and fifty-two in this mother church I baptized and put the holy oils on Ephigenia *parvola*[13] natural daughter of Rita slave of Francisco Martins. The godparents were Captain João Favacho Roubão and Luzia de Crasto, the wife of Manuel Carreira Botelho, all from this parish, and I made this record, coadjutor Manuel de Souza." And nothing else was found in the said record.

---

13. *Parvola*, or *parvolo* in the masculine form, means small or little. As a noun it can also mean child.

Finally, I certify that on the back of folio 101 of the same book there was another record with the following content: "On the sixteenth day of the month of October of the year of one thousand seven hundred and fifty-seven in this mother church of Our Lady of Nazareth of Inficcionado, the Reverend Inácio Pedro de Souza, with my license, baptized and put the holy oils on Escolástica *parvola* natural daughter of Rita slave of Francisco Martins and of unknown father. The godparents were Captain João Favacho Roubão and Archangela de Moura, freed *parda*, and I made this record, the vicar Antônio Dias Delgado de Carvalho." And nothing else was found in the said record.

Inficcionado, September 9, 1767
The Vicar, Dr. Antônio Dias Delgado de Carvalho

(v) Captain Sir Bernardo Vasconcellos Cardoso

I, João de Souza Lobo, freed *preto*, had a *negra*[14] woman by the name of Rita and to the said slave I gave a letter of freedom with the obligation that she always be with me. And there was a *branco* who advised her to challenge that obligation. I then said that if they gave me something I would remove the obligation. The *branco* said that he committed to passing me a credit if I removed the obligation.[15] And seeing this, the same slave was very happy and quickly gave me one pound of gold which she had accumulated while under my authority. The man then recorded a paper that stated that the gold was his. I would like now to see him show a paper of sale saying that I sold the *negra* to him, with witnesses: All the records he has were made by himself without any paper statement being made by me. Therefore, the said *negra* is freed because she gave me her own gold, and the truest witness is myself and my wife. And [my wife] was never her mistress because I had bought [Rita] as a new slave from the hand of João Ferreira. And [Rita], for the good services she has provided, was freed by me and has never known another owner. I had a child with her and therefore I gave her the letter and the *negra* may pursue her justice because I did not contract a deed of sale with the said *senhor* Francisco Martins. And if she was his slave while she washed his clothes why did he pay her? She certainly was not his slave. She bought her house and lived in it as a freed *preta*,[16] and she paid the royal tax, and all else that was licit. [*The letter is signed with two crosses, identified as the sign of João de Souza Lobo and*

---

14. The term *negro/a* was often used to refer to a slave of African origin. It was not interchangeable with *preto/a*, however, because it would not have been used to refer to a freed person, whereas *preto/a* could be used for either an enslaved or freed person.
15. Payment in the form of a transfer of credit was common in colonial Minas Gerais, where other forms of currency were scarce.
16. When referring to her as a free person, he identified Lobo as a *preta* rather a *negra*.

of Francisca Nunes do Rosário. The notary public wrote that the signs of the cross were made by the hand of João and Francisca.]¹⁷

Suggested Reading

Dantas, Mariana. "Market Women of African Descent and the Making of Sabará, a Colonial Town in Eighteenth-Century Minas Gerais, Brazil," *Colonial Latin American Historical Review*, Second Series 2:1 (Winter 2014): 1–25.

Furtado, Júnia. *Chica da Silva: A Brazilian Slave of the Eighteenth Century.* New York: Cambridge University Press, 2009.

Higgins, Kathleen. *"Licentious Liberty" in a Brazilian Gold-Mining Region: Slavery, Gender and Social Control in Eighteenth Century Sabara, Minas Gerais.* State College: Pennsylvania State University Press, 1999.

Lauderdale Graham, Sandra. *Caetana Says No: Women's Stories from a Brazilian Slave Society.* Cambridge: Cambridge University Press, 2002.

Document Themes

- Family
- Labor
- Law
- Race and ethnicity
- Slavery

---

17. This file can be found at the Public Archive of Minas Gerais, Collection Secretariat of the Government of the Captaincy—Colonial Section, box 8, document 14, July 24, 1775.

15

Isabel Victoria García Sues the Hacienda del Trapiche over Land Ownership (Pamplona, Colombia, 1777)[1]

In this late eighteenth-century civil court case, an enslaved woman, Isabel Victoria García, sues a Spaniard to maintain possession of a portion of land on the Hacienda del Trapiche (or Landed Estate of the Mill), formerly owned by the Jesuits, and by 1777 under the ownership of one Juan Gregorio de Almeida. The parcel of land in question was a grove of several thousand cacao trees; whomever controlled the land would also enjoy the profits from the cacao trees. The entire case runs more than one hundred folios; the excerpts chosen here emphasize the issue of an enslaved woman's legal right to use her deceased husband's property and to file suit in the court to protect it. The excerpts also provide insight into marriage and family structures of enslaved women in late colonial Colombia.

Isabel Victoria García was the widow of Francisco Borja González, an enslaved man who held the position of captain at the Hacienda del Trapiche.[2] When he died in 1767, Isabel and their children became the beneficiaries of his estate and gained the right to use and profit from the property during her lifetime. At her death, the property was meant to revert to the body of the main estate. The practice of lending enslaved peoples land to cultivate was long-standing within the Spanish empire and it would have been a breach of custom for the land to be taken away from Isabel after Francisco's death. García's claim to the land was based on customary practice by enslaved peoples at the Jesuit *hacienda*; her conviction in the legal persuasiveness of custom may have emboldened her to take the case to the court.

At the time of her suit, García had remarried. Her second husband, Salvador Noguera, was a free man, possibly of Spanish descent, who frequently represented García in the case. From a legal standpoint, García's marriage to Noguera did not invalidate her claim to the cacao grove. The *hacienda* owner,

---

1. The editors thank Wilson Pava for his transcription assistance on this document.

2. As captain, Francisco would have enjoyed status and responsibility on the Hacienda relative to other slaves. This status likely influenced how much land they worked in the parcel, as well as Isabel's status.

Almeida, argued that he only allowed García to marry Noguera after she agreed to sell her claim to the land in order to purchase her freedom.

This case transpired in the 1770s in the town of Cucutá and the city of Pamplona, Colombia, both located today in the northeast corner of the country near its border with Venezuela. Because of the rural location, the case illuminates the experience of enslaved women and their families in the context of plantation labor and agriculture, as opposed to slaves living in towns and cities and working in market settings. Near Pamplona, Isabel and her family labored over cacao trees, an important product in Colombia's economy. This time and place highlights the experience of rural enslaved peoples in society and in court. With regard to chronology, the expulsion of the Jesuits from the New World in 1767 prompted the changeover of the ownership and management of the *hacienda* from the religious order to the private individual, Juan Gregorio Almeida. Living and working conditions for an enslaved person on a Jesuit-run *hacienda* would not have necessarily been preferable to those under a private owner. Nevertheless, the following case does include some indications that the defense of rights to land possession was more challenging in the new private system with its more precarious relationship to customary practices and behavior and its severance from previous personal slave-owner relations.

The *hacienda* owner Almeida objected stubbornly to García's claim lest a legal victory by a female slave should make an example of him. Almeida used to his advantage a characteristic of colonial litigation (and one not specific to women): the preponderance of overlapping or competing jurisdictions. A local judge in Cucutá initially ruled to award possession of the parcel to Isabel Victoria García. However, when Almeida appealed the ruling, he argued that "the proceedings carried out in Cucutá . . . are considered null inasmuch as [the judge in that court] did not have authority to undertake proceedings."[3] This was a clever argument. Because the land was formerly owned by the Jesuits, it fell under the jurisdiction of the Superior Junta (Council) de Temporalidades (ex-Jesuit landholdings) of the City of Pamplona. The Junta de Temporalidades was set up as a part of royal bureaucracy to deal with the sale of the property of the Jesuits after their order was exiled from the New World.[4] Almeida argued concurrently that he never would have agreed to let his slave marry a free person, claiming, "I responded that in no way I would consent to this . . . and she told me she would give me the money, or the part of the grove that corresponded to her. . . ."[5]

---

3. Archivo General de la Nación de Colombia, Sección Colonia, Fondo Temporalidades: SC.57, 8, D9, fol. 17v.
4. Bianca Premo, *Children of the Father King: Youth, Authority, and Legal Minority in Colonial Lima* (Chapel Hill: University of North Carolina, Press, 2005), 143.
5. Fol. 39v.

Throughout the case, several rulings by different judges supported Isabel Victoria García in her claims to maintain access to the land. To some, this may seem surprising; having remarried, she had arguably severed ties with the man who had originally possessed the land. And how could an enslaved person, whom we normally assume would be deprived of all civic rights and personal privileges, marry, file a legal case, and acquire property? Under the *Siete Partidas*, thirteenth-century Iberian legal code, enslaved men and women had the right to marry.[6] If a woman was married and her owner attempted to sell her away from her husband, she could ask a judge to mandate the sale be local in order not to jeopardize her marriage. Further, enslaved peoples had the right to be litigants if mistreated by their owners, a right that was codified in the 1680 *Recopilación de Leyes de Indias* and further emphasized in a 1789 Royal *Cédula* (decree).[7] In the case before us, Isabel Victoria García is a married woman who takes a Spaniard to court to ensure her access to property. Studies have shown that enslaved women acquired property in urban areas, especially by earning money in markets. In fact, some women acquired enough property over time as a strategy to purchase their freedom.[8] However, Victoria García seeks a different kind of property: she wants to maintain what are known as usufruct rights over a cacao grove.[9] The legal rights to marry and to hold property were certainly not realized by all enslaved women. However, for some, like Isabel Victoria García, perseverance and luck might mean these possibilities became realities. Recent work by historians on enslaved people's litigation suggests that García's decision to press forward with the lawsuit was in keeping with a strong embrace of the court system by enslaved peoples.[10] Especially in the time period in which her case unfolded, the number of court cases filed by enslaved peoples spiked.[11]

---

6. On slaves and marriage, see Samuel Parsons Scott and Robert I. Burns, *Las Siete Partidas, Volume 4: Family, Commerce, and the Sea: The Worlds of Women and Merchants* (Philadelphia: University of Pennsylvania Press, 2001), 901–3.

7. See the discussion in Matthew Mirow, *Latin American Law: A History of Private Law and Institutions in Spanish America* (Austin: University of Texas Press, 2004), 81–82.

8. On this practice, see the work of Christine Hünefeldt, *Paying the Price of Freedom: Family and Labor among Lima's Slaves, 1800–1854* (Berkeley: University of California Press, 1994).

9. Usufruct, or right to use without ownership, refers to Isabel Victoria García's right to use and profit from the cacao grove that belonged to her first husband throughout her and her children's lifetimes. Upon their deaths, the use of the property reverts to the owner.

10. In particular, Bianca Premo, *The Enlightenment on Trial: Ordinary Litigants and Colonialism in the Spanish Empire* (New York: Oxford University Press, 2017).

11. Evelyne Laurent-Perrault researches this trend for enslaved women in late colonial Venezuela. See "Esclavizadas, cimarronaje y la Ley en Venezuela, 1760–1809," in *Demando Mi Libertad: Relatos de mujeres Negras y sus estrategias de resistencia en Nueva Granada, Venezuela y Cuba* (Universidad Icesi, Cali-Colombia, forthcoming).

How and where does the person and voice of Isabel Victoria García enter this legal document? What can we read between the lines about her role in the court case? Is it passive or active? How did both gender and race affect her appearance in the court case? What was the potential influence that ownership of this piece of land might have on her life? How did García's life as an enslaved woman differ from that of other enslaved women whose lives are detailed in this volume?[12] How did her experience of the law compare with those of other women?[13]

Civil Suit between Isabel Victoria García, an Enslaved Afro–Colombian Woman, and a *Hacendado* over Land Ownership. Pamplona (Colombia), 1768[14]

15.1 Decree on the Lands Left by Francisco Bonifas

I, the public notary [Raphael Barreto] of the Cabildo of the City of Pamplona, in compliance with the orders of the *Señores* (Sirs) of this Municipal Junta [de Temporalidades] in a decree dated November 24th and 25th, 1777 order the testimony be presented from the following acts, whose content is as follow: [*The case file includes original testimony on how Isabel Victoria García came to possess usufruct*[15] *rights to the cacao grove.*]

By virtue of which this decree was provided = Santander on April 19th, 1768. Pursuant to the foregoing and based on what the prosecuting attorney [*don* (sir) Juan Josef de Vargas Machuca] has set forth, all the possessions remaining after the death of Francisco Bonifas Gonzáles, slave and captain of the Hacienda del Trapiche that belonged to Pamplona's Jesuit religious

---

12. Readers could compare García's experiences to those of women discussed in Chapters 14, 17, 19, and 20.

13. Readers could compare García's experiences to those of women discussed in Chapters 2, 12, and 21.

14. Archivo General de la Nación de Colombia, Sección Colonia, Fondo Temporalidades: SC.57, 8, D9 Juan Gregorio de Almeida, owner of the *Hacienda Del Trapiche* (Mill) *del Salado*, that was property of the regulars, the ex-Jesuits of the city of Pamplona, with respect to the appeal of the municipal council and the *alcalde ordinario* (judge of first instance and town council member) of the city in the case initiated by Isabel Victoria García, slave of the aforementioned Hacienda, concerning some *groves* (small farming plots) and some cacao groves.

15. Usufruct, or right to use without ownership, refers to Isabel Victoria García's right to use and profit from the cacao grove that belonged to her first husband throughout her and her children's lifetime. Upon their deaths, the use of the property reverts to the owner.

order, must be surrendered to his widow and his heirs.[16] *Don* Juan José de Vargas Machuca declares that the widow can take advantage of the *cacagual* (cocoa plantation) for her lifetime, but at the time of her death, the assets must be fully incorporated into the main *hacienda* = as signed by Olarte [the public notary] = You are hereby notified to implement, by virtue of the above mentioned, what has already been determined, agreeing with me and allowing me to make it known to the aforementioned *junta* = May God keep you many years. Santander, April 21st, 1768. I kiss your majesty's hand. Your servant [signed] José Simón de Olarte = *don* Juan José de Vargas Machuca

Petition: Members of the *junta*: *don* Pedro Agustín de Peralta, superintendent of the Temporalidades in this city, I appear before Your Honors in accordance with the power to declare on behalf of Salvador Noguera, resident of Cucuta and husband of Isabel, slave of the Trapiche Hacienda that was the property of the Jesuit order, and widow of the slave Francisco Bonifas. It has come to my attention that the slave Isabel has been dispossessed by Juan Gregorio Almeida of the *cacagual* that she owned, under pretext of [exchanging it] for her freedom. As this is not in accordance with the order by the members of the *Junta Superior*, dated April 19, 1768, which I submit to Your Honors in its original version, and given the fact that the slave Isabel has been dispossessed, the cacao grove, and by extension, the Temporalidades may suffer damage over time. Your Honors will be well served to consider what has transpired and should grant the present scribe my petition as does the Superior Order that I attach below. And to all Your Honors, I beg you declare as I plead = Pedro Agustín de Peralta = Pamplona, October 25, 1777.

[The court acknowledged receipt of this petition and forwarded it to the superintendent of Temporalidades, don Pedro Agustín de Peralta. Soon thereafter, Salvador Noguera appeared before the junta of Pamplona to provide additional details on the case.]

15.2 Petition of Salvador Noguera

Members of Pamplona's *junta*: Salvador Noguera, resident of this jurisdiction, respectfully appearing before you as the legal representative of Isabel Victoria García, who was a slave of the Temporalidades [estate], and I declare:

---

16. There is a rich historiography on Jesuit landholdings in Latin America. For one example see Nicholas P. Cushner, *Farm and Factory: The Jesuits and the Development of Agrarian Capitalism in Quito, 1600–1767* (Albany: State University of New York Press, 1982).

as stated in the evidence, that my party stood before the *alcalde ordinario* of this city, resident of St. Joseph parish, with the resolution of the Junta Provincial de Temporalidades to request that [the formalization of] her possession of a cacao grove be granted. According to a Superior Order,[17] she inherited the property at the death of Francisco Bonifas. This same Superior Order also states that she was despotically dispossessed by Juan Gregorio Almeida, who had claimed whatever he wanted. Suspicious of this outcome, the *alcalde* declared the decree, that can be found below on page twelve and its reverse, and ordered that I be notified of his decision. Given these facts, and since it did not appear that justice had been served, I decided with a heavy heart to seek justice before Your Honors. In the interest of justice, I plead that the court protect us and mandate in due compliance with the higher resolution that we submitted to the aforementioned *alcalde*, and which the party against whom judgment has been given cannot contest. Juan Gregorio Almeida argued since the beginning that he would not consent to grant us the cacao grove if we got married and that to this my party [García] responded that she would give him the share of the grove that fell to him or its monetary equivalent determined by mutual agreement. However, this is not what happened. In fact, what happened was that he made this offer, but my party answered him that she did not consent to it but rather said she would progressively pay him with the grove's usufruct. But he argued that she had to get the full value of the cocoa and that he would then accept the payment. After having agreed, he gave us permission to get married. We then got married and moved to the *hacienda* without any trouble. However, once we got there, [Almeida] called for Isabel and said these words to her: "Well now you got yourself married, and you have a husband who can take care of you; move out of here." To this, my party responded: "Sir and my parcel of cacao which is my sweat and labor, how am I to leave it? This is not what was agreed upon with your grace." [Almeida] repeated to her that there was nothing for her in the *hacienda* and that she should move. In the light of this irony, we found ourselves forced to move and this is what we did last year on December 4, 1775.

As had initially been planned, we decided to give him a hundred and fifty *pesos*,[18] which is the price at which the grove had been evaluated. I then went to Juan Gregorio's house to ask him if he would accept the money in exchange for the grove. He answered that he would take it. For this reason, I went to the house of *don* Juan Ignacio de Salazar, resident of the parish of el Rosario, to request that he lend me the money; I told him that I would pay

---

17. This refers to the ruling made by the Superior Junta de Temporalidades in 1768 that awarded the use of cacao grove of Francisco Bonifas to Isabel Victoria García, see Section 1 "Decree."

18. Units of money; one *peso* was made up of eight *reales*.

him with the usufruct of the grove and he agreed to this. We went together to see Juan Gregorio, and Salazar told him to acknowledge that he would provide the money on the condition that he would be paid with the usufruct of the grove. Juan Gregorio answered him that he could not steal the bread from Isabel's children's mouths. Given this answer and given the fact that he enjoyed no guarantee of being paid with the usufruct of the grove, [Salazar] did not want to supply the money and left. Everything was suspended because we were not yet aware of the superior judgement mentioned earlier. As God willed it, we learned of the [judgment] just then but Juan Gregorio, empowered by his authority, took the best eight hundred and ninety-two cacao trees saying they were worth two hundred *pesos*, which corresponded to the amount the slave is worth. This is not true and goes against both logic and the law because, because [her value] and the agreement they had for it was for one hundred and fifty *pesos*.

He has confessed that he ordered, in an authoritarian manner, that he asked Javier Fernández to go to the grove and separate the number of trees whose appraisal satisfied his interest. This should not have happened because even supposing that this had been the agreement (which we do not concede it was), [his claiming of the trees] should only have transpired with the prior consultation with and consent of my party, or with the intervention of [the law]. And unless [Almeida] demonstrates [her] consent or good faith, it should not have happened. Almeida wants to get three hundred thirty-four *pesos* and four *reales* that corresponds, according to him, to the cacao grove's value calculated with the market price of three *reales* per tree. But this is mistaken because the market price is four *reales* per tree since those trees are, according to what has been declared, deemed to be in privately owned lands. For all these reasons, I beg your Honors to protect me and grant us the possession of this grove and of the house inside. I beseech you to prevent Juan Gregorio from disturbing our property; I also beg you to formally record that we harvested three times, the worth of which has benefited this *hacienda*. The value of the harvest should be used, on one hand, to cover the payment of a hundred and fifty pesos corresponding to the amount that my wife agreed to pay and, on the other, to defray the charges and fees that I had to pay because of the lawsuit brought on the refusal to give us the grove. I ask the court to order the relief requested = Salvador Noguera = For legal purposes, I beg your Excellencies to order to the public notary to provide me with a copy of my pleading = Salvador Noguera = Pamplona, October 25, 1777.

[The case then moves through motions for transfer to a different jurisdiction, because Juan Gregorio de Almeida hopes to appeal. Copies of the case files are sent and received by the relevant offices.]

15.3 Petition of Juan Gregorio Almeida in Response to the Allegations by Isabel Victoria García

Señores of the municipal Junta de Temporalidades: Juan Gregoria Almeida, having received the scribe's copy of a text presented by Salvador Noguera in the name of Isabel Victoria that claims that I wrongfully plundered Isabel of a parcel of cacao trees, I appear before your grace and state that having filed this same lawsuit before the tribunal of *señor don* Pedro Navarro, *alcalde ordinario*, resident of Cucuta. I responded to the claim in the demand on pages ten, eleven, and twelve and the *señor alcalde* had to remit the response to the Superior Provincial *Junta* by decree on September 25, 1777. [*The petition goes on to suggest that because Almeida has filed the case before another, the court should not pursue the suit and should inform his accuser that multiple suits are unnecessary and cause extra work for him and for the judges.*]

Almeida states that the case will be heard by the Superior Junta, *which is in possession of the case files, including the record of García taking possession of the parcel of land.*]

15.4 Isabel Victoria García and Felipe Noguera Take Possession of the Cacao Grove

Citation.

In Trapiche in the jurisdiction of Pamplona, on the *hacienda* of Juan Gregoria Almeida on the 17th of the same month and year, I the *alcalde,* have given possession as ordered by the *señores* of the municipal Junta of Pamplona to Salvador Noguera and Isabel Victoria, his wife, of the cacao grove [Noguera] has requested in this *hacienda* as its owner. And since [Noguera] is currently away in Pamplona I sought out the *mayordomo* (overseer) of the *hacienda* or whomever is responsible for its care. Finding there Gerbacio García, a slave, who holds the office of Captain, I read him the dispatch given to me, and the order I provided to effect the possession. I cited him in the name of his master so that he would agree. He did not sign because he said he did not know how. This was recorded for the decree. I signed it with witnesses Juan Antonio de Omaña Riva de Neira = Juan Augustín del Rincón = Ambrozio Javier de Castro =

On the same day, month, and year I, *don* Juan Antonio de Omaña de Riva de Neira, *alcalde* of the parish of Our Lady of the Rosary and *juez de comición* (investigating judge) for the *señores* of the municipal Junta de Temporalidades of the City of Pamplona give possession of a small land parcel of cacao trees to Salvador Noguera in the name of his wife, Isabel Victoria.

According to and detailed in the dispatch. This landholding is found within the sphere of this *hacienda*, and to this effect, I have come and have solicited the corresponding citation of the [*hacienda's*] principal owner, Juan Gregorio Almeida. Because he is absent, I presented the decree to Gerbacio García *mulato* (man of African and Spanish parentage) slave who holds the office of Captain with whom along with Salvador Noguera and his wife, Isabel Victoria, I went to the place where the landholding is found. It aligns on the eastern part with the (plowed) fields that they call Santa Rita, and lies next to the smallholding of Rosa, slave of the *hacienda*, connecting by a large stream down below it, giving way to the plot named San Antonio. By its base, is found the boundary of the street named Santa Barbara where there is a little house of the aforementioned Isabel except for some trees that are found midway to the little house down below that are said to belong to the main *hacienda*. And taking Noguera and his wife by the hands, I put them in possession of the whole land parcel. [*The* alcalde *formally closes the decree affirming Noguera and García's rights to ownership. Salvador Noguera, Omaña Riva de Beira and two witnesses all signed the decree on November 20, 1777, although García did not.*]

15.5 Petition of Juan Gregorio to Challenge the Possession

Señores of the Junta de Temporalidades: I, Juan Gregorio Almeida, *vecino* (citizen) of this city, according to the law, appear before your Honors and state that today I have been informed through a decree dated today by your Honors pursuant to an appeal that I made wherein your Honors declared that Salvador Noguera and Isabel, his wife, be given possession of the cacao grove. [*Juan Gregorio alleges this decree has been made in too great haste and notes that the Superior Court is still planning to review the case. He argues that it is indispensable that the junta not allow the sentence of a lower judge to stand until the higher court has heard the appeal. He also highlights García's status as an enslaved woman. He continues:*]

I beg your Honors be served to determine that which corresponds in justice respecting the enslavement of Isabel because there is some urgency in this matter at present. I do not know if I should execute the role that masters can and should execute with their slaves or if I should consider her to be free and to entirely use her own hand. I beg that what I now ask does not prejudice my case nor the awaited results from the superior court. I beg your Honors to rule what you deem appropriate. Juan Gregorio Almeida, Pamplona, November 27, 1777.

15.6 Decree in Response

Pamplona, November 27, 1777.
This party can use his slave under the terms allowed by the law. Ordered and signed by the *señores* of the municipal *junta* before me the authorizing scribe, *don* Jacome Gonzalez Arze Barreto. And I the scribe made the decree known to Juan Gregorio Almeida in person. [*A decree orders that copies of documents be transferred to the higher court, including the appeal by Almeida and the testimony of both Noguera and García, all of which had been overseen by* don *Juan José de Vargas. Attorney Juan Vicente Pérez de Paramo acted on behalf of Almeida.*]

15.7 Notification

On July 7 of the current year, *don* Juan José de Vargas[19] finding himself in his home in this parish, I, the scribe, in compliance with what was ordered in the decree that precedes this went and in person to inform him of the content and aforementioned decree. Respecting what is asked of him in the text of the decree, he says the following: That he acted as *teniente* (deputy) and *justicia mayor* (senior judge) of the city of Pamplona and its jurisdiction and at the same time as administrator of the Temporalidades during the time that Francisco de Borja, slave of the *Hacienda del Trapich*e, died. [Borja] left some goods including a small cacao grove, located on the land of the Temporalidades of which an account was made for it all and remitted to the Superior Government for its resolution. And he knows this for a fact because the *señor don* Domingo Antón de Guzman, commander of said Temporalidades, sent him a missive in which the Superior government declared that the possession of the groves, or land parcels by the slaves of the *hacienda* belonged to them during their lifetimes and their children's lifetimes, giving no reason for them to be stripped of [these lands]. In their view, they are not documents that should be intercepted because they are to be returned to the *señor comandante* and this is what he can say on the subject. To certify I, Juan José de Vargas Machuca = Alejandro Ortiz, public scribe signed. [*In subsequent folios of the lawsuit, Noguera returns to court to check on the copies. A declaration detailing the goods belonging to Francisco Borja, García's deceased husband, as well as the ruling and testimony by Isabel are all re-entered into the record.*]

---

19. The attorney introduced in the opening decree of the case.

15.8 Decree

Holy Thursday, April 19, 1768, with reflection on the exhibits by the *señor fiscal* (prosecutor) and others who are present, it is declared that [the cacao grove] should be turned over to the widow and heirs of Francisco Borja Gonzáles, slave and Captain of the Hacienda del Trapiche that the Jesuit fathers possessed, in the jurisdiction of the City of Pamplona. All the goods that remained at the time of the death of Borja. Further, it is declared that the cacao grove is only to be enjoyed for the life of the widow and with her death it is to be incorporated into the main *hacienda*.

15.9 Petition of Isabel Victoria García

Petition to the *Señor Alcalde Ordinario*

Isabel Victoria García, slave previously of the Temporalidades, legitimate wife of Francisco Borja (deceased), with due respect and according to law, I appear before Your Honor to petition with due solemnity and with the necessary oath, against the Superior Order of the Royal Provincial Junta de Temporalidades, which has declared the law that assists me respecting the goods of my late husband, which I have possessed as my own and worked [with him] with sweat and labor. Among [his goods], the most lucrative is a cacao grove of more than 6,000 trees. Two years ago, my master Juan Gregorio Almeida, owner of the main *hacienda*, vested with his own power authoritatively stole this parcel of land from me, leaving me in complete misery. If divine Majesty had not permit me to have remarried, I would be begging from door to door. For these reasons and because this Superior Order [of the Junta de Temporalidades] should give its due consideration and brought to its pure and required execution, I request the protection of Your just tribunal. I beg you be served to order as decreed and I should be left in the quiet and peaceful possession of my land. September 12, 1777. [*The next several pages are filled with court record-keeping. The only new information they contain is that García informs the court at one point that in her absence the cacao grove has become overgrown with weeds and is not being properly watered.*]

15.10 Petition of Juan Gregorio Almeida, *Vecino* of the City of Pamplona

Juan Gregorio Almeida, *vecino* of the city of Pamplona and resident in this valley of Cucuta, in response to a petition presented by Isabel Victoria García, legitimate wife of Salvador Noguera, in which she demands from me a cacao grove that I supposedly took away from her authoritatively: In accordance with the law, I appear and say that in the past year of 1776, the aforementioned proposed to me that I give her permission to marry Noguera. Attending to the serious prejudices I could endure by allowing this, I responded that the only way I would consent to this would be if she liberated herself from slavery. Afterward, she could marry whomever she wanted. To this she responded that she would give me the money, or the part of the grove that had belonged to her deceased husband. I warned her with the knowledge that the very same day she married, she would have to leave the *hacienda*. We agreed that she would give me the quantity of her value which was 200 *pesos* or the equivalent part that she had in the grove. In reality, she married Noguera and as she did not give me the *pesos* worth her value, I called *don* Francisco Xavier Fernández. I begged him to count the trees that belonged to Isabel (because the remainder was divided among her three children as the heirs of Francisco de Borja) and having counted that there were 892, I took them and paid for her freedom in accordance with what had been previously agreed. I ordered her to leave the *hacienda* to live wherever she wanted to. Never mind that the said Isabel and her husband, Noguera, persisted in entering the *hacienda* without my knowledge to harvest cacao from the aforementioned parcel, from which I have harvested very little fruit. This is from the part that corresponded to the said Isabel, because her children and she have harvested the fruit from the trees that correspond to her children, which would not have happened without this deal, nor would she have left my possession and been able to go about free as she does. And, so that your Honor also remain convinced of my motive in opposing the case with Noguera: I say that I have all the sufficient motives that slaveowners generally enjoy to resist against their slaves marrying with freedmen, derived from experience and other motives that I perceive. I am compelled to speak against this marriage for these reasons to your Honor. I beg that having satisfied the complaint, you declare and order what I have asked.

San José, September 25, 1777

[The court decides to admit the case to a Superior Tribunal and notifies both parties. García gives legal power for her husband to act on her behalf. Noguera then files a motion to ensure that Almeida would not leave the parish for any travel (especially to the City of Pamplona, to where he often claimed to travel). Next Noguera asks for copies of all of the testimony. In the ensuing pages, there is a list of the court costs that each side was responsible for paying. Almeida's attorney repeatedly petitions the court to rule in his client's favor, submitting copies of earlier witness testimony supporting his client and a copy of a plea on his behalf. The last folios of the case show Noguera and Garcia

granting power of attorney to the procuradores de número *(municipal lawyer) for representation in court. His legal minutiae is surely not the end of the case once it arrived in Pamplona, but there are no additional pages in the extant case file.]*

Suggested Reading

Cushner, Nicholas P. *Farm and Factory: The Jesuits and the Development of Agrarian Capitalism in Colonial Quito, 1600–1767.* Albany: State University of New York Press, 1982.

Echeverri, Marcela. *Indian and Slave Royalists in the Age of Revolution: Reform, Revolution, and Royalism in the Northern Andes, 1780–1825.* Cambridge: Cambridge University Press, 2016.

McKinley, Michelle A. *Fractional Freedoms: Slavery, Intimacy, and Legal Mobilization in Colonial Lima, 1600–1700.* New York: Cambridge University Press, 2016.

Document Themes

- Family
- Labor
- Law
- Property
- Slavery

16

Between Heaven and Earth: Thereza de Jesús Maria Jozé's Last Will and Testament (Cachoeira, Bahia, 1777)

Introduction and Translation by Caroline Garriott

Thereza de Jesús Maria Jozé was an elite woman born in a small rural parish of Cachoeira, a township of about twenty-six thousand inhabitants located around one hundred kilometers northeast of the city of Salvador, "The Bay of All Saints," a bustling Atlantic port which served as the political and administrative capital of Brazil until 1763.[1] In the sugarcane- and tobacco-producing hinterlands where Jesús Maria Jozé lived—a region called the Bahian Recôncavo, which was dependent upon slavery—slaves not only labored on agricultural estates and in *engenhos* (sugar mills), but also influenced religious society by forming their own Catholic brotherhoods devoted to patron saints including Our Lady of the Rosary and the black Saint Benedict.[2]

Just a few months before she died, on January 30, 1777, Jesús Maria Jozé affirmed her individual wealth as the wife of Manoel Ferreira Gomes Guimarães in her will and testament dictated before a local scribe in her farmhouse of Olho d'Agua "The Eye of Water."[3] While still a single

---

1. Beginning in 1615, Portuguese *bandeirantes* (cowboys) began colonizing the hinterland region outside of Salvador called the Recôncavo, displacing its originary indigenous populations to establish settlements along the fertile banks of rivers that fed into Salvador's port. With the rise of sugarcane and tobacco at the end of the seventeenth century, Cachoeira became the second most populous and wealthy city in the captaincy of Bahia after Salvador. In 1775, 26,980 persons, including free and enslaved populations, lived in urban and rural Cachoeira. Arquivo Histórico Ultamarino, Bahia, Castro e Almeida, cx. 47, doc. 8750, "Mappa de todas as Freguezias, que pertenecem ao Arcebispado da Bahia [. . .] Bahia 9 de janeiro de 1775," document published in the *Anais da Biblioteca Nacional,* n. 32 (1910): 288–90.

2. The city of Salvador de Bahia, "The Bay of All Saints," was a populous city with commercial ties to Europe and West Africa dependent upon slave labor. In 1819, nearly half of the Salvador's inhabitants of fifty thousand were enslaved and an estimated thirty thousand slaves resided in nearby Cachoeira. Stuart Schwartz, *Sugar Plantations in the Formation of Brazilian Society: Bahia, 1550–1835* (New York: Cambridge University Press, 1985), 400.

3. An abbreviation of Sant'ana dos Olhos D'água, a *fazenda* (rural property) with a water source where travelers such as *bandeirantes* and cattle herders passing through the arid region rested. On September 28, 1732, Domingos Barbosa de Araújo and Ana Brandão, the wealthy

woman, Jesús Maria Jozé inherited the landed property and dowry of five slaves from her parents and relatives, whose location along the river banks provided strategic access to Salvador's Atlantic port as well as to overland routes leading into the *sertão* (interior) of Minas Gerais with its gold and diamond mines. As a couple, Jesús Maria Jozé and Gomes Guimarães' conjugal patrimony included twenty-two slaves, only five of which were purchased, and five *sitios* (mixed tobacco-farms and cattle ranches). Since only wealthy persons could afford to purchase more than one slave, the fact that Jesús Maria Jozé and her husband owned twenty-two slaves signifies their economic privilege as members of the powerful planter class who controlled the region's *engenhos*.[4]

According to the 1603 civil codes known as the *Ordenações Filipinas,* the couple's legal heirs—either ascendant or descendent relatives up to the tenth degree—would inherit two thirds of their conjugal patrimony.[5] Jesús Maria Jozé and Gomes Guimarães, however, were childless. Thus, when she verbally dictated her last will before a local scribe in Cachoeira, Jesús Maria Jozé exercised her legal right to freely disburse her half of the couple's estate among relatives (siblings, nieces, cousins) as well collateral kin affiliated to her through the Catholic institution of *compadrío* (godparentage).

Following her opening declaration of her Catholic faith—a common formula in colonial-era wills—Jesús Maria Jozé expressed her individual ties to local Catholic institutions in both urban Cachoeira and the nearby port city of Salvador by describing her funeral rites and ordering requiem masses on behalf of her soul's salvation. A member of the exclusive Carmelite Third Order (a prestigious lay institution restricted to populations of Portuguese ancestry who could demonstrate their *limpieça de sangue* (purity of blood)), Jesús Maria Jozé declared that her corpse should be wrapped in the Carmelite shroud, accompanied by several priests, and escorted to her burial site in the

---

property-holders occupying the "Olhos d'água," donated lands to construct a chapel dedicated to the Santa Anna and São Domingos, in their parish of São José de Itapororocas.

4. During the late 1780s, around twenty-four slaves labored on each sugar mill in the nearby parish of São Cristovão, and throughout the sugar-producing region of the Recôncavo the average number of slaves per owner was eleven. Schwartz, *Sugar Plantations,* 94, 443.

5. Livro IV, Título LXXX. Os testamentos e em que forma se farão. Cândido Mendes de Almeida, ed. *Codigo Philippino, ou, Ordenações e leis do Reino de Portugal: recopiladas por mandado d'El-Rey D. Philippe I,* (Rio de Janeiro: Typ. do Instituto Philomathico, 1870), 900–907. Promulgated by the Spanish King Felipe II in 1603, the Philippine Civil Codes were used to govern Brazil until the 1916 institution of the first Brazilian Civil Code (*Código Civil Brasileiro*), a legal constitution revoked by law in 2002 (Lei n. 10.406) and replaced by the New Brazilian Civil Code (*Novo Código Civil Brasileiro*). For an historical analysis of legality surrounding last testaments and wills in colonial Brazil, see Júnia Ferreira Furtado, "A Morte como testemunha da vida," in *O historiador e suas fontes* (São Paulo: Editora Contexto 2011), 93–118.

parish church by at least ten clergymen as well as her affiliated brotherhoods: Our Lady of the Rosary, the Holy Sacrament, and the Blessed Souls.[6] As a wealthy woman, her funeral was an ostentatious affair and also included a sung mass (perhaps with an orchestra, choir, and musicians), and a large public procession officiated by her parish priest, several clergymen, and her Brotherhoods of Our Lady of the Rosary and Blessed Souls that were obligated to attend all members' funerals, as well as the black Brotherhood of the Glorious Senhor Saint Benedict that, since Jesús Maria Jozé was a nonmember, was paid to accompany her body to its burial.[7]

Jesús Maria Jozé further performed her Catholic identity by earmarking large sums of money for masses for the souls of her deceased relatives and slaves, as well as in honor of her preferred saints, Saint Joachim and Saint Anne. Given that Saint Anne was both a symbol of the chaste mother devoted to the spiritual instruction of children as well as the patroness of barren or sterile women, it is perhaps not surprising that Jesús Maria Jozé would identify with the elderly grandmother of Jesus Christ. After all, she herself, though lacking birth children, served as the surrogate spiritual mother for several young females affiliated to her through ritual kinship ties of *compadrio*.

To preserve the family's farming operations, Jesús Maria Jozé left her husband with the *mestiço*[8] slave named Vicente, a modest parcel of land, eight oxen, and six mules; also, she designated large sums of money, slaves, and productive estates to women not related to her by blood: Maria Vicencia, the daughter of her wealthy *compadre* (co-parent according to Catholic baptismal sponsorship) the Captain Francisco Pereira de Carvalho, as well as Maria's sister Anna Maria.[9] Given that Jesús Maria Jozé served as the *madrinha*

---

6. The number of participants within Jesús Maria Jozé's funerary cortege extended beyond her membership affiliations to include all the available brotherhoods in her parish church including the black brotherhood of Saint Benedict, which was paid 1$280 *réis* for the privilege of escorting her shrouded body to its burial site in the church.

7. The black *Irmandade do Gloriozo Senhor São Benedito* (Brotherhood of the Glorious Senhor Saint Benedict) also received 16$000 *réis* (the value of fifty masses), a material transaction which implied a spiritual obligation to perform intercessory masses on behalf of the soul of Jesús Maria Jozé.

8. Rather than a juridical designation, the term *mestiço* refers to Vicente's mixed ancestry as descendent of European and indigenous parents, or the son of a white male and a biracial woman of African-descent referred to as a *mulata*. Raphael Bluteau and Antonio de Moraes Silva, *Diccionario da Lingua Portugueza composto pelo Padre D. Rafael Bluteau, reformado, e accrescentado por Antonio de Moraes Silva, natural do Rio de Janeiro*, vol. 2 (Lisbon: Na Officina de Simão Thaddeo Ferreira, 1789), 78.

9. While the ethnic status of Vicente's parents is unclear, the fact that he was referred to as a *mestiço* implies lesser black ancestry—or at least lighter skin—than that of mixed-race children born of whites and blacks (whether Brazilian-born *creoles* or Africans) referred to as *mulatos* or

(godmother) of Francisco Pereira's two daughters, she was responsible for shaping them—from their infant baptism—into honorable women who would fulfill their Christian roles as chaste wives and virtuous mothers. By bequeathing these capital assets to serve as dowries for her unwed female kin, Jesús Maria Jozé effectively established reciprocal bonds of ritual kinship with her *compadre* Francisco Pereira while also replicating her own upward mobility as she, too, had inherited slaves and land as part of her dowry. Moreover, by declaring that any property left over from the division of two thirds of her conjugal estate in the absence (or perhaps death) of her sister Bernarda Francisca should be passed on to the daughter of her godchild Maria Vicencia, she preserved these economic and spiritual bonds that linked her to *compadre* across two generations of female descendants.

Throughout her testamentary declarations, Jesús Maria Jozé symbolically performed her status as a member of the Christian elite while strategically positioning herself within Bahia's broader religious and economic orbit. Besides bequeathing large sums of money for masses for herself, relatives, slaves, the souls of purgatory, and Saint Anne and Saint Joachim, Jesús Maria Jozé channeled the legal apparatus of her last will and testament to preserve her inheritance across future generations of elite females not affiliated by blood. Ultimately, Jesús Maria Jozé's political power was reflected through her strategic social alliances with the region's male elites and maintained through reciprocal kinship ties based on godparentage—spiritual bonds which she not only maintained over the course of her lifetime but that, even after her death, she preserved through material bequests to female kin inscribed within her last will and testament.

Reflecting on this document, readers might consider how institutional patriarchy informed the way that property was bequeathed and inherited in eighteenth-century Brazil as well as the regulations on who was able to serve as legal witnesses for the writing of wills. Similarly, gender considerations can be brought to bear on the contents of the will itself. How might Jesús Maria Jozé's will have differed, if at all, from that of an elite Portuguese man, such as her spiritual kinsman, Francisco Pereira? How did Theresa Jesús Maria Jozé actively perform her Christian identity in her will and express her spiritual kinship toward living and deceased persons?

---

pardos—a term referring to the lighter skin tone of mixed-race Afro-descended persons who were differentiated from darker-skinned *pretos* or *negros* (blacks) whether African or Brazilian-born. Since the Portuguese Crown proscribed the enslavement of indigenous populations during the 1570s, Vicente was likely the son of a white man and a light-skinned black woman and may even have been the natural son (born out of wedlock) of Jesús Maria Jozé's husband and a female slave.

16.1 Last Will and Testament of *doña* Thereza de Jesús Maria Jozé[10]

January 30, 1777
Opening
Know, all those who see this document, that in the year of Our Lord Jesus Christ 1777 on the 30th day of January of said year, I, Thereza de Jesús Maria Jozé, being of sound mind and judgment, and taking more account of death, than of life, and desiring, as a true Christian to conform myself with the will of God, I order this my will in the following manner:

Invocation of Christian Faith
First, I commend my soul to the Most Holy Trinity, which created it, and I ask that through the merits of the passion of my Lord Jesus Christ that He desire to forgive me of my sins, and I beseech the Virgin Mary, Our Lady, Mother of God, and all the saints of the celestial court, especially the Archangel Saint Michael, and my guardian angel, and my patron saint, that they intercede and beseech my Lord Jesus Christ now, and when my soul leaves this body because, as a true Christian I profess that I live and die in the Holy Catholic Faith, and to believe as I truly believe, that which the Holy Mother Church of Rome and our faith reveres and believes, and I hope to save my soul, not by my worthiness, but by the Most Holy Passion of Our Lord Jesus Christ.

Appointment of Testamentary Executor
I nominate as the general executors of my will in these interior regions of Cachoeira, in the Parish of San José de Itapororocas[11] where I was born and where I reside, in the first place my husband Manoel Ferreira Gomes Guimarães, in the second place my brother-in-law Domingo Ferreira Gomes, and in the third place my *compadre* José Pires de Carvalho.[12]

---

10. Arquivo Público de Estado da Bahia, Seção Judicial. Tribunal da Relação. Testamento. Classificação 3/1282/1751/14. 65 ff. This last will and testament is excerpted from a lengthy judicial process concerning the distribution of Thereza de Jesús Maria Jozé's estate among her many heirs. Due to the deteriorated state of the document, the folio numeration is illegible.
11. Following the Dutch Invasion, on July 3, 1655, the Portuguese Crown awarded the wealthy *bandeirante* João Peixoto Viegas with a *sesmaria* (a royal concession of lands) and the title "Morgado da Casa de São José das Itapororocas" (the *morgado* was a type of entail which served to prevent the dissolution of the landed estate). The parish of São José das Itapororocas was founded in 1694 to attend to the spiritual needs of the region's growing populations of cattle herders, tobacco farmers, as well as slaves.
12. As a widower, Manoel served as the executor of his wife's will, and was responsible for organizing Thereza's funeral, disbursing payments for pious bequests (such as requiem masses) to local priests and Catholic brotherhoods, and distributing his wife's estate among her designated heirs. Thereza's co-godparent José Pires de Carvalho was a wealthy *engenho*

Funeral and Burial Rites

My body will be shrouded in the habit of Our Lady of Carmen, and buried in the main church of this parish of Saint Joseph; and my body will be accompanied to the grave by the Reverend Vicar with eight or nine priests, and more if possible; and all of them on that day will say a Mass of *corpo presente* (to be performed before the coffin is lowered into the grave), and burial rites for my soul, and they will be given customary arms for the Mass and burial rites, and for accompanying me 10 *patacas* (silver coin worth 320$ *réis*) with a half-pound of wax;[13] and the brotherhoods of the Most Holy Sacrament, and Our Lady of the Rosary, to which I belong, and all the Crosses and Banners that might be found in my parish church, will accompany me, and they will be given the customary alms.[14]

I declare that each one of the priests who accompany my body to the grave, will say an octave of masses for my soul on the day following my burial, with alms of 320$ *réis*.[15]

I declare that if the Mass of *corpo presente* cannot be done on the day of my burial, I want it to be done as soon as possible, and by the eighth day [following my death] at the very latest; and on this day all of the priests present at the burial rite will say a mass for my soul, and for the burial rite and mass, they will be given for alms eight *patacas* (2$560 *réis*) and a half-pound of wax.[16]

---

owner, married to the daughter of an aristocratic family—the Calvacanti and Albuquerque—who owned lands across Pernambuco and in Bahia. By 1805, the Carvalho and Albuquerque clan not only monopolized privileged administrative posts within the municipal council of Salvador and Cachoeira, but also owned nine sugar mills and thousands of heads of cattle in the Recôncavo, as well as large mansions in the city of Salvador. Schwartz, *Sugar Plantations,* 277.

13. In other words, each priest present at Thereza's funeral received a lump sum of $3200 *réis* as payment for participating in her funeral cortège.

14. Though first erected in 1692 on lands donated by wealthy planters, the Carmelite Convent in Cachoeira was reconstructed between 1752 and 1757. It included a black brotherhood devoted to Bom Jesus dos Martírios (The Lord of the Martyrdoms) which, by 1761, owned its own burial vaults within the convent. The construction of the Church of the Third Order of the Our Lady of Mount Carmel, which annexed the Carmelite Convent, was financed by wealthy merchants, planters, and businessmen and completed in 1773, just a few years before Thereza's death.

15. While the mass of *corpo presente*—performed before the open tomb to commend the deceased person's soul to the afterlife—was a lengthy and opulent mass, funeral masses included all octave masses, which were any masses performed within eight days of burial.

16. Thereza's funeral was an expensive affair as the officiating priest charged 12$000 *réis*, and the brotherhoods of Our Lady of the Rosary and Santas Almas, which escorted her body to the tomb, were paid 2$000 *réis* in outstanding membership dues. Moreover, given that she was not a member, the black brotherhood of Saint Benedict was paid 1$280 *réis* for the privilege of accompanying Jesús Maria Jozé's funerary cortege.

Masses

I declare that they request six chaplets[17] of Masses be celebrated for my soul [three hundred masses]; and two chaplets of Masses for my deceased parents [one hundred masses]; and two chaplets of masses for my deceased slaves [one hundred masses]; and two chaplets of masses for the souls in purgatory [one hundred masses]; and one chaplet for the Senhor São Joachim [fifty masses]; and one chaplet for the Senhora Saint Anna [five hundred masses], with 12$000 *réis* of alms for each chaplet.[18]

I declare that all of these masses be said within eighteen months of my death: and my executor can have them said in whichever place seems best, and most desirable, and where the best accounts can be given me during my life to say a Chaplet to Senhora Santa Anna, and to the Senhor Saint Joachim, and if upon my death one or another of the chaplets has already been discharged, or both chaplets are already said; I want that same quittance to be taken into account by my executor, so that it is not necessary for him to request they be celebrated a second time.

Patrimony: Lands and Property (Slaves and Equipment)

I declare that I am married to Manoel Ferreira Gomes Guimarães and from our marriage we do not have children, nor any direct [legally enforced] heirs to inherit my estate.

I declare as a couple we possess the following properties: four *fazendas* (rural properties) with their own lands, which we purchased from João de Teixera de Argolo. Specifically, the Mangabeira farm in which we cultivate tobacco, [and] the farms of Pindoba[19] or Sitio Novo and Queimada, which at present are vacant (dispossessed); in these *fazendas* we have some heads of cattle; and horses; and two pairs of domestic bulls; and we bought from the aforementioned seller a plot of land on the skirts of the River Jacuípe called São Jorge, where Francisco Nogueira Arão and his nephew Luis da Costa

---

17. A chaplet of masses consisted of fifty masses officiated by priests before designated altars inside churches or convents. During the eighteenth century, the Third Order of the Carmelites awarded its membership body—both living and dead—with one hundred and fifty requiem masses (three chaplets) pronounced on Sundays and religious holidays. In her will, however, Jesús José ordered an additional three chaplets be pronounced on behalf of her soul in whichever church or convent the executor of her will deemed appropriate.

18. The executor of Jesús Maria Jozé's will was thus required to pay a grand sum of 132$000 *réis* in requiem masses, the estimated value of two *creole* (Brazilian-born) slaves.

19. *Pindoba* is a word of Tupi origin which likely refers to hooked reed poles used for fishing and for collecting *graviola* fruits from *pindaíba* trees. Alexandre de Mello Moraes, *Corographia historica, chonographica, genealogica, nobiliaria, e politica do imperio deo Brasil*, vol. 2 (Rio de Janeiro: Typografia Americana de J. Soares de Pinho, 1858), 234.

currently reside;[20] and in the *fazenda* called Borda da Mata de Baixo, we also have a parcel of lands; and developments shared together with the rest of the heirs, partly given to me legitimately from my parents Mathias Pereira Bernardes and Marianna Pereira de Castro; and partly given at the bequest of my uncle João Pereira Bernardes; and the *fazenda* called Ilha in the parish of Santa Anna do Camizão which I purchased from the Reverend Priest Pedro de Sylva Dias when I was still unmarried.

I declare that we possess as a couple twenty-two slaves, both male and female, and among these Antonio Crioulo, Bernardo Crioulo, Jacinto Crioulo, Joanna Crioula, and Jozé Criolo were not inherited.[21] Moreover, we also have two oxen-carts; farm instruments, and any home furnishings that may be found upon my death.

Debtors and Debts

I declare that from a lawsuit that we won against them João Hornato and his uncles owe us 70$000 *réis;* and João Ribeiro owes us the greater part of the interest from a loan advance worth 140$000 *réis*.

I declare that we as a couple owe the following debts: From a debt we developed from a contract we made with the brotherhood of the Holy Sacrament in the main parish church of Saint Joseph, so that they would discharge us from membership obligations under which all brothers are subjected [we owe] 100$000 *réis* with interest; and to the mill of the aforementioned parish 50$000 *réis*; for a loan advance with interest from Miguel Alfonso, money which we used to buy provisions 50$000 *réis*; for a loan advance from Jozé Ferreira de Castro 50$000 *réis*; in the city of Bahia we also owe the merchant Luis da Costa Gomes with whom we have accounts, the debts that are recorded in his book.

Distribution of Estate Among Heirs

I leave the executor who accepts my will, as prize and compensation for all the labor [trouble] he will have with it, 300$000 *réis*.[22]

---

20. While Francisco Nogueira Arão and his nephew may have been tenant farmers, who paid rent to Thereza and Manoel from their agricultural surplus, it is also possible that they were skilled employees who administered part of the couple's estate while overseeing slave laborers.
21. The *creole* (Brazilian-born) slaves Joanna and Antonio were worth seventy thousand and sixty thousand *réis* respectively, while African-born slave Ignacia was evaluated at only forty thousand *réis* according to a 1782 postmortem inventory of Thereza's estate. The fact that the Pindoba ranch was assessed at four hundred thousand *réis* suggests the high value of slaves in comparison to land. Slaves constituted 50 percent of the value of agricultural estates in most eighteenth-century postmortem inventories. Alida Metcalf, *Family and Frontier in Colonial Brazil: Santana de Parnaíba, 1580–1822* (Berkeley: University of California Press, 1992), 106–7.
22. This amount is the purchasing value of around four Brazilian-born slaves at the time. A 1782 inventory of Jesus Maria Jozé's estate included her property in slaves, which were

I leave the following alms: For my brother the Reverend Priest João Pereira 150$000 *réis*. For my cousin Catherina Alvez the *crioulinha* named Maria.[23] For my niece Maria, the daughter of Manuel de Pinho, I leave the *crioulinha* named Anna, as well as 100$000 *réis* in cash. For my niece Joanna Maria Francisca who is the keeper of my brother's house, I leave the *crioulo* slave named Domingos. For my goddaughter Antonia Maria, wife of Manuel Jozé das Santos [I leave] 20$000 *réis* as alms. I leave for my nieces, the daughter of my *compadre* Francisco Pereira, my goddaughter Maria Vicencia 100$000 *réis* in cash and the farm Queimada with the lands that pertain to it demarcated in this form: divided on the western the part with the boundaries established by its first seller Capitão João Rodrigues Adorno,[24] and in the middle from the northern to the northeastern part my farm is split by the surrounding proprietors, thus upon my death with this delineation my god-niece can take possession of it, as her own property, and it will remain so by virtue of this clause; I leave 150$000 *réis* for the sister of my goddaughter, my other niece affiliate with my *compadre* Francisco Pereira.[25]

---

appraised by public officials at market value. The fact that Antonio and Joanna (*creoles*) were appraised at 60$000 and 70$000 *réis*, respectively, while the African slave Ignacia, whose ethnic affiliation was noted as *gêge* (a West African ethnic group), was valued at only 40$000 réis, shows the relatively high price of Brazilian-born slaves to African slaves at this time.

23. The term *crioulinha* is a diminutive form of *crioula* and refers, in this case, to a Brazilian-born black slave who was still a minor—an unwed female under fourteen years of age. During the early colonial period and throughout the nineteenth century, the term *crioulo* [creole] was applied to Brazilian-born blacks to distinguish them from Africans. The cultural and linguistic associations between blackness and slavery in the Portuguese Empire is reflected by the fact that Afro–Brazilian freedmen, even if born into freedom, were referred to as *crioulos forros* or *libertos* (manumitted or liberated blacks).

24. Beginning in 1654, the Captain João Rodrigues Adorno established himself in the region, and in 1673 he erected a small hermitage with a chapel dedicated to Nossa Senhora de Rosário on his property, which was eventually converted into the parish church. In 1688, he and his wife *dona* Úrsula de Azevedo donated lands to the Carmelite Order so that they could begin the construction of their convent. Completed in 1692, the Carmelite convent and church and its adjoining Carmelite Third Order was renovated during the mid-eighteenth century and the church's interior decoration—which includes remarkable collection of Portuguese *azulejos* (decorative ceramic tiles)—continued through 1780. Maria Helena Ochi Flexor, ed., *O Conjunto do Carmo de Cachoeira [The Carmo architectonic ensemble of Cachoeira]* (Brasília: IPHAN/Monumenta, 2007), 34–83.

25. Captain Francisco Pereira was obligated by bonds of *compadrazgo* (godparentage) to not only instruct Jesús Maria Jozé in the Catholic faith but also to materially provide for her well-being. She, in turn, was discharging her mutual obligation as godmother to his daughter through this bequest.

I declare that out of gratitude for the great love and affection with which my husband Manoel Ferreira Gomes always treated me, I leave him the *mestiço* Vicente, and fifty *varas* (175 feet of land),[26] eight domesticated oxen, six mules, and in the lack of any of these items their value of in cash, so that he can take this amount as inheritance, or all the value of these items as one third of my inherited and acquired possessions.

I declare that my executor will record and satisfy these suffrages,[27] and the other bequests and legacies as declared in my will, first by levying and setting aside the expenditures from my funeral from the one third of my inherited possessions, and exempting from these accounts my acquired possessions; which without anything more being necessary, shall be disbursed and signed by him.[28]

I declare that my executor will satisfy in their entirety of all the dispositions and legacies that are specified in this my will within five months, and so long as these remain unfulfilled, he cannot be obliged to attend to any other thing.

I declare that I institute as the heirs of the two parts [two thirds] of my inherited possessions my brother the Reverend Priest João Pereira and my sisters Joanna Maria Pereira de Castro and Bernarda Francisca Pereira and Maria Jozé Sá, verifying the third part [one third] of my estate is equally divided among them.

I declare that after the bequests and legacies declared in this my testament are all satisfied, I institute my sister Bernarda Francisca as the heir of whatever remains from the two parts [two thirds] of my acquired goods, and I state that whatever is left, and remains from the two parts [two thirds], granted to my brother the Reverend Priest João Pereira, and my cousin Catherina Alvez, and my niece the daughter of Manuel de Pinho, and my nieces—my goddaughter Maria Vicencia and her sister[29]—the daughters of my *compadre* Francisco Pereira, and my niece Joanna Maria Francisca, I institute each one as heirs of solely the aforementioned legacies and nothing else, such that these

---

26. This is roughly the size of a subsistence farm or a sugarcane plot in which eight oxen were needed to transport one cart loaded with heavy cane or timber.

27. Suffrages were intercessory prayers or masses pronounced on behalf of the deceased's souls intended to swiftly deliver them from purgatory into heaven.

28. A 1782 inventory evaluated Jesús Maria Jozé's total estate after subtracting150$000 réis (the money devoted to funerary rites and pious legacies) to 450$242 *réis* to be divided equally among her four siblings.

29. On February 26, 1779, the Captain Francisco Pereira acknowledged that because they were unmarried, he served as the administrator of his two daughters' inherited properties. He also provided his elite daughters' full names: *doña* Maria Vicencia de Jesus and *doña* Anna Maria da Purificação.

legacies will be recorded during the division of the property from the two parts [two thirds] of my acquired goods.

I declare that if any of the third part [one third] of my acquired goods should remain, I institute my sister, the aforementioned Bernarda Francisca Pereira, as the heir of all that remains, but if in my life she is absent, all the inheritance that I left her upon my death I restitute to be passed on to the daughter of Maria Vicencia, my aforementioned niece.

Closure

I declare that all that I have ordered written is my last and final wish, and I now ask my executors as a service to God and as a favor to me, to accept this my testament and seek to retain and fulfill what is contained in it, and with it I nullify any other will, or codicil made before this one, and I beg that the justices, ecclesiastical and secular alike, will assist me in carrying out executing what is ordered in it [my will], and if necessary I grant my executors with all the powers of attorney if required of them; and for this testament at my request I had Simão da Cunha Barboza serve as witness and I ordered it written by him, and since it is in the form which I ordered it in my farm of Santo Antonio, I signed it with my sign, along with the afore-mentioned scribe, who wrote it on the thirtieth day of January, the year of the birth of Our Lord Jesus Christ, one thousand seven hundred and seventy seven [1777].

[signature of Thereza Jesús Maria Jozé]

As the witness that wrote it

[signature of Simão da Cunha Barboza]

Suggested Reading

Ferreira Furtado, Júnia. *Chica da Silva: A Brazilian Slave of the Eighteenth Century.* New York: Cambridge University Press, 2009.

Metcalf, Alida C. *Family and Frontier in Colonial Brazil: Santana de Parnaíba, 1580–1822.* Berkeley: University of California Press, 1992.

Myscofski, Carole A. *Amazons, Wives, Nuns and Witches: Women and the Catholic Church in Colonial Brazil 1500–1822.* Austin: University of Texas Press, 2013.

Reis, João José. *Death Is a Festival: Funeral Rites and Rebellion in Nineteenth-Century Brazil,* trans. H. Sabrina Gledhill. Chapel Hill: The University of North Carolina Press, 2003.

Schwartz, Stuart B. *Sugar Plantations in the Formation of Brazilian Society: Bahia, 1550–1835.* New York: Cambridge University Press, 1985.

Document Themes

- Family
- Law
- Property
- Religion

17

Natividad, *Negra*, Sues Her Owner for Freedom (Lima, 1792)[1]

Accusations of forced sex by an owner–priest and a demand to be freed from him constitute the heart of a lawsuit filed by the enslaved woman, Natividad, in late eighteenth-century Lima.[2] To modern-day readers, the opening statement may seem to fly in the face of common understandings about the legal powers of enslaved peoples, and in particular, enslaved women. Yet the complaint of Natividad, while unique in its particular details, should be read in the context of an augmentation in the number of lawsuits and petitions initiated by enslaved women in this period. The priest, Doctor *don* Juan de la Reinaga, rejected Natividad's claims and offered a defense that relied on stereotypes about unruly behavior by enslaved women. In both the original petition and the ensuing case (of which only a portion survived), details about Natividad's experiences allow us to reconstruct a sense of the pressures suffered on a daily basis by enslaved women, as well as about the kin resources and legal discourses to which enslaved women might appeal for assistance.

Higher numbers of enslaved women appeared in courts in the late eighteenth century in part due to a Royal Decree passed in 1789 which made practical changes allowing enslaved peoples more room to maneuver in the courts.[3] Recently, historians have argued that there was a broader trend in this time period that was not solely based on this decree but which substantially shifted how minors (women, indigenous peoples, enslaved peoples)

---

1. The editors acknowledge our gratitude to Bianca Premo for providing us with this document. See analysis of the case in Premo, *The Enlightenment on Trial: Ordinary Litigants and Colonialism in the Spanish Empire* (New York: Oxford University Press, 2017), 203.

2. For additional context on the lives of enslaved women in Lima, see Michelle A. McKinley, *Fractional Freedoms: Slavery, Intimacy, and Legal Mobilization in Colonial Lima, 1600–1700* (New York: Cambridge University Press, 2016) and Christine Hünefeldt, *Paying the Price of Freedom: Family and Labor among Lima's Slaves, 1800–1854* (Berkeley: University of California Press, 1994).

3. See discussion of the 1789 *Instruction on the Education, Treatment and Occupation of Slaves,* in Premo, *The Enlightenment on Trial,* 198. Also, Evelyne Laurent-Perrault researches this trend for enslaved women in late colonial Venezuela. See "Esclavizadas, cimarronaje y la Ley en Venezuela, 1760–1809," in *Demando Mi Libertad; Relatos de mujeres Negras y sus estrategias de resistencia en Nueva Granada, Venezuela y Cuba* (Universidad Icesi, Cali-Colombia, forthcoming).

looked to the judicial system to seek redress and freedom. In doing so, these people were instrumental in creating the intellectual current we now know as the Enlightenment.[4] As Bianca Premo contends, these historical actors made the Enlightenment by promoting "the preeminence of secular law as they opted to use the king's civil courts for formal trials" rather than by using other jurisdictions or extrajudicial options. They also "contributed to the notion that the value of the law was intrinsic . . . [because of] its very status as law."[5]

It was within this context, then, that Natividad took deliberately crafted legal action to free herself from the priest, Reinaga, who owned her and with whom she alleged a sexual relationship. We might anticipate that the courts would be more likely to side with the priest in this case who was, after all, her master and her superior in colonial society's race, gender, and class hierarchies. Her petition strove to counter those factors that worked in Reinaga's favor. Natividad's original petition used language and reason to deflect attention away from Reinaga's status and shone light on his failure to live up to the model expected by Spanish men, especially those who were members of the clergy. Even the choice of the court to which Natividad appealed suggests strategy on her part. With attention to the details we notice that the main judge mentioned throughout the case is an ecclesiastical, or church, judge. Natividad did not strive to have this lawsuit heard in a civil court, but rather wanted it tried before the eyes and ears of other religious men whom, she hoped, would judge Reinaga more harshly because of his failures to adhere to the vows of the priesthood. Moreover, if we analyze the language of the petition carefully, we see that it is the priest who was really on trial here, for his abuse of Natividad. Because slaves represented property as well as income, Reinaga repeatedly insisted that Natividad should be forced to pay him a bond for her daily wages. Many urban slaves labored outside of their masters' homes during the day and had to give a set amount of money, daily or weekly, to those masters.

The particulars of violence alleged by Natividad, striking in terms of her significant suffering, are emblematic of what enslaved women suffered daily in the colonial world. Contemporaries viewed the infliction of physical abuse by masters as a prerogative rather than a crime. Imprisonment in bakeries, where people worked shackled near hot ovens, served as a frequent punishment for enslaved men and women in the urban Andes who dared to resist their masters. And rape was a common tool that male slaveowners used to further subjugate their female slaves. This dark violence of daily life lurked in stark contrast to the reach for reason and legal justice that Natividad sought.

---

4. See the novel argument in Premo, *The Enlightenment on Trial.*
5. Premo, *The Enlightenment on Trial,* 14–15.

When Natividad tried to move beyond her unbearable situation with Reinaga, was the law on her side? This question does not have a simple answer. Enslaved women and men did have rights before the law according to early modern Spanish legal code. Natividad could bring a case against her master for abuse and ask to be sold to another master. She went further, however, by taking her case to the religious courts and asking for her freedom. This was a harder case to make.

Readers studying this document could consider what networks and strategies Natividad employed to try to gain her freedom from Reinaga. Who assisted her to present her case and what does that suggest about how men and women worked together? More generally, what does Natividad's case reveal about gender-specific struggles for enslaved women? Compare this with the case of the enslaved woman Isabel Victoria García in Chapter 15. How did the experience of slavery and paths to manumission differ across these geographic locations?

17.1 Petition of Natividad, Slave of *Licenciado don* Juan de Reinaga about the Recognition of Her Freedom[6]

Illustrious *Señor*:

I, Natividad, *negra* (black woman), slave of *licenciado* (licentiate) *don* (sir) Juan de la Reinaga, priest of this Archbishopric, appear before the feet of your Illustrious *Señor* (Lord) with the greatest remorse and I say: that clearly my master forgot the obligations of his position, about Christianity and about authority when, on different occasions, he proposed his dishonest relations.[7] Taking advantage of the honesty and example that he is expected to embody, for many days I resisted, not condescending to an impurity so abominable. Ultimately, I was compelled by the violence of a determined master and also by my longing to obtain the freedom that the same *licenciado* promised me on repeated occasions. I had to allow his troublesome request and commit the offense that I had valiantly resisted until, exhausted from the persuasions of he who ruled me, I allowed this sexual congress. It endured over a long period, during which he repeatedly affirmed his solemn promise to grant

---

6. Archivo Arzobispal de Lima: Autos de Natividad, esclava del licenciado don Juan de Reinaga, presbítero domiciliario del arzobispado, sobre que le reconzca su libertad que obtuvo por el concubinato que tuvo con su amo, Causas de Negros, 33, no. 3, 1792.

7. The original language in the document is *"communicacion torpe,"* which she used to refer to sexual relations.

[me] freedom, without which condition I would not have consented to this illicit concubinage, not the first time, nor ever thereafter.

With the days passing in my unhappy fate, no offer of manumission was initiated, and at the same time, the most abominable happening suddenly impeded any end to the aforementioned excesses. I tried to remove myself from the situation and reject the new and effective intentions of my master. Because he recognized my firm renunciation [of the earlier behavior], my master seized on this offense as a lack of respect and disobedience. He imprisoned me in a bakery,[8] where they shaved my head, believing perhaps that in this way they would conquer my perseverance. Disappointed that these punishments could not conquer my just condemnation and dread, my master moved me and imprisoned me in his *hacienda* (landed estate) which is called Manchay. Holding me there with all his severity, my Master impulsively ordered that his *mayordomo* (overseer) give me twenty-five lashes that I indeed suffered. Thereafter, my master, the *licenciado,* punished me by his own hand for nine continuous days so that I spilled copious blood from the *simplegadas*[9] outside of the oppressive prison where I was kept, called the Rabo de Zorro. My master, determined to prevail, attached me to an iron bar that was available and took me from this city for that purpose, according to what I was notified.

To avoid offending the pious ears of your Illustrious *Señor,* it does not seem useful to me to elaborate further on this simple and truthful account. Your superior understanding will mean that you will have understood that this case compels me to act by in the very least soliciting that you grant me the freedom that corresponds to me. Because according to legal principles, the slave owner that compels or introduces his slave to dishonest commerce by that same act must grant that slave the benefit of manumission. Further, that the slave who consented to this favor, of course, acquires that pardon due to the lack of restraint of the master, primarily when the motive of promise of freedom was involved.

Dispensing with those (aspired) legal statutes through which immediately are determined the illustrious benefit,[10] the other action that concerns me is the claim against my Master *licenciado don* Juan de la Reinaga for sexual assault. No one can ignore either our view or the conviction of the *Señor* that if a slave sins, or even more, is complicit in sinning, ([because they believe that] merit and reason requires that the slave endure spiritual cruelty), this

---

8. For a detailed discussion of bakeries as punishment for enslaved men and women, see Carlos Aguirre, "Violencia, castigo y control social: esclavos y panaderías en Lima, siglo XIX," *Pasado y Presente* (Lima), 1988, 1.

9. This colloquialism may refer to the anus.

10. In other words, her freedom from slavery.

is because they mean for their masters to sell them for a fair price and with good conditions as I now aspire. If I am denied a declaration of freedom that I have previously proven that indisputably compels [my freedom], how much less will I be concerned with the spiritual and corporal punishments that I have suffered for not wanting to persevere in the impure sins that my master inflicts upon me and tries to have me carry out under the anguish of punishments, prisons, and unmerciful cruelty.

I could very well lodge my appeal before the *Señores* of the Real Audiencia (Royal Court) where the law of God has directed that slaves demand freedom whenever they seek the sanctuary and refuge that the law grants. But I wish that the secular[11] courts should hear about the recklessness, indifference, and tyrannies so foreign to leniency[12] and self-restraint that an ecclesiastical priest professes. Thus, I renounce the indulgence of royal law and bring my case before the just commission of Your Most Illustrious Lord, who is very competent to reform the immoderate powers[13] of a priest and decree what is in the interest of the pious cause of liberty that I claim. And in fact, there are no grounds for granting the sale of my person,[14] [as opposed to granting her freedom] according to the law. For all of these reasons:

To Your Excellency, I ask and beg that you see fit to admit this petition, as is appropriate, and demand that I be declared free. Moreover, grant me relief so that *licenciado don* Juan, my master, sells me for a just price and under good conditions according to what justice demands. Swearing to God, Our Lord and to this sign of Christ, I declare that I do not behave maliciously in this petition. Also, I state that, cautiously, I fear that my master will make sure to capture me and punish me using the highest form of authority in vengeance for my petition. And it is precisely for this kind of behavior that I have denounced his actions against modesty and the kind of honest example that would elicit much more respect from his slaves. Therefore, to Your Illustrious Sir, I ask and beg that you demand that *licenciado don* Francisco de la Reinaga be notified, that for no reason or excuse [should he] follow me, trouble me, nor capture me, leaving me helpless. Rather I should be ready to make use of my rights and justice which I demand above.

[sign of the cross]

---

11. Here she refers to secular courts or civil course in contrast to the ecclesiastical courts, which she has petitioned in this document.

12. *Legnidad* in the original.

13. *Gobernaciones* in the original.

14. Natividad literally says there are no grounds to grant the sale of her *cabeza* (head).

17.2 Response of *Licenciado don* Juan de Reinaga, Priest and Slave Owner

In the City of Kings of Peru on May 31, 1792: *Licenciado* Juan José Negrón, lawyer in this Real Audiencia, *juez ordinario* (judge) of the Holy Inquisition, *Examinador Sinodal* (synod examiner), *Cura Rector* (priest, rector), *Provisor y Vicario General* (judge and Vicar General) of this Archbishopric,[15] in virtue of the verbal dispatch to your Illustrious *Señor,* Your Grace the Archbishop: My *señor,* I order that you transmit to the *licenciado don* Juan de Reinaga that he should not aggravate the punishment of this party and inflict no greater harm because of this appeal and the release that is solicited by the other party. Further, [you should] consider the surety of her person and daily wages before you give a decision. Signed before me [by] Doctor Nuñez and Francisco Gutiérrez Gallegos.

Doctor Juan de la Reinaga responding to the notification that your grace has sent me about the petition of Natividad, my slave: I say: that I am ready to answer it and to prove its falsehood, demonstrating with the most distinguished witnesses, the agreeable treatment that I give and have always given to her and to all my slaves. Likewise, I will prove the well-known, practice of notorious prostitution, disorder, and scandal of this servant. But in order to execute this, it is necessary (in keeping with the forewarned about this point) that the slave stand surety for this slander with her person and her wages with a known person and to my satisfaction.[16] Having protested with this reply as I have said, therefore I ask and beg your highness demand that the aforementioned slave give the surety that I ask and justice be done.

don Juan de la Reinaga

In the city of Kings in Peru June 18, 1792: Before *Señor* Doctor *don* Juan José Negrón, this petition was read and seen by your honor, who ordered that the *negra* Natividad, slave of the Doctor *don* Juan de la Reinaga, be notified to give surety for her person and daily wages to the satisfaction of the said *don* Juan, and he signed it.

I, *don* Juan de la Reinaga, in the lawsuit initiated by a *negro* whose name I do not know,[17] in the name of Natividad, my slave, I say: that to the document presented by this [*negro*] your Honor ordered that I be sent notification; and responding to him, I say that I was ready to respond to

---

15. *Licenciado* Juan José Negrón's title is repeated every time his name is mentioned in the documents, though this is the only instance in which the editors have included it in its entirety.
16. Here the priest and owner Reinaga is demanding that a bond be guaranteed for Natividad before moving forward with this complaint since she has, in his opinion, slandered him.
17. At this point in the case, Reinaga claims that a *negro* (Afro–Peruvian man) has entered the petition on the part of Natividad.

the lawsuit and persuade him of its falsehood with the most distinguished witnesses and evidence; but before making these declarations [I wanted to] guarantee the servant, her person and her wages, as is anticipated in similar cases.

I sent this request to your honor and the court was informed. I did not direct it to the said servant (because as I have said she did not make the presentation) but to the above-mentioned *negro,* on the chance that he came to this tribunal to inquire into the ruling that had been given in the lawsuit, as the notary could certify. It has been much more than one month since this court carried out these proceedings, and neither the *negro* nor the servant have complied with what your honor ordered. She [Natividad], in the shadows of her fanciful lawsuit, is living in her excesses. I am deprived [of her wages] because of the almost five times in which she has fled her service. It will continue thus if your honor does not order that she is put in a bakery. In that way, she can give surety as is decreed and, thereafter, your honor can continue deliberating the pending lawsuit. Therefore, to your honor I ask and beg that you order as I request and as justice demands. Signed, *don* Juan de la Reinaga [*The court receives and reads Reinaga's petition on July 27, 1792 as presented by his lawyer.*]

17.3 The Court Looks for Natividad

I, the under-signed public notary of this Archbishopric Court, attest that in the lawsuit that a *negra* named Natividad pursues against Doctor *don* Juan de la Reinaga, her legitimate master, in which she attempts to be declared as free in virtue of various deeds that against Doctor *don,* her master she presents in a document that in my name a *negro* named Mariano de Castas, *criollo* (Peruvian-born), presented to his illustrious Honor the Archbishop, my lord. In virtue of the verbal dispatch that the Illustrious Señor [Archbishop] sent the *Señor Provisor* he supplies a decree of the following tenor:

In the City of Kings in Peru on May 31, 1792, I, *Señor* Doctor *don* Juan José Negrón, in virtue of the verbal dispatch that the Illustrious Archbishop, my lord, decreed, order you transmit [to] *licenciado don* Juan de la Reinaga who should be promptly notified that he should not aggravate the petitions of this party nor inflict more damages for this case and for the release that is solicited in the other count, that of guaranteeing the person and wages [of Natividad], a ruling will be made and he signed it: *don* Negrón = before me, Francisco Gutiérrez Gallegos = On the same day that Doctor *don* Juan de la Reinaga was notified in person of the content; based on this notification the said Doctor presented a letter asking for justice that the *negra* Natividad give

surety for her person and daily wages for the continuation of the lawsuit, pro-
testing her excuses, this was verified, in whose petition his Lord decreed an
Auto of the following tenor: In the City of Kings of Peru on June 18, 1792:
before *licenciado don* Doctor Juan José Negrón, this petition was read. And
seen by your Lord, he ordered that the *negra* Natividad, slave of Doctor *don*
Juan de la Reinaga, be notified, and he signed it *don* Negrón = Before me.
Francisco Gutiérrez Gallegos. This Auto was not communicated in person
to the said *negra* Natividad because she is not known nor has she presented
herself in this court. Nor is the location or existence of her dwelling known,
so the content [of the Auto] was made known, on the same day and date,
to the referred *negro* Mariano who presented the written copy of the lawsuit
and the one who came to pursue these proceedings and he to whom, on one
of these occasions, I made the decree known. However, from this time until
the present day, neither Natividad nor the interlocutor Mariano have come
to counterclaim, and for the record as is appropriate under the law, I give the
present decree at the order of the *Señor Procurador* and Vicar General of the
City of the Kings of Peru on July 27, 1792.

Justo de Taboada
Public Notary

In the City of the Kings of Peru on July 28, 1792: Doctor *don* Juan
José Negrón, having seen this certification of the record. I order that the
present notary locates the *negra* Natividad, slave of Doctor *don* Juan de
la Reinaga, with the intent of letting her know in person the proceedings
that transpired on June 18 of this present year, certifying what will be the
results of the proceedings. He signed it: *don* Negrón before me, Francisco
Gutiérrez Gallegos.

I, the public notary of this Audiencia, certify that I requested that the *negro*
named Mariano Bravo speak with Natividad, *negra*, slave of Doctor *don* Juan
de la Reinaga, to tell me her location and to make known to her in person the
act decreed by the *Provisor* and Vicar General on June 18 of this present year
as is justified and ordered by the act of 28 of July of this same year. Having
seen Mariano Bravo and asked after the house or dwelling of Natividad, he
told me that he knew nothing of her. It had been many days since he had seen
her, because he had a leg injury. Further, he said he did not know which was
her house, nor in which place one could find her. He maintained his ignorance of her whereabouts even after I made known to him the punishments
that could be unleashed upon him for concealment [of information]. At the
same time, he let me know that he was the brother of the *negra* Natividad and
that his surname by which he was known was Bravo; actually, it was also Solis
but nobody knows him as such. For the record and validity that applies, I

give the present order of the Lord *Procurador* (legal representative) and Vicar General in the Kings of Peru August 3, 1792.

Justo de Taboado, Public Notary

Suggested Reading

McKinley, Michelle A. *Fractional Freedoms: Slavery, Intimacy, and Legal Mobilization in Colonial Lima, 1600–1700.* New York: Cambridge University Press, 2016.

Premo, Bianca. *The Enlightenment on Trial: Ordinary Litigants and Colonialism in the Spanish Empire.* New York: Oxford University Press, 2017.

Townsend, Camila. "Angela Batallas: A Fight for Freedom in Guayaquil." In *The Human Tradition in Colonial Latin America*, Second edition, ed. Kenneth J. Andrien. New York: Rowman and Littlefield, 2013.

Document Themes

- Labor
- Law
- Race and ethnicity
- Slavery
- Sexuality and gender

18

A Colonial Cross-Dresser (Mexico, 1796)

In the spring of 1796, Mexico City resident María Vicenta Vargas raised her concerns about another parishioner's behavior, detailed in the complete file documents reproduced here, to her parish priest. Vargas had informed her priest that when taking communion during Holy Week, she had witnessed Gregoria "la Macho" Piedra participating in the holy rite, but doing so dressed in the clothing of a man. Even more alarmingly, rather than ingesting the communion host, Vargas had also witnessed Piedra smuggling it out of the church in her hand. The priest with whom Vargas had spoken had ordered Piedra seized and held in the "jail of the court" awaiting further investigation.

One of the Inquisition officials questioned Vargas and queried the prefect of the Royal Prison about Piedra's past and present behavior. The latter revealed that Piedra had come to legal authorities' attention on several other occasions. Piedra had been held in custody four times in the city jail, once for three months in the jail of the Acordada, in the Hospicio de Pobres for two months, and twice before in the jail of the court. Piedra's crimes had consisted in having taken communion more than once, dressing as a man, and brawling.

La Macho's file documents that Gregoria Piedra dressed as both a man and a woman, but preferred to dress as a man. Transvestism occurred, but was rarely recorded, in colonial Latin America. Historians have recently uncovered a number of cases of both male and female cross-dressers across the colonial period in both secular courts and inquisition trials.[1] Although witnesses

---

1. Serge Gruzinski, "The Ashes of Desire: Homosexuality in Mid-Seventeenth-Century New Spain," in *Infamous Desire: Male Homosexuality in Colonial Latin America*, ed. Pete Sigal (Chicago: University of Chicago Press, 2003), 205, uncovered eight cases of male transvestites in the colonial era. Zeb Tortorici discusses several other cases in *Sins Against Nature: Sex and Archives in Colonial New Spain, 1530–1821* (Durham, NC: Duke University Press, 2018). Laura A. Lewis, "From Sodomy to Superstition: The Active Pathic and Bodily Transgressions in New Spain," *Ethnohistory* 54:1 (Winter 2007), 155. fn 66 has found equal numbers of female and male cross-dressers in Mexican archives. Geoffrey Spurling, "Under Investigation for the Abominable Sin: Damián de Morales Stands Accused of Attempting to Seduce Antón de Tierra de Congo (Charcas, 1611)," in Richard Boyer and Geoffrey Spurling, eds. *Colonial Lives: Documents on Latin American History, 1550–1850* (New York: Oxford University Press, 2000), 112–129, located another man accused of cross-dressing in early seventeenth-century Charcas, while Thomas A. Abercrombie encountered a story of a late sixteenth-century

described defendants in these cases as having cross-dressed, both church and secular courts prosecuted them for other crimes—most often sodomy, but in Piedra's case, sacrilege. Transvestism, although prohibited in at least two obscure Spanish and New World ordinances, was a marginal criminal act, rarely prosecuted.[2] Male transvestism appears to have disturbed members of colonial society more than female cross-dressing because the former act, unlike the latter, was associated with suspicion of homosexuality.[3]

There is some suggestion in the following texts that Gregoria Piedra professed a preference for a masculine gender identity; witnesses describe her as preferring men's clothing to women's, as enjoying men's pass-times, and as publicly brawling, although we must be careful to not impart anachronistic thinking about gender on historical subjects living in different times from our own. It is also possible that Piedra enjoyed switching from one public identity to another; one witness describes Piedra as dressing interchangeably between "the clothing of men and of women according to what suits her criminal plans." It is also difficult to know from the surviving materials, as in the case of Gregoria Piedra's more well-known antecedent, the cross-dressing early seventeenth-century Basque "lieutenant" nun, Catalina de Erauso, whether Gregoria la Macha's preference for dressing as a man implied a preference for same-sex sexuality. Inquisitorial authorities and regular citizens did acknowledge (and vigorously prosecute) same-sex relations when they occurred between men, but same-sex relations between women was much more likely to remain unperceived and unacknowledged.[4] Even in cases which more

---

cross-dressing woman: "Affairs of the Courtroom: Fernando de Medina Confesses to Killing His Wife (Charcas, 1595)," in Boyer and Spurling, *Colonial Lives*, 54–76. Catalina de Erauso, the "lieutenant nun" is the most well known early seventeenth-century cross-dresser. For Erauso's story, see Catalina de Erauso and Michele Stepto, *Lieutenant Nun: Memoir of a Basque Transvestite in the New World* (Boston: Beacon Press, 1997).
2. One late eighteenth-century Spanish law and one mid-sixteenth-century royal ordinance directed at Nahuas prohibited transvestism: Antonio Calvo Maturana, *Impostores: sombras en la España de las Luces* (Madrid: Cátedra, 2015) 266, 270; Barry D. Sell and Susan Kellogg, "We Want to Give Them Laws: Royal Ordinances in a Mid-Sixteenth Century Nahuatl Text," *Estudios de Cultura Náhuatl* 27 (1997), 327, 330. But famously, when Pope Urban VIII learned of Catalina de Erauso's transvestism, practiced along with the maintenance of her virginity, he granted her permission to continue to dress as a man as long as she promised to desist from her violent activities. A similar ruling befell the late eighteenth-century Mexican Mariano Aguilar, whose case is discussed further below.
3. Lewis, "From Sodomy to Superstition," 141.
4. Martin Nesvig, "The Complicated Terrain of Latin American Homosexuality," *Hispanic American Historical Review* 81:3–4 (2001) 689–729; Chad Thomas Black, "Prosecuting Female-Female Sex in Bourbon Quito," in Zeb Tortorici, ed., *Sexuality and the Unnatural in Colonial Latin America* (Oakland: University of California Press, 2016), 141–161; and Ronaldo Vainfas and Zeb Tortorici, "Female Homoeroticism, Heresy, and the Holy Office in Colonial Brazil," in Tortorici, ed, *Sexuality and the Unnatural*, 77–94.

explicitly dealt with sexuality, such as that of one late eighteenth-century transvestite, Mariano Aguilera, the church appears to have been virtually incapable of perceiving female homosexuality.[5] In some historic cases, as in La Macho's, however, allegations that defendants had specifically impersonated male members of the military, did concern state authorities.[6]

Witnesses in Piedra's case alleged she had committed two spiritual crimes: smuggling the communion host out of church, and removing and selling communion letters. Ecclesiastical law required priests to distribute printed letters that certified parishioners had taken communion to members of their congregations at Easter. They were to be signed by individual curates, and read: "Taken communion in the parish church of *N.* in the year *N.*" The letters were meant to be resubmitted to the curate the following Sunday.[7] Another witness also claimed that Piedra had blown out the candle of a religious processant who paraded in front of her. In all three actions, La Macho violated one of the seven religious sacraments (Baptism, Confirmation, Confession, the Eucharist, Marriage, Holy Orders, Last Rites) that the colonial church placed at the center of colonial religious orthodoxy. One eighteenth-century theological guide detailed the various means by which the Eucharist might be desecrated or rendered invalid.[8] If consecrating the host with grape juice rather than wine was classified as a "grave sin," how much worse would it be for a layperson to smuggle outside a half-eaten host? Piedra was challenging the authority of the Counter Reformation church, which, particularly in Latin America, insisted on the efficacy of both systematic observation of the Holy Sacraments, and the public's participation in ostentatious public rites, as means of cementing orthodox piety amongst inhabitants of its New World possessions.[9]

Piedra's investigators did not charge Piedra with sodomy (same-sex relations), but did insinuate Piedra's proclivity to identify as masculine. The prison prefect described Piedra as *"una mujer hombrada"* (a manly woman),

---

5. María Elena Martínez, "Sex and the Colonial Archive: The Case of 'Mariano' Aguilera," *Hispanic American Historical Review* 96:3 (2016), 421–43.

6. François Soyer, "The Inquisitorial Trial of a Cross-Dressing Lesbian: Reactions and Responses to Female Homosexuality in 18th-Century Portugal," *Journal of Homosexuality* 61 (2014), 1529–1557; Tortorici, *Sins Against Nature.*

7. See description in Diego Sánchez Carralero, *Constituciones synodales del priorato de Santiago de Ucles* (Murcia: Felipe Díaz Cayuelas, 1742), 250–51.

8. Francisco Echarri, *Directoria moral que comprehende, en breve, y claro estilo todas las materias de la theologia moral* (Gerona: Por Pedro Morera, 1755).

9. On baroque Catholicism in Mexico, see Brian Larkin, *The Very Nature of God: Baroque Catholicism and Religious Reform in Bourbon Mexico* (Albuquerque: University of New Mexico Press, 2010); on challenges to such orthodoxy, see Nora E. Jaffary, "Sacred Defiance and Sexual Desecration: María Getrudis Arévalo and the Holy Office in Eighteenth-Century Mexico," in Tortorici, ed. *Sexuality and the Unnatural,* 43–57.

as someone known to participate in activities (brawling and street games) more often associated with men than women, and also as a person preferring the company of women to that of men. In outward appearance, Piedra performed identification with manliness and masculinity. Can we necessarily conclude from this, as at least one scholar has done, that Piedra also preferred homo to heterosexual amorous or sexual relations?[10] Are there indications that Piedra's contemporaries made this assumption? Several witnesses claimed Piedra dressed in men's clothing in order to facilitate her "criminal plans." What crimes do witnesses suggest Piedra was trying to commit and how would dressing as a man rather than a woman have made them easier or more appealing to Piedra in some other way? What does the correspondence from her investigation reveal about how Piedra's contemporaries perceived sexuality and gender? What associations did the term "macho" convey here? A contemporary dictionary defined the term in the following way: "Macho. By implication is called the man of excessive force and resistance."[11] It also bears considering which actions of Piedra's most disturbed her contemporary peers and judges. Were her choices of clothing and pastimes more disturbing than the sacrilegious acts described? Did they see her acts of religious defiance as linked to her refusal to conform to the virtues (or the appearance) of idealized femininity?[12]

18.1 María Vicenta Vargas Denounces Gregoria[13]

[*left margin:* Received on 30 March 1796 Inquisitors Mier y Bergosa]

[*right and left margin*]: Respecting the proximity to San Diego in which the denouncer, María Vicenta Vargas, was located, our *calificador* (theological evaluator), *fray* (brother) José Francisco Valdés examined her according to procedure about the passage referred to in this denunciation and about her knowledge of the whereabouts of the denounced party, her surname, and personal identification. He asks to be informed by the prefect of prisons,

---

10. Úrsula Camba Ludlow assumes that because she was a cross-dresser, Piedra must have been a lesbian. See "Gregoria la Macho y su 'inclinación a las mujeres': reflexiones en torno a la sexualidad marginal en Nueva España, 1796–1806," *Colonial Latin American Historical Review* 12:4 (Fall 2003), 480.

11. Real Academia Española, *Diccionario de Autoridades,* Tomo IV, (1734). http://web.frl.es/DA.html

12. For discussion of a contemporary figure who challenged both sexual and sacred convention, see Jaffary, "Sacred Defiance and Sexual Desecration," 43–57.

13. The excerpts are drawn from Archivo General de la Nación, Inquisición, vol. 1349, exp. 29 fs, 336–344; exp. 30, fols. 357–357v.

Montejano, clarifying all that is known respecting this denounced party, her surname, where she is or where she has lived, but without her perceiving that this is done on behalf of the Holy Office.

On Holy Monday the 21st of March, a woman presented herself to me named María Vicenta Vargas, who is married to Joseph Antonio Reyes, and lives in the *pajería* (straw shop) facing the Alameda,[14] on the walkway in front of Corpus Christi,[15] and she has come to make a denunciation: Having come to take communion on this day in the parish church of the Sagrario, she observed close to her that a woman named Gregoria dressed in men's clothing was taking communion and that immediately after receiving the sacred host, she put her hand to her face and furtively took it out from her mouth between her fingers, and that when she saw the denouncer observing her, she hid this with an action of admiration and surprise, and at that moment, Gregoria stood up and left the church and she [Vargas] did not see what she did with the holy sacrament that she took out between her sacrilegious fingers.

Surprised, as is to be expected by such an irreligious and sacrilegious affront, I [the writer of the report, *don* José Nicolas Larragoiti] took it upon myself to learn from other subjects who this Gregoria is and where she is seen and where she lives, and I have informed myself in order to give an account of it here so that [Gregoria] will be punished for this horrific and very unusual crime.

In consequence of this duty, a sergeant of the regiment del Comercio named Joseph de Acosta apprehended [Gregoria] on Holy Friday the 25th of the current month, dressed in the clothing of a man, while she was watching the procession that passed by on this day and she was even ridiculing it, according to what the sergeant informed me. And having put her in the jail of the court, since he arrested her near to it, he informed me of this and gave an account of it to the Governor of the Real Sala del Crimen (the High Criminal Court), *don* Juan Francisco de Anda, requesting that he order [Gregoria] to be held in prison and declared that an account should be made to the Holy Office of the Inquisition which body I consider appropriate to acquire knowledge about this crime since [Gregoria] is suspected for her faith, especially considering other circumstances which will be discussed.

[Gregoria] is of such depraved and perverse customs, according to what I have learned that she has been in all the prisons of this city many times for many misdeeds which she has committed under the cloak of various disguises, because she has always dressed interchangeably in the clothing of men and of women according to what suits her criminal plans and I have been told

14. A central park in Mexico City.
15. An eighteenth-century convent for indigenous women (discussed in Chapter 13), located on what is now Avenida Juárez on the south side of the Alameda.

that [Gregoria] has even established herself at the Plaza of soldiers dressed in a uniform.

Recently, in 1794, [Gregoria] was denounced in this parish for coming, at the time of religious obligation, to frequently take communion dressed sometimes in the clothing of a man, and other times in that of a woman so that she would not be recognized afterward, with the goal of obtaining *cédulas* (official letters) to sell them, which deed she confessed to me and to my colleague doctor and *maestro* (master) *don* (sir) Joseph María Alcalá, and we informed the senior ecclesiastical judge of this archbishopric about it and he put her in prison for it and brought a case against her.

This is what has happened and I inform you, my lords, about it so that if you judge it appropriate you give an account of it to the Holy Office so that they take the corresponding measures, in light of which the cited Gregoria remains imprisoned in the royal jail of the court.

My lord, may you live many years. Parish of the Sagrario, Mexico, March 30, 1796. Doctor *don* José Nicolas Larragoiti

18.2 The Inquisition's Theological Qualifier, *Fray* José Francisco de Valdés, Examines María Vicenta Vargas

[*left margin:*] To *señor* doctor *don* Juan de Mier

In this convent of San Diego de México on April 4 1796 a woman appeared before the reverend father and theological qualifier *fray* José Francisco Valdés, having been called, and swore to tell the truth. She said her name is María Vicenta Vargas, she is married to José Antonio Reyes, native of Puebla and citizen of Mexico, and works as a servant. She does not know how old he is because she says she does not know how to count, nor does she know her own age.

Asked if she knows or presumes the reason why she has been called, she answered that it is because on the last Holy Monday of this year when she came to take communion at the church del Sagrario and she was close to the altar rail she saw a woman arrive dressed in the clothing of a man to take communion and that when she left the altar rail, she walked with her hand over her face and she took the host, which the denouncer saw she had between her fingers, and she kept watching her face and Gregoria was also watching her. And that after this she saw that Gregoria made a sign with her hand and this denouncer looked to see to whom she made it and saw that it was to a boy, and that after this [Gregoria] got up and left the church in the company of this boy leaving some strips of cotton cloth that she had brought with her there, and she went laughing out of the church with this same boy. She was asked from where she knows Gregoria and she answered that she has known her since she was a girl when the denouncer went for *atole*[16] at her house. And although she knows her name is Gregoria, she does not know her surname.

Asked if she knows where Gregoria lives and what her social status is and how she lives her life and what work she does, she responded that she knows nothing about this because since the time when she knew her when she was a girl she has never had contact with her. And this is the truth according to the oath which she has taken. And having read her this statement she said that it was well written and that she does not act out of malice and she promised to keep this secret. And since she does not know how to write, the father and qualifier signed it for her.

[signature] *fray* José Francisco Valdés, qualifier

María Vicenta Vargas
Before me, *Fray* Santiago Ayala Henas, notary

[Vargas subsequently ratified her testimony without amending it except to clarify that she had previously made the same denunciation to other authorities twice previously. The officers of the Inquisition wrote the prefect of the Royal Prison three times requesting more information about Gregoria: her surname, the places she had lived and with whom, how she lived and what kind of conduct they had observed of her in prison, and the details of her appearance, and eventually, about any details respecting her prior imprisonments. In compliance the prefect submitted the following description.]

18.3 The Prison Prefect Describes Gregoria and Gregoria's Companion

In obedience to your request of April 1 of this present year of 1796, I have taken the steps that appear to me appropriate to inform myself about the news that you solicit about the prisoner, Gregoria, who has been arrested and is in the Royal Jail of the Court by order of one of the priests of the Sagrario because on this past Holy Monday, she took communion in this church in the clothing of a man and immediately afterward passed her hand over her face and took from her mouth the sacred form and one person saw her and observed this action that she did with the sacred form. This person denounced her to one of the priests who arranged for Gregoria's apprehension and she was found on the afternoon of that day watching the procession

---

16. A rich rice drink.

of the Holy Mother near the jail where she is at present, in whose act of devotion she showed contempt by putting out the candle of one of those who went with one illuminated, making fun (apparently) of this devout act; this act moved [the priest] to worry and he requested the Sergeant, *don* José Acosta, to apprehend her.

She is *una mujer hombrada* (a manly woman), *prieta* (dark-skinned), with the face of a man, body and behavior of the same, curly hair, limbs, skin, markings, and skin tone typical of a *mulata* (woman of African and Spanish descent). Her surname is Piedra, she was born in the Plazuela de las Vizcaínas and she has lived much of her life in this part of town, in the streets San Juan, Puente de Peredo and Callejón de la Baca, and in these byways, she is known as Gregoria la Macho, and she has been seen in both kinds of clothing although more often in that of men, playing *pelota*,[17] *picado*, and *rayuela*,[18] accompanied more often by women than by men. She has been put in the jail of this city on four occasions for having worn men's clothing, for fighting, and for brawling. She was put in the Acordada[19] about three months ago, and has also been in the Poor House. Two years ago, she was taken from the same church of the Sagrario for having taking communion twice, once in the clothing of a man and once as a woman and was put then in the ecclesiastical jail and from there transferred to the city jail and it appears that she did this in order to sell the [communion] letters. She has been imprisoned in the jail of the court previously for her repeated quarrels. She claims that some while ago she was a soldier in the regiment of the blacks or in the cavalry.

In prison, nothing remarkable has been observed except the bother caused by keeping her separate from the women, but she has prayed the holy rosary, and she devoted herself to God and the saints. As for the confrontation she had with her denouncer, she entirely denies the accusation made against her.

This is all the information that I have uncovered here within the jail as well as outside it, which I, in my customary capacity place in your hands so that you may judge from it how best to proceed. April 6, 1796.

May god keep you for many years my illustrious *Señor*,

Illustrious *Señor*

I kiss the hand of your Illustriousness, your most affectionate and blessed chaplain, *Bachiller* (graduate) Agustín José Montejano Larrea

---

17. A Basque ball game played on a large court and brought to Mexico in the eighteenth century.
18. A game that involves throwing coins into a hole in a brick.
19. An eighteenth-century criminal court, first formed in 1715 for the countryside but extended to the capital in 1756.

[left margin note:] On the 9th of the same month, Montejano was instructed in writing to learn and inquire in the most opportune manner about anyone who might know the boy described by the denouncer with whom the denounced left the church and to whom she signaled.

[In the court's second letter to prefect Montejano Larrea, the Inquisition requested further details about the boy who had accompanied Piedra. His response follows:]

In obedience to the preceding order, I have used every means available to verify who the boy was who accompanied Gregoria Piedra on the day that she took communion in the Sagrario and by these steps I have only acquired a little information and it is that on the afternoon that she was apprehended, she was with a boy of medium size, barefooted, wearing leather breeches and he did not appear at the jail and only the woman did who brought food knowing that the judge was requesting her. He has stayed away and has not reappeared. I had hoped to bring in this boy and I informed myself about where he lived but he has since moved houses and I have not found out where he is. I will remain in communication with you if I learn anything further and in the mean time I hope that god keeps you for many years.

April 26 1796

I kiss the hand of Your Illustriousness, your affectionate and blessed chaplain,

Bachiller Agustín José Montejano y Larrea

[In response to the Inquisition's third request for further information about Piera Prefect Montejano Larrea observed the following:]

Most Revered Father *Comisario Fray* José Francisco Valdés,
My Dear *Señor*,

With respect to the order that you, my father, have communicated to me in your letter of the 4th of this month, I have attempted to inform myself with the necessary details to produce, as far as I am able, the report that you seek from me . . .

[The next paragraph of his letter repeated the same description as above about why Gregoria Piedra had been imprisoned in the Royal Jail of the court. The remainder of his letter repeated nearly verbatim the text of his first report, although he elaborated in a little more detail in his closing description of some of Piedra's past actions and present preferences:]

. . . Her surname is Piedra, and in this there has been no variation. She says that she was a soldier for a while, either in the regiment of *pardos* (blacks) or in the cavalry. In jail, she has only been observed showing an inclination to women (*solo se le ha obserbada la inclinación á las mujeres*), and this has given her something to do (*por este lado ha dado que aser*). She has been seen praying the holy rosary and sending her soul to saints, and in the matter of the events with the denunciant, she denies it entirely.

He signs his letter as above.

[The final document in the file is a note directed to Inquisitor don *Juan de Mier signed by Thomas Calderón, an officer in the* Real Sala *dated December 17, 1802 noting only that he is sending the accompanying file about Piedra's case to the court which he says should have been previously sent in December 1796 according to the regulations of the* Real Sala, *the business of the court had impeded the file's earlier transfer.]*

Suggested Reading

Few, Martha, "'That Monster of Nature': Gender, Sexuality, and the Medicalization of a 'Hermaphrodite' in Late Colonial Guatemala," *Ethnohistory* 54:1 (Winter 2007), 159–76.

Jaffary, Nora E. *False Mystics: Deviant Orthodoxy in Colonial Mexico*. Lincoln: University of Nebraska Press, 2004.

Lewis, Laura A., "From Sodomy to Superstition: The Active Pathic and Bodily Transgressions in New Spain," *Ethnohistory* 54:1 (Winter 2007), 129–57.

Martínez, María Elena, "Sex and the Colonial Archive: The Case of 'Mariano' Aguilera," *Hispanic American Historical Review* 96:3 (2016), 421–43.

Tortorici, Zeb, ed. *Sexuality and the Unnatural in Colonial Latin America*. Oakland: University of California Press, 2016.

———. *Sins Against Nature: Sex and Archives in Colonial New Spain, 1530–1821*. Durham, NC: Duke University Press, forthcoming.

Velasco, Sherry, *The Lieutenant Nun: Transgenderism, Lesbian Desire, and Catalina de Erauso*. Austin: University of Texas Press, 2000.

Document Themes

- Law
- Religion
- Sexuality and gender

19

Ana Gallum, Freed Slave and
Property Owner (Florida, 1801)

Introduction and Translation by Jane Landers

The following documents are drawn from a lengthy probate case of a frontier planter and translator of indigenous languages named Joseph or Jacob or Job Wiggins, who died in Spanish Florida. From the testimonies in this case we know that when Florida was still a British colony (1763–1784), Job Wiggins bought a young Senegalese slave from the British firm of Panton, Leslie & Company that held the monopoly on the Indian trade in Florida. Wiggins subsequently freed the young woman variously known as Ana Gallum, Nancy/Nansi Wiggins, and Ana Wiggins, and married her in a Protestant ceremony somewhere near Rollestown, Florida.[1] Spanish officials who took control of the colony in 1784 did not recognize this marriage because it was not sanctified by the Catholic Church, but Ana and Wiggins lived together for approximately eighteen years before his death and had seven children who lived, all of whom were baptized in the Catholic Church.

When Wiggins died in 1797, Ana was left in charge of their surviving minor children and an estate that included a furnished plantation house, twelve hundred acres of land, farm equipment, almost one hundred head of cattle, and thirteen slaves living in six cabins. Because Wiggins died intestate, the Spanish governor ordered a tribunal to determine Ana's rights and those of the couple's children. Ana was interviewed multiple times by Spanish court and treasury officials and although she was illiterate, assisted by an amanuensis, and by her extended network of advocates, Ana also filed multiple petitions of her own in this process, as did her eldest daughter, Patty. Ultimately, in 1801, Ana's inheritance rights and those of her surviving mixed-race, and technically illegitimate, children were upheld.[2]

---

1. To avoid confusion she is normally referred to as "Ana" in this chapter.
2. Testamentary Proceedings of Jacob Wiggins, November 14, 1797, East Florida Papers (hereafter EFP) microfilm reel 134, P. K. Yonge Library of Florida History, University of Florida (hereafter PKY). I would like to thank James Cusick, Curator, Florida History, PKY, for providing me with a scanned copy of this 142-folio document.

Women of all ethnicities, backgrounds, and legal conditions, including free and enslaved women of African descent, like Ana, took advantage of their access to law in Spanish Florida. They clearly understood the significance of law in Spanish society; the intimate nature of the tribunal, which consisted of the governor, his legal counsel, and the royal notary, and the small size and interrelatedness of the community may have minimized petitioners' fears about approaching the court. If the women who approached the court were illiterate, as Ana was, they could use the services of a friend or of the government notary to file petitions or complaints. In those cases, the women's "Xs" would be accompanied by the signature of the person assisting and by the notation "at the request of _____ who cannot write." If they required the assistance of translators this fact, too, was duly noted in the documents. Many women in colonial Florida, however, were multilingual, especially women of African descent.

Just as they learned new languages, women of African descent learned to manipulate Spanish law, customs, and gender conventions to their advantage. Once free, women of African descent living in Spanish colonies, like Ana, enjoyed the legal and customary rights held by Spanish women. They operated small businesses; litigated in the courts; and bought and sold property, including slaves. Some, like Ana, and the better-known Anna Madgigine Jai Kingsley, became plantation mistresses.[3]

European–African unions such as Job and Ana's were common and accepted in Florida, much as they were on the African coast and in other areas of Latin America. Even in cases involving concubinage, rather than legal marriage, Spanish law and community consensus protected widows and heirs, and the Catholic Church also interceded "paternally" on behalf of mothers of African descent. Spanish settlers across the Americas left substantial property to their common-law wives and natural children,[4] and the community usually respected the desires of the deceased, as well as the rights of the bereaved. Many of Florida's wealthiest ranchers, planters, government

---

A number of African women living in Florida in this period also came from the interior of Senegal, most notably Anna Madgigine Jai. Daniel L. Schafer, *Anna Madgigine, Jai Kingsley: African Princess, Florida Slave, Plantation Slaveowner* (Gainesville: University Press of Florida, 2003).

Baptisms of Patricia Wiggins (b. 1782), María Wiggins (b. 1785), Benjamin Wiggins (b. 1788), and Abigail Juana Wiggins (b. 1789) all on Feb. 13, 1795; Baptisms of Ana María Wiggins (b. May, 15, 1792) and Jorge José Wiggins (b. July 10, 1795) both on Nov. 8, 1797 (Black Baptisms, Catholic Parish Records [hereafter CPR], microfilm reel 284 J, PKY). A number of witnesses also alluded to a son, William Wiggins, who was killed by Indians shortly before Wiggins' death.

3. Jane Landers, *Black Society in Spanish Florida* (Urbana: University of Illinois Press, 1999).

4. This phrase alludes to the allegation that their parents were unmarried. For the distinction between "natural" and "illegitimate" children, see Chapter 1, footnote 7.

officials, and merchants had large *mulato* (of African and European parentage) families (sometimes in addition to their white families) and recognized their *mulato* children, educated them, and provided for them in their wills. Among the prominent Florida planters, merchants, and government officials with African wives or consorts and mixed-race children were Zephaniah Kingsley, James Erwin, John Fraser, Francis Richard, Luis Mattier, Francisco Xavier Sánchez, John Sammis, Oran Baxter, Juan Leslie, Eduardo Wanton, the brothers Jorge J. F. Clarke and Carlos Clarke (who was married to Ana's daughter), and the physicians Tomás Tunno and Tomás Sterling. John Leslie of the British trading firm Panton & Leslie, the government translator Miguel Ysnardy (who was himself of mixed-race heritage), the militia commander Carlos Clarke, and the physician Tomás Tunno were among others testifying that Job Wiggins had always recognized Ana and their children as his family, that Ana and the children had, in fact, been responsible for greatly augmenting Wiggins' estate, and that Wiggins always intended for them to inherit his estate. All also testified that they knew of no other legitimate wife or heirs who might make claims on the estate.[5]

In the years after her husband's death, Ana continued to manage the estate she inherited and she appeared frequently in the legal records of the day, buying and selling horses and slaves.[6] But Ana's life on the plantation was not an easy one. Two years after Wiggins' death, Ana reported to the governor's tribunal that she had been raped by Pedro Casaly, who had come to her plantation to get a horse. On his way back to town, Casaly was drowned, but Ana was left pregnant. She appealed to the court for financial assistance for the son that was born of the rape, as she claimed to have no money. The governor, and everyone else in the community, knew Ana held substantial property and had important and wealthy "family" on whom she could depend, namely the important white consorts of her daughters, so no government assistance was forthcoming.[7] In 1811, Ana Wiggins petitioned the government for lands

---

5. Interestingly, English witnesses like the priest Thomas Hassett, and the court-appointed executor James Forrester mistakenly gave Ana's birthplace as Bengal, rather than Senegal. Daniel L. Schafer, *Zephaniah Kingsley Jr. and the Atlantic World: Slave Trader, Plantation Owner, Emancipator* (Gainesville: University of Florida Press, 2013). Kimberly S. Hanger found many similar cases of cross-racial inheritance in Spanish New Orleans. *Bounded Lives, Bounded Places: Free Black Society in Colonial New Orleans, 1769–1803* (Durham, NC: Duke University Press, 1997).

6. The free black militiaman Jorge Sanco brought suit against Ana (alias Nansi) Wiggins to try to force the manumission of his wife, Rosa, which Ana contested. Petition of Jorge Sanco, June 4, 1810, Civil Proceedings, EFP, microfilm reel 160, PKY. Rose appears as twenty-three years old on an inventory of Ana's estate, f. 120.

7. Testamentary Proceedings of Jacob Wiggins, op. cit.; Declaration of Ana Gallum, October 3, 1799, ibid.; Baptism of Pedro Casaly (b. Sept. 18, 1799) on Sept. 5, 1800. The child is listed as the natural son of Pedro Casaly and Ana Wiggins, free black from Senegal. Catholic Parish

on which to work four slaves and live with her twelve-year-old son, but the acting governor replied that she already owned lands on the St. Johns River and ordered her to get that acreage into cultivation or lose it.[8]

Compare Ana's case to the stories of women in Chapters 2, 14, 15, and 17 in this collection. How does Ana's use of the law compare to the attempted uses by other enslaved or formerly enslaved women in colonial Latin America? What attitudes toward their marital partnership did Job Wiggins' peers express in these legal proceedings? Do you think the relationship between Ana's family and that of their slaves would have differed from relations between white slave-owning families and their slaves? How so or why not?

19.1 Declaration of Miguel Ysnardy, Testamentary Proceedings, Jacob Wiggins, November 14, 1797[9]

[All witnesses called to testify in the case followed the format of an interrogatory, with each witness swearing first on the Cross, and then responding to a set of questions posed by a Spanish official.]

Miguel Ysnardy, public interpreter, swore on God and the Cross that by law he promised to tell the truth about all he knew that was asked of him; and regarding the particulars contained in this case he said the following.

To the first question he said: He has resided in the Province since 1782, when it still belonged to the British Crown and it was then he met Job Wiggins, although he can't be certain that at that time he was already living conjugally with the *morena* (black woman) Ana Gallum, he understood that he bought her from the House of Panton Leslie as a young girl and that he freed her later and that he knows that they always lived as if married until his death and that he had children of both sexes with her, which the declarant saw because he dealt often with Wiggins and went to his house and saw that he raised and fed them

Registers on microfilm reel 284 J, PKY. These records are also available online at the Slave Societies Digital Archive http://www.slavesocieties.org/

8. Petition of Nancy [sic] Wiggins, July 3, 1811, and reply by Governor Juan José de Estrada, July 9, 1811, Spanish Florida Land Records, Record Group 599, Series 992. Brief translations of the various Wiggins' land claims were also done by the Historical Records Survey, Works Projects Administration and published by the State Library Board, Tallahassee, FL, May 1941. These are available on the Florida Memory site of the State Library & Archives of Florida. https://www.floridamemory.com/collections/spanishlandgrants/

9. East Florida Papers, Reel 134, P. K. Yonge Library of Florida History, University of Florida, f. 88 v. The editors have rearranged the ordering of some of the documents in the following transcriptions to follow chronological order.

as if his children treating them in this manner, unlike the slaves he had in the house although they were of the same color, who were assigned to serve him. And to the second question, he referred to his first answer. And to the third question he said he knows that Wiggins' estate grew considerably in the last years he lived, when because he was already old and could not work as much as in his youth, although one would have expected the contrary. And the witness attributes this to the management of the *negra* Ana; and that of her children and of Wiggins, now grown who worked to conserve and augment the goods; To the next [fourth question] he answered that the great friendship and history he had with the deceased Wiggins aids his knowledge and he is certain that he was never legitimately married nor does he know he had any other children than those he had with the *morena* Ana Gallum and he remembers that years ago, two strangers appeared at his [Wiggins'] plantation saying they were his relatives, one of whom left shortly afterwards because Wiggins did not recognize him as a relative and the other whom he did recognize stayed but died some three years later. To the fifth and last question he stated: That the witness, for the love and high esteem he observed that Wiggins had for Ana and her children, that as he said were also his own [Wiggins'], he believed and still believes it was that only they should enjoy the fruits of their labor, inheriting all the goods at his death, and the witness always understood that although he never heard Wiggins voice it, and he responds that all he has said is the truth according to his oath: he is fifty-eight years old, is under no legal charges and he signed understanding the contents of this declaration

Licenciado Ortega   Miguel
Ysnardy   Isaac Wickes
Before me, Jose de Zubizarreta, Government Scribe

19.2 Declaration of *don* Miguel O'Reilly, November 20, 1797[10]

Don (Sir) Miguel O'Reilly, *cura beneficiado Vicario Juez Ecclesiastico* (ordained priest and ecclesiastical judge) of the Parish Church, Plaza and Province of St. Augustine, Florida, certify that in the second book of the archive in my charge, are found the following entries of baptisms of *pardos* and *morenos* (blacks) on page 40, second entry, page 41, first, 2nd, and 3rd entries and page 94, 1st and 2nd entries, numbers 76, 77m 78, 79, and 285 are found the following persons:

---

10. Testamentary Proceedings, Jacob Wiggins, November 14, 1797, East Florida Papers, Reel 134, P. K. Yonge Library of Florida History, University of Florida, f. 17–18.

Friday, February 13, 1795 I, *don* Thomas Hassett, *cura beneficiado Vicario Juez Ecclesiastico* of the Parish Church, Plaza and Province of St. Augustine, East Florida baptized and put the holy oils on a free *parda* (black girl) of thirteen years, natural daughter of *don* Joseph Wiggins, native of England, and of the free *negra*, Ana Gallum, native of Bengal [sic]; and I performed all the ceremonies of our Holy Mother Church, and named her Patricia, her godfather was Doctor *don* Thomas Travers, resident of this city and I advised him of his spiritual relationship and obligations, and I signed it this day and month.

Thomas Hassett

[On Friday, February 13, 1795, don *Thomas Hassett, baptized three more children of Joseph Wiggins and Ana Gallum. The first was María, their ten-year-old* mulata *daughter; the second was their seven year-old* mulato *son, Benjamin; and the third was their six-year-old* mulata *daughter, Juana Abigail. Serving as godfather for all three children was Doctor* don *Thomas Travers. On Wednesday, November 8, 1797,* don *Miguel baptized Joseph and Ana's* mulata *daughter Ana María, who was born on May 15, 1792, and their* mulato *son, Jorge José, born on July, 10, 1795. Don* Carlos Clarke[11] *and* doña *Ana Sanders served as Ana María's godparents and* don *Lorenco Solana and* doña *Maria Scott served as godparents for Jorge José.]*

19.3 Inventory of Wiggins Plantation, November 21, 1797[12]

On the same plantation and on the same day and year [January 26, 1797] the Captain of the Militia, *don* Bernardo Segui, in virtue of the commission he received and with the assisting witnesses *don* Juan Forester [sic] and William Wignes [sic], lists the goods belonging to the deceased for inventory as follows:

Credits:
A debt by Juan Mor [Moore][13] resident of the Rivera de San Juan for twenty *pesos* and five *reales* (coins worth one eighth of a *peso* each)

---

11. *Don* Carlos Clarke, commander of the free black militia of Fernandina, Florida, also of English ancestry, raised a mixed-race family with Ana's daughter, Beatriz. Landers, *Black Society.*
12. Testamentary Proceedings, Jacob Wiggins, January 26, 1797, East Florida Papers, Reel 134, P. K. Yonge Library of Florida History, University of Florida, f. 3V-6.
13. Juan Moore was a free black militiaman whose enslaved family fled Georgia and received religious sanctuary in Spanish Florida. Landers, *Black Society.*

Inventory: (wealthy)

<u>Slaves</u>

First, a *negro* (black man) named Francisco, seventy years old

Item,[14] a *negra* named Bety, fifty years old

Item, a *negrita* (black girl) named Rose, eight years old

Item, another *negrita* named Fanny, four years old

Item, a *negro* named Bob, twenty-seven years old

Item, a *negra* named Seillia [Celia], thirty-eight years old

Item, a *negra* named Amie, seventeen years old

Item a *negro* named Dicke, fifty-five years old

Item, a *negra* named Carolina, fifty years old

Item, a *negro* named Champion, fifty-four years old

Item, a *negra* named Chloe, thirty-eight years old

Item, *negrita* named Tenah, seven years old

Item, another *negrito* named Chason, five years old

Item, another *negrito* named Dick, five years old

Item, a *negra* named Venus, thirty-eight years old

<u>Horses</u>

First, a sorrel horse with the usual brand

Item, another red horse [*with brand drawn, letters IF inside a circle*] on its right flank

<u>Cattle</u>

First, thirty head of young bulls and bulls, branded with the brand $\overline{3E}$; usually about seventy head of cattle and calves; forty head of male and females about two years old, sixty of the same one year old, all marked with the same brand

<u>Note</u>

Regarding the said cattle, it having been impossible to see them, you can more or less see they do not account for this year's calves

<u>Pigs</u>

First, two pigs with piglets

Item, two deer

Item, about thirty head [of pigs] that wander in the forests endangered by tigers[15] and other animals

<u>Canoes</u>

First, a canoe with two oars

Item, another useless canoe

---

14. *Item* in the original, meaning next in a list.

15. Likely panthers.

<u>Corn</u>
One hundred bushels of corn

<u>Rice</u>
A barrel and a half of rice weighing 800 pounds

<u>Yams</u>
Forty bushels of *muniatos* (yam-like or cassava-like tubers)

<u>Furniture</u>
First, two beds, each with their mattress
   Item, three tables of pine
   Item, three benches of pine, useless
   Item, three cauldrons of iron
   Item, one coffee pot of iron
   Item, one rifle to shoot birds
   Item, five hatchets
   Item, four grills
   Item, four small hatchets
   Item, two carpenter's tools[16]
   Item, one hand saw
   Item, one saw to cut boards
   Item, another to chop
   Item, two palm leaf baskets
   Item, two knives for making shingles
   Item, one cooper's hammer
   Item, two cooper's washers
   Item, five large drills
   Item, one stone grinder
   Item, eight wedges of iron

A plantation of their habitation with one house with a kitchen where the family lives, two houses of [illegible word] and one *Espensa*[17] six [word illegible] of *negros*
   Item, sixty fenced acres of land
   Item, one thousand forty acres of pine. These lands he gave to his woman [Ana Wiggins] to inhabit

In the same plantation on the sixth of the same month and year the Captain of Militias, one Bernardo Segui with the assisting witnesses having inventoried the property of the deceased Jacobo Wiggins, named *don* Juan Forester [sic], resident of the Rivera de San Juan, as executor of the goods

---

16. The text looks like *suelas* in the original, which might refer to a carpenter's, or shoe-maker's sole.
17. This phrase is hard to decipher. An *Espensa* is an expense.

corresponding to the same inventory until the disposition of the tribunal and he signed in the presence of the assisting witnesses Juan Forrester

Bernardo Segui, Lorenzo Yanes, Lorenzo Solana

19.4 Declaration of Ana Gallum, November 21, 1797[18]

Ana Gallum, free *morena*, before Your Excellency as legally permitted, present myself and state: That I was married in the custom of the Anglicans, when they dominated the province, to *don* Joseph Wiggins, resident of the place called Rolls Town, about thirteen leagues from this Plaza, who being now dead left thirteen slaves, cattle and other effects on the plantation he owned, all without doubt for my use, and that of his six living children as his only and legitimate heirs. But in the month of February of this year [1797], the Militia Captain, *don* Bernardo Seguy [sic] came to the plantation to inventory said property and placed it in the control and administration of *don* Juan Forrester who had put one Luis (James Lewis) in charge of everything on my said plantation. But this man wants to be owner of everything and blocks my use and benefit of the most minimal thing, giving my children and me only one ration of corn such as the rest of the *negros* receive and we are experiencing the greatest miseries and cruel treatment. In virtue of this [situation], I come to receive the powerful aid of Your Excellency having presented the sad situation in which I find myself and of course I believe that said Lewis is not authorized to enact such a thing, for which reason I find myself needing to make the following requests of Your Excellency.

First, that your Excellency immediately order the said Lewis to leave my plantation because no stranger can better care for a property than I who has helped conserve and augment [it] with my labor and sweat; that because the Wiggins estate incudes six natural children registered in this Parochial Church as found in the baptismal books, of which four are minors, two daughters, one of eight years and the other of six years, and two boys, one of ten years and the other of three, that you name me as their guardian, as I should be. Because there is nobody better than I, and for the benefits that redound to me, who could better care for the properties of these minors, this having been my same home which for the period of twenty-two years I have been working and augmenting that which is now inventoried. And respecting my

---

18. Testamentary Proceedings, Jacob Wiggins, September 11, 1797, East Florida Papers, Reel 134, P. K. Yonge Library of Florida History, University of Florida, f. 12–13.

two children older than twelve years, they ask that a guardian be named this very day. And, finally, that you concede me the free administration of all my goods as the legitimate widow of the said Wiggins and give me after examination the same inventories [of goods] that are about to be registered, or failing that, the necessary sustenance to allow me and my children to exist without misery, and to this end I ask Your Excellency the right that I am due to the said property, and to the papers left due to the death of the said Wiggins who I always heard say would leave all to his children.

For all these reasons I humbly ask Your Excellency agree to order as I have asked, what I ask is just, and I swear I do not proceed out of malice but according to the [legal] requirements.

For the interested party who does not know how to write, Dimas Cortes

19.5 Declaration of Patricia Wiggins, November 21, 1797[19]

Patricia Wiggins, free *parda* (black woman), for herself and in the name of María, her sister, as is my right by law, present myself to your Majesty and state: That as the document I present states, I am the natural daughter of *don* Joseph Wiggins, now deceased, who was the owner of the plantation situated about nine leagues west of this Plaza, in the area called Rolls Town. To my knowledge, my father never made any testamentary disposition of the thirteen slaves, cattle and other goods that he left. As a result, those goods are now by the dictate of this Tribunal inventoried and placed in the care and management of *don* Juan Forrester, and we are not allowed the use of any of them.

I ask Your Majesty to appoint me a *curador* (legal defender) because I have no known person in this Plaza to take charge of this matter, to represent my rights, and it is justice that I seek, and I swear that I do not proceed out of malice but according to the [legal] requirements. . . .

At the request of the interested party who does not
know how to sign, Dimas Cortes

---

19. Testamentary Proceedings, Jacob Wiggins, November 23, 1797, East Florida Papers, Reel 134, P. K. Yonge Library of Florida History, University of Florida, f. 15.

19.6 Declaration of *don* Juan Leslie, November 21, 1797[20]

In the city of St. Augustine, Florida on the 27th of November 1797, I, the scribe notified *don* Juan Leslie of what is contained in the earlier document and informed by this he stated: That he is not sure he has the will in his possession, that in truth the deceased Wiggins made it during the English dominion [of Florida] using a qualified attorney or official and the undersigned certifies as to the authenticity of the said Wiggins' will because he read that disposition in which he named as his only and universal heirs his natural children with a *negra* named Ana Gallum who was at that time his slave and to whom he also gave liberty in the cited will. All of which he confirms is certain and true according to his religious oath according to law, for God Almighty and on the Sacred Bible, according to the Protestant sect he professes, adding that he remembers that the deceased Wiggins in that testament named *don* William Panton, the testator's partner, as guardian of said children and their mother and of their goods, until such time as they were old enough to manage them. [The testator] is forty-seven years of age, a resident and a merchant in this city. He is married and is under no legal penalties and what he has testified is the best he can remember of what transpired more than twelve years ago when Wiggins made the said will and he signed it and I witnessed, Juan Leslie

Before me: Jose de Zubizarreta, Government Scribe

[These proceedings run more than a hundred double-sided folios, a number of which are dedicated to the signatures of the officials and persons testifying and recording all those who were notified of the testimony. The royal scribe occasionally summarized all the earlier testimonies. A number of the folios are illegible but the format is fairly consistent and many of the subsequent testimonies are similar to Leslie's. Residents, often those who had fictive or actual kinship connection to the free black community, testified about their relationship or connection to Joseph Wiggins and about the length of time they had known he and Ana Gallum to have lived together as a couple. They also testified as to their knowledge that it was always Wiggins' wish to have Ana and their children inherit his property, Some witnesses commented on Ana's successful

---

20. Testamentary Proceedings, Jacob Wiggins, November 14, 1797, East Florida Papers, Reel 134, P. K. Yonge Library of Florida History, University of Florida, f. 19 *don* Juan Leslie was a leading merchant in St. Augustine and director of the important Panton Leslie Trading Company, from whom Wiggins had initially purchased Ana. Leslie was another resident of English ancestry, who although married, had children with his slave and he also served as commander of the free black militia. Landers, *Black Society*, 150, 207, 242.

management of his estate. Folios 25–28 offer an interesting accounting of items Wiggins purchased from the Panton Leslie Company and of his outstanding debt to the company. The following examples focus on testimonies regarding Ana Gallum's rights to Wiggins' property.]

19.7 Declaration of *don* Dimas Cortes, Testamentary Proceedings, Jacob Wiggins, January 1798[21]

Don Dimas Cortes, on behalf of *don* Rafael Espinosa, named guardian of the minors Patricia Wiggins and her brothers and sisters, natural children of *don* Joseph, now dead, formerly a new vassal of Your Catholic Majesty in this province, in the inventory of goods left by his death ordered by Your Excellency's Tribunal, following the law and representing the best interests of said minors, before you appear and state: That I have been informed that your order of the ninth of this month, in which you declare that the said Wiggins died intestate; and that the said minors should justify the legal basis they have for challenging their natural births[22] and illegitimacy recorded in their respective baptismal entries.[23] Such justification, *Señor Gobernador*, would be impossible for anybody to provide especially since it is not optional, nor would it lead to the desired objective, and the only thing that can be proven, and that which is very clear in the cited baptismal entries, against which nothing else can prevail, is that the minors are truly the natural children of *don* Joseph Wiggins, resident who lived in the Province from the time it was under the dominion of the King of Great Britain; that he remained in the province even after July 12, 1784 when your Majesty's troops took possession of the province; and that under the Protestant sect he professed (and in which he died) he lived in a conjugal union with his *morena* slave whom he later freed and with whom he had numerous children and who helped him over almost thirty years of labor augment his wealth that is now inventoried and in deposit and possession of a stranger. This being the case, I do not want nor should I want for now any other thing except that as quickly as possible, Your Excellency definitively declare to whom the inventoried goods belong, preserving the rights of my minors (should it be the case that they are not named the legitimate heirs of all) so that by my representation they may protest and appeal where it is most convenient, for although the poverty of options in

---

21. East Florida Papers, Reel 134, P. K. Yonge Library of Florida History, University of Florida, f. 31. The precise day in January is not indicated on the document.
22. Underlining in the original.
23. Underlining in the original.

this place is known, there are many possibilities in Havana by which they can appeal if it should be necessary before the Royal Throne if by chance (as I have heard some rumors) these goods are adjudicated to the Royal Hacienda in accordance with the Laws.

For these [the Laws] if they so disposed, must be very different in other cases and by no means apply in this Province, to which Your Majesty [the King] conceded the privilege to receive new settlers of whatever faith, as long as the public faith was solely Catholic. Many other exemptions also appear in this case, that in another time I will allege and aided by other information I will be able to better claim, the main ones being that it appears in this inquiry that the deceased made a will in the time of the British, according to the declaration on f. 19; and if he did in fact make one, it must exist wherever they moved their archives; so there is much to claim and in consequence it cannot be said that Jacobo Wiggins died intestate. It would certainly appear a very hard thing for Your Excellency to appropriate the goods resulting from the sweat and industry of farmers and deprive legitimate natural children of their enjoyment, who are now loyal vassals of His Majesty in the Province and who have joined the brotherhood of the Church, all of them being very young, in addition the law favors the mother, for the work and increase during the time of the couple's union, and that of her oldest son who, sadly, the Indians killed.

And as for the credit of *don* Juan Leslie for the two bills that he has presented, I agree that these seem very correct and for all these reasons, I implore your Majesty to definitely rule as I have asked, it is justice I seek and I swear not to proceed from malice, and all the rest. . . .

And, because you have not yet ruled anything regarding the request that Ana Gallum, mother of these minors, made to you in her petition of the 21st of November last on f. 12, asking that the inventoried goods be assigned to her with the corresponding bond as agreed to by the executor in his own petition of f. 20 and the Royal Accountant in his representation, if it please Your Majesty, this just request should take effect or give this function to another administrator because in the control of the current one [*don* Juan Forrester], who has had it for almost a year, I consider for many reasons it has been extremely prejudicial to the increase of the property and the rights of the heirs. I request justice, Dimas Cortes

[In subsequent folios, a number of other individuals to whom Wiggins owed money came forward to record their claims to Ana's inheritance. On f. 40 the widow María Hambly registered a claim on two cows and their offspring; on f. 41–42v don Juan Forrester, an associate of the Panton Leslie Company also made additional claims on the Wiggins' estate. On f. 43–44v Ana Gallum petitioned the governor for assistance stating that she and her children were in dire need of "clothing and other indispensable items" and

asking that she be given "a dozen cows with their calves, two negro men named Bob and Champion, and the negress Betsi for domestic service" until such time as the court ruled. Ana's supporter, Dimas Cortes, and two other witnesses, Juan Gutiérrez and Lorenzo Solano, inventoried the Wiggins' plantation a second time on October 21, 1798 on f. 55–61, recommending that since Ana had no other way to pay Wiggins' debts, she sell most of her cattle herd to satisfy them. On f. 66 dated November 29, 1798, Ana asked the court to wait until spring for the sale (after the birth of calves) and on f. 68–69, don Juan Forrester, of the Panton Leslie Company, agreed. Ana subsequently sold a number of cattle to don Fernando Arredondo and Antonio Huertas, among others, while she and the children continued to live on their plantation.]

19.8 Declaration of Manuel Zamorano, Royal Accountant, September 14, 1798[24]

[I,] the Accountant of the Army and the Royal Treasury, as *fiscal* (crown attorney), in response to Your Majesty's [the Governor] order of the fourteenth of September, have reviewed the official proceedings resulting from the death of Jacobo Wigins [sic], resident of this province, to assign his properties and goods in favor of those who appear to be his legitimate heirs and from what it appears I say: As a result of the declarations received from Jaime Luis, Juan Muray [sic] that said Wigins [sic], a new vassal of His Catholic Majesty was unmarried but did leave seven children who he had with a free *morena* named Nancy [i.e., Ana Gallum]; and that the will of their father was always to leave them in possession of his properties when he died. I am of the opinion that if Your Honor's Tribunal applies the relevant laws touching on this matter, and declares that natural children, such as those that present themselves here, are due the same inheritance as those born of a legitimate marriage, then whatever Wigins [sic] left should be placed in the control of the said *morena*. But if by law, they do not enjoy the same rights as those [legitimate children], it falls on Your Majesty to assign what the inventory states exists to the named trustee, *don* Juan Forrester, declaring invalid the wishes of Jacobo Wigins [sic], as there is no testament. And if all that exists are the declarations of those who testified, Your Majesty will decide what you judge to be most just. San Agustin de la Florida, twentieth of November of seventeen ninety-seven.

Gonzalo Zamorano

---

24. Testamentary Proceedings, Jacob Wiggins, November 23, 1797, East Florida Papers, Reel 134, P. K. Yonge Library of Florida History, University of Florida, f. 14.

[This case was only concluded in 1801, three-and-a-half years after Wiggins' death, but in the end, Governor Enrique White agreed with the many who testified on Ana Gallum's behalf that Wiggins intended Ana and the children to inherit his estate, but reminded her that she was forbidden from alienating any of the estate and was still responsible for her remaining debts, including to her daughter, Patricia.]

19.9 Declaration of *don* Enrique White, Testamentary Proceedings, Jacob Wiggins[25]

In the city of St. Augustine, Florida, on the fourteenth of July, 1801: *Señor don* Enrique White, Colonel of the Royal Armies and Governor, Civil and Military of it and this Province, for Your Majesty: Having reviewed the declarations and inventories and estimates of the goods left at the death of Job Wiggins, resident in this Province since the time of the British dominion, which pertain to the Royal Treasury; and to the free *morena* Ana Gallum, and to her children Ysavel, María, Benjamin, Juana, Ana and Jorge, that she had with Wiggins, living in conjugal marriage according to the Protestant sect, decree: that it is clear in these declarations that the named children, and no others, were had by and raised by Wiggins with the named Ana, and that also no other children are known, nor are any other relatives known who would have rights to legitimately inherit, should declare and does declare, that the named six children and one other] who in the declarations is named William and who died at the hand of the Indians after his father died, are heirs in equal parts to the goods left by his death, and that also is [heir] in two parts equal to that of her children their mother Ana, for earnings or as best required by law, in consideration of the clear findings in the declarations, not only because it was the wish of Wiggins shortly before his death, but also there is some proof that he stated this in a will that two very reputable witnesses signed in the times of the British dominion, whose [the will's] location is unknown, and the children of the *morena*, Ana, all being still minor and she the tutor and legal guardian.

[The governor then ordered that Ana be named administrator of the inheritance from Wiggins' estate and that she absolutely be forbidden from alienating any of the inventoried goods, adding that it would without doubt be worse to place the administration in the hands of another. Ana would

---

25. East Florida Papers, Reel 134, P. K. Yonge Library of Florida History, University of Florida, f. 107 v.

administer the estate remaining after deducting all legal charges incurred by officials taking testimony, inventorying the estate, and certifying the legal paperwork, and after deducting nineteen pesos and one real due to her adult daughter, Patricia.]

Signed Enrique White, *Licenciado* Josef de Ortega: before Me: Jose de Zubizarreta, Government Scribe.

Suggested Reading

Candido, Mariana P. "Concubinage and Slavery in Benguela, 1750–1850." In *Slavery in Africa and the Caribbean: A History of Enslavement and Identity Since the 18th Century*, ed. Olatunji Ojo and Nadine Hunt (London: I.B. Tauris, 2012), 65–84.

Hanger, Kimberly S. *Bounded Lives, Bounded Places: Free Black Society in Colonial New Orleans, 1769–1803* (Durham, NC: Duke University Press, 1997).

Landers, Jane. "African-American Women and Their Pursuit of Rights through Eighteenth-Century Spanish Texts." In *Haunted Bodies: Gender and Southern Texts*, ed. Anne Goodwyn Jones and Susan V. Donaldson (Charlottesville: University of Virginia Press, 1998), 56–76.

———. *Black Society in Spanish Florida* (Urbana: University of Illinois Press, 1999, 2001, 2002, 2005).

McKinley, Michelle A. *Fractional Freedoms: Slavery, Intimacy, and Legal Mobilization in Colonial Lima, 1600–1700* (New York: Cambridge University Press, 2016).

Schafer, Daniel L. *Anna Madgigine, Jai Kingsley: African Princess Florida Slave, Plantation Slaveowner* (Gainesville: University Press of Florida, 2003).

Document Themes

- Family
- Labor
- Law
- Race and ethnicity
- Religion
- Sexuality and gender
- Slavery

20

A Female Slave Owner's Abuse of an
Enslaved Woman (Neiva, Colombia, 1803)[1]

A legal investigation into slave abuse raises questions about both the limits of slave owners' powers and about gendered understandings of violence in the setting of Colombia at the turn of the nineteenth century. The following texts are excerpted from an 1803 criminal suit from Nueva Granada (current-day Colombia, Panama, and Venezuela) charging that a Spanish woman, *doña* (lady) Ana María Vargas, had physically abused Simona, an enslaved black woman, to the point of death. The Colombian National Archives classifies the following excerpt in its catalogue as a "*sumaria*," denoting the central investigative portion of a legal case that was preceded by the case's opening denunciation, and which was normally followed by the *juicio plenario* (plenary suit, where all evidence was fully examined) and the *sentencia* or sentence.[2] The *sumaria*, which became a crucial innovation in Spanish law beginning in the mid-sixteenth century, consisted in magistrates' investigative inquiries into the cases they tried. Conventionally, such processes opened with a magistrate's declaration about a specific crime about which he had learned from a denunciation or accusation or his own knowledge, followed by his analysis of its occurrence undertaken by interviewing several witnesses.

The materials contained in this file document a case already in progress. The denunciation or accusation, alleging that Vargas was responsible for Simona's death, has already been made. We cannot ascertain from these documents who had initiated the inquiry, but they imply that a man called *don* (sir) Diego Antonio Gutiérrez, a scribe, had initiated the case. The portion of the *sumaria* reproduced here opens with a notice from *alcalde ordinario* (municipal judge) Josef Silvestre Rodríguez Durán to all his peer *alcaldes ordinarios* in the city of San Sebastían de la Plata, informing them of an order issued by the Audiencia (court) of New Granada requiring that certain elements be included in any presiding *alcalde*'s investigation of Simona's death. Luis de Oballe, *doña* Ana María Vargas's hardworking legal defender, had successfully lobbied the

---

1. Archivo General de la Nación de Colombia, Colonia, Miscelánea: SC.39, 65, D. 57, "Sumaria criminal por maltratos a esclava y causar su muerte." The editors acknowledge with thanks Frida Osorio Gonsen's translation assistance with this document.
2. Charles R. Cutter, *The Legal Culture of Northern New Spain, 1700–1810* (Albuquerque: The University of New Mexico Press, 1995), 105.

Audiencia to require the *alcalde ordinario de primero voto* (he of higher rank) in La Plata who handled the investigation to include the various stipulated questions detailed below in his inquiry. Much of the following document, then, consists in the list of questions that Oballe had specified the directing magistrate should put to the witnesses to be examined in the case. We might conclude from the extent and tenor of the questions that Vargas and her family had been alarmed by indications in the initial proceedings that Vargas stood a chance of being found guilty of excessively abusing Simona or causing her death. Her *procurador* (legal defender) certainly went to intricate lengths to ensure that the court be made aware of context he considered relevant to Vargas's defense. He framed many of the questions he instructed the *alcalde ordinario* to put to witnesses with a negative construction, as in his sixth proposed question: "If when [Simona, the slave] was brought back to the house of Zerrano for the second time, was she not so furious that she tore apart even the animals that went into her room." He framed his queries in this way either because evidence given in the original denunciation revealed this information, which he wished to substantiate, or because he was aware of it from private conversations with *doña* Vargas, the party he represented.

Doña Vargas was married to Pedro Zerrano, identified as the owner of Simona, a slave. Vargas, Zerrano, and their daughters lived on a *hacienda* (estate), in the town of Timaná, located the southern tip the *cordillera central* (central mountain range) in current-day Huila department, which was called the province of Neiva in the colonial period. The case was tried in the nearby larger municipal center of San Sebastián de la Plata. The Zerrano–Vargas family's ownership of an African slave in this location would have been somewhat unusual at this time and in this part of Colombia. Representing just under 8 percent of the total population, the enslaved population amounted to sixty-five thousand people according to Nueva Granada's 1778–1780 census.[3] While this represented one of the largest slave populations in mainland Spanish America by the late colonial period, the concentration of slaves differed markedly within regions in the kingdom with the slave population concentrated much more heavily in the provinces of Popayán, Cartagena, Choco, and Antioquía, working particularly in the mining and sugar sectors. By the early nineteenth century, the African slave population in Neiva, where Simona worked and died, was just over 2 percent of the province's total. The 1825 census listed 1,237 slaves among Neiva's total population of 47,157.[4]

---

3. Anthony McFarlane, *Colombia Before Independence: Economy, Society, and Politics Under Bourbon Rule* (Cambridge: Cambridge University Press, 1993), Table 1, 353.
4. Russell Lohse, "Reconciling Freedom with the Rights of Property: Slave Emancipation in Colombia, 1821–1852, with Special Reference to La Plata," *The Journal of Negro History* 86:3 (Summer 2001), 204.

Most of this population would likely have worked in the dominant economic ventures of the region: cattle raising, cacao cultivation, and gold and salt mining. The Zerrano–Vargas household, however, apparently employed Simona more often as a domestic laborer.

The circumstances of this case are also unusual in that they describe a female member of a slave-owning family engaging in the physical punishment of an enslaved person. New research has begun to examine women's roles as slave owners in Spanish American society, but most work has focused on women's participation in the emancipation of slaves rather than on the ways they participated in the institution of slavery even to the point of inflicting physical discipline on slaves, as discussed in this text.[5] Spanish law permitted owners to physically discipline their slaves, but prohibited owners from killing them. The *Siete Partidas,* the thirteenth-century legal code that served as the most important foundation of the law in Spanish America, specified that while owners could punish slaves, owners who unintentionally caused their deaths could be sentenced with five years' banishment, and those who had actually intended to kill their slaves were subject to capital punishment, the same penalty for parents who murdered their children.[6] It is unlikely that Vargas would have been sentenced in such terns. Spanish American magistrates tended to sentence more lightly than prescribed by the *Siete Partidas.* Nevertheless, the extensive intervention of the Audiencia in shaping the investigative magistrate's interview questions suggests that both her defender and the *Audiencia* itself took seriously the implications of Vargas's actions and their possible ramifications and went to extensive lengths here to pre-empt a guilty sentence.

Other elements of the case may be more representative of the history of African slavery in Colombia, including Simona's evident repeated resistance to her condition. The evidence of the sole witness, Toribio Clavijo, whose testimony is reproduced in the excerpt of the *sumaria* below, confirms that Simona had repeatedly tried to flee from servitude. Other material alludes to the violence with which she resisted capture and pacification as well as her husband's reputation as a *cimarron,* or renegade slave. Simona and her husband, like many of those enslaved in Nueva Granada, chose revolt and resistance, while others, like Isabel Victoria García (see Chapter 15) opted for adaptation to the slave regime. Although recent researchers are hesitant to characterize late colonial Colombia as definitively experiencing a dramatic rise in slave rebellion, an older historiography contends that slave resistance

---

5. Susan Migden Socolow, *The Women of Colonial Latin America* (Cambridge: Cambridge University Press, 2000), 139.

6. Alan Watson, *Slave Law in the Americas* (Athens: University of Georgia Press, 1989), 45.

and escape had become so frequent in this period that it had acquired the characteristics of a colonial civil war between slaves and slave owners.[7]

This document, because of its fragmentary nature, poses particular challenges for those seeking to reconstruct the history of enslaved women and female slave owners. We do not hear in it from either Simona or from *doña* Ana María Vargas themselves, nor do we possess the case in its entirety, so we do not know what kind of evidence different witnesses presented against Vargas, nor if the efforts of her *procurador* succeeded in securing her absolution. Nevertheless, the *sumaria* can still be analyzed for several purposes. What do we learn from it about late colonial conceptions of normative femininity, both for African slave women and Spanish women of the upper class? Which aspects of behavior deemed unfeminine did various parties described here seek to curtail or reframe? What specific evidence had earlier witnesses apparently provided to the court about the details of the case that *doña* Vargas's *procurador* sought to challenge and why? Aside from the legal issues presented in this case, its details allow for the reconstruction of some aspects of the lived experience of slavery in the context of this *hacienda*. What details can you extract from it that help you reconstruct the living and working conditions?

20.1 *Alcalde don* Josef Silvestre Rodríguez Durán Informs la Plata's Magistrates about How to Investigate Simona's Case[8]

[*Sealed paper:* 1804 and 1805]

Don Josef Silvestre Rodríguez Durán, *alcalde ordinario de primer nominación* (of first nomination) in this city of San Sebastián de la Plata and its jurisdiction, for His Majesty, may God preserve His Highness.

To the *Señores* (sirs) *Alcaldes Ordinarios* of the city of Buga,[9] and to any other ministers which may be presented with this suit, I make known that the honest servants[10] of the Audiencia (Court) and Royal Chancellery of the Kingdom of New Granada, have issued a royal provision whose content literally states the following: *Don* Carlos, by the grace of God, . . . [*this is followed by the long list of the titles of the Spanish king and all the places over which*

---

7. Jaime Jaramillo Uribe, "Esclavos y señores en la Sociedad Colombiana del siglo XVIII," Anuario Colombiano de Historia Social y de la Cultura, 1:1 (January 1963), 42. Available at http://revistas.unal.edu.co/index.php/achsc/article/view/29620/29858. Accessed May 16, 2017.

8. Archivo General de la Nación de Colombia, Colonia, Miscelánea: SC.39, 65, D. 57 "Sumaria criminal por maltratos a esclava y causar su muerte."

9. A city in western Colombia's current Valle del Cauca department.

10. *SS* in the original, which might represent, as translated here, "*Seguros Servidores.*"

he held royal authority]. Insofar as the indicated criminal case was received and put to judgement before my viceroy, president, regent and the *oidores* (judges) of my Audiencia and Royal Chancellery in this Kingdom of New Granada, and was represented in the following way:

Most powerful *Señor*: Luis de Oballe, *procurador del numero*[11] and legal representative for *doña* María Vargas y Flores, *vecina* (citizen) of Timaná, in a case about the ill-treatment attributed to her of a slave named Simona, from which the slave's death is said to have followed appears before Your Highness to declare: that as part of the evidence that forms this legal process, I beg that Your Highness will be well served, prior to the *fiscal* (prosecuting attorney)'s *citación* (subpoena), to issue a Royal Provision instructing the *alcalde ordinario de primer voto* of the city of La Plata to proceed with the following inquiries: First, to confirm whether *don* Diego Antonio Gutiérrez recognizes as his own and by his hand the letter written in la Plata, dated the 15th of April, 1803 and addressed to *don* Felix Zerrano certifying a copy of the baptismal certificate of *doña* Antonia and *doña* Margarita Zerrano, daughters of the party I represent. Further,[12] that the judge and a scribe interview witnesses from the *hacienda* of San Miguel which belongs to *don* Pedro Zerrano, and also examine the place where the body of Simona, slave of Zerrano, was buried according to the information that could be obtained, to study the gorge located eight blocks from the house, next to the ravine called Las Museñas, and provide a detailed account of the location or place where Simona's bones were found and their distance from the aforementioned house. Further, to receive information from the witnesses that will be presented to him about the following questions:

First if they have news about the lawsuit. 2nd: Their age and identifying information.[13] 3rd: Their knowledge of Simona, who was *don* Pedro Zerrano's slave, and of her temperament, nature, and habits and if she had a wild and depraved nature and was inclined principally to run away such that her owners could not put up with her and if she was always escaping from their house. 4th: If as a result of this, he discovered that *don* Pedro Zerrano tried to send her back, together with her husband, to her previous owner, *don* Nicolas de Cabrera, who, instead of agreeing to this, lowered the price another one hundred pesos from his original price so that the two pieces were sold for their most negligible value.[14] 5th: If the *negra* (black woman), because of her

---

11. *Procuradores de número* were professionals licensed to practice law who were less fully educated than the lawyers and who often handled the initial submission of legal cases.
12. "*Pared*" in the original, which in this context, I have translated as "further" throughout.
13. The original says that witnesses should provide their "*generales de la ley,*" their identifying information (name, home address, occupation, and marital status).
14. A *pieza*, or piece referred to an able-bodied slave.

numerous childbirths and her escapes was not destroyed and emaciated to such an extent that she appeared to be a skeleton and if her womb was on the outside of her body (*tenia su matriz fuera*).[15] 6th: If when she was brought back to the house of Zerrano for the second time, was she not so furious that she tore apart even the animals that went into her room. 7th: How many times was she punished for the two escapes, how many lashes she received, with what instruments, by whose hand, and in what position; and whether she was hanging, stretched out, tied up, etc. 8th: If, even after receiving only one moderate punishment which *doña* Ana María de Vargas herself administered after they brought her the second time, [Simona] was not fulfilling her womanly duties in the house, such as grinding corn and cooking it and putting the copper pot on the fire. 9th: If she did not go down to fetch water in the drinking jug and was accompanied only by a daughter of *doña* Ana María or someone else from the house to prevent her from running away, until one day, when she resisted when she was at the spring accompanied by *doña* Rosa and María Muñoz, so that they had to bring her by force because she said that not even all the devils in the world could make her return to this house. If this occurred when *doña* Ana María Flores[16] was already very ill, with fever and swollen feet, and just about to give birth; if she gave birth the next day and if two days later she felt a terrible pain in her side to the point where she lost consciousness, and if she was brought on the third day to la Plata and did not know anything about the slave for a long time, nor had any contact with her because she did not convalesce from her unhealthy condition nor return to the *hacienda* for two months. 10th: That Rosalía Liscano should say whether, when *doña* María de Vargas was just recovering from her illness and was speaking one day about the *negra,* she [Rosalía] told her that the *negra* had already died and if this was the first news she had had about it. And if she did not ask her then what she had died from and if she said that she did not know. And if she did not reply that that was how it was that she had been advised, and if she had answered that it was because they had not left her. 11th: They should say if Vargas had not always been a sick woman and weak and incapable of giving harsh punishment. If, in her house, her slaves had been given bad treatment with respect to food and clothing. If her daughter, *doña* Rosa, is not of a docile and mild-mannered temperament. 12th: They should say if the aforementioned *don* Diego Antonio Gutiérrez is not an avowed enemy of the house because of an altercation he had with *don* Toribio Zerrano concerning his father's will. 13th: If the aforementioned Gutiérrez has not been the scribe of La Plata and since when, and if he has not for this reason addressed documents to all the *alcaldes ordinaries* including *don* Miguel Mariano González who was a scribe as well in the

---

15. Presumably, the judge is to ask if Simona had a prolapsed uterus.
16. I.e., Vargas, whose full name was *doña* María Vargas y Flores.

preceding year, and if he received detailed information regarding this case that the *señores* of the court of the Real Audiencia sent him. 14th: If they know how this information was obtained and if the witnesses were left in liberty or if they were intimidated or threatened, and by whom; and if they swore a legal oath; and who examined them, and who issued and wrote out their statements; and if these were read to them after being written in order that they could see what they had declared; and if before this they had been able to see the statements of some other witnesses so as to not make variations in their statements. 15th: That they should say if *don* Joaquin Benites is not also an avowed enemy of Toribio Zerrano because of opposing interests and if la Muñoz is not a beggar and drunk during the day. And if Juan Romualdo Villarroel is known in Zerrano's house or has been seen entering it before or after the events of this case with some frequency. 16th: That *don* Gerónimo Gonzáles should say if it was not he who brought back the slave Simona to the house of *doña* Ana María de Vargas the second time that she ran away, having caught her as *alcalde* then of la Santa Hermandad[17] and if the slave was mistreated or hurt because of the lashes. 17th: They should say whether doctor *don* Fernando de Vargas, priest of La Plata, as uncle of *doña* Ana María, did not visit her house with great frequency to help her with whatever task she needed. 18th: They should say if the reason for having sent the slave who was the husband of Simona to be sold at the gateway to the Chocó[18] was because he was a *cimarrón*. 19th: That *don* Toribio Clavijo should testify about the events in this case of which he is well aware, and especially to ask him if, after many days after having been informed by the news from Liscano, whether (*doña*) Vargas asked him (Clavijo) what had happened, and if he, no doubt, out of fear for the delicate condition in which he saw her, answered that nothing had happened. And if this important witness is not in that jurisdiction, the respective judge should be urged to request statements about all the pertinent questions, and that once the investigation is done, to send his report to this High Court and that it is kept for an appropriate time in the interest of justice through which I beg Your Highness to decree as I ask I swear in what is required etc. I also ask that the certification by the city council of La Plata be kept for a time. I swear as above.[19]

Doctor Camilo Torres, Luis de Ovalle.

---

17. John Leddy Phelan, *The People and the King: The Comunero Revolution in Colombia, 1781* (Madison: University of Wisconsin Press, 1978), 177, describes Nuevo Granada's *Santa Hermandad* as "both a rural police force" and "a court of first instance exercising original jurisdiction in the rural hinterland of an urban or village nucleus."

18. The Chocó, now a Pacific coastal department in northwest Colombia, was a historic center of Nuevo Granada's African slave population.

19. *Juro ut supra* in the original.

[The court's fiscal and the alcalde ordinario de primer voto of la Plata, Josef Silvestre de Rodríguez y Durán, agreed to implement the Audiencia's decree. Rodríguez y Durán also obtained the testimony of the key witness, don Torivio Clavijo. His deposition constitutes the remainder of the sumaria:*]*

On the same day, month, and year, [March 22, 1804], in accordance with what was ordered, I *don* Josef María Cárdenas, called Toribio Clavijo, *vecino,* to testify in the presence of witnesses and in the absence of a scribe. He took an oath in due form required by law for Our *Señor* God and he made the sign of the cross by whose power he swore to tell the truth about that which and would be questioned, in accordance with the *ynterragatorio yncerto* (unresolved interrogation) within his knowledge touching the written commission.[20] He declares that he has heard about the lawsuit and is not in a position of personal conflict of interest with respect to it.[21] He is forty-four years old. And in response to the second question he says that he personally knew the *negra* (black woman) Simona, who was *don* Pedro Josef Zerrano's slave, and who had an arrogant temperament and therefore a bad nature. She did not treat her *señora* (mistress) with the respect due to her despite the latter's forgiveness of her many faults. He declares that Simona's customary practice was to go about absconding for no known reason. In response to the third question, he states that everything is true in this question and he refers to what he has already expressed. To the fourth question, he says it is true that because *don* Pedro José Zerrano found out about Simona's bad attributes, he tried to return her along with her husband to her previous owner, *don* Nicolás de Cabrera; but the latter, in order to avoid again owning such slaves in his house, preferred to reduce by one hundred pesos the price he had originally charged for them. To the fifth question, he answers that it is true and he attests that he has seen the slave Simona *aniquilada* (destroyed) when *don* Pedro Zerrano brought her under his control and that she suffered the illness of having her womb outside her body. She did not recover from this, and he is persuaded that this was because of her continual flights. In response to question six: that he was aware of the facts because he heard them said to the servants of the house. To the seventh: that in the case of the two principal escapes that are dealt with here, he did not see the punishment of the *negra,* Simona, but that he did know that the first time some fellow called Coellar punished her by order of the *señora doña* Ana María de Vargas, and according to what she told the declarant, that she, by her own hand disciplined [Simona] the second time with some short lashings which he takes to

---

20. The text literally refers here to a "*deprecatorio,*" a commission of specific functions that the judge in a suit makes to another judge of equal seniority to fulfill a prescribed legal step.
21. The text reads: "*los generales de la ley no le tocan.*" See Chapter 8, footnote 9.

be how it happened considering that he perceives the said *señora* to be sick and delicate and incapable of excessive punishment. In response to the ninth, he says that in equal terms it is true that after her escape, Simona the *negra* was punished so that she would not run away and that she was controlled to prevent her from escaping again. That concerning the resistance of the *negra* and its consequences, he did not see this but he did hear it said from those of the house that all the rest that is asked about in this question is true and he states that it is true for having seen it. To the eleventh question, he responds, because he did not speak about the tenth question, and refers to what he declared in response to the seventh question, that he knows this from having seen that in the house of *doña* Ana María Vargas the slaves were not mistreated with excessive punishments; that food was regular and the same with clothing. The declarant knows that the temperament of *doña* María Rosa Zerrano, daughter of *doña* Ana María, is docile and mild-mannered as he was asked. And in response to question twelve: that he can not give any other reason than that provided for *don* Diego Antonio Gutiérrez's bad faith against *don* Pedro Zerrano and his family. And in response to question thirteen: that *don* Diego Antonio Gutiérrez, first was a scribe, and then wrote to the judges of la Plata, as documents certify. In response to question fourteen: that he does not know about it. To the fifteenth question: that he does not know and only knows that María Muños is a poor woman who was subjected to serve *señora doña* Ana María Vargas for her maintenance and that it is true that she has the vice of drinking. To the seventeenth question for not having spoken about the preceding one, he said that it is true that doctor *don* Fernando de Vargas, as he was her uncle, frequently visited the house of *doña* Ana María, his niece, and he believed that everyone in her house would have helped her with any work that needed doing. And in response to the eighteenth question: he confirms the content of the question. And in response to the nineteenth question, he refers to the declaration he made on the 15th of January of this year concerning this same case and he says that this is the truth as he declared in under oath, which he affirms and ratifies. And once his statement was read to him, he signed it with me the judge and the witnesses as I certify. [signature] Cárdenas [signature] José Toribio Clavijo; witnesses: guard Cazerez, [signature] Miguel Bermeo

---

Suggested Reading

Helg, Aline. *Liberty and Equality in Caribbean Colombia, 1770–1835.* Chapel Hill: University of North Carolina Press, 2004.

McFarlane, Anthony. *Colombia Before Independence: Economy, Society, and Politics Under Bourbon Rule.* Cambridge: Cambridge University Press, 1993.
Uribe-Uran, Victor M. *Fatal Love: Spousal Killers, Law, and Punishment in the Late Colonial Spanish Atlantic.* Stanford, CA: Stanford University Press, 2015.

Document Themes

- Family
- Labor
- Law
- Sex and gender
- Slavery

21

María del Carmen Ventura's Criminal Trial for Infanticide (Zacualtipan, Mexico, 1806)

The criminal trial for the crime of infanticide María del Carmen Ventura underwent at the close of the colonial era in a small Mexican community reveals much about contemporary notions of maternity and femininity, the localized operation of criminal justice in the era of the Enlightenment, and the social experiences of non-elite women in this setting. Ventura was a poor woman of Spanish descent who lived in the small community of Zacualtipan, in the current state of Hidalgo, Mexico, at the turn of the nineteenth century. Although legally married, Ventura had lived apart from her husband for twelve years at the time that a *encargado de justicia* (judicial official) in her community opened a criminal investigation against her because he suspected her of having committed infanticide.

Both legal theory and statute regulating criminal practice in the colonial period handled with considerable severity both the crimes of infanticide and the closely related charge of intentional abortion. Medieval and Early Modern Castilian legal texts, including the foundational Castilian legal code, King Alfonso X's *Siete Partidas*, decreed that those found guilty of committing infanticide should receive the death penalty. One eighteenth-century Spanish medico–juridical tract that took its inspiration from the *Partidas* asserted that those convicted of infanticide should be "sewn into a hide with a rooster, a dog, a snake and a monkey and tossed in the sea or a river."[1]

Although the crime was theoretically treated harshly, in the setting of colonial Mexico, as María del Carmen Ventura's trial illustrates, community members and judicial officials adopted a more equivocal view of the act. Ventura's was one of the only twelve cases of infanticide historians have uncovered in the setting of New Spain. Unlike other violent crimes—homicide, assault, or rape—infanticide was not a crime that community members felt compelled to bring to the attention of judicial authorities in the colonial era, perhaps because they did not often perceive its occurrence. As in Ventura's case, very few women in colonial Latin America, even at the close of the colonial period,

---

1. Cristóbal Nieto de Piña, *Instruccion medica para discerner, se el feto muerto, lo ha sido dentro, o fuera del utero* (Madrid: *don* Manuel Nicolas Vazques, n.d.), quoted in Nora E. Jaffary, *Reproduction and Its Discontents in Mexico: Childbirth and Contraception from 1750 to 1905* (Chapel Hill: University of North Carolina Press, 2016), 109.

gave birth assisted by medical doctors. Most commonly, however, women were attended at childbirth by a midwife, like Isabel Hernández (see Chapter 11). But many also gave birth either alone or assisted by female acquaintances and for these reasons, details about unexpected births or misbirths, when they occurred, would easily escape legal or medical monitoring by agents of the colonial state. We cannot know from the evidence presented in this case whether Ventura's child died of natural causes immediately after birth, or whether she had facilitated this act by ingesting an efficacious abortifacient such as *cihuapatli* (the aster flower) or *altamisa* (altamisia), that would induce early labor. This was a practice to which women frequently resorted in colonial Mexico, although its history has only been recently brought to light.[2]

The attitude many of the court officials involved in Ventura del Carmen's case is also typical of those judges adopted toward those accused of both abortion and infanticide. Conviction for either crime was the exception rather than the rule in the colonial period.[3] We may be observing the beginnings of a late colonial change in attitude about such matters in Ventura's case, however. In this instance, a local judicial officer, *don* José López de Anaya, initiated the case against her because of his indignant suspicion that she had killed her newborn child. His supposition was based on the grounds that he had noticed that her publicly known pregnancy had ended both abruptly and secretly. Notice, however, that coincident with the heightened suspicion about Ventura that Anaya voices here, we also see evidence in the defense presented by both her *curador* (legal defender) and Real Audiencia (Royal Court) lawyer Victoriano Umaran y Arenzaza of Enlightenment-influenced rhetoric in defense of her rights.[4]

Ventura's case is also illustrative of some aspects of non-elite women's lives in late colonial Mexico. We learn from these records that while it may have been possible for women to apply for church-sanctioned marital separation from unsatisfactory husbands (see Chapter 11), the voluntary and unofficial dissolution of marriage that Ventura and her spouse had enacted was subject to societal censure, and, according to her *curador*, to a position of economic precariousness as well.[5] Although she normally lived in a small community

---

2. See Jaffary, *Reproduction and Its Discontents*, 33–34, 79–85.
3. See Jaffary, *Reproduction and Its Discontents*, 104–37.
4. For further discussion of such ideas and their mobilization in the late colonial era, see Bianca Premo, *The Enlightenment on Trial: Ordinary Litigants and Colonialism in the Spanish Empire* (New York: Oxford University Press, 2017).
5. Silvia M. Arrom, "Desintegración familiar y pauperización: Los indigentes del Hospicio de Pobres de la ciudad de México, 1795," in *Familia y vida privada en la historia de iberoamérica*, ed. Pilar Gonzalbo Aizpuru and Cecilia Rabell Romero (Mexico: UNAM-Colegio de México, 1996), 119–31, has documented that women who remained single in late colonial Mexico suffered from economic disadvantages when compared to their married peers.

outside of the urban capital, Ventura's economic prospects would not have differed greatly from those of the better documented urban population of late eighteenth-century Mexico City. By the late eighteenth century, poor people constituted approximately 85 percent of Mexico City's population. They worked as its manual laborers, domestic servants, seamstresses, cooks, healers, paupers, and prostitutes, workers whose labor was morally condemned although not prohibited by law in the colonial world.[6] Despite María del Carmen Ventura's limited financial means, readers might be surprised to learn of the degree of geographic mobility she experienced. At the beginning of her trial, she was living in Zacualtipan, Hidalgo, a community roughly two hundred kilometers northeast of Mexico City. But at some point in the month between early November and early December 1806, Ventura had escaped from a private house where she was being held to join her former lover in Mexico City. None of the administrators handling her case found it remarkable that a plebeian woman of limited financial means (and apparently failing health), managed to make this rather substantial journey, with her son. The reverse journey (visualized in Map 4), which she likely did on foot, took her two weeks to complete. We might conclude that although we often assume that the rural poor of generations past would have normally lived immobile lives, Ventura's example challenges that assumption.

María del Carmen Ventura's trial allows readers to perceive the everyday functioning of justice on the local level in New Spain. Her case opens in her own small community where it is first appraised by the *encargado de justicia,* Josef López de Anaya. López de Anaya then submitted his findings to his district supervisor, *don* Ignacio Muñoz, the senior magistrate of the larger neighboring community of Mextitlan (referred to in the text as a *cabecera,* a "head town"), a predominantly indigenous community that by 1797 was populated by 7,313 indigenous tributaries, and a small number of non-indigenous families, as well just over 600 *mulato* (person of African and European parentage) tributaries.[7]

Midway through Ventura's case, another official, *don* Francisco Lezama, charged with the administration of justice in Mextitlan, took over Muñoz's duties due to the latter's "illness and absence." Lezama communicated regularly with officials in the Mexico City's primary criminal court, the Sala de Crimen of the Real Audiencia, where numerous officials also weighed in on

---

6. This was in contradistinction from bawds—those who procured prostitutes for others—whose work was prohibited. Nicole von Germeten, "Mexican Bawds: Women and Commercial Sex in the Viceroyalty of New Spain," *Latin American History: Oxford Research Encyclopedia, Latin American History* (latinamericanhistory.oxfordre.com).

7. Peter Gerhard, *A Guide to the Historical Geography of New Spain* (Norman: University of Oklahoma Press, 1993), 186. Because only adult men paid tribute, we can assume the indigenous population was, in fact, much larger.

both the gravity of the crime with which Ventura was charged and the likelihood that she had committed it.

Readers might consider what the correspondence of these judicial officials reveals about the extent to which the state was able to scrutinize the behavior of regular inhabitants of colonial Latin American society. How much privacy or anonymity does it seem regular inhabitants of Mexico's rural communities experienced?

María del Carmen Ventura's case is also interesting because of the information it conveys about contemporary expectations of gendered behavior. What does her trial reveal about which of her actions and attributed attitudes most disturbed her peers and her judges? What elements of her activities or traits do not seem to have elicited the condemnation of her judges? What attitude does the case reveal about contemporary attitudes toward prostitution, motherhood, and women's financial independence?

21.1 Writ of the Opening of the Hearing[8]

In the town of Encarnación Zacualtipan de la Sierra 28 July, 1806. I, *don* (sir) José López de Anaya, *teniente* (deputy) charged with the administration of justice here by *señor* (sir) *don* Ignacio Muñoz, the *Justicia Mayor Subdelegado* (senior judge and administrator) of this district and commander of its militias, and acting, as prescribed by law, as the receiver of witnesses in the absence in this place of a royal and public notary, certify the following.

That in the royal court under my charge, Mariana del Carmen Ventura, a member of this community and legitimate wife of José Hernández (alias *el Güero*) from whom she has been separated for some time, appeared for verbal judgment. The present judge, observing that she is not now pregnant as he had seen her to be just a few days earlier, and forming a poor judgment of her depraved conduct because she is held in public opinion to be of bad reputation, orders the opening of this hearing. In virtue of this, María del Carmen Ventura is brought before me by the *ministro de vara* (a municipal officer) of this jurisdiction, and is compelled to account for the pregnancy that she experienced since being separated from her husband and she must declare under the oath of the sacred religion by whom she was impregnated, where the baby can now be found, if she has given birth to others during this matrimonial separation, from whom she was impregnated in these cases, and where [these babies] may be found. In light of this, so that the swift administration

---

8. Archivo General de la Nación, Criminal, vol. 251 exp. 10, fols. 274–308.

of justice will demonstrate the truth, it is ordered that [Ventura] be apprehended in the usual way and be made to account for these charges to the *Señor Justicia Mayor Subdelegado* of the district without delay. I order and sign the opening of this hearing with the others and give faith.

[signature] Josef López de Anaya.

21.2 María del Carmen Ventura's First Appearance

[María Ventura del Carmen is brought before teniente López de Anaya, admonished to tell the truth, and asked to provide the court with an account of the babies she has given birth to since her separation from her husband.]

She said she is called María del Carmen Ventura, she is of the Spanish *calidad*[9] and is married to José Hernández alias el Güero, of the same *calidad*, from whom she has been voluntarily separated because there was disagreement between them about the dissolute behavior of the declarant. And it is true that during the time of her separation from her marriage up until now, she has given birth to three babies. The first, four years ago when she was imprisoned in the royal jail of Mextitlan for a wound that she gave to her lover, Venancio Ruíz. She miscarried there, without having had time to put the water of baptism on the baby,[10] and this creature was the child of her lover, Venancio. The second, she had two years ago, more or less, when she was exiled from this town by the previous *Señor de Justicia Mayor Subdelegado*, and living in one of the outlying communities of the town of Mextitlan, she had an illicit friendship with a young soldier from there called José Larios, alias Pozos (who has since died), from which resulted a baby boy that her compatriot Petra Espindola baptized in her own house because she [Ventura] was sick. And that they then went to bury him in the cemetery of the church but, in truth, she does not know where he was buried. The third child she gave birth to two months ago, more or less, in her own home in this town, and she had him with Manuel Hernández, an unmarried militiaman. The baby was a boy and she gave

---

9. The term *calidad*, or quality, denoted a person's overall social status with respect to racial, economic, social, and reputational attributes.

10. To avoid sending to hell the souls of unbaptized infants who died shortly after childbirth, birthing mothers or the midwives who assisted them were obliged to baptize babies immediately after childbirth if it appeared they might die before priests could arrive to provide a proper burial.

birth to him alone in the middle of the night, without a midwife nor any other person except her legitimate son, Pedro. The baby was born alive, and having shown signs that he was going to die, she took a mouth full of water and sprayed it in his mouth saying "in the name of the Father and the Son and the Holy Spirit" and then he died. Only her son Pedro saw this, he, who the next morning at about midday made a hole at the foot of her bed where he buried the baby by her order and where the cadaver must be still. For now, this is all that she can declare about that which she has been asked. This hearing remains open in case further investigation is necessary. She says she is thirty years old and does not sign the transcript herself because she does not know how to read.

[María del Carmen Ventura remained imprisoned while several court officials went to her home to excavate the corpse of the baby which she then identified as the one to which she had recently given birth. Teniente López de Anaya ordered Ventura's son, Pedro Hernández, brought before him and consulted with the local priest about reburying the corpse. The latter advised that since the baby had not been formally baptized, he could not be given a Christian burial, and must be buried outside of the church cemetery, without cross or any ceremony.

On 30 July, 1806, López de Anaya sent a summary of the case along with Ventura herself to the regional judicial administrator, don Ignacio Muñoz, Justicia Mayor Subdelegado of the district of Mextitlan. Muñoz decreed that Ventura should remain in the royal jail of Mextitlan under the custody of its alcalde, that she ratify her initial declaration, and that a curador be assigned to represent her. Finally, Muñoz declared that he would send her dossier on to the Viceroyalty's central court, the Sala del Crimen in the Real Audiencia in Mexico City for assessment. On August 4, Ventura, as typically occurred, was given the opportunity to name a curador herself and she named one don Anselmo Ferreira, a Spanish resident of Zacualtipan. Ferreira declined the position because of his "notorious illnesses." Ventura affirmed she had no other suggestions and on August 8 Muñoz assigned Antonio Morales, a resident of Zacualtipan to serve as her curador. Morales, too, declined explaining that his work as a muleteer "who traveled ordinarily on the road" prevented him from taking the position. A different judicial administrator in Mextitlan, don Francisco Lezama, who replaced Muñoz, eventually assigned don Manuel de los Reyes Mateos, administrator of mail tax, to act as Ventura's curador. Reyes Mateos requested that copies of all materials relating to her case be sent to him so he could prepare her defense.]

21.3 *Don* Manuel de los Reyes Mateos's Defense of María del Carmen Ventura

In the town of Zacualtipan on 12 of January, 1807 before the official charged with justice in this jurisdiction of Mextitlan [Francisco de Lezama] is presented the following document:

[left margin:] document

Don Manuel de los Reyes Mateos, administrator of the royal tax on mail in the *cabecera* of Mextitlan, acting as *curador ad litem*[11] for María del Carmen Ventura, imprisoned in the Royal Jail for the unfounded, capricious suspicion of infanticide. In compliance with the law, I declare that you must order a reversal of the so-called preparatory proceedings of the *encargado de justicia* in this case. I declare [Ventura] to be innocent of those things which he [the *encargado*] has wished to invent about her for the following reasons.

The *encargado* opened the proceedings without being directed to do so by a sentence or by a request from a third party and only on the basis of his own suspicions, and these are far removed from all rational (I speak with all due respect) and Christian and humane sentiment. A woman who is pregnant and then ceases to be so, can be, and indeed must be in this state either because she has reached the end of her normal term of pregnancy or because by some accident before the end of it she miscarries prematurely. What other party than his own malicious perversity suggested to the *encargado* that this could only happen when the babies were murdered? Merely by reading the cited proceedings it becomes apparent that he followed no procedure but rather acted with malice contrary to the divine precepts that command us to judge those around us charitably and not to suspect them without foundation and not to be suspicious of the actions of others without sufficient proof.

It is a more than obvious principle that to bring a person to judgment, a case should be opened because someone is caught in the act of committing the crime, or the case has been requested by a *pedimento de parte* (accusation) or by a denunciation. In these cases, the accused party must justify themselves. But if a person is investigated only because of the suspicion of a judge or arbitrarily (or by another impulse), the case will always end with the defendant being found guilty.[12] And I may presume to ask what connection [the

---

11. *Ad litem* is Latin for "for the suit" and indicates a party appointed to act on behalf of a minor.

12. Reyes Mateos' objections here are perplexing, because Spanish law recognized the right of a magistrate to initiate legal investigations. Such cases were classified as those that opened "*de oficio*." Charles R. Cutter, *The Legal Culture of Northern New Spain, 1700–1810* (Albuquerque: University of New Mexico Press, 1985), 114. Indeed, judges were obliged to prosecute crimes against the public order, including all forms of homicide, to satisfy the need for "public

encargado] might have in this matter, because while prostitution has created a bad reputation for the party I am defending, is this alone sufficient reason to charge her with infanticide? Why were no witnesses called to be examined? I well know that there are many ways to create criminal cases, but we must always arrive at a result that illuminates the truth and the crime imputed to my party should not derive merely from the rash suspicions of a judge.

He could, as already indicated, begin with the defendant's declaration, but not even this demonstrates that infanticide occurred on the three occasions of her pregnancies; on the first occasion, she gave birth in health and the baby was baptized; the second two were misbirths, a common occurrence, so how can he name the prisoner guilty of repeated infanticides? Who instructed this man to investigate how many times a married woman had given birth and who had fathered the children? Is it not likely that his practice results in grave injuries to peoples' lives and the dissolution of their marriages? I know that not even in the *Tribunal Sagrado de la Penitencia* are the names of accomplices requested, but this official, to better demonstrate his talent, discovered a new method of proceeding in his investigation.[13]

Regarding the procedures for exhumation, what proof was revealed demonstrating infanticide? He wished to show, perhaps that the body had been thrown to the dogs? Could it not be that the body was not buried outside because as a mother she wished to save it from this unhappy end? If one wishes to conclude that she buried the body in order to hide her moral weakness, why would she have shown herself in the streets pregnant? With what proof will the rash, unfounded, and malicious charges of the *encargado de justicia* demonstrate that she is an imposter?

The only thing to which the party I represent has confessed in good faith in her declaration is prostitution, but although it is very certain that she cannot be excused in moral terms, in legal ones, does not her situation of financial need mitigate judgment against a woman abandoned by her husband and who has no recourse to provide for her sustenance, especially in these lands where it is almost impossible to survive on the miserable salary that domestic labor produces?

For this reason, you must see fit to command that which I have requested: judge that the party that I represent has already served a sentence of six months' imprisonment in a place unknown to her, one in which nothing exists from which prisoners can support themselves, for a charge that, by her declaration, should result in her being placed in liberty. This is even more

---

vengeance." Victor M. Uribe-Uran, *Fatal Love: Spousal Killers, Law, and Punishment in the Late Colonial Spanish Atlantic* (Stanford, CA: Stanford University Press, 2016), 45.

13. By *Tribunal Sagrado de la Penitencia*, Reyes Mateos was likely referring to the sacrament of confession, sometimes referred to as occurring within the "tribunal of penance."

urgent given that her husband is also in the royal jail of the royal tribunal of the Acordada at the present, while the couple has two children, one of them a maiden of fifteen years, who, since she does not have shelter nor anyone to care for her at the moment, circulates in the streets in search of help for her mother without any other company than that of her little brother, exposing herself to the circumstances and ends that are to be expected in such unending circumstances.

For these reasons, I beg that your highness decree and order as such.

Manuel de los Reyes Mateos

[Having considered Reyes Mateos' plea, Mextitlan's judicial officer, don Francisco Lezama, deemed that Ventura's dossier should be sent to the assessor of the Real Audiencia in Mexico City, licenciado (licentiate) *and lawyer* don Victoriano Umaran y Arenzaza.]

21.4 Assessor Victoriano Umaran's Opinion

To the *Señor* charged with the administration of justice in the district of Mextitlan, *don* Francisco Paredes de Lezama:

Even a fleeting examination of the legal trial of the prisoner María del Carmen Ventura reveals that her case was opened without precedent either by an accusation or a denunciation but only because of the passing suspicion held by the *encargado* of Zacualtipan that she had twice executed infanticide during her twelve-year separation from her husband. This, only because on two occasions she seemed different to him. He noted that she had been pregnant, and then a few days later was no longer pregnant without any sign whatsoever that she had been.

This act, that the prisoner presented as that of repeated adultery, cannot and must not be elevated to the status of infanticide. Her presumption of having presented herself in this town in a way that publicly registered her moral weakness as well as what was enclosed in her womb inclines judgment to believe her. We must conclude that she did not perpetuate such a crime, since only two motives could have pushed her to do what she is charged with after giving birth to the infant: the shame that is proper to her sex or the fear of punishment.

Both motives are absent in her. The love that nature engenders in parents for the preservation of their children, has in her surpassed its highest grade (according to the views of the authors) in valuing more the lives of the infants than even her own, and even more than her own being, since she sacrificed her own modesty and the loss of her public estimation for them. One must be persuaded that she did not commit the murder of any of the three infants to which she says she has given birth in her two-page declaration.

In her declaration, she asserts that during her marital separation, two of these infants were born alive but perished shortly thereafter and that she miscarried the third when she was imprisoned in the jail of the *cabecera* [Mextitlan]. She does not reveal any reason why she would have intentionally procured their death. . . . [*Assessor Umaran then discussed the importance of judges using only concrete evidence rather than conjecture and inference to judge crimes, particularly hidden private crimes.*]

. . . In the case formed against María del Carmel [sic], the evidence—her confession and the exhumation of the cadaver—is scarce and is contradictory to the judgment formed by the *encargado*. From the first, as has been noted, nothing can be deduced of a criminal nature; rather her declaration merely showed that the deaths of her children occurred through natural causes. Regarding the second, the body revealed no sign of the intentional privation of life either during the act of birth or after it.

Further and even more importantly than all of this, is the fact that when the misbirth occurred inside the jail, no one denounced the defendant for charges of having procured an abortion. It is unreasonable to believe that if [infanticide] had been her depraved intention that nobody upon learning of the act, denounced her for it so that her impunity would not remain habituated to such efforts.

Indeed, since there is no proof of them, María del Carmel [sic] is not the culprit of these infanticides, and if there is evidence of adultery into which she has frequently fallen, as she has openly confessed, she merits the indulgence and generosity of the law in these acts. But the licentious prostitution or libertinage in which she has lived since the abandonment of the obligations of her state [of marriage] opened the doors to her punishment and for the *encargado de justicia,* the opportunity to prosecute her despite her link to the ties of marriage, for the grave scandal that her adultery caused in her neighborhood.

She must be expected to reform her obscene practices, and given that she suffers great pain in prison because she says she is innocent of the infanticides, and given that her extended time in prison has purged her of the practice of prostitution, it would serve you to order her put in liberty, while a person known to be a good Christian watches over her and supervises her activities, conduct, and care of her children, so that when her husband is freed from the jail he is held in by order of the Royal Tribunal of the Holy Brotherhood it will be possible to reunite them in marriage and avoid greater harm or deviation for her smaller children for whom they must set a good example. Mexico, April 20 1807. *Licenciado* Victoriano Umaran.

[in a different hand:] Between the lines (*entre renglones*) = This determination is given to the *Real Sala* for its approval or revocation.

> *[The* justicia mayor *of Zacualtipan, subdelegado Ignacio Muñoz noted on May 11, 1807, that he had received the assessment and requested that the officers of the Real Sala direct him further how to proceed. On October 7, 1807,* licenciado *Manuel de la Bandera, an official of the Sala de Crimen in the Real Audiencia, wrote to* don *Ignacio Muñoz, to say that the justices of the Sala de Crimen advised him to examine Pedro, María del Carmen Ventura's son. Muñoz confirmed receipt and obedience of this directive on November 2, 1807. Two days later,* don *Francisco de Lezama, Muñoz's occasional delegate because of absence or illness, "acting as the receiver of witnesses because of the absence of a notary," notified the Real Audiencia that he had ordered María del Carmen Ventura removed from the municipal jail in which she had been held and installed in a private home because she was ill. Ventura had escaped from this house and had traveled to Mexico City where Lezama learned she was serving her former lover, the soldier Manuel Hernández, a member of the infantry regiment of Zelaya. Lezama sent one José Abrego along with his notification to the Real Sala de Crimen and a request that the central court order Ventura's recapture and return to Mextitlan, upon which journey Abrego would accompany her. The* alcalde ordinario de primero voto *(first instance judge) in the Sala de Crimen received and complied with Lezama's directive. Ventura was re-imprisoned in the public jail in Mexico City on December 3, 1807. Following this are a series of letters sent by the administrators of justice in several small towns located between Mexico City and Mextitlan, reporting on the passage of Ventura and her conductor, José Abrego, through each location.]*

Reports from the Local Alcaldes

Court of Popotla, January 21 1808

The prisoner María del Carmen Ventura, was been sent today by the *alcalde ordinario de primero voto* of the capital of Mexico to this, my court, so that she may be conducted through the mountains to the town of Mextitlan. By virtue of this command, when she passed through, I ordered her processed by the *teniente* of the Villa and Sanctuary of Our Lady of Guadalupe so that he would execute his obligation to receive her. This, I, *don* Ramón de la Rosa y Serrada, *teniente* of the said place execute, and I sign with those of my court and give faith.

Map 4: Itinerary of María del Carmen Ventura

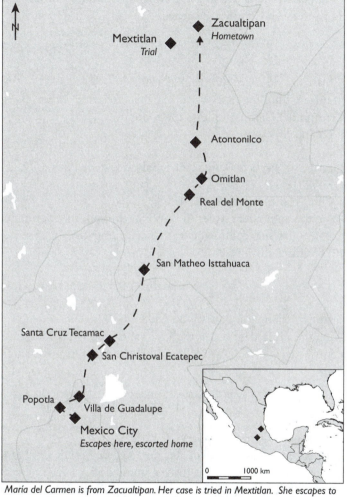

María del Carmen is from Zacualtipan. Her case is tried in Mextitlan. She escapes to Mexico City and is then brought back home by an official escort.

Megan Rohrer | 2017
GADM | Robinson Projection

Ramón de la Rosa y Serrada.
De . . .[14] Toribio Sánchez
With the assistance of Antonio García.

Villa de Guadalupe January 22 1808
The suspect María Venura del Carmen, continues her imprisonment under transit for San Cristoval Ecatepec.

[signature] Anguilo

San Christoval Ecatepec, January 23 1808
Maintaining, fulfilling, and executing the antecedent order, the prisoner María Ventura del Carmen follows the route through the mountains to the town of Tecamac.

[signatures] Francisco Somarriba, Salvador de la Batista, Pedro García

Santa Cruz Tecamac January 23 1808
Fulfilling the antecedent order of traveling through the mountains María Ventura continues her confinement on her journey to the town of Santa Anita and to affirm this I sign.

[signature] Pablo de la Cruz, Governador

San Matheo Isttahuaca, January 24 1808
Fulfilling the antecedent order, with the route through the mountains that María Ventura del Carmen must follow for the town of Asuyatla and to verify this I sign.

[signature] Julian Thomas, Governador

Court of Real del Monte, January 26 1808
This suspect, with her custodian, destined for the Real de Omitlan, passed through here. The *teniente* of this place requested that I receive her. I command this. I, *don* José de la Serna, *teniente* of this Real del Monte. I sign.

[signature] José de la Cerna

---

14. There is an illegible word here; it might be *custodio* (custodian).

Court of Real de Omitlan January 26 1808
This suspect passed with her custodian for the town of Atotonilco el Grande. This I commanded. I, the *teniente* of this Real de Omitlan, and to affirm it I sign.

[Signature] José María Baca

Royal Court of Atontonilco January 27 1808
This suspect and her custodian passed *en route* to the judge of the town of Santa Monica and is ordered to be conducted to the appropriate judge there. I claim and affirm this along with those of my assistance and I certify.

[signatures] Francisco Rubín, of assistance Juan Diego de la Orta, assistant, Juan Agustín Montez

[María del Carmen Ventura returned to the town of Mextitlan on February 3, 1808, and justicia mayor subdelegado *Muñoz ordered her deposited in the house of* don *Manuel Cordova. The court also ordered Ventura's son, Pedro, to return to Mextitlan from Mexico City where she had left him in the care of his older sister. Ventura informed the court on March 2 that she believed Pedro had delayed his return to Mextitlan because of illness. On May 30, 1808,* Pedro appeared before Muñoz and described how one night his mother had awoken him and asked him to light a fire and asked for water. *She* told him that she had given birth to a child who had been born dead and she had requested that he dig a hole in which to bury the body. *Pedro Hernández signed his own testimony.*

A midwife, Josefa Morales, a Spaniard, testified before Muñoz on May 31, 1808. Morales declared that she had arrived to aid Ventura *in her most recent childbirth only after the latter had given birth, but said the baby had been "born dead, or died of natural causes." A second woman,* María Bonifacia Larios, *also appeared on the same day to testify that Ventura had asked her* one month before the birth *to be the* godmother of the baby *when she was pregnant, but had* written her after the birth *to say the child had* been stillborn. *Another witness, Ana Petra Espindola, testified that she had known that Ventura had had an affair with a man, Larios, in Mextitlan that had resulted in the pregnancy of an earlier child. The baby in this case had been born near death and so sick that even though they had* "put powder in its eyes and nostrils," it had died, but they had had permission from the curate to bury it in the cemetery even though the infant had not been properly baptized. *On October 10, 1808,* María Magdalena, a midwife who had attended Ventura at the birth of this child confirmed that it had been born "more dead than alive." *On October 26, Francisco Lezana Mextitlan's* encargado de justicia *remitted all*

263

these testimonies to the Real Sala del Crimen in Mexico City for further judgment.

The file seems to have sat unattended for the next eighteen months. Not until the spring of 1810 did the alcaldes del crimen *of the Real Audiencia take any action on Ventura's case. On May 10, 1810, the* fiscal *(prosecutor) of the Real Audiencia decreed that María del Carmen Ventura was "not found guilty of any of the instances of infanticide for which she had been accused, instead they all seem to be the result of natural deaths." He ordered her freed. Eleven days later, another officer of the court declared that María del Carmen Ventura should be liberated because of Royal Pardon. Fol. 289 of the dossier is inserted out of order amid the pages constituting the assessor's judgment. It is dated June 6, 1810, signed by* licenciado *Ignacio Muñoz, and records that María del Carmen Ventura has been placed in freedom by virtue of the order that the Real Sala communicated to Muñoz, and that the parish curate is charged with overseeing her conduct.]*

Suggested Reading

Jaffary, Nora E. *Reproduction and Its Discontents in Mexico: Childbirth and Contraception from 1750 to 1905.* Chapel Hill: University of North Carolina Press, 2016.

Lavrin, Asunción, ed. *Sexuality and Marriage in Colonial Latin America.* Lincoln: University of Nebraska Press, 1989.

Premo, Bianca, *The Enlightenment on Trial: Ordinary Litigants and Colonialism in the Spanish Empire.* New York: Oxford University Press, 2017.

von Germeten, Nicole, *Violent Delights, Violent Ends: Sex, Race, and Honor in Colonial Cartagena de Indias.* Albuquerque: University of New Mexico Press, 2013.

Document Themes

- Family
- Law
- Migration and mobility
- Sexuality and gender

Glossary

Abbreviations used in the Glossary are as follows:
N = Nahuatl, P = Portuguese, Q = Quechua, S= Spanish

acsu (Q): tunic worn as part of women's dress in the Andes.

adze (S): carpentry tool.

agua de rostro (S): water for washing faces.

alcalde/alcalde ordinario (S): municipal-level first instance judge elected from town council.

alcalde mayor (S): district judge and district governor (synonymous with *corregidor*).

alguacil (S): bailiff.

altamisa (S): artemisia; an herb inducing early labor.

amantecas (S): featherwork pieces.

arroba (S): unit of liquid measure equivalent to 4.26 gallons; and dry measure equivalent to 25 pounds.

atole (S): drink made from rice.

audiencia (S): governmental unit with judicial and administrative power; usually the highest court within a colonial district.

avasca (Q): cloth of coarse alpaca wool.

ayllu (Q): Andean kin unit.

bachiller (S): graduate of a baccalaureate program.

bandeirantes (P): men who explored territory in Brazil; sometimes translated as cowboys.

barbero (S): barber–surgeon.

barraganía (S): semi-permanent common law relationship customary in medieval and early modern Iberia.

bayeta de la tierra (S): domestic, as opposed to imported, cloth.

beaterio (S): house of women who have taken informal religious vows.

birque (S): large earthen vessel.

bobo (S): freshwater fish found in the rivers of Mexico and Guatemala.

branco (P): white; person of Portuguese or European descent.

cabecera (S): head town of a municipality or parish.

cabildo (S): municipal council.

cacagual (S): cocoa plantation.

cacique/cacica (S): hereditary indigenous chieftain or lord; the term is from the Arawak.

calidad (S): signifier of social position in terms of class, race, reputation, wealth, social connections, and character.

calificador (S): theological qualifier (officer of the Inquisition).

Capitán General (S): regional royal official with military and civil powers.

carga (S): bushel.

cédula (S): written decree; usually a royal decree.

chacara (S): farm or lot of land that can be tilled (term used in the Andes).

chicha (S): fermented drink made from corn; common in the Andes.

chichilpatle (N): bitter medicine.

chumbe (Q): woolen belt used to cinch a woman's tunic in the Andes.

cihuapatli (N): the aster flower; a powerful abortifacient (also sp. suapatle).

cimarrón (S): runaway enslaved person or community of runaway enslaved people.

coco (Q): silver drinking vessel, typically used for drinking native corn beer.

cofradía (S): lay religious brotherhood, usually founded for a specific devotion.

comisario (S): inquisitorial agent acting as first-instance judge at the local level.

compadrazgo (S): godparentage.

compadre (S): godparent (co-parent according to Catholic baptismal sponsorship); also close friend

compadrío (P): godparentage.

conquistador (S): conqueror.

contrayerba (S): medicinal plants.

cordillera central (S): central mountain range.

corpo presente (mass of) (S): mass performed before coffin is lowered into the grave.

corral (S): yard, animal pen.

corregidor (S): district judge; district governor (synonymous with *alcalde mayor*).

coyol (N): type of palm, for consumption.

crioulo/a (P): person of mixed African and European descent yet perceived to have a lighter skin tone.

crioulos forros (P): manumitted blacks.

crioulos libertos (P): free blacks.

crioulinho/a (P): diminutive form of *crioula*.

cuartos (S): copper coins.

cumbe (Q): finely woven wool cloth.

cura (S): rector, parish priest.

cura beneficiado (S): ordained priest.

curandero/a (S): healer.

curador (S): court-appointed guardian and legal defender.

depósito (S): legal practice of keeping women in custody prior to marriage or during ecclesiastical divorce proceedings.

doctrinas (S): indigenous parishes administered by regular clergy.

don (S): customary title of sir.

doña (S): customary title of lady.

donada (S): convent servant, usually a woman of color, who professed simple vows.

doncella (S): young woman who is unmarried and a virgin.

encomendero (S): recipient of an *encomienda*.

encomienda (S): crown grant to an *encomendero* of the tribute and labor of indigenous people in a specified location.

engenhos (P): sugar mills in Brazil.

expensa (S): expense.

examinador sinodal (S): synod examiner, for a Church council.

fanega (S): unit of dry measure equal to 1.5 bushels.

fazenda (P): landed estate.

fiscal (S): prosecutor.

fray (S): brother (religious).

gobernador (S): official with similar power to a *corregidor*, sometimes refers to position of authority held by an indigenous person.

guayra (Q): native Andean smelting process using clay ovens. Also, the women who carried out the task of smelting ore.

hacienda (S): landed estate.

hamaca (S): hammock.

hechicería: (S): witchcraft.

hechizera/hechicera (S): witch; spell-maker.

hija/o natural (S): daughter or son born outside of marriage to a man and woman who are not married to others and who are recognized by their father.

indio/india (S): indigenous person

indio/a ladino/a (S): indigenous man or woman who has acculturated particularly in terms of learning the Spanish language.

indios carboneros (S): indigenous men who sold wood, llama dung, or other combustibles.

informe (S): formal report mandated by the Real Audiencia.

interrogatorio (S): questions, typically in written format, to be answered by witnesses.

juez comisario (S): examining judge in a court of the Inquisition.

juez de comición (S): investigating judge.

juez eclesiastico (S): ecclesiastical magistrate.

juicio plenario (S): plenary suit.

junta (S): ruling body, usually refers to a council.

justicia mayor (S): deputy of the governor or *corregidor* who has judicial authority within the local *cabildo*.

letrado (S): lawyer; learned person.

licenciado (S): an honorific title indicating the bearer held a university licentiate degree.

lliclla (Q): shawl worn as part of women's dress in the Andes.

limpieza de sangre (S)/*limpieça de sangue* (P): blood purity determined through religious identity as a Christian.

madre mui baja (S): prolapsed uterus.

madrinha (P): godmother.

maestre de campo (S): field commander, one step below captain general.

maestro (S): master, one who has acquired skill or learning in a given field.

mala vida (S): literal translation is "bad life"; reference to chronic mistreatment of a woman by her male partner or spouse.

maltratos (S): abuse.

mandas forzosas (S): obligatory donations, for example to the poor or to orphans, required of those who made wills.

marco (S): unit to measure weight (and value) of silver; each *marco* weighed half a pound.

matadero (S): slaughterhouse.

mate de yerba (S): herbal tea.

mayordomo (S): overseer.

mestiço (P) : person of mixed Portuguese and African parentage. In the Brazilian context, implies lesser black ancestry—or at least lighter skin—than that of mixed-race children born of whites and blacks referred to as *mulatos* or *pardos*.

mestiza/o (S): person of mixed Spanish and indigenous parentage.

morena/o (S): mixed-race person of predominantly African descent.

morisca/o (S): new convert from Islam to Christianity.

mora/o (S): Muslim inhabitant of the Mediterranean.

mulata/o (S): person of mixed Spanish or Portuguese and African parentage. In Brazil, can refer to lighter-skinned mixed-race Afro-descended persons.

morgado (P): a type of entail which served to prevent the dissolution of the landed estate.

mujer hombrada (S): manly woman.

muniatos (S): a yam-like or cassava-like tuber.

nación (S): an abstract grouping based on place of origin, residence, or imperial affinity.

ñanaca (Q): woven head covering worn as part of women's dress in the Andes.

natural (S): can refer to an indigenous person or, especially in the sixteenth century, a person who belongs to or is an original inhabitant of a place or broader "culture."

negra/o (S): black; person of African descent.

negrita/o (S) black child.

oidor (S): judge of the Real Audiencia.

oitava (P): one-eighth of an ounce.

parda/o (S,P): Brazilian Portuguese: person of mixed African-European descent; Spanish America: person of African descent.

parvolo/a (P): child; also small, little.

pataca (P): silver coin worth 320$ *réis*.

pelota (S): a Basque ball game played on a large court and brought to Mexico in the eighteenth century.

perulero (S): a merchant or other trader who has made money in Peru.

peso (S): unit of money; one *peso* was made up of eight *reales*.

piezas (S): cannonballs.

piña (S): a cone of refined silver, unminted.

pirua (Q): corncrib.

poder (S): power of attorney, specifically legal power of one person over another.

Predicador General (S): ecclesiastical officer; preacher general.

preta (P): black; person of African descent.

principales (S): hereditary indigenous elite

probanza (S): petition, proof.

procurador (S): legal representative.

provisor (S): chief ecclesiastical judge of a diocese.

pulque (N): fermented cactus beverage.

quero (also kero) (Q): wooden drinking vessel for corn beer.

rayuela (S): game that involves throwing coins into a hole in a brick.

reales (S): units of currency denoting one eighth of one *peso*.

Real Acuerdo (S): official body composed of the viceroy and officers of the Real Audiencia.

Real Audiencia (S): highest (royal) court within the jurisdiction of Spanish kingdoms.

real cédula (S): royal decree.

Real Sala del Crimen (S): High Criminal Court.

recogida (S): a woman who leaves her home, by will or by force, to enter a secluded community; the quality of being secluded from the world.

recogimiento (S): the act of seclusion or withdrawal; a building or house of seclusion for spiritual retreat.

réis (P): plural of *real,* the currency of colonial Brazil.

relaciones (S): legal, certified accounts.

responsos (S): sung prayers for the dead.

rígida condición (S): controlling nature of a person.

sacha (Q): a plant native to the rainforest in Bolivia/Peru.

senhor/a (P): lord or lady, sir or madam.

señor/a (S): lord or lady, sir or madam.

señor comandante (S): senior military commander

señorío (S): lordship, or similar political domain over a territory.

sentencia (S): legal sentence.

sesmaria (P): a royal concession of lands.

Siete Partidas (S): expansive medieval legal code drafted in the thirteenth century under Alfonso X and used in Iberia and colonial Latin America.

sitios (P): mixed tobacco farms and cattle ranches.

solar (S): urban land lot.

sor (S): a religious sister; nun.

sumaria (S): initial investigative portion of a legal case.

subdelegado (S): royal district governor position instituted during the Bourbon Reforms of 1780s; replacement for *alcalde mayor* and *corregidor.*

Superior Junta de Temporalidades (S): court set up as part of royal bureaucracy to sell the property of the Jesuits after their expulsion from the New World in 1767.

tacha (S): in a judicial case, the disqualification of a witness.

temascal (N): pre-Columbian "houses of heat" or sweat houses.

teniente (S): deputy.

teniente corregidor deputy to a district governor.

tlacuache (Q): a powder of dried opossum tail.

tocadas (S): relics that contained spiritual powers.

tomín (S): coin, unit of currency, subdivision of the *real.*

topos (also *tupus*) (Q): dress pins, usually silver, that attach the shawl to the tunic worn as part of a woman's dress in the Andes.

varas (S): measure equal to about three feet of cloth in Peru.

vecina/o (S): citizen or permanent resident of a city with attendant privileges and responsibilities.

vicaria (S): assistant abbess.

vicario (S): assistant to the parish priest.

vicario general (S): vicar general, assistant to a bishop.

vida (S): spiritual biography.

vida maridable (S): married life, meaning specifically to fulfill obligations of man and wife.

Villa Imperial (S): literally, imperial village, an honorific status granted by the Spanish Crown to certain cities in the New World, such as Potosí for its silver.

yanacona (Q) an indigenous person (usually a man) responsible to a Spanish master and without kin ties to a specific *ayllu* (Andean kin-based community).

Bibliography

Abercrombie, Thomas A. "Affairs of the Courtroom: Fernando de Medina Confesses to Killing his Wife." In *Colonial Lives, Documents on Latin American History, 1550–1850*, ed. Richard Boyer and Geoffrey Spurling (pp. 54–76). New York: Oxford University Press, 2000.

Aguirre, Carlos. "Violencia, castigo y control social: esclavos y panaderías en Lima, siglo XIX." *Pasado y Presente* (Lima) 1:1 (1988), 27–37.

Alberro, Solange. *Inquisición y sociedad en México, 1571–1700*. México: Fondo de Cultura Económica, 1988.

Altman, Ida. *Emigrants and Society: Extremadura and America in the Sixteenth Century*. Berkeley: University of California Press, 1989.

————. *Transatlantic Ties in the Spanish Empire: Brihuega, Spain and Puebla, Mexico, 1560–1620*. Stanford, CA: Stanford University Press, 2000.

Altolaguirre y Duvale, Angel de. *Colección de documentos inéditos de ultramar* Series II, Tomo XXI. Nendeln: Kraus Reprint Limited, 1967.

Arenal, Electa, and Stacey Schlau, eds. *Untold Sisters: Hispanic Nuns in Their Own Works*. Albuquerque: University of New Mexico Press, 1989.

Arrom, Silvia Marina. *The Women of Mexico City, 1790–1857*. Stanford, CA: Stanford University Press, 1985.

————. "Desintegración familial y pauperización: Los indigentes del Hospicio de Pobres de la ciudad de México, 1795." In *Familia y vida privada en la historia de iberoamérica*, edited by Pilar Gonzalbo Aizpuru and Cecilia Rabell Romero, 119–31. Mexico: UNAM-Colegio de México, 1996.

Azcona Pastor, José Manuel. *Possible Paradises: Basque Emigration to Latin America*. Reno: University of Nevada Press, 2004.

Baber, R. Jovita. "Law, Land, and Legal Rhetoric in Colonial New Spain: A Look at the Changing Rhetoric of Indigenous Americans in the Sixteenth Century." In *Native Claims: Indigenous Law against Empire, 1500–1920*, ed. Saliha Belmessous (pp. 41–62). New York: Oxford University Press, 2012.

Behar, Ruth. "Sexual Witchcraft, Colonialism, and Women's Powers: Views from the Mexican Inquisition." In *Sexuality and Marriage in Colonial Latin America*, ed. Asunción Lavrin (pp. 178–206). Lincoln: University of Nebraska Press, 1989.

Bennett, Herman L. *Africans in Colonial Mexico: Absolutism, Christianity, and Afro-Creole Consciousness, 1570–1640*. Bloomington: Indiana University Press, 2003.

Bergad, Laird W. *Slavery and the Demographic and Economic History of Minas Gerais, 1720–1888*. Cambridge: Cambridge University Press, 1999.

Black, Chad Thomas. "Prosecuting Female-Female Sex in Bourbon Quito." In *Sexuality and the Unnatural in Colonial Latin America*, edited by Zeb Tortorici (pp. 141–61). Oakland: University of California Press, 2016.

Bluteau, Raphael, and Antonio de Moraes Silva. *Diccionario da Lingua Portugueza composto pelo Padre D. Rafael Bluteau, reformado, e accrescentado por Antonio de Moraes Silva, natural do Rio de Janeiro*, vol. 2. Lisbon: Na Officina de Simão Thaddeo Ferreira, 1789.

Boyd-Bowman, Peter. "Patterns of Spanish Immigration to the Indies Until 1600," *The Hispanic American Historical Review* 56:4 (November, 1976), 580–604.

Boyer, Richard. "Catarina María Complains that Juan Teioa Forcibly Deflowered Her." In *Colonial Lives, Documents on Latin American History, 1550–1850,* edited by Richard Boyer and Geoffrey Spurling (pp. 155–65). New York: Oxford University Press, 2000.

——. *Lives of the Bigamists: Marriage, Family, and Community in Colonial Mexico.* Albuquerque: University of New Mexico Press, 1995.

——. "Women, *La Mala Vida,* and the Politics of Marriage." In *Sexuality and Marriage in Colonial Latin America,* ed. Asunción Lavrin (pp. 252–86). Lincoln: University of Nebraska Press, 1989.

Bristol, Joan Cameron. *Christians, Blasphemers, and Witches: Afro-Mexican Ritual Practice in the Seventeenth Century.* Albuquerque: University of New Mexico Press, 2007.

Burkett, Elinor. "Indian Women and White Society: The Case of Sixteenth-Century Peru." In *Latin American Women: Historical Perspectives,* ed. Asunción Lavrin (pp. 101–28). Westport, CT: Greenwood Press, 1978.

Burns, Kathryn. *Colonial Habits: Convents and the Spiritual Economy of Cuzco, Peru.* Durham, NC: Duke University Press, 1999.

——. "Forms of Authority: Women's Legal Representations in Mid-Colonial Cuzco." In *Women, Texts, and Authority in the Early Modern Spanish World,* ed. Marta V. Vicente and Luis R. Corteguera (pp. 149–64). Aldershot, UK: Ashgate, 2003.

——. *Into the Archive: Writing and Power in Colonial Peru.* Durham: Duke University Press, 2010.

Calvo Maturana, Antonio. *Impostores: sombras en la España de las Luces.* Madrid: Cátedra, 2015.

Camba Ludlow, Úrsula. "Gregoria la Macho y su 'inclinación a las mujeres': reflexiones en torno a la sexualidad marginal en Nueva España, 1796–1806." *Colonial Latin American Historical Review* 12:4 (Fall 2003), 479–97.

Candido, Mariana P. "Concubinage and Slavery in Benguela, 1750–1850." *Slavery in Africa and the Caribbean: A History of Enslavement and Identity Since the 18th Century,* ed. Olatunji Ojo and Nadine Hunt (pp. 65–84). London: I.B. Tauris, 2012.

Chaves, María Eugenia. "Slave Women's Strategies for Freedom and the Late Spanish Colonial State." In *Hidden Histories of Gender and the State in Latin America,* ed. Elizabeth Dore and Maxine Molyneux (pp. 108–26). Durham, NC: Duke University Press, 2000.

Chipman, Donald E. *Moctezuma's Children: Aztec Royalty under Spanish Rule, 1520–1700.* Austin: University of Texas Press, 2005.

Chowning, Margaret. *Rebellious Nuns: The Troubled History of a Mexican Convent, 1752–1863.* New York: Oxford University Press, 2005.

Christensen, Mark, and Jonathan Truitt. *Native Wills from the Colonial Americas: Dead Giveaways in a New World.* Salt Lake City: University of Utah Press, 2015.

Chuchiak, John F. IV, ed. *The Inquisition in New Spain, 1536–1820: A Documentary History.* Baltimore, MD: Johns Hopkins University Press, 2012.

Classen, Albrecht, and Connie Scarborough, eds. *Crime and Punishment in the Middle Ages and Early Modern Age: Mental-Historical Investigations of Basic Human Problems and Social Responses.* Göttingen, Germany: Hubert & Co., 2012.

Córdova y Salinas, Diego de. *Crónica franciscana de las Provincias del Perú,* 1651. Reprint. Ed. Lino G. Canedo. Washington, DC: Academy of American Franciscan History, 1957.

Cook, Alexandra Parma, and Noble David Cook. *Good Faith and Truthful Ignorance: A Case of Transatlantic Bigamy.* Durham, NC: Duke University Press, 1991.

Cruz, Anne J., and Rosilie Hernández, eds. *Women's Literacy in Early Modern Spain and the New World.* London: Routledge, 2011.

Cushner, Nicholas P. *Farm and Factory: The Jesuits and the Development of Agrarian Capitalism in Quito, 1600–1767.* Albany: State University of New York Press, 1982.

Cutter, Charles R. *The Legal Culture of Northern New Spain, 1700–1810.* Albuquerque: University of New Mexico Press, 1995.

Dantas, Mariana. "Market Women of African Descent and the Making of Sabará, a Colonial Town in Eighteenth-Century Minas Gerais, Brazil." *Colonial Latin American Historical Review,* Second Series 2:1 (Winter 2014), 1–25.

Deeds, Susan M. "Double Jeopardy: Indian Women in Jesuit Missions of Nueva Vizcaya." In *Indian Women of Early Mexico,* ed. Susan Schroeder, Stephanie Wood, and Robert Haskett (pp. 255–72). Norman: University of Oklahoma Press, 1997.

de Erauso Catalina, and Michele Stepto. *Lieutenant Nun: Memoir of a Basque Transvestite in the New World.* Boston: Beacon Press, 1997.

Díaz, María Elena. *The Virgin, the King, and the Royal Slaves of El Cobre: Negotiating Freedom in Colonial Cuba, 1670–1780.* Stanford, CA: Stanford University Press, 2002.

Díaz, Monica. "The Indigenous Nuns of Corpus Christi: Race and Spirituality." In *Religion in New Spain,* ed. Susan Schroeder and Stafford Poole (pp. 179–92). Albuquerque: University of New Mexico Press, 2007.

———. *Indigenous Writings from the Convent: Negotiating Ethnic Autonomy in Colonial Mexico.* Tucson: University of Arizona Press, 2010.

Díaz, Mónica, and Rocío Quispe-Agnoli, eds. *Women's Negotiations and Textual Analysis in Latin America, 1500–1799.* New York: Routledge Press, 2017.

Echarri, Francisco. *Directoria moral que comprehende, en breve, y claro estilo todas las materias de la theologia moral.* Gerona: Por Pedro Morera, 1755.

Echeverri, Marcela. *Indian and Slave Royalists in the Age of Revolution: Reform, Revolution, and Royalism in the Northern Andes, 1780–1825.* Cambridge: Cambridge University Press, 2016.

Few, Martha. "'That Monster of Nature': Gender, Sexuality, and the Medicalization of a 'Hermaphrodite' in Late Colonial Guatemala." *Ethnohistory* 54:1 (Winter 2007), 159–76.

———. *Women Who Live Evil Lives: Gender, Religion, and the Politics of Power in Colonial Guatemala.* Austin: University of Texas Press, 2002.

Fisher, Andrew, and Matthew D. O'Hara, eds. *Imperial Subjects: Race and Identity in Colonial Latin America.* Durham, NC: Duke University Press, 2009.

Furtado, Júnia Ferreira. *Chica da Silva: A Brazilian Slave of the Eighteenth Century.* New York: Cambridge University Press, 2009.

———. "A Morte como testemunha da vida." In *O historiador e suas fontes* (pp. 93–118). São Paulo: Editora Contexto, 2011.

Gallagher, Ann Miriam, R.S.M. "The Indian Nuns of Mexico City's *Monasterio* of Corpus Christi, 1724–1821." In *Latin American Women: Historical Perspectives,* ed. Asuncíon Lavrin (pp. 150–72). Westport, CT: Greenwood Press, 1978.

Gauderman, Kimberly. *Women's Lives in Colonial Quito: Gender, Law and Economy in Colonial Spanish America.* Austin: University of Texas Press, 2003.

Gerhard, Peter. *A Guide to the Historical Geography of New Spain,* Revised Edition. Norman: University of Oklahoma Press, 1993.

Gonzalbo, Pilar. *Familias iberoamericanos: historia, identidad, y conflictos.* Mexico, DF: El Colegio de México, Centro de Estudios Históricos, 2001.

Graubart, Karen B. "Catalina de Agüero: A Mediating Life." In *Native Wills from the Colonial Americas: Dead Giveaways in a New World,* ed. Jonathan Truitt and Mark Christensen (pp. 19–39). Salt Lake City: University of Utah Press, 2015.

———. *With Our Labor and Sweat: Indigenous Women and the Formation of Colonial Society in Peru, 1550–1700.* Stanford, CA: Stanford University Press, 2007.

Gruzinski, Serge. "The Ashes of Desire: Homosexuality in Mid-Seventeenth-Century New Spain." In *Infamous Desire: Male Homosexuality in Colonial Latin America,* ed. Pete Sigal. Chicago: University of Chicago Press, 2003.

Gunnarsdóttir, Ellen. *Mexican Karismata: The Baroque Vocation of Francisca de Los Ángeles, 1674–1744.* Lincoln: University of Nebraska Press, 2004.

Hanger, Kimberly S. *Bounded Lives, Bounded Places: Free Black Society in Colonial New Orleans, 1769–1803.* Durham, NC: Duke University Press, 1997.

Haskett, Robert. "Activist or Adulteress? The Life and Struggle of Doña Josefa María of Tepoztlan." In *Indian Women of Early Mexico*, ed. Susan Schroeder, Stephanie Wood, and Robert Haskett (pp. 145–64). Norman: University of Oklahoma Press, 1997.

Haslip-Viera, Gabriel. "The Underclass." In *Cities and Society in Colonial Latin America,* ed. Louisa Schell Hoberman and Susan M. Socolow (pp. 285–312). Albuquerque: University of New Mexico Press, 1986.

Helg, Aline. *Liberty and Equality in Caribbean Colombia, 1770–1835.* Chapel Hill: University of North Carolina Press, 2004.

Higgins, Kathleen. *"Licentious Liberty" in a Brazilian Gold-Mining Region: Slavery, Gender and Social Control in Eighteenth-Century Sabará, Minas Gerais.* State College, PA: Pennsylvania State University Press, 1999.

Hünefeldt, Christine. *Paying the Price of Freedom: Family and Labor among Lima's Slaves, 1800–1854.* Berkeley: University of California Press, 1994.

Jaffary, Nora E. *False Mystics: Deviant Orthodoxy in Colonial Mexico.* Lincoln: University of Nebraska Press, 2004.

———. *Reproduction and Its Discontents in Mexico: Childbirth and Contraception from 1750 to 1905.* Chapel Hill: University of North Carolina Press, 2016.

———. "Sacred Defiance and Sexual Desecration: María Getrudis Arévalo and the Holy Office in Eighteenth-Century Mexico." In *Sexuality and the Unnatural in*

Colonial Latin America, edited by Zeb Tortorici (pp. 43–57). Oakland: University of California Press, 2016.

Jesús, Ursula de, and Nancy E. van Deusen. *The Souls of Purgatory: The Spiritual Diary of a Seventeenth-Century Afro-Peruvian Mystic, Ursula de Jesús*. Albuquerque: University of New Mexico Press, 2004.

Johnson, Lyman J., and Sonia Lipsett-Rivera, eds. *The Faces of Honor: Sex, Shame and Violence in Colonial Latin America*. Albuquerque: University of New Mexico Press, 1998.

Jouve-Martín, José R. "Death, Gender, and Writing: Testaments of Women of African Origin in Seventeenth-Century Lima, 1651–1666." In *Afro-Latino Voices: Narratives from the Early Modern Ibero-Atlantic World, 1550–1812*, ed. Kathryn Joy McKnight and Leo Garafalo (pp. 105–25). Indianapolis, IN: Hackett Publishing Company, 2009.

Kalyuta, Anastasya. "La casa y hacienda de un señor mexica. Un estudio analítico de la 'Información de *doña* Isabel de Moctezuma.'" *Anuario de Estudios Americanos* 65:2 (2008), 13–37.

Kamen, Henry. *The Spanish Inquisition: A Historical Revision*. New Haven, CT: Yale University Press, 2014.

Kanter, Deborah E. *Hijos del Pueblo: Gender, Family, and Community in Rural Mexico, 1730–1850*. Austin: University of Texas Press, 2008.

Kellogg, Susan. *Weaving the Past: A History of Latin America's Indigenous Women from the Prehispanic Period to the Present*. New York: Oxford University Press, 2005.

Kellogg, Susan, and Matthew Restall, eds. *Dead Giveaways: Indigenous Testaments of Colonial Mesoamerica and the Andes*. Salt Lake City: University of Utah Press, 1998.

Klein, Herbert S., and Ben Vinson III. *African Slavery in Latin America and the Caribbean*, 2nd Edition. New York: Oxford University Press, 2007.

Landers, Jane. "African-American Women and Their Pursuit of Rights through Eighteenth-Century Spanish Texts." In *Haunted Bodies: Gender and Southern Texts*, ed. Anne Goodwyn Jones and Susan V. Donaldson (pp. 56–76). Charlottesville: University of Virginia Press, 1998.

———. *Black Society in Spanish Florida*. Urbana: University of Illinois Press, 1999, 2001, 2002, 2005.

Lanyon, Anna. *The New World of Martin Cortés*. Cambridge, MA: Da Capo Press, 2003.

Larkin, Brian. *The Very Nature of God: Baroque Catholicism and Religious Reform in Bourbon Mexico*. Albuquerque: University of New Mexico Press, 2010.

Lauderdale Graham, Sandra. *Caetana Says No: Women's Stories From a Brazilian Slave Society*. Cambridge: Cambridge University Press, 2002.

Laurent-Perrault, Evelyne. "Esclavizadas, cimarronaje y la Ley en Venezuela, 1760–1809." In *Demando Mi Libertad; Relatos de mujeres Negras y sus estrategias de resistencia en Nueva Granada, Venezuela y Cuba*. Universidad Icesi, Cali-Colombia, forthcoming.

Lavallé, Bernard. *Amor y opresión en los Andes coloniales*. Lima: IEP, 1999.

Lavrin, Asunción. *Brides of Christ: Conventual Life in Colonial Mexico*. Stanford, CA: Stanford University Press, 2008.

————. "Indian Brides of Christ: Creating New Spaces for Indigenous Women in New Spain," *Mexican Studies/Estudios Mexicanos* 15:2 (Summer 1999), 225–60.

————, ed. *Latin American Women: Historical Perspectives*. Westwood, CT: Greenwood Press, 1979.

————, ed. *Sexuality and Marriage in Colonial Latin America*. Lincoln: University of Nebraska Press, 1989.

Lewis, Laura A. "From Sodomy to Superstition: The Active Pathic and Bodily Transgressions in New Spain," *Ethnohistory* 54:1 (Winter 2007), 129–57.

————. *Hall of Mirrors: Power, Witchcraft, and Caste in Colonial Mexico*. Durham, NC: Duke University Press, 2003.

Libby, Douglas. "A Culture of Colors: Representational Identities and Afro-Brazilians in Minas Gerais in the 18th and 19th Centuries." *Luso-Brazilian Review* 50:1 (June 2013), 26–52.

Lipsett-Rivera, Sonya. *Gender and the Negotiation of Daily Life in Mexico, 1750–1856*. Lincoln: University of Nebraska Press, 2012.

Lockhart, James. *Spanish Peru, 1532–1560: A Colonial Society*. Madison: University of Wisconsin Press, 1968.

Lohse, Russell. "Reconciling Freedom with the Rights of Property: Slave Emancipation in Colombia, 1821–1852, with Special Reference to La Plata." *The Journal of Negro History* 86:3 (Summer 2001), 203–27.

Mamayo, Andrés de. *Tratados breves de algebra y garrotillo*. Valencia: Por Juan Chrysostomo Garriz, 1621.

Mangan, Jane E. *Transatlantic Obligations: Creating the Bonds of Family in Colonial Era Peru and Spain*. New York: Oxford University Press, 2016.

————. *Trading Roles: Gender, Ethnicity and the Urban Economy in Colonial Potosí*. Durham, NC: Duke University Press, 2005.

Mannarelli, María Emma. *Private Passions and Public Sins: Men and Women in Seventeenth-Century Lima*. Trans. Sidney Evans and Meredith D. Dodge. Albuquerque: University of New Mexico Press, 2007.

Martínez, María Elena. *Genealogical Fictions: Limpieza de Sangre, Religion, and Gender in Colonial Mexico*. Stanford, CA: Stanford University Press, 2008.

————. "Sex and the Colonial Archive: The Case of 'Mariano' Aguilera." *Hispanic American Historical Review* 96:3 (2016), 421–43.

McFarlane, Anthony. *Colombia Before Independence: Economy, Society, and Politics Under Bourbon Rule*. Cambridge: Cambridge University Press, 1993.

McKinley, Michelle A. *Fractional Freedoms: Slavery, Intimacy, and Legal Mobilization in Colonial Lima, 1600–1700*. New York: Cambridge University Press, 2016.

McKnight, Kathryn Joy. *The Mystic of Tunja: The Writings of Madre Castillo, 1671–1742*. Amherst: University of Massachusetts Press, 1997.

Mello Moraes, Alexandre de. *Corographia historica, chonographica, genealogica, nobiliaria, e politica do imperio deo Brasil*, vol. 2. Rio de Janeiro: Typografia Americana de J. Soares de Pinho, 1858.

Mendes de Almeida, Cândido, ed. *Codigo Philippino, ou, Ordenações e leis do Reino de Portugal: recopiladas por mandado d'El-Rey D. Philippe I*. Rio de Janeiro: Typ. do Instituto Philomathico, 1870.

Metcalf, Alida C. *Family and Frontier in Colonial Brazil, Santana de Parnaíba, 1580–1822.* Second Ed. Austin: University of Texas Press, 2005. First Ed.: Berkeley: University of California Press, 1992.

Mirow, Matthew. *Latin American Law: A History of Private Law and Institutions in Spanish America.* Austin, TX: University of Texas Press, 2004.

Myers, Kathleen Ann. *Neither Saints nor Sinners: Writing the Lives of Women in Spanish America.* New York: Oxford University Press, 2003.

Myscofski, Carole A. *Amazons, Wives, Nuns and Witches: Women and the Catholic Church in Colonial Brazil 1500–1822.* Austin: University of Texas Press, 2013.

Nalle, Sarah. "Literacy and Culture in Early Modern Castile." *Past and Present* 125 (November 1989), 65–96.

Nazzari, Muriel. *Disappearance of the Dowry: Women, Families and Social Change in São Paulo, Brazil, 1600–1900.* Stanford, CA: Stanford University Press, 1991.

Nesvig, Martin. "The Complicated Terrain of Latin American Homosexuality." *Hispanic American Historical Review* 81: 3–4 (2001), 689–729.

Numhauser, Paulina. *Mujeres indias y señores de la coca: Potosí y Cuzco en el siglo XVI.* Madrid: Ediciones Catedra, 2005.

Ochi Flexor, Maria Helena, ed. *O Conjunto do Carmo de Cachoeira [The Carmo architectonic ensemble of Cachoeira].* Brasília: IPHAN/Monumenta, 2007.

O'Toole, Rachel. *Bound Lives: Africans, Indians, and the Making of Race in Colonial Peru.* Pittsburgh, PA: University of Pittsburgh Press, 2012.

Owens, Sarah E. *Nuns Navigating the Spanish Empire.* Albuquerque: University of New Mexico Press, 2017.

———. "Transatlantic Religious." In *The Routledge Research Companion to Early Modern Spanish Women Writers,* ed. Nieves Baranda and Anne J. Cruz (pp. 315–27). New York: Routledge, 2018.

Owens, Sarah E., and Jane E. Mangan, eds. *Women of the Iberian Atlantic.* Baton Rouge: Louisiana State University Press, 2012.

Owensby, Brian P. *Empire of Law and Indian Justice in Colonial Mexico.* Stanford, CA: Stanford University Press, 2008.

Penyak, Lee M., and Walter J. Petry, eds. *Religion and Society in Latin America: Interpretive Essays from Conquest to Present.* New York: Orbis Books, 2009.

Perry, Mary Elizabeth. *Gender and Disorder in Early Modern Seville.* Princeton, NJ: Princeton University Press, 1990.

Phelan, John Leddy. *The People and the King: The Comunero Revolution in Colombia, 1781.* Madison: University of Wisconsin Press, 1978.

Poole, Stafford. *The Guadalupan Controversies in Mexico.* Stanford, CA: Stanford University Press, 2006.

Poska, Allyson M. "Elusive Virtue: Rethinking the Role of Female Chastity in Early Modern Spain." *Journal of Early Modern History* 8:1–2 (2004), 135–46.

———. *Gendered Crossings: Women and Migration in the Spanish Empire.* Albuquerque: University of New Mexico Press, 2016.

———. *Women and Authority in Early Modern Spain: The Peasants of Galicia.* New York: Oxford University Press, 2006.

Powers, Karen. *Andean Journeys: Migration, Ethnogenesis, and the State in Colonial Quito.* Albuquerque: University of New Mexico Press, 1995.

―――. *Women in the Crucible of Conquest: The Gendered Genesis of Spanish American Society, 1500–1600.* Albuquerque: University of New Mexico Press, 2005.

Premo, Bianca. *Children of the Father King: Youth, Authority, and Legal Minority in Colonial Peru.* Chapel Hill: University of North Carolina Press, 2005.

―――. *The Enlightenment on Trial: Ordinary Litigants and Colonialism in the Spanish Empire.* New York: Oxford University Press, 2017.

Rama, Angel. *The Lettered City.* Durham, NC: Duke University Press, 1996.

Rappaport, Joanne. *The Disappearing Mestizo: Configuring Difference in the Colonial New Kingdom of Granada.* Durham, NC: Duke University Press, 2014.

Real Academia Española. *Diccionario de autoridades.* Vols. 1–6. Facsimile. Madrid: Gredos, 1963.

Reis, João José. *Death Is a Festival: Funeral Rites and Rebellion in Nineteenth-Century Brazil,* trans. H. Sabrina Gledhill. Chapel Hill: University of North Carolina Press, 2003.

Reséndez, Andrés. *The Other Slavery: The Uncovered Story of Indian Enslavement in America.* Boston: Houghton Mifflin Harcourt, 2016.

Rostworowski, María. *La mujer en la época prehispánica.* Lima: Instituto de Estudios Peruanos, 1988.

Salomon, Frank. "Indian Women of Early Colonial Quito as Seen Through Their Testaments." *The Americas* 44:3 (1988), 325–41.

Sánchez Carralero, Diego. *Constituciones synodales del priorato de Santiago de Ucles.* Murcia: Felipe Díaz Cayuelas, 1742.

San José, María de, Kathleen Ann Myers, and Amanda Powell. *A Wild Country Out in the Garden: The Spiritual Journals of a Colonial Mexican Nun.* Bloomington: Indiana University Press, 1999.

Schafer, Daniel L. *Anna Madgigine, Jai Kingsley: African Princess, Florida Slave, Plantation Slaveowner.* Gainesville: University Press of Florida, 2003.

―――. *Zephaniah Kingsley Jr. and the Atlantic World: Slave Trader, Plantation Owner, Emancipator.* Gainesville: University of Florida Press, 2013.

Schroeder, Susan, Stephanie Wood, and Robert Haskett, eds. *Indian Women of Early Mexico.* Norman: University of Oklahoma Press, 1997.

Schwartz, Stuart B. "The Manumission of Slaves in Colonial Brazil: Bahia, 1684–1745." *The Hispanic American Historical Review* 54:4 (November 1974), 603–35.

―――. *Sugar Plantations in the Formation of Brazilian Society: Bahia, 1550–1835.* New York: Cambridge University Press, 1985.

Scott, Samuel Parsons, and Robert I. Burns. *Las Siete Partidas, Volume 4: Family, Commerce, and the Sea: The Worlds of Women and Merchants.* Philadelphia: University of Pennsylvania Press, 2001.

Seed, Patricia. *To Love, Honor, and Obey in Colonial Mexico: Conflicts over Marriage Choice, 1574–1821.* Stanford, CA: Stanford University Press, 1988.

Seixas, Margarida. "Slave Women's Children in the Portuguese Empire: Legal Status and Its Enforcement." In *Women in the Portuguese Empire: The Theatre of*

Shadows, ed. Clara Sarmento (pp. 63–80). Newcastle, UK: Cambridge Scholars Publishing, 2008.

Sell, Barry D., and Susan Kellogg. "We Want to Give Them Laws: Royal Ordinances in a Mid-Sixteenth-Century Nahuatl Text." *Estudios de Cultura Náhuatl* 27 (1997), 325–67.

Sigal, Pete. *The Flower and the Scorpion: Sexuality and Ritual in Early Nahua Culture.* Durham, NC: Duke University Press, 2011.

———. *From Moon Goddesses to Virgins: The Colonization of Yucatecan Maya Sexual Desire.* Austin: University of Texas Press, 2000.

———, ed. *Infamous Desire: Male Homosexuality in Colonial Latin America.* Chicago: University of Chicago Press, 2003.

Silverblatt, Irene. *Moon, Sun, and Witches: Gender Ideologies and Class in Inca and Colonial Peru.* Princeton, NJ: Princeton University Press, 1987.

Socolow, Susan Migden. *The Women of Colonial Latin America.* Cambridge: Cambridge University Press, 2000.

Sousa, Lisa. *The Woman Who Turned into a Jaguar, and Other Narratives of Native Women in Archives of Colonial Mexico.* Stanford, CA: Stanford University Press, 2017.

Soyer, François. "The Inquisitorial Trial of a Cross-Dressing Lesbian: Reactions and Responses to Female Homosexuality in 18th-Century Portugal." *Journal of Homosexuality* 61 (2014), 1529–57.

Spurling, Geoffrey. "Under Investigation for the Abominable Sin: Damián de Morales Stands Accused of Attempting to Seduce Antón de Tierra de Congo (Charcas, 1611)." In *Colonial Lives: Documents on Latin American History, 1550–1850*, ed. Richard Boyer and Geoffrey Spurling (pp. 112–29). New York: Oxford University Press, 2000.

Stavig, Ward. *The World of Túpac Amaru: Conflict, Community, and Identity in Colonial Peru.* Lincoln: University of Nebraska Press, 1999.

Stern, Steve J. *Peru's Indian Peoples and the Challenge of Spanish Conquest: Huamanga to 1640.* Madison: University of Wisconsin Press, 1982.

———. *The Secret History of Gender: Women, Men, and Power in Late Colonial Mexico.* Chapel Hill: University of North Carolina Press, 1995.

Sweet, James H. *Recreating Africa: Culture, Kinship, and Religion in the African-Portuguese World, 1441–1770.* Chapel Hill: University of North Carolina Press, 2003.

Thomas, Samuel S. "Early Modern Midwifery: Splitting the Profession, Connecting the History." *Journal of Social History* 43:1 (2009), 115–38.

Tigges, Linda, ed., and J. Richard Salazar, trans. *Spanish Colonial Women and the Law: Complaints, Lawsuits, and Criminal Behavior; Documents from the Spanish Colonial Archives of New Mexico, 1697–1749.* Santa Fe, NM: Sunstone Press, 2016.

Tortorici, Zeb, ed. *Sexuality and the Unnatural in Colonial Latin America.* Oakland: University of California Press, 2016.

———. *Sins Against Nature: Sex and Archives in Colonial New Spain, 1530–1821.* Durham, NC: Duke University Press, 2018.

Townsend, Camilla. "Angela Batallas: A Fight for Freedom in Guayaquil." In *The Human Tradition in Colonial Latin America, Second edition*, ed. Kenneth J. Andrien (pp. 305–20). New York: Rowman and Littlefield, 2013.

———. *Malintzin's Choices: An Indian Woman in the Conquest of Mexico*. Albuquerque: University of New Mexico Press, 2006.

Twinam, Ann. *Public Lives, Private Secrets: Gender, Honor, Sexuality, and Illegitimacy in Colonial Spanish America*. Stanford, CA: Stanford University Press, 1999.

Uribe, Jaime Jaramillo. "Esclavos y señores en la Sociedad Colombiana del siglo XVIII." *Annuario Colombiano de Historia Social y de la Cultura* 1:1 (January 1963), 3–62.

Uribe-Uran, Victor M. *Fatal Love: Spousal Killers, Law, and Punishment in the Late Colonial Spanish Atlantic*. Stanford, CA: Stanford University Press, 2016.

Vainfas, Ronaldo, and Zeb Tortorici. "Female Homoeroticism, Heresy, and the Holy Office in Colonial Brazil." In *Sexuality and the Unnatural in Colonial Latin America*, ed. Zeb Tortorici (pp. 77–94). Oakland: University of California Press, 2016.

van Deusen, Nancy E. *Between the Sacred and the Worldly: The Institutional and Cultural Practice of* Recogimiento *in Colonial Lima*. Stanford, CA: Stanford University Press, 2002.

———. *Global Indios: The Indigenous Struggle for Justice in Sixteenth-Century Spain*. Duke, NC: Duke University Press, 2015.

———. "Indios on the Move in the Sixteenth-Century Iberian World." *Journal of Global History*, 10:3 (November 2015), 387–409.

———. "The Intimacies of Bondage: Female Indigenous Servants and Slaves and Their Spanish Masters, 1492–1555." *Journal of Women's History*, 24:1 (2012), 13–43.

———. "'Wife of my Soul and Heart, and All my Solace,' Annulment Suit between Diego Andrés de Arenas and Ysabel Allay Suyo." In *Colonial Lives, Documents on Latin American History*, 1550–1850, ed. Richard Boyer and Geoffrey Spurling (pp. 130–40). New York: Oxford University Press, 2000.

———. *The Souls of Purgatory: The Spiritual Diary of an Afro-Peruvian Mystic, Ursula de Jesús*. Albuquerque: University of New Mexico, 2004.

Velasco, Sherry. *The Lieutenant Nun: Transgenderism, Lesbian Desire, and Catalina de Erauso*. Austin: University of Texas Press, 2000.

Vergara, Teresa. "Growing Up Indian: Migration, Labor, and Life in Lima (1570–1640)." In *Raising an Empire: Children in Early Modern Iberia and Colonial Latin America*, ed. Ondina E. González and Bianca Premo (pp. 75–106). Albuquerque: University of New Mexico, 2007.

Villella, Peter B. *Indigenous Elites and Creole Identity in Colonial Mexico, 1500–1800*. New York: Cambridge University Press, 2016.

von Germeten, Nicole. "Mexican Bawds: Women and Commercial Sex in the Viceroyalty of New Spain." *Latin American History: Oxford Research Encyclopedia, Latin American History* (latinamericanhistory.oxfordre.com).

———. *Violent Delights, Violent Ends: Sex, Race, and Honor in Colonial Cartagena de Indias*. Albuquerque: University of New Mexico Press, 2013.

Watson, Alan. *Slave Law in the Americas*. Athens: University of Georgia Press, 1989.

Index